New Zealand's Foreign Policy under the Jacinda Ardern Government
Facing the Challenge of a Disrupted World

Editors

Robert G Patman
Peter Grace
Balazs Kiglics
Dennis Wesselbaum

University of Otago, New Zealand

NEW JERSEY • LONDON • SINGAPORE • BEIJING • SHANGHAI • HONG KONG • TAIPEI • CHENNAI • TOKYO

Published by

World Scientific Publishing Co. Pte. Ltd.
5 Toh Tuck Link, Singapore 596224
USA office: 27 Warren Street, Suite 401-402, Hackensack, NJ 07601
UK office: 57 Shelton Street, Covent Garden, London WC2H 9HE

Library of Congress Control Number: 2024000569

British Library Cataloguing-in-Publication Data
A catalogue record for this book is available from the British Library.

NEW ZEALAND'S FOREIGN POLICY UNDER THE JACINDA ARDERN GOVERNMENT
Facing the Challenge of a Disrupted World

Copyright © 2024 by World Scientific Publishing Co. Pte. Ltd.

All rights reserved. This book, or parts thereof, may not be reproduced in any form or by any means, electronic or mechanical, including photocopying, recording or any information storage and retrieval system now known or to be invented, without written permission from the publisher.

For photocopying of material in this volume, please pay a copying fee through the Copyright Clearance Center, Inc., 222 Rosewood Drive, Danvers, MA 01923, USA. In this case permission to photocopy is not required from the publisher.

ISBN 978-981-12-8515-8 (hardcover)
ISBN 978-981-12-8516-5 (ebook for institutions)
ISBN 978-981-12-8517-2 (ebook for individuals)

For any available supplementary material, please visit
https://www.worldscientific.com/worldscibooks/10.1142/13646#t=suppl

Desk Editors: Aanand Jayaraman/Yulin Jiang

Typeset by Stallion Press
Email: enquiries@stallionpress.com

Printed in Singapore

© 2024 World Scientific Publishing Company
https://doi.org/10.1142/9789811285165_fmatter

Dedication

This book is dedicated to the memory of Mr. Terence O'Brien who served New Zealand with distinction for over 40 years as a diplomat and as a founding director of the Center for Strategic Studies at Victoria University of Wellington. He is greatly missed, but those that knew him can continue to draw strength and inspiration from the memory of his courage, sense of fairness, and scholarly conviction that international relations encompasses much more than the interests of great powers.

© 2024 World Scientific Publishing Company
https://doi.org/10.1142/9789811285165_fmatter

Foreword

As a former Prime Minister of New Zealand (1999–2008) and the former Administrator of the United Nations Development Programme (2009–2017), I have had the chance to combine a life-long interest in international relations with the experience of contributing to policy-making in this field.

I believe that we now stand at an inflexion point in global affairs. Russia is attempting to annex as much of Ukraine as it can, the long-running Israeli-Palestinian conflict has exploded again, there are significant geopolitical tensions in the Asia-Pacific, and the building climate crisis is not matched by commensurate action to tackle that existential threat to life on earth. Taken together, these developments and more present challenges to New Zealand as it seeks to safeguard its prosperity and well-being.

This book therefore is both important and timely. It is important because it focuses on how Jacinda Ardern's Labour Government conducted New Zealand's foreign policy in a challenging geopolitical environment while simultaneously addressing COVID-19 — the worst global pandemic since the Great Influenza between 1918 and 1920. These were severe tests for any government. The editors of this book have brought together a team of specialists to consider how the foreign policy of the Ardern Government influenced its COVID-19 response and how the government navigated some major security and diplomatic challenges along the way.

The book is timely because the world is confronted by a growing number of problems which do not respect borders and cannot be resolved by countries acting alone. In this context, there is a need for more international co-operation and for smaller powers to assume more responsibility to help to make that happen. In showing courage, empathy, support for science, and a distinctive worldview based on a commitment to multilateralism, the Ardern Government showed that it was possible for a relatively small country to make a positive impact on the world stage. This book shows that when the world was disrupted by the pandemic in 2020, New Zealand under the Ardern Government was able to provide international leadership through its response.

I commend this volume with its diverse perspectives to all seeking to understand how New Zealand has positioned itself in turbulent times, and I commend those who saw the importance of producing it now. Continuity of approach has characterised New Zealand's foreign policy for the most part. Time will tell whether that continues to be the case. This volume provides a baseline for making comparisons.

Helen Clark
November 7, 2023

© 2024 World Scientific Publishing Company
https://doi.org/10.1142/9789811285165_fmatter

About the Editors

Robert G. Patman is one of the University of Otago's Inaugural Sesquicentennial Distinguished Chairs and a specialist in international relations in the Politics Programme. He is the director of the Master of International Studies (MIntSt) programme. He has authored or edited 13 books with most recent being a co-edited volume titled *From Asia-Pacific to Indo-Pacific: Diplomacy in a Contested Region* (Palgrave Macmillan, 2021). Robert is also an Honorary Professor of the New Zealand Defence Command and Staff College and makes regular contributions to the national as well as global media on international issues.

Peter Grace is a teaching fellow in the Politics Programme at the University of Otago, New Zealand. He is co-director of the annual Otago National Security School. His forthcoming book is *The Intel Intellectuals: How Social Scientists Helped Create the Central Intelligence Agency, 1950–1953*. Peter's research interests include intelligence history, international relations theory, and public preparedness for national crises.

Balazs Kiglics is a teaching fellow in the Languages and Cultures Programme at the University of Otago, New Zealand. His doctoral thesis explored the role of values in Japanese elite perceptions of contemporary Japan–China relations. He also coordinates the annual Otago Foreign Policy School and Otago National Security School. Balazs has co-edited the volumes *New Zealand and the World: Past, Present and Future* and *From Asia-Pacific to Indo-Pacific: Diplomacy in a Contested Region*. His research interests include Japanese and Chinese studies, international relations of the Indo-Pacific, and intercultural communication.

Dennis Wesselbaum is an associate professor in Economics at the University of Otago, the President of the New Zealand Association of Economists, Editor-in-Chief of *New Zealand Economic Papers* and Associate Editor of *Humanities & Social Sciences Communications*. He earned a Diploma in (Theoretical) Economics from the University of Kiel and received his Doctorate (Doctor rerum politicarum) from the University of Hamburg. In between, he worked as a researcher for the Kiel Institute for the World Economy. Dennis is a theoretical macroeconomist by training but has both theoretical and empirical interests across various fields. His research activity is split between macroeconomic topics and the interaction between climate, environment and society. His research is interdisciplinary in nature and covers macroeconomics (especially monetary and fiscal policy), economic development, labour, health and environmental impacts.

© 2024 World Scientific Publishing Company
https://doi.org/10.1142/9789811285165_fmatter

About the Contributors

Marion Crawshaw is a former New Zealand Pacific diplomat with postings to Fiji, Solomon Islands (twice) and Papua New Guinea, the latter two as High Commissioner. Early career work in trade and economics shifted to security and development issues. In Wellington she managed New Zealand's bilateral Pacific relationships including in the Regional Assistance Mission to Solomon Islands, established a knowledge management programme in MFAT and spent two years in NZ Police setting up a Policy Group. Marion retired in 2017 and in 2018 completed a Master of Professional Business Analysis in the School of Information Management at Victoria University of Wellington. She is a senior fellow at the VUW Centre for Strategic Studies.

Bethan Greener is professor of International Relations at Massey University. Her research centres on security provision, with a recent focus on the use of the military in support to pandemic responses, how militaries support foreign policy objectives, and New Zealand foreign and defence policy. Her work has been published in journals such as *Critical Military Studies*, *International Peacekeeping*, *Asia Pacific Viewpoint*, and *International Relations* and she is currently working on a major international team research project on gender in military contexts in partnership with the New Zealand Army.

Clifford A. Hart, Jr. is a retired US diplomat and New Zealand permanent resident, served as the National Security Council's China Director at the White House, US Consul General to Hong Kong and Macau, and US Special Envoy for the Six-Party Talks on North Korean nuclear weapons. Over a

33-year diplomatic career, Ford served three other times in China and once each in the Soviet Union and Iraq. For Ford's work on North Korea, President Obama accorded him the personal rank of ambassador. As a private citizen, Ford consults on government relations and speaks and writes on geopolitics. He does not represent the United States or any other government, and the following analysis expresses his personal views only.

Alice C. Hill is the David M. Rubenstein senior fellow for Energy and the Environment at the Council on Foreign Relations. She previously served in the White House as Special Assistant to President Barack Obama and Senior Director for Resilience Policy on the National Security Council, where she led the development of national policy to build climate resilience. Prior, Hill served as senior counselor to the Secretary of the US Department of Homeland Security where she developed the department's first-ever climate adaptation plan. She is the author of *The Fight for Climate After COVID-19* (Oxford University Press) and co-author of *Building a Resilient Tomorrow* (Oxford University Press).

Philip C. Hill is a medical doctor, with specialisation in public health and infectious diseases. He is a researcher and fellow of the Royal Society of New Zealand. He is the first McAuley Professor of International Health at the University of Otago. He established and co-directs the Otago Global Health Institute of over 100 researchers across the University. Professor Hill has published around 260 articles and collaborates with research partners in Africa, Asia, Europe, South America and the Pacific. He served on four ministerial advisory committees during the COVID-19 pandemic, leading key reports on system performance and recommendations to protect New Zealanders.

Suzannah Jessep is the Chief Executive of the Asia New Zealand Foundation. Prior to that, she served as New Zealand's Deputy High Commissioner to India, Sri Lanka, Bangladesh and Deputy Ambassador to Nepal and as New Zealand's Deputy High Commissioner to Vanuatu. During her 13 years in the Ministry of Foreign Affairs and Trade, she also served in the Ministry's Australia, Pacific and Europe Divisions, and in the area of Antarctic and security policy. She is a Board member of the New Zealand Institute of International Affairs (NZIIA), Chairs the Trade for All Ministerial Advisory Group, and sits on the Advisory Boards of the New Zealand Contemporary China Research Centre (NZCCRC) and the New Zealand India Research Institute (NZIRI).

Hon Nanaia Mahuta became the first woman in 2020 as the first woman to hold the Foreign Affairs portfolio in New Zealand under the leadership of Jacinda Ardern. She also served as the Minister of Local Government and Associate Minister for Māori Development until 2023. As a mother and a constituent MP with more than 20 years political experience, Nanaia is a tribal member of Waikato-Tainui, Ngāti Maniapoto and Ngāti Manu and her parliamentary experience has enabled her to contribute to and champion the collective aspirations of Māori and all New Zealanders.

Geoffrey Miller is a geopolitical analyst and writes on current New Zealand foreign policy and related geopolitical issues. He is currently working on a PhD at the University of Otago on New Zealand's relations with the Gulf states. He has written extensively for the Democracy Project, hosted by Victoria University of Wellington, and his analysis has been published regularly by outlets including The Diplomat, the New Zealand Institute of International Affairs and Radio New Zealand. Geoffrey has lived in Germany and the Middle East and is a learner of Arabic and Russian.

Robert Scollay is an honorary associate professor of Economics at the University of Auckland, where he was also the Director of New Zealand's APEC Study Centre until his retirement at the end of 2021. He is currently the vice-chair of the New Zealand Committee of the Pacific Economic Cooperation Council (NZPECC), and was formerly international coordinator of the PECC Trade Policy Forum. His research has focused on international trade policy, with an emphasis on regional trade agreements and regional economic integration, especially in the Asia-Pacific and South Pacific regions, as well as on multilateral trade issues.

Nicholas Ross Smith is a senior research fellow at the University of Canterbury, currently based at the National Centre for Research on Europe. His research coalesces around the regional implications of great power competition with a particular interest in the foreign policies of relatively smaller states that find themselves caught in the middle. His work has been published in *The Journal of Politics*, *International Affairs* and *Global Policy* (among others). He is also currently the academic lead of the Jean Monnet Network research project (2022–2025), 'What role for the EU in the Indo-Pacific (EUIP)?'

Reuben Steff is a senior lecturer of International Relations and Global Security at the University of Waikato, New Zealand. His research encompasses US–China Great Power Competition, the implications of Artificial Intelligence for international security, nuclear deterrence theory, and NZ geopolitics. He has publications in multiple journals, regularly participates in policy development processes, and is the author of four books, including *Emerging Technologies and International Security: Machines, the State and War* (Routledge, 2020). His forthcoming book is *Indo-Pacific Geopolitics in an Era of Intensifying Great Power Competition: A New Zealand Security Strategy Perspective* (Palgrave Macmillan, due 2024).

Lisa Tumahai is the deputy chair of He Pou ā Rangi — Climate Change Commission, Aotearoa New Zealand's independent climate change advisory body and the Kaiwhakahaere (Chairperson) of the Tribal Parliament of Te Rūnanga o Ngāi Tahu. She has served in the Tribal Parliament for over 20 years and has held the role of Kaiwhakahaere for the last seven. She is also an active and important leader for her hapū, Ngāti Waewae, and a commercial director for her Papatipu Rūnanga (Marae entity) on Te Tai Poutini West Coast.

© 2024 World Scientific Publishing Company
https://doi.org/10.1142/9789811285165_fmatter

Acknowledgements

The editors owe a debt of gratitude to a significant number of people and institutions for assistance in the preparation of this book. The inspiration for this volume evolved largely from the theme chosen for the 55th University of Otago Foreign Policy School. As co-directors of that school and editors of this book, we wish to acknowledge the generous support that helped make this book possible.

First, we would like to thank our colleagues on the Academic Committee of the 55th School: Professor Marcelle Dawson, Dr Katerina Standish, Associate Professor Jacqueline Leckie, Professor Ben Schonthal and Professor Paola Voci. They not only provided encouragement and practical support in the planning of the 55th School, but also agreed to chair various sessions and thus played a large part in making a success of the occasion.

Second, we would like to thank all the contributors to this book. They constitute a distinguished team of specialists. They graciously accepted our editorial guidelines and took the time to revise their initial drafts into polished and stimulating chapters.

Third, we wish to express our sincere thanks for the encouraging and patient support for the project given by the staff at World Scientific Publishing. That assistance was greatly appreciated by the editors.

Fourth, we wish to thank all those organisations whose support and sponsorship helped bring together our team of contributors. Without this support, it would have more difficult to bring this book to fruition. We are grateful to the New Zealand Ministry of Foreign Affairs and Trade, Wellington; the Konrad Adenauer Stiftung, Canberra; the Delegation of the European Union to New Zealand; the Asia New Zealand Foundation, Wellington; the US Embassy, Wellington; and the University of Otago.

Finally, and most importantly, we should especially like to thank our families and friends, particularly Beth, Martha, Pattama, Ruth, Ingrid, and Bernd. Throughout the period of producing this book, their support was indispensable.

© 2024 World Scientific Publishing Company
https://doi.org/10.1142/9789811285165_fmatter

Contents

Dedication		v
Foreword		vii
About the Editors		ix
About the Contributors		xi
Acknowledgements		xv
Introduction		xxi
Part I	**Setting the Scene: The Ardern Government's Foreign Policy Agenda**	**1**
Chapter 1	Foreign Policy of Jacinda Ardern's Government in the Era of COVID-19: Minister Mahuta's Vision for Aotearoa New Zealand's Foreign Policy *Nanaia Mahuta*	3
Part II	**The Geopolitical and Economic Context of COVID-19**	**21**
Chapter 2	New Zealand and the Indo-Pacific: Adaptation to Changing Geopolitics *Clifford A. Hart, Jr.*	23

Chapter 3	The Taniwha and the Dragon: New Zealand's Relationship with China under the Ardern Government at a Time of Growing Geopolitical Uncertainty *Nicholas Ross Smith*	43
Chapter 4	Trade Policy under the Ardern Government *Robert Scollay*	63
Part III	**The Promise and Possibilities of Ardern's COVID-19 Pandemic Stance**	**97**
Chapter 5	The New Zealand Public Health Response to COVID-19 and International Implications for Managing Future Pandemic Threats *Philip C. Hill*	99
Chapter 6	Climate Considerations *Alice C. Hill*	131
Chapter 7	Climate Policy in Jacinda Ardern's New Zealand: A Ngāi Tahu Perspective *Lisa Tumahai*	139
Chapter 8	Big Global Issues and Soft Power: New Zealand and the Pacific *Marion Crawshaw*	159
Part IV	**Security and Foreign Policy Directions for New Zealand during the COVID-19 Era**	**171**
Chapter 9	National Security, COVID-19 and New Zealand Foreign Policy *Bethan Greener*	173
Chapter 10	The Ardern Government's Independent Foreign Policy at a Time of Great Power Competition and Australia–China Tensions *Reuben Steff*	191
Chapter 11	New Zealand's Asia Story: The Curious Case of New Zealand–India Relations *Suzannah Jessep*	221

Part V	**Conclusion: Implications for the Foreign Policy of Ardern's Government**	**243**
Chapter 12	The Era of COVID-19 and Beyond: Some Reflections on the Implications for the Foreign Policy of Jacinda Ardern's Government *Geoffrey Miller*	245

Index 265

© 2024 World Scientific Publishing Company
https://doi.org/10.1142/9789811285165_fmatter

Introduction

The purpose of this book is to examine the foreign policy of Jacinda Ardern's New Zealand Government between 2020 and early 2023 when a disruptive event, the COVID-19 pandemic, intersected with an evolving and often tumultuous post-Cold War global environment. By speaking of Ardern's foreign policy, we are referring to decisions and actions that involved, to some appreciable extent, relations between her Labour-led government and other international actors (Frankel, 1963: pp. 1–3). In many ways, it is a good time to consider the development of New Zealand's foreign policy during this period. While COVID-19 continues to impact the world, Ardern has now left the international stage. In a surprise announcement on 19 January 2023, she indicated she was resigning as the fortieth Prime Minister of New Zealand and leader of the Labour Party (Ardern, 2023). The subsequent outpouring of tributes from overseas government figures revealed Ardern's leadership was widely seen as internationally significant. Amongst other things, she was praised for her courage, human decency, and empathy which, in the words of Kamala Harris, the current US Vice-President, 'inspired millions around the world' (Khan, 2023). Few, if any, New Zealand leaders had made a greater impact on the world stage than Ardern during what was an eventful five and a half years as the country's prime minister.

The Ardern Government inherited a New Zealand foreign policy characterised by continuity and change. For the first four decades of the post-1945 era, the United States had displaced Britain as the principal strategic partner of New Zealand as the former colonial power retreated to Europe after the 1956 Suez Crisis and the 1968 decision to withdraw the Royal

Navy from areas 'East of Suez' (Patman, 1997: p. 13). At the same time, New Zealand Governments since 1945 have firmly supported the international rules-based order (sometimes known as the liberal international order) embodied in institutions such as the United Nations and the norm of multilateralism. Such an order is understood by decision-makers in Wellington to be an indispensable element in maximising New Zealand's capacity to conduct an active foreign policy. However, by the mid-1980s, the advent of globalisation coincided with profound changes in New Zealand's national identity and its world view. Sweeping deregulation of the economy and an ambitious attempt to improve relations between Māori and Pākehā through the Crown's recognition of indigenous rights have been linked to the assertion of a non-nuclear security policy, the expansion of free trade, and the reinvigoration of support for human rights and multilateral institutions. These developments have been largely rationalised in terms of a principled, independent New Zealand foreign policy which has emphasised the importance of closer relations with Pacific Island states and the wider Indo-Pacific region in which they are located.

Conceptualising New Zealand as a 'Small State'

Traditionally, New Zealand official representatives and scholars have largely depicted their country as a small state. Such entities are typically defined as those nations which are limited in terms of the size of their territory, population, economic and military capabilities (Brady, 2019: p. 2). Writing in 1980, John Henderson identified what he saw as the essential characteristics of small states. These include the following: low participation in international affairs due to limited capabilities; a narrow scope of interest in international relations; a heavy focus on economic affairs; strong support for internationalism, including the formation of alliances, multilateral institutions and a rules-based order; a moral emphasis in the international arena; and a risk-averse foreign policy approach (Henderson et al., 1980). Such characteristics, it has been argued, oblige a small state to recognise 'it cannot obtain security primarily by use of its own capabilities' (Rothstein, 1969: p. 29) and that it must rely fundamentally on forming alliances with more powerful states, sometimes playing one major power off against another, placing faith in international agreements, or adopting a position of neutrality. In other words, a small state is deemed to be one 'whose leaders consider that it can never, acting alone or in a small group, make a significant impact on the [international] system' (Vital, 1967). In this context, Baldur Thorhallsson has developed the concept of 'shelter' to capture the process in which small states actively seek 'direct and visible diplomatic or military backing' from a more powerful state or multilateral organisation (Thorhallsson, 2019: pp. 380–385).

However, New Zealand has manifested some, though by no means all, of the characteristics commonly associated with a small state's foreign policy. While it has a relatively small but highly developed economy and only modest military capabilities, it possesses a territorial area that is slightly larger than that of the United Kingdom, lays claim to the world's fifth-largest maritime space, and has a population size (5.1 million) which is similar to that of minor powers such as Norway, Ireland or Finland. To be sure, New Zealand's championing of free trade and its enthusiasm for GATT, the World Trade Organization (WTO), the Comprehensive and Progressive Agreement for Trans-Pacific Partnership (CPTPP) and bilateral Free Trade Agreements (FTAs) could be said to reflect a strong economic focus. Similarly, New Zealand's Nuclear Free Zone, Disarmament, and Arms Control Act of 1987 and Wellington's refusal to support the George W. Bush Administration's illegal invasion of Iraq in March 2003 might be interpreted as being consistent with the moral focus of small states.

Nevertheless, it is clear New Zealand has diverged in a number of ways from Henderson's model of small state foreign policy behaviour. First, its distinctive geography means it is not subject to any direct threat in the post-Cold War era, and this has given Wellington some freedom of manoeuvre on a range of international issues. For example, New Zealand was the first developed state to sign an FTA with China, in 2008. Second, New Zealand appears to be a relatively significant power in the context of the Pacific Island states (Jackson, 2005: p. 198). As well as retaining the status of an administrative trustee power and having constitutional responsibilities towards the Cook Islands, Niue and Tokelau, New Zealand allocates more than 60 per cent of its development aid to this region, and this makes it the third-largest aid donor there after Australia and the United States. Third, New Zealand's foreign policy has consistently had a broad disposition in the post-1945 era. The country has been an active player in international governance arrangements, which includes the United Nations, international peacekeeping or the Antarctic Treaty System amongst others. In addition, New Zealand has demonstrated a commitment to multilateral security activities. These include its post-war membership of the Five Eyes intelligence-sharing partnership and serving as a partner of NATO since 2012. Fourth, and not unrelated, New Zealand has shown a presence on the international stage that is out of all proportion to the status normally associated with a small state. In the post-Cold War era, it has twice won a non-permanent seat on the UN Security Council, in 1993–1994 and 2015–2016. Meanwhile, New Zealand citizens have secured a number of leadership positions in international organisations and boosted the country's influence on the global stage. Don McKinnon, the former New Zealand Foreign Minister, served as Secretary-General of the Commonwealth; Mike Moore, a former New Zealand Prime Minister, held a three-year 'split term' as Director-General of the WTO; Alan Bollard, former Governor of the Reserve Bank of New Zealand, served as Executive Director of Asia-Pacific Economic Cooperation (APEC); and Helen Clark, a former New Zealand Prime Minister, served as the Head Administrator of the UN Development Programme (UNDP) and competed strongly for the position of Secretary-General of the United Nations in 2016.

Ardern's Foreign Policy before COVID-19

The gulf between New Zealand's self-image as a small state and the way the country was perceived externally significantly widened during the early years of Ardern's leadership. After the September 2017 general election and the formation of a Labour-led coalition government, the new Prime Minister quickly demonstrated a style of leadership that captured considerable international attention and admiration. Ardern enthusiastically embraced and clearly communicated a New Zealand world view based firmly on multilateralism and a rules-based international order, but also showed some deft diplomatic skills and the ability to learn from mistakes in managing relations with two superpowers that did not always have a similar understanding of those interests and values.

The first major overseas trip by Ardern was in November 2017 when she attended the APEC summit in Vietnam. The meeting provided Ardern with her first face-to-face encounter with President Donald Trump, a populist advocate of an 'America First' foreign policy stance that emphasised the rights and privileges of great powers in world politics. According to Ardern, Trump had 'genuinely been interested' in the New Zealand election and the two leaders apparently engaged in some light-hearted banter at the meeting after Trump suggested she had 'caused a lot of upset' in her country (Ainge Roy, 2017). The contrast in the international perspectives of Ardern and Trump became plain when the two leaders addressed the UN General Assembly in September 2018. While Trump rejected 'the ideology of globalism' in favour of 'patriotism', 'sovereignty' and 'independence', Ardern said the 'concept of looking outwardly and beyond ourselves, of kindness and collectivism' was an essential starting point for addressing challenges like climate change that were 'truly global in their nature and impact' (Trump, 2018; Ministry of Foreign Affairs and Trade, 2018). But the New Zealand Prime Minister was careful to avoid any direct public criticism of President Trump's foreign policy stance at the United Nations or elsewhere.

In January 2017, Washington had announced its withdrawal from the Trans-Pacific Partnership (TPP). This was a major blow to Wellington and a number of other states that had worked hard to accommodate American interests in this proposed arrangement. Historically, New Zealand governments have been trying for years to secure a bilateral free trade agreement with Washington and played a leadership role in advancing the idea of the TPP, a multilateral trade agreement encompassing the United States and 11 other states from the Asia-Pacific region. But pointing to the North American Free Trade Agreement (NAFTA) experience, President Trump argued that multilateral FTAs like the TPP disadvantaged America and simply lead to the outsourcing of US jobs to partner countries. But if the Trump Administration expected America's exit to kill the TPP initiative, it was disappointed. The Labour–New Zealand First coalition government negotiated with the other ten members of the proposed TPP agreement to activate a multilateral FTA without the US, and in March 2018 Trade Minister David Parker signed what was now called the CPTPP in Chile (Parker, 2018). Meanwhile, the Trump Administration went further than the Obama Administration in its public hostility to the WTO, a key institution as far as New Zealand was concerned in promoting multilateral rules-based trade, and appeals to the Trump Administration by Ardern's Labour-led coalition government to exempt New Zealand from US tariffs imposed on imports of steel and aluminium largely fell on deaf ears.

At the same time, Ardern agreed with many other international leaders that President Trump's reported reference to 'shithole' nations in a meeting on immigration with US lawmakers was 'hugely offensive' (Satherley, 2018); indicated she accepted rather than endorsed Trump's unilateral action of unleashing more than 100 American missiles against facilities belonging to the Assad regime following the alleged use of chemical weapons during the Syrian war; and expressed some strong political reservations about the Trump Administration's somewhat erratic policy stance toward Kim Jong-un's dictatorship in North Korea. Nevertheless, Ardern's leadership worked hard during the first years of her premiership not to allow points of disagreement with the Trump Administration to adversely affect what was a generally positive bilateral relationship between the two states.

The first Ardern Government also faced the challenge of managing New Zealand's important relationship with China at a time of increasing Chinese assertiveness in the Indo-Pacific region and intensifying superpower rivalry. In what was a nuanced policy response, the Ardern leadership sought to avoid the narrow range of choices said to confront small states in such circumstances. Wellington showed little inclination to rely exclusively on balancing against China's growing presence, in particular, in the Pacific region by strengthening its military–strategic relationship with the Trump Administration or alternatively bandwagoning with China in this region (Gee & Patman, 2021). Rather, Ardern's coalition government tried to maximise New Zealand's diplomatic autonomy and leverage by combining both elements, of balancing and accommodation, in its policy towards China.

On the one hand, the Labour-led coalition in Wellington announced the 'Pacific Reset' in March 2018. It involved a substantial increase of New Zealand's development assistance to the region. This would be increased over four years by NZ$714 million and the Reset also included the establishment of 14 new diplomatic and development posts, and a significant increase of high-level New Zealand diplomacy in the region (Cabinet External Relations and Security Committee, 2018). While Winston Peters, the New Zealand Foreign Minister, did not identify China by name in launching the Reset, his emphasis on regional coordination with Australia and his plea to the United States to step up its engagement in the South Pacific (Peters, 2018) made it plain it was China's growing regional role that was the most important reason for the Reset. At the same time, Ardern's Labour-led coalition's Strategic Defence Policy Statement of July 2018 marked a major departure in the way New Zealand conducted relations with its biggest trade partner, China. The document explicitly identified Beijing as a potential threat to the international rules-based order, which has long been considered a vital safeguard for New Zealand's national interests (Ministry of Defence, 2018).

Furthermore, having publicly identified links between the Chinese Ministry of State Security and cyber intrusions in New Zealand, the Director-General of the Government Communications Security Bureau (GCSB) recommended in late 2018 that China's telecommunications giant, Huawei, should not be permitted to participate in the development of New Zealand's 5G telecommunications network. That outcome followed similar decisions by three other Five Eyes partners — the United States, Canada and Australia — and led to warnings by China's diplomats that New Zealand's decision to exclude Huawei could have consequences for the bilateral economic relationship. Moreover, the Ardern Labour-led coalition suspended its extradition treaty with Hong Kong in late July 2020 after China passed national security legislation which significantly restricted the democratic rights of Hong Kong residents and, in Wellington's view, clearly breached the 'one country, two systems' agreement of 1997 (Manch, 2020, July 28). This suspension followed similar moves by other members of the Five Eyes alliance and was condemned by the Chinese Embassy in Wellington 'as a gross interference in China's internal affairs' (Chinese Embassy, 2020).

On the other hand, the Labour-led government attempted to engage with China in a way that was distinguishable from other members of the Five Eyes alliance. While Beijing has been very energetic in pressing the Belt and Road Initiative (BRI) in the South Pacific region, New Zealand did not follow the path of other Western states in spurning it. Rather, the Ardern coalition government signed a non-binding cooperation agreement in 2017, and by 2019 the Prime Minister publicly indicated she was prepared to offer a dialogue with Beijing on the evolution of the BRI. The way in which the Labour-led coalition handled the decision to exclude Huawei from developing New Zealand's 5G network was also instructive. Unlike the United States, Canada and Australia, which openly rationalised the rejection of Huawei's involvement in their 5G projects in national security terms, the GCSB minister said New Zealand's decision was based on technical requirements, that Wellington had no concerns about the closeness of Huawei to the Chinese Government, and the future participation of Huawei in the 5G network could not be ruled out (Radio New Zealand, 2018).

These points were reiterated in April 2019 when Prime Minister Ardern visited Beijing. In the words of President Xi Jinping, Ardern's visit 'proved the special commitment of [New Zealand] to relations with China' (Young, 2019). As well as positive talks with President Xi, the New Zealand Prime Minister met with her counterpart Li Keqiang and Foreign Minister Wang Yi. Amongst other things, the two sides agreed to accelerate work on upgrading the 2008 New Zealand–China FTA, a process that was completed three years later. Overall, Prime Minister Ardern's visit seemed to put bilateral relations back on a positive track after the Huawei controversy. In contrast, Beijing's relations with the other members of the Five Eyes alliance generally remained much more strained after they had banned Huawei from their respective 5G networks. Moreover, while New Zealand followed its Five Eyes partners in suspending its extradition treaty with Hong Kong on 28 July 2020, it was the last to do so within this intelligence-sharing partnership (Manch, 2020, July 9). It was clear that while Wellington shared many of the strategic concerns of its Five Eyes partners, it reserved the right to express them in a distinctive fashion that was more typical of a minor power than a small state.

However, it was the compassionate but decisive response of Ardern to a white supremacist terrorist attack, which killed 51 people at two mosques in Christchurch in March 2019, that more than anything established her reputation as a leader on the international stage during this period. In the immediate aftermath of the attack, the Prime Minister reached out to and showed great solidarity with the Muslim victims of this atrocity. 'They are us. The person who has perpetuated this violence against us is not. They have no place in New Zealand', Ardern said (Ardern, 2019). The power of her public response came not only from warmly embracing the survivors and the families of the victims but also from symbolic gestures such as wearing the hijab and refusing to use the name of the main suspect (Malik, 2019). In contrast to the robotic, scripted and often insincere responses of some political leaders to comparable tragedies overseas, images of Ardern reacting as a decent, empathetic human being at a time of national trauma helped to unify New Zealand and won her considerable global admiration.

In addition, the Ardern leadership took measures immediately after the Christchurch atrocity that signalled the government's determination to make New Zealand a safer country. By 11 April 2019, the New Zealand parliament had succeeded in passing urgent legislation that banned all military-style semi-automatic weapons and assault rifles — the sort of arms used by the Christchurch terrorist — and introduced a buy-back scheme to take such weapons out of circulation (Schwartz, 2019). A month later, Ardern collaborated with French President Emmanuel

Macron to launch an initiative known as the Christchurch Call to Action in Paris to curb online extremism. During the previous decade and a half, new digital networks and social media platforms such as Facebook and Twitter had provided opportunities for extremist organisations to propagate their ideas to wider audiences and thus radicalise and recruit 'lone actors' to carry out violent acts of terrorism. It was this environment that helped to generate the terrorist attacks in Christchurch in 2019, conducted by an attacker equipped with GoPro technology to record and share the images of his atrocity online with other white supremacists (Patman, 2021). By 2022, the Christchurch Call initiative had won the support of more than 55 governments, including the Biden Administration in the United States.

The leadership qualities of empathy and decisiveness were also evident in Prime Minister Ardern's public responses to the White Island/Whakaari volcanic eruption in December 2019 which killed 22 tourists, many of them Australian, and two local guides, and to her handling of relations with neighbouring Australia. In a statement that was widely praised internationally, Ardern said the overseas visitors among those killed on the island 'are forever linked to this place and our nation and we will continue to hold [them] close' (Taylor, 2020). Meanwhile, Ardern pulled no punches when it came to strains in relations with New Zealand's closest ally, Australia, generated by Canberra's policy of deporting New Zealand citizens who had been sentenced to more than a year in prison, regardless of how long they had lived in Australia. In an extraordinary joint appearance in Sydney, Ardern bluntly told her Australian counterpart, Scott Morrison, that 'Australia is well within its rights to deport individuals who break its laws — New Zealand does the same … But we have a simple request. Send back Kiwis, genuine Kiwis — do not deport your people and your problems' (Walls, 2020). While Morrison was apparently unmoved by Ardern's candid message, her stance demonstrated that New Zealand was not prepared to be bullied by a bigger partner on this issue. Such defiance was admired in New Zealand, in many parts of Australia and the wider world.

Ardern's Foreign Policy during COVID-19

Having mounted the world stage through her empathetic handling of the 2019 Christchurch mosque attacks, Prime Minister Ardern then garnered global headlines for her administration's bold COVID-19 response. Lauding her staunch resolve, the *New York Times* wrote in April 2020 as follows:

> Leadership may be hard to define, but in times of crisis it is easy to identify. As the pandemic has spread fear, disease and death, national leaders across the globe have been severely tested. Some have fallen short, sometimes dismally, but there are also those leaders who have risen to the moment, demonstrating resolve, courage, empathy, respect for science and elemental decency, and thereby dulling the impact of the disease on their people. The master class on how to respond belongs to Jacinda Ardern, the 39-year-old prime minister of New Zealand (*New York Times*, 2020).

Credited with being only the second woman in the modern era to have a baby while leading a country (Benazir Bhutto of Pakistan was the first), Ardern represented a foil to the narcissistic self-interestedness of the Trump era. The 'politics of kindness' she espoused appeared to be backed by a strong ideological approach steeped in over a century's progressive Labour Party foreign policy, which had championed the League of Nations' collective security in the 1930s and spurned Cold War nuclear posturing in the 1980s. This was what the world was looking for in a leader. 'Wherever I go', the New Zealand movie actor Sir Sam Neill told *Time* magazine, 'people say, "You think we could have Jacinda this week? Could we just borrow her for a while?"'. The magazine's front cover had trumpeted 'Know us by our deeds' and claimed 'Jacinda Ardern has the world's attention. How will she use it?' (Luscombe, 2020).

'Proof of power', wrote the political scientist Joseph Nye, 'lies not in resources, but in the ability to change the behavior of states', thus coining the expression *soft power*. If, as Nye believed, traditional forms of power like military and economic strength were being replaced by co-optive power — or the 'power of ... ideas' that can 'shape others' preferences' — then by 2021 Aotearoa New Zealand was arguably one of the most powerful countries in the world (Nye, 1990: pp. 155, 166).

Were there ever a time when Aotearoa New Zealand could help lead the world through the many challenges it faced — from geopolitical tensions, peace and greater prosperity through trade, countering the effects of poverty and poor health and education outcomes on indigenous populations, or tackling the mounting storms of climate change — then it appeared Ardern was ready to seize the moment. The opportunity to 'shape others' preferences' would obviously be embedded in foreign policy, and it came at a time when Ardern had appointed the country's second indigenous and first woman foreign minister, Nanaia Mahuta, a signal that Aotearoa New Zealand intended to do things differently, and with an emphasis on promise-keeping and inclusive values.

Part I   Setting the Scene: The Ardern Government's Foreign Policy Agenda

Any survey of the Ardern Government's foreign policy during COVID-19 must recognise the uncertainty the pandemic brought, not only in how to deal with the crisis, but also the ripple effects it brought to geopolitics. In Chapter 1, Minister of Foreign Affairs and Trade Mahuta is candid about the problems presented to the Ardern Government by COVID-19 and the rising geopolitical competition evidenced by Russia's invasion of Ukraine. Foreign policy during a global pandemic when borders are closed, issues are complex and dynamic, and many of the routine tools and fora for diplomacy are unavailable, is a deeply challenging thing to navigate — but Mahuta believes Aotearoa New Zealand has done so, with much success. The Ardern Government's vision for a country in and of the Pacific is a defining feature of how this country equips itself to navigate a way forward and strengthen its core relationships and resilience characteristics for this time. Foreign policy at a time of heightening geostrategic contests, and indeed assaults on the most fundamental tenets of international law, state sovereignty, territorial integrity and human rights, as we have witnessed in Russia's actions against Ukraine, is an equally challenging thing — but Aotearoa New Zealand is responding with absolute clarity, commitment, speed, and humanity, together with its many partners. And foreign policy during this critical moment for accelerated climate change action, which requires an unprecedented level of global agreement, leadership, and shared effort, is perhaps the single most important item on our country's international agenda — but here, too, Aotearoa New Zealand is taking up this challenge at home and abroad, with determination and clarity of purpose, argues Mahuta. An intergenerational perspective to our foreign policy means that we are more deliberate in our approach and in the connectivity between the societal norms we seek to uphold and the modernisation of our international architecture. The aforementioned challenges are exacerbating a range of worrying international trends, including the following: a troubling rise in inequality and in hunger; the development and resilience challenges within our Pacific region; tensions and growing militarisation, including within the Indo-Pacific; and a rules-based international system under pressure, with its multilateral and regional institutions often lacking the tools, will or support to respond effectively to these emerging challenges. These are difficult times, and Aotearoa New Zealand should not expect them to grow easier or less complex in the period ahead. They are likely to test the boundaries of the country's relationships and foreign policy settings. Aotearoa New Zealand will need to do things differently. The responses of the past two years have seen us chart wholly new territory. Our country will need to continue to adapt and innovate, and we will need the very best our foreign policy can deliver for Aotearoa New Zealand.

Part II The Geopolitical and Economic Context of COVID-19

In Chapter 2, Clifford A. Hart, Jr. takes a long and critical look at Aotearoa New Zealand's policy towards its security alliance with the United States and its trade relationship with China. Wellington has taken practical steps which confirm Aotearoa New Zealand's deep concerns about Chinese behaviour, says Hart. However, he believes there remains a substantial gap between the Ardern Government's declaratory policy and its practical responses to the deteriorating geopolitical environment in which it finds itself. There remains the question of how deeply rooted is Wellington's new geopolitical mindset. Senior Aotearoa New Zealand leaders have expressed unmistakable concerns about China but, Hart argues, failed to place them in a clear strategic context.

Meanwhile, Nicholas Ross Smith argues in Chapter 3 that the Aotearoa New Zealand Government has been taking an asymmetrical hedging strategy towards China and the United States, and may struggle to maintain this position in the future. His chapter begins with an historical overview of Aotearoa New Zealand's relationship with China, coupled with an appraisal of the relationship during Ardern's first term as Prime Minister, particularly the 'mature relationship' with China which is underpinned by deepening trade dependence. Thereafter, Aotearoa New Zealand's relationship with China is theoretically assessed by examining the wider geopolitical dynamics found in the Indo-Pacific, with a specific utilisation of the Regional

Security Complex Theory. Finally, a discussion of the future challenges and directions of Aotearoa New Zealand's relationship with China in light of the continued changing geopolitical dynamics of the Indo-Pacific is offered. However, the Sino-Aotearoa New Zealand relationship is significantly challenged by the growing geopolitical uncertainty of the Indo-Pacific and Aotearoa New Zealand's putative China strategy — part of a broader asymmetrical alignment hedging strategy — which may become untenable in the near future. Smith says this will have seismic implications for Aotearoa New Zealand's relationship with China moving forward.

In Chapter 4, Rob Scollay argues that while Aotearoa New Zealand's trade environment continued much along the same path as before in some respects, the Ardern Government faced two disruptive challenges: how to deal with the United Kingdom's leaving the European Union in 2020 and President Trump's 'America First' trade policy, particularly his decision to withdraw the United States from the TPP. The Ardern Government navigated these problems firstly by adopting a more inclusive approach to setting trade policy (one that recognised the partnership with, and obligations to, Māori under Te Tiriti o Waitangi, the Treaty of Waitangi of 1840), and secondly by emphasising Aotearoa New Zealand's commitment to multilateralism (and to championing plurilateralism — a 'likemindedness' strategy) by helping rescue TPP from the ashes and concluding negotiations on the Regional Comprehensive Economic Partnership. In the midst of Brexit, and the imposition of Trump's discriminatory tariffs on Aotearoa New Zealand steel and aluminium, the Ardern Government also had to deal with the immediate disruptions to trade supply chains brought on by the COVID-19 crisis, the diminution of the WTO Dispute Settlement Body, a 'remote' APEC conference, and the negotiation of an FTA with the European Union. While Aotearoa New Zealand continued to feel the heat of a trade environment in crisis over COVID-19, the touchpaper remained China: export dependency grew over this period at the same time as questions over China's role in the coronavirus outbreak, its clampdown on democracy in Hong Kong and its treatment of the Uyghurs in Xinjiang became hot geopolitical issues.

Part III The Promise and Possibilities of Ardern's COVID-19 Pandemic Stance

The Ardern Government's handling of the COVID-19 pandemic earned Aotearoa New Zealand plaudits from much of the Western world.

In Chapter 5, Philip C. Hill argues that Aotearoa New Zealand's experience in dealing with COVID-19 can rightly be considered an overall success story. However, like all countries, its public health response to COVID-19 has been a mix of successes and failures. In this chapter, Hill provides a basic summary of the epidemiology of COVID-19, followed by a description of key aspects of the public health response. This is then followed by a description of specific initiatives undertaken in the Aotearoa New Zealand public health response that are of some significance. Finally, the local and international implications for managing future pandemic threats are discussed.

Alice C. Hill believes there are parallels between COVID-19 and climate change. Tackling climate change requires collective action among international governments, local communities, non-governmental organisations (NGOs), the private sector, business leaders, and others. In Chapter 6, Hill argues that a national adaptation plan can increase the coordination among these groups by identifying the roles that each could play. Other nations across the globe have heeded the call to create national adaptation strategies. China unveiled its strategy in 2013, as did Russia in 2019. Unfortunately, the United States currently lacks a national climate adaptation plan. Without a national adaptation plan, states tend to wait for disasters to happen before they address the risk.

Chapter 7 considers what a Māori-centred climate policy would look like. Lisa Tumahai cites Ardern's claim that climate change would be her generation's 'nuclear-free moment'. This, says Tumahai, is a clear implication that Aotearoa New Zealand would become a climate action beacon for the world. It is plain that climate action needs to be prioritised and policies enacted with a high degree of urgency; however, equal weight and immediacy must be given to partnership with *tangata whenua* (Māori people). A Māori-centred climate policy will help ensure a lasting societal shift that does not inflict detrimental effects on the most vulnerable. Tumahai is optimistic that this important *mahi* (work) can be carried out contiguously in a way that will lead to a harmonious and equitable transition to a more resilient, economically sound and climatically viable Aotearoa New Zealand.

In Chapter 8, Marion Crawshaw argues it is important for Aotearoa New Zealand to put 'people relationships' first when tackling the Pacific's growing worries about its future. She critically analyses Aotearoa New Zealand's claim to soft power before looking at a number of 'big global issues' and their impact on the Pacific region. Crawshaw then discusses some of the soft power tools that Aotearoa New Zealand has available in its Pacific relationships. She concludes with an argument for the widening of those tools beyond development assistance, including the establishment of institutions that can more deeply embed Pacific knowledge connections and relationships in Aotearoa New Zealand itself, not just in the Pacific Island nations.

Part IV   Security and Foreign Policy Directions for New Zealand during the COVID-19 Era

In Chapter 9, Bethan Greener looks at the pandemic as a national security problem. Despite, at face value, looking like a public health issue, the COVID-19 pandemic has presented or exacerbated challenges to both national security and foreign policy. Greener looks at three particular components: supply chain resilience for vaccines and protective gear; measures to ensure economic security; and rising concerns about social cohesion. The possibility of future pandemics, she concludes, means Aotearoa New Zealand must continue to focus on these issues and weave preparedness into both its foreign policy and national security strategies.

Reuben Steff suggests in Chapter 10 a framework of *strategic liberalism*. This is entirely consistent, he says, with the open and inclusive partnership model designated by Foreign Minister Mahuta and Prime Minister Ardern. It recognises a harmony of interests between the United States and Australia on the one hand and China on the other, rather than a pessimistic, determinist narrative. Steff sees Aotearoa New Zealand taking a lead in diplomacy and institution building in the Indo-Pacific and, after outlining a brief history of the problem, suggests the creation of a new research and teaching institution to facilitate co-operation in the region; a proposal that Aotearoa New Zealand hosts a high-level summit meeting between the United States, Australia and China; that Aotearoa New Zealand take up associated or observer status in the Quad and AUKUS; and also that there be a greater focus on shared institutions promoting a global public health-care system, a tax system, and an international crisis-management and quick-response system to handle global crises.

If Aotearoa New Zealand is going to take a stronger role in the Indo-Pacific, it needs to understand the key players better and build relationships that are more than just transactional, argues Suzannah Jessep. In Chapter 11, she explores the development of Aotearoa New Zealand's relations with India and South Asia more widely. Jessep looks at the factors that have helped and hindered the growth of the relationship and shines a light on the opportunities that exist to rejuvenate the bilateral partnership, based on deepening knowledge, growing targeted people-to-people connections and changing the lens through which Aotearoa New Zealand has become accustomed to viewing India. Jessep concludes by highlighting a set of 'engagement principles' that the Ardern Government and its successors could employ to guide the relationship with India going forward.

Part V   Conclusion: Implications for the Foreign Policy of Ardern's Government

Geoffrey Miller concludes that the polarisation that affected the world in general over the pandemic period — seen in the global debates over lockdowns, masks and vaccines — also affected geopolitics. He believes that COVID-19 and the upheaval of 2020 may mark the end-point for Aotearoa New Zealand's previously successful strategy of riding the waves of globalisation and viewing foreign policy primarily through a trade lens. Looking back, COVID-19 may have not directly changed Aotearoa New Zealand's foreign policy, but it certainly provided the background music for some fundamental shifts.

Without a doubt, the uncertainty that the COVID-19 pandemic created globally required Aotearoa New Zealand to define its foreign policy more clearly. Australia's decision to call for an investigation into the origins of the virus in Wuhan was a pivotal point, as both Foreign Minister Mahuta and Prime Minister Ardern were repeatedly challenged on Aotearoa New Zealand's policy towards an increasingly aggressive authoritarian and illiberal China. The punishing sanctions levelled by Beijing against Australia for calling for an inquiry; an energised Biden Administration demanding a cohesive approach towards China; and the Five Eyes intelligence-sharing partnership being corralled into acting as a voice against China's repressive internal politics, all pressured the Ardern Government to be specific about where its red lines lay.

Ardern, after all, was a seasoned communicator with a reputation for speaking plainly. The great test for Aotearoa New Zealand foreign policy over this period was to refine the language used to describe the country's geopolitical relationships in such a way as to minimise offence and backlash, acknowledge tensions, and leverage Ardern's soft power in a way that opened doors for the rebuilding of a much-weakened rules-based order.

An example came towards the end of Ardern's six-year prime ministership. Responding to Russia's 2022 invasion of Ukraine, Ardern recognised it for what it was — a large, authoritarian state exercising the principle of 'might is right' against a smaller, democratic state. This event drew together many of the elements of Ardern's foreign policy: her belief that a decline in the rules-based order was an existential threat to small states; that such states needed a multilateral platform like the United Nations to 'level the playing field'; and that trade was an important tool in finding common understanding and expressing disagreement. In the case of the latter, her government moved quickly to pass legislation to autonomously sanction Russia, a move that was unlikely to have happened if the United Nations had not had its hands tied by Russia using its veto in the Security Council. Ardern said at the time that Russia's 'use of its UN Security Council position to block consideration of the invasion is morally bankrupt' and it 'demonstrates why we must continue to seek reform of the UN' (Patman, 2023). As one of the first countries to formally recognise Ukraine's plight, Aotearoa New Zealand implemented a travel ban on Russian officials, cut back diplomatic engagements and by mid-March 2022 had extended NZ$6 million in humanitarian aid to Ukraine, as well as sending military personnel to the United Kingdom to help train Ukrainian recruits.

Ardern retired from politics in January 2023, just two-thirds into her second term. Visibly exhausted, but smiling throughout her resignation announcement, she told the country there she 'no longer had enough left in the tank to do the job justice' (Mahon-Heap, 2023). But Aotearoa New Zealand's foreign policy has its own momentum, which Ardern clearly boosted but never solely provided its main impetus. Ardern very clearly articulated Aotearoa New Zealand's position in the international system, an essential foundation for what is a very uncertain future. This book endeavours to tell the story of how that foreign policy position was decided.

References

Ainge Roy, E. (2017, November 17). Jacinda Ardern retorts to Donald Trump: "No one marched when I was elected." *The Guardian*. www.theguardian.com/world/2017/nov/17/jacinda-ardern-to-donald-trump-no-one-marched-when-i-was-elected.

Ardern, J. (2018, September 28). Full speech: "Me too must become we too" — Jacinda Ardern calls for gender equality, kindness at UN. *One News*. www.1news.co.nz/2018/09/27/full-speech-me-too-must-become-we-too-jacinda-ardern-calls-for-gender-equality-kindness-at-un.

Ardern, J. (2019, March 15). Jacinda Ardern on the Christchurch shooting: "One of New Zealand's darkest days." *The Guardian*. www.theguardian.com/world/2019/mar/15/one-of-new-zealands-darkest-days-jacinda-ardern-responds-to-christchurch-shooting.

Ardern, J. (2023, January 19). Prime Minister Jacinda Ardern announces resignation. www.beehive.govt.nz/release/prime-minister-jacinda-ardern-announces-resignation.

Brady, A.-M. (Ed.) (2019). Small can be huge: New Zealand foreign policy in an era of global uncertainty. In *Small States and the Changing Global Order: New Zealand Faces the Future*. Cham: Springer.

Cabinet External Relations and Security Committee, New Zealand (2018). The Pacific Reset: The First Year. Minute of Decision, ERS-18-MIN-0028. Wellington: Cabinet External Relations and Security Committee. www.mfat.govt.nz/assets/OIA/R-R-The-Pacific-reset-The-First-Year.PDF.

Chinese Embassy, Wellington (2020, July 28). Response to Media Query by Spokesperson of Chinese Embassy in New Zealand on Hong Kong Issue. The Embassy of the People's Republic of China in New Zealand. nz.china-embassy.gov.cn/eng/zxgxs/202007/t20200728_886724.html.

Frankel, J. (1963). *The Making of Foreign Policy: An Analysis of Decision-Making*. London: Oxford University Press.

Gee, A. & Patman, R. G. (2021). Small state or minor power? New Zealand's Five Eyes membership, intelligence reforms, and Wellington's response to China's growing Pacific role. *Intelligence and National Security*, 36(1), 34–50.

Henderson, J., Jackson, K., & Kennaway, R. (Eds) (1980). *Beyond New Zealand: The Foreign Policy of a Small State*. Auckland: Methuen.

Jackson, R. (2005). Multilateralism: New Zealand and the United Nations. In Patman, R. G. & Rudd, C. (Eds.), *Sovereignty under Siege? Globalization and New Zealand*. Aldershot: Ashgate.

Khan, A. J. (2023, January 20). Mother, politician, trailblazer. How Jacinda Ardern became an icon for millions. *NBC News*. www.nbcnews.com/news/world/jacinda-ardern-resigns-new-zealand-prime-minister-mother-icon-rcna66485.

Luscombe, B. (2020, February 20). A year after Christchurch, Jacinda Ardern has the world's attention. How will she use it? *Time Magazine*. time.com/5787443/jacinda-ardern-christchurch-new-zealand-anniversary.

Mahon-Heap, J. (2023, January 19). Jacinda Ardern didn't have "enough left in the tank" — how to tell when you're running on empty. *Stuff*. www.stuff.co.nz/life-style/wellbeing/300788082/jacinda-ardern-didnt-have-enough-left-in-the-tank--how-to-tell-when-youre-running-on-empty.

Malik, N. (2019, March 28). With respect: How Jacinda Ardern showed the world what a leader should be. *The Guardian*. www.theguardian.com/world/2019/mar/28/with-respect-how-jacinda-ardern-showed-the-world-what-a-leader-should-be.

Manch, T. (2020, July 9). New Zealand to "review" its relationship with Hong Kong, as Five Eyes Countries Respond to Beijing's national security law. *Stuff*. www.stuff.co.nz/national/politics/122089304/new-zealand-to-review-its-relationship-with-hong-kong-as-five-eyes-countries-respond-to-beijings-national-security-law.

Manch, T. (2020, July 28). New Zealand suspends extradition treaty with Hong Kong, China calls it "serious violation" of international law. *Stuff*. www.stuff.co.nz/national/politics/122268160/new-zealand-suspends-extradition-treaty-with-hong-kong-china-calls-it-serious-violation-of-international-law.

Ministry of Defence, New Zealand (2018). Strategic Defence Policy Statement 2018. Wellington: Ministry of Defence. www.defence.govt.nz/assets/Uploads/8958486b29/Strategic-Defence-Policy-Statement-2018.pdf.

Ministry of Foreign Affairs and Trade, New Zealand (2018, September 28). New Zealand national statement to United Nations General Assembly. www.mfat.govt.nz/en/media-and-resources/new-zealand-national-statement-to-united-nations-general-assembly.

New York Times (2020, April 30). In a crisis, true leaders stand out. www.nytimes.com/2020/04/30/opinion/coronavirus-leadership.html.

Nye, J. (1990, Autumn). Soft power. *Foreign Policy, 80*, 153–171.

Parker, D. (2018, March 9). New Zealand Sets Out Progressive and Inclusive Trade Approach at CPTPP Signing. www.beehive.govt.nz/release/new-zealand-sets-out-progressive-and-inclusive-trade-approach-cptpp-signing.

Patman, R. G. (1997). Introduction. In Patman, R. G. (Ed.), *New Zealand and Britain: A Special Relationship in Transition*. Palmerston North: Dunmore.

Patman, R. G. (2021, July 31). NZ still has important role in the global challenge of violent extremism. *Stuff*. www.stuff.co.nz/national/christchurch-shooting/125916643/nz-still-has-important-role-in-the-global-challenge-of-violent-extremism.

Patman, R. G. (2023, February 24). Is New Zealand doing enough for Ukraine? *Newsroom*. www.newsroom.co.nz/ideasroom/is-new-zealand-doing-enough-for-ukraine.

Peters, W. (2018). Pacific Partnerships — Georgetown Address, Washington, DC. www.beehive.govt.nz/speech/pacific-partnerships-georgetown-address-washington-dc.

Radio New Zealand (2018, November 29). Minister: GCSB decision about risk assessment, not China. www.rnz.co.nz/news/political/377048/minister-gcsb-decision-about-risk-assessment-not-china.

Rothstein, R. (1969). *Alliances and Small Powers*. New York: Columbia University Press.

Satherley, D. (2018, January 15). Donald Trump's s**thole comments "hugely offensive" — Ardern. *Newshub*. www.newshub.co.nz/home/world/2018/01/donald-trump-s-s-thole-comments-hugely-offensive-ardern.html.

Schwartz, M. S. (2019, April 10). New Zealand passes law banning most semi-automatic weapons. *npr*. www.npr.org/2019/04/10/711820023/new-zealand-passes-law-banning-most-semi-automatic-weapons.

Taylor, P. (2020, December 9). White Island volcano anniversary: Ardern leads nation in mourning tourists who died. *The Guardian*. www.theguardian.com/world/2020/dec/09/white-island-volcano-anniversary-ardern-leads-nation-in-mourning-tourists-who-died.

Thorhallsson, B. (2019). Small states and the changing global order: What small state theory can offer New Zealand foreign policymaking. In Brady, A.-M. (Ed.), *Small States and the Changing Global Order: New Zealand Faces the Future*. Cham: Springer.

Trump, D. (2018, September 25). Remarks by President Trump to the 74th Session of the United Nations General Assembly. trumpwhitehouse.archives.gov/briefings-statements/remarks-president-trump-74th-session-united-nations-general-assembly.

Vital, D. (1967). *The Inequality of States: A Study of Small Power in International Relations*. Oxford: Oxford University Press.

Walls, J. (2020, February 28). PM Jacinda Ardern to Scott Morrison: "Do not deport your people, and your problems" to NZ. *New Zealand Herald*. www.nzherald.co.nz/nz/pm-jacinda-ardern-to-scott-morrison-do-not-deport-your-people-and-your-problems-to-nz/2HK4OGNEKGSQAC55AU3UKBMX44.

Young, A. (2019, April 2). PM in China: Jacinda Ardern meets Xi Jinping. *New Zealand Herald*. www.nzherald.co.nz/nz/news/article.cfm?c_id=1&objectid=12217953.

Part I

Setting the Scene: The Ardern Government's Foreign Policy Agenda

© 2024 World Scientific Publishing Company
https://doi.org/10.1142/9789811285165_0001

Chapter 1

Foreign Policy of Jacinda Ardern's Government in the Era of COVID-19: Minister Mahuta's Vision for Aotearoa New Zealand's Foreign Policy

Nanaia Mahuta

Māku anō e hanga i tōku nei whare,
Ko te taahūhū he hīnau, ko ngā poupou he māhoe, he pateté,
Me whakatupu ki te hua o te rengarenga,
Me whakapakari ki te hua o te kawariki
Nā Kīngi Tāwhiao[1]

We live in challenging times.

Eighteen months into my term as minister, the international context for the conduct of foreign policy has been as challenged and challenging as at any point in recent history.

Foreign policy during a global pandemic, when borders are closed, issues are complex and dynamic, and many of the routine tools and fora for diplomacy are unavailable, is a deeply challenging thing to navigate — but we have done so, with much success; and we are stronger and wiser for the experience.

---

[1] I will build my own house: The ridge-pole will be of *hinau* and the posts of mahoe (whiteywood) and *patate* (umbrella tree). Raise the people on *rengarenga* (spinach); strengthen them with the fruits of the *kawariki* (coprosma) — King Tāwhiao (1860–1894).

Our vision for ourselves as a country in and of the Pacific is a defining feature of how we equip ourselves to navigate a way forward, strengthen our core relationships, and strengthen our resilience characteristics for this time.

Foreign policy at a time of heightening geostrategic contest, and indeed assaults on the most fundamental tenets of international law, state sovereignty, territorial integrity, and human rights, such as we have witnessed in President Vladimir Putin's actions against Ukraine, is an equally challenging thing — but we are responding with absolute clarity, commitment, speed, and humanity, together with our many partners.

And foreign policy during this critical moment for accelerated climate change action, which requires an unprecedented level of global agreement, leadership and shared effort, is perhaps the single most important item on our international agenda — but here, too, we are taking up this challenge (*wero*), at home and abroad, with determination and clarity of purpose.

An intergenerational perspective to our foreign policy means that we are more deliberate in our approach and in the connectivity between the societal norms we seek to uphold and the modernisation of our international architecture.

These challenges are exacerbating a range of worrying international trends, including a concerning rise in inequality and in hunger; the development and resilience challenges within our Pacific region; tensions and growing militarisation, including within the Indo-Pacific; and a rules-based international system under pressure, and its multilateral and regional institutions often lacking the tools, will, or support to respond effectively to these emerging challenges.

These are difficult times and we should not expect them to grow easier or less complex in the period ahead. They are likely to test the boundaries of our relationships and foreign policy settings. *We will need to do things differently.* The responses of the past two years have seen us chart wholly new territory. We will need to continue to adapt and innovate and we will need the very best our foreign policy can deliver for New Zealand.

In this chapter, I reflect on how we can maximise the effectiveness and impact of our foreign policy. I believe we do so when:

- We ground our foreign policy in who we are as a nation and where we are from — the Pacific.
- We are clear-eyed on our enduring interests.

- We are up front about our values, and they are present in our policy and actions.
- We are creative, agile, innovative.
- We invest in and deepen our relationships.
- We learn from experience — including from COVID-19.

Ko Matariki tonu te tohu — we should be ourselves and use our full toolkit.

As I pen this chapter, we again approach the season of Matariki, when the arrival of this very international constellation (the Pleiades) on Aotearoa's horizon heralds the new year in the Māori calendar. It is a time to draw from ancestors, celebrate connections, and reflect on the year that has been and those who have passed on. It is also a time to look ahead, to ready the tools and traps, waka (canoes) and nets that will be needed in the coming season.

I have made explicit my intention that Aotearoa New Zealand's foreign policy should be grounded in the principles that we aspire to and apply at home. As a liberal democracy, we privilege fundamental human rights and work actively to sustain and strengthen our democratic institutions. We also engage in principles of partnership, recognition of *rangatiratanga* (sovereignty) *mana* (authority or prestige) — our own and that of others, active participation and protection.

Aotearoa's founding document, *te Tiriti o Waitangi* (the Treaty of Waitangi of 1840), and the relationship it intended between Māori and the Crown have been with us for more than 180 years. Our journey as a nation has not been straightforward — it remains a 'challenge space' that often strikes at the fabric of who we are and who we want to become. The nexus of the contested friction has shaped us and we have grown from it. It has taught us that, as a society, we need to work hard to understand the strength of different perspectives with common objectives, the opportunity in understanding each other through shared experience; and the growth that comes from respect. It has taught us that, where there has been conflict or harm, there must be acknowledgement and restitution if there is to be reconciliation.

Like our voyaging ancestors, it is a journey we are destined to make. In navigating it, we are, in the process, drawing on traditional tools and developing new ones.

This toolkit includes values unique to us, reflecting a *tirohanga* Māori (view), but relevant beyond our shores. These values resonate as dimensions of our international identity and foreign policy. They include the following:

- *Manaakitanga* (kindness, care, the spirit of reciprocity and our common humanity).
- *Whanaungatanga* (connectedness and relationship to others).
- *Mahi tahi* and *kotahitanga* (working towards a common purpose, shared objectives and unity).
- *Kaitiakitanga* (stewardship and intergenerational well-being).

These values all emphasise the creation of meaningful, mutual, enduring relationships where mana and sovereignty are acknowledged. They can apply equally to relationships between individuals and peoples, as between countries and governments, large and small.

They demand a broad, long-term, integrated view — one that acknowledges complexity and connectedness and understands both our own situation and interests, and those of others. Indeed, they reflect the nature of the foreign policy challenges we face. Those too are complex, interconnected and long-term, and have many mutual and competing interests at stake. Our values serve our foreign policy well.

We Are of *Te Moana-nui-a-Kiwa* (the Pacific)

Aotearoa New Zealand is a Pacific country. We share an ocean, a past and a future with our Pacific *whanaunga* (relations). Our Pacific connections run through language, peoples, history, culture, politics and shared interests. We share *kaitiaki* (stewardship) responsibilities for *Te Moana-nui-a-Kiwa* — the Blue Ocean continent — and know that what we do today sets the course for our *tamariki* (children) and *mokopuna* (grandchildren).

We desire a peaceful, stable, prosperous, and resilient Pacific in which New Zealand is a true partner. Our *Tiriti o Waitangi* experience is relevant. It has taught us about the challenges and the benefits of building enduring and evolving partnerships.

From Reset to Resilience

In 2018, the Pacific Reset was a deliberate decision to deepen our focus on and commitment to our region. It recognised that strength and success as a region relies on *kotahitanga* (common objectives) and *mahi tahi* (working together). The Reset reaffirmed our partnership with Pacific nations and gave coherence and focus to more than 30 government agencies working with our Pacific neighbours. It sought to bolster the engagement of like-minded partners in support of the region.

We know that the region is facing an array of challenges and changes — social, environmental, economic and security. This government has moved to a 'Pacific Resilience Approach' as the natural next step, working with our partners to tackle these challenges. The approach is consistent with our domestic focus on well-being and resilience; it recognises the overlap between domestic and international issues and policy responses.

It is also driven by resilience realities we share by virtue of our place in the region: our *hononga* (connectivity) with the Pacific peoples; our collective *kaitiakitanga* (stewardship) responsibilities for shared resources; our economic and health connectivity with the region; and our common security interests, including the transboundary nature of threats facing the Pacific, among which are climate change.

The approach looks to intergenerational outcomes; it commits to partnerships that acknowledge the inherent *mana* and sovereignty of each country, and the importance of openness, trust, respect, and understanding of different perspectives.

It recognises that each has a different starting point and outlook. We aim to build on Pacific peoples' own capabilities, using local and culturally relevant approaches, and strengthening the capacity of partner countries to chart their own journeys. With the Sustainable Development Goals (SDGs) as a common horizon, we prioritise our cooperation and resources on those issues that matter most for the region, and with Pacific countries' own sustainable development plans.

This is not just the right and respectful way to engage. It is the only way if we are to give meaning to our *whanaungatanga* and build the trust that underpins common action.

Being of the Pacific shapes our outlook and priorities in the world. Aotearoa New Zealand has an obligation to support Pacific countries to have influence beyond the region and to amplify Pacific voices and concerns in international fora. It means we consistently seek to both defend and advance the voices and interests of small island developing states. It shapes our policies in all areas, including on climate, oceans, security, development and, most recently, COVID-19.

We Must Be Clear-Eyed on Our Enduring Interests

Aotearoa New Zealand is a small, open, outward-oriented Pacific country, deeply engaged in our region and in the world. We value things we believe to be universally important, including democracy, freedom, human rights, sustainability, inclusion, and tolerance. We depend on a rules-based international system that gives voice, agency and protection to smaller countries. Our prosperity has been built around an open trade environment. And our security is linked to the ability of all nations, large and small, to solve problems peacefully through diplomacy and dialogue, eschewing the threat or use of force. As a small country, our relationships matter and we aim to be a principled, consistent and constructive partner.

In the following, I reflect on four enduring and interwoven strands in our foreign policy:

1. A Rules-Based International Order That Reflects New Zealand's Values and Allows Us to Advance Our Interests

From the very origins of the United Nations, New Zealand has been an active player — working with others to conceive, build and reform institutions that allow states and actors to come together and tackle common challenges through dialogue and common endeavour.

Successive governments have recognised our powerful interest in an international system that can agree on rules that protect the rights of people and states and provide a platform to address common and transboundary issues. Aotearaoa, and our fellow Pacific countries, benefit disproportionately from institutions that allow states an equal voice and vote.

New Zealand is a committed global citizen: with our values as a compass, we work with and through the multilateral system and international organisations to promote and protect democratic values, human rights, peaceful relations, disarmament, the environment, international development, the reduction of poverty and inequality, and the rule of law.

Importantly, we believe that collective action leads to more effective, durable and equitable solutions.

We are similarly committed to fora at the regional level which agree on norms, navigate differences and promote dialogue, common action and peaceful development. We are an integral member of the Pacific Islands Forum and place a high value on its unity and purpose. We are an active and principled player in the Indo-Pacific and we recognise and support the central place of the Association of Southeast Asian Nations (ASEAN) and the connecting role of the Asia-Pacific Economic Cooperation (APEC).

We will lean into these organisations and work hard to foster collaboration. Leaning into the rules-based international order means pulling our weight and taking on leadership roles, as we have through hosting APEC in 2021. Aotearoa New Zealand will also look for other opportunities to put itself forward to advance our interests and values, including through putting our hand up to take a seat at the table within key multilateral processes.

It is not news that a fraying consensus and contested geopolitics have placed stress on multilateral and regional systems and collective rule-making. The United Nations, among others, faces many challenges to its effectiveness and speed. However, the United Nations has shown time and again that it is still the critical organisation when dealing with global and transboundary issues: it has unrivalled convening power, serves as a meeting place to develop collective political will, and is the place where global rules are discussed and agreed, and acquire legitimacy.

If we look to a suite of issues that demand an intensified and coordinated global response — such as in the areas of space, oceans, artificial intelligence, autonomous weapons, cyber, digital cooperation, climate, and biodiversity — we see the need for *more* collective action, not *less*.

I believe we can find cause for optimism, though it is an optimism that will demand a determined and sustained effort by all. We have seen what can be achieved when we work together to find global solutions to global problems, including in a COVID-19 context. We have seen much unity of action in response to the situation in Ukraine. We continue to make progress in and alongside global climate negotiations.

Global initiatives are possible when all of the great powers participate and cooperate, but smaller countries also need to engage constructively and ensure solutions work for all.

Much of our work to bolster the rules-based system lies in supporting and strengthening that system. But sometimes it requires defence of that system and its most fundamental rules; this may carry costs.

We have witnessed, this year, how willing much of the world has been to condemn and sanction Russia for its flagrant violation of Ukraine's sovereignty and territorial integrity, the rights of Ukrainian citizens, international humanitarian law, and indeed the UN Charter. The response has been without recent precedent in scale and significance; it has affirmed the importance of fundamental protective rules and a collective will to uphold them.

New Zealand too, has taken the unprecedented step of passing legislation to apply direct economic sanctions against Russia. We have done so because it is in our interests to stand clearly against these aggressive acts and breaches of international law, where we assess that the UN Security Council is unlikely to act or has acted insufficiently. We are part of an international community, sharing the responsibility to act in concert with others to ensure that its most fundamental rules and protections are upheld. Our values tell us this is the right thing to do.

On Human Rights

While new rules and norms are needed, some of our most long-standing ones need just as much attention.

Human rights are the bedrock of an international order tasked not only with mediating the interests of states but also protecting and advancing the human dignity of all people, individually and collectively, irrespective of the context or situation in which they live.

This foundational element of the international system is at risk.

Human rights are universal, inalienable and indivisible, yet far too many experience little of that universality. This year, I addressed the UN Human Rights Council, the first such speech by a New Zealand Foreign Minister since its inception. I used this opportunity to address the human rights dimensions of Russia's invasion of Ukraine, among other deeply concerning situations. I underlined our collective responsibility to uphold human rights, including in the light of COVID-19 and climate impacts.

2. A Security Environment That Keeps New Zealand's People and Activities Safe, and Supports the Safety of Our Region

A second enduring strand of our foreign policy is our need for peace and security. I have already addressed the rules-based international system as a critical underpinning to peace and security.

International and regional security rests on the ability of the international community to protect people and livelihoods, build relationships and norms that avoid the resort to armed conflict, and to respond quickly and effectively to conflicts when they do occur.

Aotearoa New Zealand is a committed partner in these efforts, globally and regionally. We participate actively in the international campaign against terrorism, contribute to international peacekeeping operations and promote work on women, peace and security. We collaborate on a spectrum of transnational crime issues from people trafficking to cybersecurity. We lead the Christchurch Call to eliminate terrorist and violent extremist content online.

In our region, this means partnering with Pacific countries to support the unity and role of the Pacific Islands Forum as the pre-eminent body in the regional political architecture. It means fostering the support of partners who align behind Pacific values and interests. It means taking forward the undertakings of the Boe Declaration and the Pacific's broad interpretation of security. And it means responding to Pacific issues and requests when they arise.

The Indo-Pacific is a contested space, and the security stakes are high. I have likened the Indo-Pacific to a marae — a meeting space where all should be respected and have speaking rights, where there must be rules and protocols that govern behaviour and provide for openness, inclusivity, sovereignty, and transparency. New Zealand has a place and a voice on that marae. We are embedded within the regional architecture, particularly APEC, the East Asia Summit and the ASEAN Regional Forum, and we promote an open, inclusive, stable, and prosperous region that will serve the interests of all.

New Zealand also has a proud tradition of sustained advocacy for disarmament, arms control and non-proliferation. We are party to all multilateral treaties and conventions prohibiting weapons of mass destruction and limiting the production, proliferation and use of inhumane conventional weapons.

The threats posed by such weapons are not new, but recent events have shown just how present they remain. The spectre of nuclear weapons use has been raised and the possibility of equally abhorrent chemical and biological warfare remains. While the risk of miscalculation and escalation grows, civilians are already suffering from the use of inhumane conventional weapons in flagrant violation of the fundamental principles of international humanitarian law — both in Ukraine and in other conflicts around the world. Now is not the time to question the value of disarmament and arms control, or to put compliance with international humanitarian law in the 'too-hard basket'. Although the challenges are formidable, we must be undaunted in our efforts to make real and urgent progress on these critical issues.

3. International Conditions and Connections That Allow New Zealand and Our Region to Prosper

Aotearoa New Zealand has long been a trading nation, and this government is committed to ensuring that trade delivers for all New Zealanders and contributes to addressing global and regional issues of concern.

Regional and global economic development is an objective in its own right and an important means to reduce poverty, drive opportunity and achieve the SDGs. But our economic prospects also rest with the economic stability, progress and connectivity of our region and the world.

We remain committed to free trade and open markets and we advocate and model liberal economic norms that drive economic development. We seek international trade rules, centred on the World Trade Organization, that, alongside domestic policies, support sustainable and inclusive economic development. We seek to expand opportunities for Aotearoa New Zealand in overseas markets, to deliver more jobs, better wages, innovation, and productivity for all New Zealanders.

Fortunately, our region is home to others who share that commitment. APEC has championed the WTO and connected Asia-Pacific economies for over thirty years. As noted earlier, we had the honour of hosting APEC — virtually — in 2021, using the opportunity to focus on resilience, the pandemic response and protecting the region's prosperity in light of COVID-19 economic impacts. I am proud of Aotearoa New Zealand's success in bringing together 21 economies — representing 38 per cent of the world's people and 48 per cent of world trade — to demonstrate the relevance of this forum to both immediate and long-term issues of sustainability, inclusion and the economic well-being of the region and beyond.

Successive governments have worked to achieve a suite of trade agreements that underpin New Zealand's market access; this continues apace. The Regional Comprehensive Economic Partnership entered into force in 2022, promising to deepen our trade and economic integration with 15 economies in the Indo-Pacific and almost a third of the world's population. The signing of the United Kingdom–New Zealand Free Trade Agreement (FTA) sees 67.8 per cent of our goods and services trade now covered by an FTA, a figure which will grow significantly with the conclusion of a European Union–New Zealand FTA. We continue to lift ambition within existing agreements, such as via the recent signing of the enhanced FTA with China.

This work is not complete. There are important gaps in coverage, particularly with respect to the United States, India and emerging markets beyond our region. We continue to aspire to high-quality, comprehensive free trade agreements with these economies which in addition to bringing economic benefits can also strengthen and broaden these important relationships.

FTAs are insufficient on their own. Many constraints to trade lie behind the customs desk, in the form of non-tariff and regulatory barriers. This is a growing priority as we seek to maximise the real returns from FTAs. In just the six months to December 2021, cross-agency work successfully resolved seven non-tariff barriers that were impacting New Zealand exporters and cover an estimated trade value of NZ$700 million.

And our trade agenda goes well beyond FTA coverage and reducing barriers. The government is fully seized of the importance of trade as a means to support a wider set of social and economic objectives, at home and abroad.

The inextricable links between trade policy and climate change are recognised in New Zealand's sustained advocacy on fossil fuel subsidy reform. It is perverse that governments worldwide subsidise fossil fuel use at a cost of US$500 billion annually. Removing these subsidies is seldom easy — they are institutionalised and politically sensitive. But their removal would greatly hasten the transformation required, while freeing up vital resources to support affected businesses and communities and invest in a just transition and critical health, education services and environmental protection.

Trade must be inclusive if we are to address rising inequality and support all to realise their full potential. It must recognise the value of action on gender parity in the workplace and support adoption of gender-responsive policies and business practices that will enable women and girls to participate in, and benefit from, the COVID-19 recovery.

Aotearoa New Zealand is determined to promote inclusive economic development, including the intergenerational well-being of indigenous peoples — in alignment with shared indigenous values. An inclusive trade agenda which empowers indigenous peoples is an economic opportunity.

The Māori economy, worth NZ$70 billion, has already emerged as one of the fastest growing and most export-oriented parts of the New Zealand economy. It is in all our interests for this part of Aotearoa New Zealand's economy to thrive.

This work is becoming tangible. This year saw Aotearoa achieve the ground-breaking inclusion of an indigenous trade chapter within the

United Kingdom–New Zealand FTA and the conclusion of the Indigenous Peoples Economic and Trade Cooperation Arrangement among several APEC economies. These achievements would not have been possible without deepening engagement with Māori to ensure Māori interests are reflected in Aotearoa New Zealand's trade policy.

4. Global Action on Climate and Sustainability Issues That Matter to New Zealand

In the words of the [former] Prime Minister, climate change is this generation's nuclear-free moment. Alongside biodiversity loss and pollution, it is a 'triple threat' to human health and prosperity. Climate change is something we can only address as a global community. As extreme weather events intensify, sea levels rise and temperatures increase, irreversible biodiversity losses compound, and the extent and impact of pollution become ever more pervasive, the economic and non-economic costs of inaction are rising rapidly. This triple threat can only be addressed as a global community. Like the nuclear-free movement, this is a *moment* that must become a *momentum*.

Aotearoa New Zealand brings a concerted intergenerational perspective to climate and global environmental issues. Protection of global biodiversity, the health of our oceans, the environmental integrity of Antarctica, or the action required across a suite of forms of pollution are as much development, economic, social, and security issues as they are environmental. They threaten future generations even more than our own — they must be determined foreign policy priorities.

On climate change, this government has shown its commitment to leadership and policy coherence at home, in the region and internationally. We have placed keeping global warming to 1.5° C at the heart of our responses across all levels. Achieving this temperature goal collectively is critical for all, especially our Pacific neighbours.

We continue to work actively with others to promote ambitious global action. We have secured progress through the UN Framework Convention on Climate Change, including finalised guidelines to implement the Paris Agreement. We are mainstreaming climate change across our foreign policy, including in trade and development cooperation.

At home, Aotearoa New Zealand is one of the few countries to have a target of net zero emissions, with significant reductions in biogenic methane by 2050, enshrined in law. The Climate Change Response (Zero Carbon) Amendment Act 2019 provides a framework to transition to a low-emissions, climate-resilient economy and play our part in realising the Paris Agreement goals. This year we have published our first emissions reduction plan, outlining tangible actions across every sector over the next 15 years.

In the region, Pacific countries have recognised climate change as the greatest threat to their livelihoods, security and well-being. The projected impacts are immense: loss of coastal infrastructure and land to sea level rise; more intense weather events and the damage these do to development progress; failure of crops and fisheries; and the loss of coral reefs and mangroves. Aotearoa is working with the region on climate change policy, global advocacy and development cooperation. In 2021, we played a key role supporting work toward the Pacific Islands Forum Leaders' Declaration on Preserving Maritime Zones in the Face of Climate-Change Related Sea-Level Rise.

We have committed NZ$1.3 billion over 2022–2025 to support countries most vulnerable to the effects of climate change. This is a four-fold increase on our previous commitment, ensuring that New Zealand pulls its weight on financial support for climate resilience and transitions in developing countries. Over half will be spent in the Pacific and on adaptation. This is vitally important for our Pacific partners, who contribute negligibly to emissions but, as small island states, face huge adaptation costs.

Of the climate finance increase, NZ$800 million is additional to our ongoing Official Development Assistance. New Zealand's development cooperation has withstood a concerning international trend toward declining budgets, evidence of New Zealand's sustained commitment to our region and to tackling global challenges. I see our development cooperation as core to our support for realising the 17 SDGs. With their integrated, partnership and intergenerational focus, the SDGs are well aligned with my foreign policy vision.

We Should Learn from COVID-19

There is nothing like a pandemic to underline the world's interdependencies and vulnerabilities. From citizens' health and interpersonal connections to countries' economies, transport links, supply chains, and vaccine access, none were insulated. Nor could any respond on their own.

We should be proud of New Zealand's response, which delivered some of the best health and economic outcomes of any country. I am proud of the role that our foreign policy played: managing the impact of border closures on key relationships and markets; providing an unprecedented level of support to New Zealanders stranded offshore; providing up-to-the-minute intelligence on disease and response measures worldwide to inform New Zealand's response; mitigating COVID-19 health and economic risks to the Pacific while maintaining a gateway to the Pacific and Antarctica; negotiating equitable access to vaccines globally and for New Zealand; and helping to protect critical transport and supply chains to New Zealand and the Pacific.

But COVID-19 also confirmed some deeper truths.

Our Values Matter

The advent of the pandemic drove swift and significant shifts in Aotearoa New Zealand's policy and priorities. But it did not shake us from our core values. Instead, we drew on them to inform our choices. We have seen tangible benefits from applying values of *manākitanga* (kindness and generosity), *kaitiakitanga, mahi tahi* and *kotahitanga* with their emphasis on relationships, resilience and the long term. Our health response, our support to the Pacific, our economic resilience, and our collective engagement at the regional and multilateral levels all benefited from being true to these values.

Our Pacific Policy Matters

From the outset, Aotearoa New Zealand's COVID-19 response included a firm Pacific dimension, aware of the high risk posed to small Pacific countries with limited health capacities and economic vulnerability. We worked intensively with Pacific governments to support their efforts to prepare for, respond to and start to recover from the impacts of the pandemic.

The Pacific featured centrally in our vaccine strategy. We committed to supporting a roll-out in the region, particularly in the Cook Islands, Niue and Tokelau, as well as wider Polynesia, over the same time frame as New Zealand. We worked at the global level, with the region and Australia, and through direct contributions to ensure the Pacific could access vaccines for full coverage. Across the region, New Zealand used existing institutional connections to support vaccination programmes, personal protective equipment (PPE) supply, hospital upgrades, laboratory and testing assistance, medical equipment, isolation and quarantine facilities, and even the deployment of medical teams.

Pacific countries have taken a dramatic economic hit from the loss of economic activity and revenue, the near shutting-down of tourism and the financing of the COVID-19 response. New Zealand has responded with scaled-up support, including NZ$142 million of development cooperation funding reprioritised to support Pacific COVID-19 response in the 2020–2021 financial year. In total, since the start of the pandemic, we have provided almost NZ$325 million in emergency budget support to help Pacific countries withstand this shock.

We have also worked to secure early and equitable access to New Zealand for our Pacific neighbours. Amended visa provisions under the Recognised Seasonal Employer scheme provided options for Pacific workers unable to return to their home countries. And we reinstated the scheme when it could be done safely.

We will continue to support our partners through COVID-19 outbreaks and to 'build back better' in line with the Pacific resilience approach. This is Pacific *whanaungatanga* and resilience in action.

Multilateralism Matters

The World Health Organization and the associated global health architecture played an important but imperfect role. It was, in the end, undersupported, underfunded and insufficiently empowered to fully do its job. But the pandemic also provided examples of strong collective action. The COVID-19 Vaccines Global Access Facility (COVAX) is a worldwide multilateral initiative set up to ensure equitable access to vaccines. It recognised the risk early and seized the initiative to design a mechanism with sound principles and high ambition. Aotearoa New Zealand has been a strong supporter, contributing NZ$26 million, and contributing to the delivery of over one billion vaccine doses to 144 countries in COVAX's first year of delivery.

There remains significant disparity between vaccination rates in high-income and low-income countries and much work to be done to help countries strengthen their health systems. But this would have been far worse had COVAX deliveries not rebalanced supply toward those in need and supported vaccine roll-outs.

The lesson is that the multilateral system can identify critical issues, develop responses and resources, and have a real impact. But all must enable and support the system. New Zealand is actively engaged in processes under way to empower and improve the resilience of the global health architecture to ensure that we are better prepared for the next pandemic.

Trade and Economic Connections Matter

The pandemic placed extreme stress on global supply chains, took a heavy economic toll on many countries, and will cast a long shadow on trade, supply chains and markets.

But the rules-based trading system, open markets and trade connectivity, and a progressive and inclusive trade response, also underpinned New Zealand's resilience. We were able to protect trade and supply chains to ensure New Zealanders had access to essential goods and could export. With other APEC economies, we kept markets open and made trade easier — reducing red tape and accelerating border clearance procedures. We worked to ensure trade assisted the pandemic response by unilaterally suspending tariffs on medical products, PPE and vaccine-related goods.

Our focus now is on recalibrating trade policy for the new environment. The strength and sustainability of New Zealand's COVID-19 economic recovery will depend on our connections. With one in four New Zealanders' jobs dependent on exports, we will continue to prioritise efforts to provide secure access to a diverse range of international markets for the benefit of all.

At a time when many are tempted to look inwards toward a self-sufficient model of resilience, it is in our interest to defend multilateral, rules-based trade, push back against protectionism, and advance a model that recognises the potential for progressive and inclusive trade to build mutual resilience.

Our Relationships Matter

New Zealand's long-standing network of international relationships was something we drew on heavily. Our close connections and presence across the Pacific allowed us to navigate issues quickly. Our intimate relationship with Australia allowed us both to co-ordinate a host of high-pressure policy and operational shifts. Our relationships across the Indo-Pacific underpinned our own and the region's economic and health response. Our multilateral and Pacific credentials mattered around the COVAX table, and our successful pandemic management provided a platform to engage further. When facing a squeeze between demand and supply of critical PPE, pharmaceuticals, vaccines or test kits, or when we needed to repatriate New Zealanders from difficult locations, we looked to close partners for mutual help, and they delivered.

Such relationships are not built overnight. They are the product of history and investment, and of being principled, predictable and trusted. They mattered during COVID-19; they will matter again.

We Need to Innovate and Respond

Before I finish, I will highlight three areas where I feel New Zealand's foreign policy needs to evolve further:

- *Working across the silos*: Foreign policy and the institutions and fora it works with and through often align by theme or issue, whether that be security, environment, development or trade. But the space for this kind of separation is long past. The challenges we face and solutions required do not respect such boundaries. *We must get better at working across disciplines and agencies to ensure lasting solutions to complex challenges.*
- *Creativity and innovation*: We know that the challenges ahead will not be solved by existing approaches. We must learn from the past, but, as COVID-19 has shown, we must bring new thinking and take risks. This is an area New Zealand has always excelled in — it comes with being small and independently minded. *Our foreign policy must be entrepreneurial where it matters.*
- *Navigating the contest of power*: Thirdly, as I outlined at the start, we live in a period of geostrategic contest during which we should expect New Zealand to face difficult choices and less room to move. *We need to hold fast to our values, be clear about our interests and work deftly to pursue both our safety and our prosperity.*

He taonga tuku iho; he taonga tupu ake (it is an inheritance; it is a legacy of growth).

In closing, the present feels to be carrying much portent. The health impact of the pandemic has not finished and its economic shadow will be long and uneven. The world faces long-standing and new challenges and has an ambitious agenda. We have yet to make the historic climate transition all committed to under the Paris Agreement. Security concerns have grown and the rising strategic anxiety that we and others feel in our region and globally will complicate and add drag and risk to progress.

I have made the case for the even greater presence of Aotearoa New Zealand's domestic experience, values and Pacific identity in our foreign policy. I believe they serve our interests well, as has been borne out during COVID-19. The pandemic has reminded us that international cooperation founded on partnership and mutual respect is a necessity, not an aspiration: *Mo te iti, me te rahi (for the greater benefit of the most vulnerable and the most diverse).*

I have argued for the importance and continuity of Aotearoa New Zealand's core foreign policy interests, even as they evolve to meet new challenges. But I have also argued for greater emphasis on human rights, inclusion, and intergenerational thinking and action within those interests. And I see areas where we need new thinking.

But ultimately, my argument is that at a time of great global uncertainty, the temptation to turn inwards, in the hope of protecting narrowly defined national interests, is real. To do so would be to act from a place of fear and failure. The lessons of COVID-19 have been hard but clear, and really quite familiar. Global challenges require global solutions. Regional challenges require regional solutions. Pacific challenges require Pacific solutions. Our interests can really only be advanced through our relationships with others.

Now is a time for Aotearoa New Zealand to be as active in the world as we have ever been. We can bring real value to our region and the world. We have no choice but to continue to posture ourselves as an active, principled and engaged international actor if we are to build a safer, more prosperous and more sustainable future for New Zealanders.

In the words of my ancestor Tāwhiao, *kei ngā tōpito e wha o te ao ōna hoa* (his friends will come from the four corners of the world). This expression was made when he grappled with the changing nature of his world and the onset of new migrants to the shores of Aotearoa. Their requisite skills, talents and perspectives challenged the norms of his world, but Tāwhiao believed that if united in purpose, then much could be achieved through working collectively and collaboratively together.

Pai Mārire (goodness and peace)

Part II

The Geopolitical and Economic Context of COVID-19

Chapter 2

New Zealand and the Indo-Pacific: Adaptation to Changing Geopolitics

Clifford A. Hart, Jr.

From Asia-Pacific to Indo-Pacific

This chapter addresses the geopolitical context for New Zealand's foreign policy — that strategic level where perceptions of power relationships among states and the intentions of their governments shape the international order and influence prospects for peace, prosperity and values. It focuses on the common geopolitical concerns of stability and national security.

From the early 1970s, the ebbing of immediate security threats and a search for alternatives to the British market profoundly shaped New Zealand's external policies. Wellington by the late 1980s characterised itself as part of an 'Asia-Pacific' community, reflecting a surge in the economic importance of north-east and South East Asia and linking the Americas — particularly the United States — into the region. A reforming People's Republic of China (PRC) was an important player but not a central one, and there was hope that integration into this community could shape Beijing's potential power in healthy directions. Labour and

National-led governments alike focused on multilateral connections in the Asia-Pacific — including the Asia Pacific Economic Cooperation forum (APEC) and, in particular, the Association for SouthEast Asian Nations (ASEAN).

By the mid-2000s, China's rapid emergence as a power began reshaping Asian geopolitics. As both Asia-Pacific and Indian Ocean leaders began reassessing their strategic references, conceptually merging the two regions became all but inevitable. The Asia-Pacific was a recent, ad hoc construct; the Indo-Pacific dropped the artificial distinction between two closely linked areas and invoked a centuries-old notion. The Indo-Pacific incorporated the remainder of China's bordering regions outside the former Soviet Union and maritime areas of strategic importance to Beijing. It also brought into play India, the other Asian giant, and its chronically fractious relationship with the PRC.

Japan's Prime Minister Shinzo Abe played a central role in the reframing. As early as 2005, he began speaking of the need to manage the challenge of a rising China through co-operation spanning the Indian and Pacific Ocean communities. In 2007, he initiated the Quadrilateral Security Dialogue among Washington, Tokyo, Canberra and Delhi. While the 'Quad' was premature and soon slipped into dormancy, the Indo-Pacific reframing was an idea whose time had come.

China's impact on regional geopolitics occurred in two overlapping and reinforcing stages. First, the years after Beijing's 2001 accession to the World Trade Organization (WTO) witnessed an extraordinary surge in the PRC's aggregate power. Between 2000 and 2015, its gross domestic product more than doubled as a percentage of global GDP, and it goods exports more than tripled as a portion of the world total (International Monetary Fund, 2023; Nicita & Razo, 2021). Alongside this growth, Beijing prosecuted a historic military modernisation programme. The PRC's defence budget increased by nearly nine times between 2000 and 2015,[1] and its military capabilities improved dramatically.

Even had the PRC been an established democracy with an unambiguous record of support for the rules-based international order, this power shift would have required significant adaptations, regionally and globally. As it was, China's authoritarian regime, problematic history with its neighbours, and ideological grievance narrative raised concerns about

---

[1] Or 4.7 times in 2020 constant US dollars. Stockholm International Peace Research Institute. (2023).

what it intended to do with its new capabilities. It was in this environment that Prime Minister Abe mooted the Indo-Pacific framework and the Quad took its first steps.

The second development was a major shift in Chinese policies that became clearer from the late 2000s, and probably began earlier. A range of factors contributed: growing national strength, looming economic and demographic challenges, resistance to the atrophy of Leninist institutions, and damage to American leadership inflicted by the Global Financial Crisis (GFC) were certainly among them. It is not insignificant that the Chinese Communist Party leadership in 2007 selected Xi Jinping as heir apparent to its General Secretaryship, although the full consequences of this were not then clear, even at home.

Far less ambiguous was Beijing's abrupt shift the next year from a South East Asian charm campaign to forceful assertion of its sweeping claims in the South China Sea (SCS). The claims were not new, but the PRC's behaviour prompted widespread concern about a body of water of global importance to which six regional countries had competing claims.

The overall direction of Chinese policy even then remained unclear for a while. Xi Jinping's November 2012 elevation to the General Secretaryship even prompted speculation the PRC was on the cusp of renewed reform and opening-up. In retrospect, important indicators at the time suggest Beijing had already decided at last to move beyond former paramount leader Deng Xiaoping's admonition to moderate China's behaviour and avoid sparking concerns about its rise.

In 2012 and 2013, China became more assertive around the Japanese-administered Senkaku Islands in the SCS, claimed by Beijing as the Diaoyu. Also in 2012, PRC survey vessels prevented the Philippine navy from intervening against illegal Chinese fishing along the Philippines' Scarborough Shoal. Starting in 2013, Beijing began what proved to be a massive campaign of island building in the SCS, both to strengthen its claims to sovereignty and to support military and other forces to defend those claims. In 2016, Beijing rejected an international tribunal's finding against its claims to the SCS.

These and other actions by Beijing further energised interest in an Indo-Pacific framework, even as countries found their trading relationships with China surge. Australia in its 2013 *Defence White Paper (DWP)* became the first country officially to embrace an Indo-Pacific policy. A re-elected Abe rolled out a parallel initiative in 2016, underscoring the breadth of the 'vision' by announcing it at a conference in Kenya. When the Trump Administration embraced the Indo-Pacific in 2017, the concept was already well advanced in the region.

New Zealand's embrace of the Indo-Pacific framework was gradual, with important considerations slowing its adoption. Aotearoa is necessarily focused on foreign trade, and by 2016 China had surpassed Australia as its top trading partner. A construct even implicitly critical of Beijing was therefore problematic. Wellington moreover was also loath to abandon the Asia-Pacific framework, which from the late 1980s had held out hope to New Zealand as a source of regional stability and order. Wellington expended significant effort in encouraging regional institutions, especially ASEAN and its affiliated fora. Aotearoa was therefore reluctant to expand its geopolitical perspective, despite Beijing's worrisome behaviour and the meagre returns of the Asia-Pacific framework.

New Zealand Perspectives

Wellington brought to these challenges its own foreign policy realities: limited resources and a distinctive kiwi flavour in its diplomacy. Both shaped but did not block its response to shifting regional geopolitics.

As a comparatively small state, New Zealand's net power and influence are necessarily limited. While its armed forces are professional and competent, even with a less modest defence budget they would be hard pressed to protect New Zealand's own territories and its Exclusive Economic Zone (EEZ), the world's fifth-largest, much less other declared kiwi interests — the Southern Ocean, Antarctica, the realm territories in the South Pacific, the Pacific Island states, and its sole remaining ANZUS ally, Australia (Jackson, 2018).

As with many other small countries, military co-operation with other states is an indispensable dimension of New Zealand's national security strategy. Also like many small countries, Aotearoa's foreign policy heavily emphasises international institutions, process and law. Its declaratory policy stresses the latter and speaks less frequently about security co-operation.

Some observers unkindly suggest New Zealand has stopped thinking strategically altogether (Graham, 2019). The view is of course unjustified on the economic front, where Wellington has a strong record of leveraging its limited influence to manage challenges and opportunities alike. Except within responsible government agencies, however, national security debate clearly grew less sophisticated and more sanguine from the early 1970s. South East Asia's stabilisation and the 1972 United States–PRC rapprochement marked the beginning of an extended period during which Asia peacefully emerged as the world's most dynamic economic region. New Zealand worked hard to take advantage of resulting opportunities.

In this environment, Labour Prime Minister David Lange in 1985 felt comfortable gambling on — and losing — Aotearoa's alliance with the United States. With no apparent harm to national security, even the National Party in 1990 embraced Lange's anti-nuclear position. Especially after the Soviet Union's demise, kiwis increasingly took their security for granted. National Party leaders in the 1990s were happy to accept a peace dividend at the expense of defence spending. After returning to power in 1999, Labour reoriented the country's armed forces toward peacekeeping and stabilisation missions, scrapping New Zealand's air combat capabilities altogether. Prime Minister Helen Clark in 2001 hailed New Zealand's 'remarkably benign' security environment.

New Zealand's geographic isolation almost certainly plays a significant role in encouraging a broadly sanguine popular view of national security. It has been a very long time since a hostile state's conventional military forces posed a direct threat to kiwi waters or soil.

In addition, Aotearoa's internal identity debate has promoted an emotive attachment to a progressive, independent foreign policy and inspired a general discomfort with competition in the international arena. Especially since the 1986 end of the US alliance, declaratory commitment to an independent foreign policy has become obligatory for all New Zealand governments. In its diplomacy, Wellington has skilfully and sincerely nurtured this identity to advance foreign policy goals, such as its successful 2014 campaign to join the UN Security Council.

Aotearoa's foreign and national security policies are, nonetheless, conventional, neither especially more nor less independent than those of most countries. Hardly a neutral state, New Zealand remains a treaty ally of Australia, has a revived defence partnership with Washington and co-operates with a range of other countries on national security. However much domestic sensitivities incline the Beehive (New Zealand Parliament) to de-emphasise comment on this co-operation, it remains vital to New Zealand interests.

The National Party and the New Geopolitics

New Zealand's 2008 general election occurred as China's rise began to roil Asian geopolitics. Kiwi candidates seemed undisturbed by these distant controversies. In fact, like those in many countries, they were decidedly focused on the potential benefits of even closer relations with Beijing, especially with regard to trade. The Leader of the Opposition, John Key, nonetheless importantly campaigned on a commitment to promulgate a new DWP and take a fresh look at national security needs.

When the DWP appeared in November 2010, 13 years after the previous one, Defence Minister Wayne Mapp described New Zealand's security environment as 'far from benign', though without much elaboration. Earlier that month, the Wellington Declaration had laid out an ambitious programme for political co-operation with the United States, and the Washington Declaration in 2012 normalised military contact. New Zealand's participation in US bilateral and multilateral exercises rapidly intensified. US Marines and soldiers arrived for exercises in the North Island in 2012, and New Zealand Defence Force (NZDF) personnel joined the Dawn Blitz amphibious exercises in California the following year.

The National Party-led government's security outreach extended well beyond Washington. A New Zealand–India joint statement at the end of Prime Minister Key's June 2011 visit to New Delhi provided for strengthened security co-operation, and he warned against 'complacency' in the Asia-Pacific region. In Brussels just two weeks before the Washington Declaration, Prime Minister Key signed a NATO partnership agreement. Japan and New Zealand in 2013 agreed on a strategic co-operative partnership statement and signed a memorandum of intent on defence co-operation.

Beijing's SCS island-building clearly grabbed Wellington's attention. Defence Minister Gerry Brownlee and Foreign Minister Murray McCully in 2015 and 2016, respectively, expressed New Zealand's clearest public concerns to date about PRC behaviour. Tellingly, neither yet mentioned China by name.

In fact, highlighting the balance Wellington was trying to strike, on a visit to Beijing soon after his 2015 remarks, Brownlee signed a five-year engagement plan with the People's Liberation Army. He applauded this as the first of its kind between China and a Western military, adding to the list of 'firsts' New Zealand leaders at the time still cited as proof of a special relationship between the PRC and Aotearoa.

Concerns in Wellington about the geopolitical environment — though without attribution to Beijing — were nonetheless crystallising by the mid-2010s. The July 2016 DWP tabled a 15-year, NZ$20 billion modernisation programme. In November, the USS *Sampson*, a destroyer, became the first American warship to visit New Zealand since the collapse of the alliance. The absence of significant controversy about the event highlighted increased popular comfort with security co-operation with Washington, though kiwi and US officials carefully described *Sampson*'s visit in non-combat terms.

Just as noteworthy, Wellington in June 2017 assigned one of its two frigates, HMNZS *Te Kaha*, to substitute for a damaged American destroyer in the USS *Nimitz* Carrier Strike Group (CSG). New Zealand characterised its offer as reciprocation for *Sampson*'s assistance during the Kaikoura earthquake the year before, but the two events were incomparable. The integration of a New Zealand warship into a CSG on patrol in the North Pacific directly involved kiwi forces in the operation of one of the premier instruments of US global power.

This remarkably uncontroversial step occurred in the final months of the National-led coalition. As it approached the 2017 election, National could, had it wanted, have claimed credit for significantly shifting New Zealand's defence policy and having begun to highlight, albeit implicitly, a growing Chinese threat to Aotearoa's welfare. Defence documents and international co-operation strongly suggest national security and foreign policy officials were already alert to the emerging reality.

It is less clear what ministers thought they were doing. Long-distance deployment of NZDF assets would have required cabinet approval, as of course did the DWPs and other defence documents. The paucity of official statements on national security by senior leaders, however, does not permit a clear judgment on what drove their thinking. Key's latest major speech on national security was in 2014, and addressed international terrorism.

Labour–New Zealand First Take Up the Baton

The Labour–New Zealand First coalition that emerged from the 2017 general election brought together an odd leadership on international matters: Prime Minister Jacinda Ardern, an idealistic, youthful Labour politician heavily focused on her progressive agenda, and Deputy Prime Minister Winston Peters, a crusty septuagenarian populist who resumed the position of Foreign Minister he had occupied nearly a decade before under the previous Labour-led government.

While foreign policy played no significant role in the 2017 campaign, China indirectly did through a controversy over the impact of foreign residential housing purchases on prices. National had denied the problem's existence, but Labour campaigned on it, and substantial anecdotal evidence pointed to significant purchases by, among others, PRC investors. Although Australian purchases likely played a far larger role, this may have been the first point at which average kiwis had reason to contemplate the downsides of China's rise for their daily welfare.

Evidence of PRC efforts to interfere in New Zealand domestic politics also had grown substantially by 2017. The University of Canterbury's Professor of political science Anne-Marie Brady's controversial essay on the topic that year energised the debate, helping increase awareness of Beijing-directed operations to influence the news media, academia and politics (Brady, 2017).

Increasing concerns about China among other partners — especially Australia and the United States — also influenced Wellington. Political differences with these governments shaped but did not halt increasing kiwi security co-operation with them. Discomfort with Donald Trump's administration was widespread in New Zealand, within government and outside. Kiwi stereotypes of Australian pugnacity likely clouded public appreciation of the challenges their closest ally was facing in dealing with China.

The 2017 election nonetheless drove a reassessment of the PRC. After nine years of National-led government, a new administration looked afresh at nearly a decade of increasingly aggressive PRC behaviour. While acutely aware of China's economic importance to New Zealand, the new coalition lacked National's dominating focus on business. Its vital New Zealand First coalition partner — especially Peters himself — harboured a long-standing distrust of the PRC. The resulting changes in kiwi behaviour, if not declaratory policy, occurred broadly on the same timeline as those of its close security partners.

That shift was well under way early in the new government. Peters in March 2018 announced a renewed emphasis on New Zealand's engagement with the Pacific Islands — the 'Pacific Reset' — which he allowed was motivated in part by concerns about PRC influence in the region.

Even clearer was the defence ministry's 6 July 2018 release of its *Strategic Defence Policy Statement*, which in unprecedented language identified the PRC as a significant challenge to New Zealand's interests. As one observer put it, Wellington's public position on China had at last begun catching up with officials' long-held views (Capie, 2018).

At least as significant, three days later the government announced the purchase of four Boeing P-8A Poseidon long-range maritime patrol aircraft to replace its ageing fleet of five Lockheed P-3K2 Orions. This was not merely an overdue refresh of Aotearoa's maritime rescue and civilian surveillance capabilities. With its massive NZ$2.3 billion price tag, the acquisition was also a generational recommitment to co-operation with the United States, which builds and flies P-8As, and other partners who also operate them, including Australia, Japan and India. There is every reason to expect the Poseidons to fly for as long as the Orions — nearly 60 years — and to sustain a high level of technical, operational and intelligence co-ordination with the other countries throughout.

Further signs in 2018 indicated a more cautious approach toward China. In October, new restrictions on foreign purchases of existing homes went into effect. The Government Communications Security Bureau (GCSB, New Zealand's signals intelligence agency) in November blocked the kiwi telecom firm Spark's use of the PRC firm Huawei's equipment to introduce 5G wireless services into Aotearoa. The next month, the GCSB publicly associated the Chinese Government with malicious cyberattacks against commercial targets in New Zealand.

Beijing in early 2019 registered its dissatisfaction, apparently delaying Prime Minister Ardern's inaugural visit to China, postponing a long-planned 'Year of Chinese Tourism' event, discouraging PRC tourists from visiting Aotearoa, and even possibly forcing the mid-course return to Auckland of a Shanghai-bound Air New Zealand flight. With both sides interested in avoiding further deterioration, the tourism promotion launch was soon rescheduled and the Prime Minister's visit in early April gave Beijing adequate reassurance of New Zealand's intentions. Ardern, for example, agreed to advance a work plan on the Belt and Road Initiative, Xi's hallmark foreign investment project, agreed under National. Defence Minister Ron Mark in Beijing in July signed a 'memorandum of arrangement' on defence co-operation, though its scope was notably limited to humanitarian assistance and peacekeeping. China agreed to upgrade the 2008 Free Trade Agreement with New Zealand.

While Beijing and Wellington thereby managed their emerging differences, the Ardern Government continued to stake out positions that could not have pleased Beijing. In July 2019, New Zealand joined 21 other countries in a letter to the President of the UN Human Rights Council expressing concern about PRC human rights violations in Xinjiang. Prime Ministers Ardern and Abe in September agreed to further the New Zealand–Japan strategic co-operative partnership and study a 'security information sharing agreement'. US and New Zealand special forces exercised together in the North Island in November, and the Ardern

Government in December introduced legislation barring foreigners from donating more that NZ$50 to political parties and candidates.

In early 2020, on the eve of the COVID-19 pandemic, New Zealand continued to enhance co-operation with other states to balance Chinese behaviour. In January, it participated in a joint anti-submarine warfare exercise off Guam with Australia, Japan, the Republic of Korea and the United States. In February, in what would be a New Zealand Foreign Minister's last trip abroad for 19 months, Peters in New Delhi embraced Indo-Pacific framing during his meeting with Foreign Minister Subrahmanyam Shankar and endorsed collective action to protect shared principles and concerns. On the last day of the month, with the pandemic beginning to shut down the world, Prime Ministers Ardern and Scott Morrison in Sydney for their annual meeting released a joint statement pledging their 'mutual efforts to support an open, inclusive and prosperous Indo-Pacific region'.

COVID-19

By the time the Prime Ministers met, New Zealand had already imposed its first restrictions on travellers, and a person arriving from Iran became Aotearoa's first confirmed Covid case. Events moved quickly.

On 16 March, Prime Minister Ardern warned the pandemic could cause a recession sharper than the one during the 2008 GFC, and Otago University epidemiologists assessed the virus's uncontrolled spread could kill as many as 11,000 kiwis. The next day, the government announced a NZ$12.1 billion response package, and New Zealand for the first time in its history closed its borders to all but citizens and residents. Embracing an elimination strategy, the government imposed a national lockdown at just before midnight on 25 March.

For a country heavily dependent on trade, tourism and international education, the situation was alarming. It was unknown whether an effective vaccine would ever become available, and there was widespread uncertainty about the resilience of global supply chains, including the food supply chain so important to the kiwi economy and public welfare. The tourism industry threatened to slip into free fall.

It is therefore remarkable COVID-19 did not prompt a significant course correction in Aotearoa's geopolitical realignment. By June 2021, China accounted for 31 per cent of New Zealand's goods and services, greater than its dependence on the British market in 1973 when London joined the European Economic Community. The PRC's trade coercion of

Australia, even more dependent on the Chinese market than New Zealand, provided an object lesson in the cost of upsetting Beijing. China in early 2019 had already put New Zealand on warning. It is hardly surprising that some kiwi members of the business community and politicians faulted Wellington for upsetting China and threatening Aotearoa's prosperity.

In the event, however, the Labour-led government did not shift course. Concerns about the PRC's regional coercion and interference likely predominated in kiwi policy circles. Deteriorating Chinese human rights conditions also contributed to changing popular and political views. New Zealand was already on record criticizing Beijing's incarceration of a million Muslims, mostly ethnic Uyghurs, in concentration camps in Xinjiang. The PRC's 30 June 2020 imposition of a 'national security law' on Hong Kong and systematic dismantling of liberal institutions there probably was even more important in shaping popular views. Many kiwis had visited Hong Kong, worked or lived there, or knew people who had. Given shared kiwi and Hong Kong values, Beijing's swift suppression of dissent after dramatic protests in 2019 touched a sensitive nerve among many New Zealanders.

Wellington in April 2020 expressed support for Taiwan's World Health Organization (WHO) observer status, an especially delicate issue for Beijing. On 5 June, Defence Minister Mark confirmed New Zealand's purchase of five Lockheed C-130J-30 Super Hercules transport aircraft, another commitment to interoperability with friends, especially Australia. On 23 June, Mark participated in a videoconference of Five Eyes defence ministers, which released a statement on co-operation to protect the international rules-based order, support the 'Indo-Pacific' community and respect states' sovereign rights. Two naturalised Chinese New Zealander members of parliament, one each from National and Labour respectively, in July announced their departure from politics in the wake of accusations they had colluded with PRC officials to promote official Chinese influence in New Zealand. At the end of July, Wellington suspended its extradition agreement with Hong Kong, ended the territory's special treatment for sensitive exports, and updated Aotearoa's travel alert for the jurisdiction.

While continuing to align with Australia, the United States and other countries in responding to PRC activities, Wellington nonetheless maintained a restrained declaratory policy on China. It was silent when the Trump Administration in its May 2020 China strategy document called for a whole-of-government and society response to the PRC. It did not embrace Canberra's July 2020 *Defence Strategic Update* finding that Australia could no longer assume a ten-year strategic warning time as a basis for defence planning (though New Zealand's 2021 *Defence Assessment* acknowledged this change in its discussion of a more demanding strategic environment).

While still too nuanced for some Australian and American observers, Wellington's public position on China nonetheless also continued to shift. The Prime Minister's 20 July remarks to the China Business Summit in Auckland — an overwhelmingly PRC-friendly event — noted 'different perspectives' on Xinjiang, Taiwan's lack of WHO access and Hong Kong. The Prime Minister expressed confidence the 'mature' relationship between Wellington and Beijing would permit continued co-operation despite inevitable disagreements between countries with different political systems. Trade Minister David Parker reminded the assembled business leaders New Zealand's 'brand' also involved respect for human rights.

As usual, foreign policy did not figure prominently when New Zealanders went to the polls on 17 October for a general election. In a remarkable victory affirming approval of Prime Minister Ardern's pandemic leadership, Labour won an outright majority in parliament. New Zealand First lost all its seats, and Labour regained full control of the foreign ministry portfolio for the first time since 2005.

Questions about the government's foreign policy arose early on, when its new foreign and trade ministers, Nanaia Mahuta and Damien O'Connor, appeared to fault Canberra for its difficulties with Beijing. The Foreign Minister in December 2020 seemed to imply New Zealand might be able to negotiate a truce between Canberra and Beijing during the November 2021 APEC summit, which Wellington would host. More significant was O'Connor's 26 January 2021 television interview, during which he stated Canberra 'should follow us and show respect' and be 'cautious with wording' in dealing with Beijing. The remarks reportedly prompted a 24-hour damage control scramble within the New Zealand Government and between Wellington and Canberra, and official Australian resentment may have lingered for weeks (Galloway, 2021).

The new government also sparked controversy on 10 January 2021, when it did not join a Five Eyes statement on Hong Kong, even though it unilaterally expressed similar concerns. Foreign Minister Mahuta reinforced the controversy in April when, after a speech at the New Zealand China Council, she answered an Australian journalist's question about the January Five Eyes decision. Mahuta's assertion that Wellington had reservations about expanding the intelligence partnership's remit was, in fact, consistent with kiwi policy, but the remarks prompted further speculation about New Zealand intent.

These controversies reflected not a considered change in policy but a lack of experience on the new Foreign Minister's part and ill-chosen comments by the Trade Minister. Wellington continued through this period to take public positions contrary to Beijing's liking. In March, for instance, it released joint statements with Australia expressing 'grave concerns' about the PRC's treatment of the Uyghurs and again protesting against changes to Hong Kong's political system.

Indeed, the Foreign Minister's choice to take up the Five Eyes question distracted from the very sober 19 April speech about China she had just delivered. Before a leading kiwi advocate of relations with the PRC, Mahuta laid out a veritable jeremiad of New Zealand worries about Beijing, including excessive reliance on its market, China's threats to the rules-based international order, forced labour, abuse of indigenous peoples' rights, Pacific debt, lack of mutual respect, human rights violations, Hong Kong and the Uyghurs.

The Foreign Minister's remarks anticipated Prime Minister Ardern's 3 May speech before the 2021 session of the annual China Business Summit in Auckland. As at the summit the year before, Ardern underscored China's importance and applauded successes in the New Zealand–PRC relationship. She nonetheless characterised Chinese behaviour as increasingly problematic for the region and for New Zealand itself. 'Managing the relationship' was not 'always going to be easy', and there could 'be no guarantees', Ardern observed. Chinese actions, the Prime Minister stated, were becoming 'harder to reconcile' with New Zealand's interests and values. Many countries 'across the Indo[-]Pacific region' and beyond were grappling with this new reality.

Prime Minister Ardern embraced the 'Indo-Pacific' framework two months later, in a 14 July 2021 speech before the New Zealand Institute for International Affairs. While kiwi leaders had used the term with increasing frequency since 2018, the Prime Minister now characterised the Indo-Pacific as 'central to our interests', and she placed Aotearoa 'in a larger ecosystem of nations and regions that includes East Asia, the Pacific, the Indian sub-continent and the Pacific Rim'. Within this huge framework, Prime Minister Ardern also carefully situated New Zealand in the Pacific.

The Prime Minister did not explicitly link her embrace of the Indo-Pacific to China. In fact, she did not provide a clear justification for the new framework at all, and, in a sense, this ambiguity placed the speech in the mainstream of contemporary New Zealand foreign policy rhetoric. Ardern imparted a distinctly kiwi flavour to the Indo-Pacific by insisting it be open and inclusive, and she closed her remarks with a nod to New Zealand's 'independent, principled foreign policy'.

The closest Ardern came to relating China to the new framework was when she suggested many countries were embracing the Indo-Pacific 'in reaction to more challenging geopolitics'. Like Wellington's generic use of 'strategic competition' in official statements, this appeared to be code for problematic PRC behaviour and other countries' responses to it. Even a cursory reading of the speech made clear the Prime Minister was not positioning her country as a neutral bystander to a contest among morally equivalent antagonists. By embracing the Indo-Pacific, Aotearoa was joining a broad collection of countries seeking to balance PRC power, albeit in terms that accommodated domestic foreign policy sensibilities.

Further evidence of Wellington's new course was readily available. Defence Minister Peeni Henare on 4 May announced the Royal New Zealand Navy (RNZN) would participate in the Pacific and East Asia operations of the United Kingdom's *Queen Elizabeth* CSG. In a *Guardian* interview published 24 May, Foreign Minister Mahuta cautioned: 'it may only be a matter of time before the storm gets closer to us' (McClure, 2021). Also on 24 May, speaking before the India New Zealand Business Council, Mahuta called for stronger defence and security ties with New Delhi and invited co-operation with India to ensure the Indo-Pacific remained open and free. On 29 May, New Zealand as a third party joined Australia's WTO dispute with China over punitive barley tariffs.

Prime Minister Ardern's 31 May annual meeting with her Australian counterpart was clearly intended to dispel any lingering doubts about differences over China. Their joint statement laid out a broad range of PRC-related concerns: Xinjiang, Hong Kong, the SCS, the Indo-Pacific region, political interference and economic coercion. China dominated the leaders' Queenstown press conference, where Prime Minister Morrison asserted: 'there will be those who seek to undermine Australia and New Zealand's security by trying to create points of difference that are not there'. Prime Minister Ardern observed: 'at no point in our discussions today did I detect any difference in our relative positions on the importance of maintaining a very strong and principled position'.

Given Canberra's forceful views on the PRC, this exercise in kiwi–Aussie solidarity was significant. At a minimum, Wellington intended its assertion of its position on China in the weeks before the 31 May meeting as a corrective to any apparent alliance disunity. A more interesting question is whether the correction was not merely in appearances but in substance as well. Given the depth of the trans-Tasman relationship, it is at least plausible that friction with Canberra in early 2021 forced New Zealand's new Labour Government to undertake a significant review of its China policy settings.

At any rate, developments through the remainder of 2021 were consistent with those pre-summit signals. On 19 July, GCSB Minister Andrew Little released a statement criticising Chinese hacking, including by state-sponsored actors. On 3 August, in a 'note verbale' to the UN Commission on the Limits of the Continental Shelf, New Zealand went 'much further' than it ever had before in rejecting Beijing's SCS claims (Capie, 2021).

Wellington tacitly approved of the 15 September announcement of AUKUS, the historic Australia–United Kingdom–United States arrangement to share advanced defence technology, starting with nuclear propulsion for Canberra's submarine fleet. While making obligatory nods to New Zealand's Pacific perspective and ban on nuclear-powered vessels, Prime Minister Ardern welcomed 'increased engagement of the UK and US in the region' and affirmed that the new grouping would have no impact on Wellington's co-operation with any of its Five Eyes partners.

Meanwhile, replenishment ship HMNZS *Aotearoa* proceeded to exercises off Okinawa as part of the *Queen Elizabeth* CSG with two US CSGs and Japanese, Dutch and Canadian naval forces. The kiwi frigate HMNZS *Te Kaha* (effectively, half of New Zealand's maritime combat force) and *Aotearoa* transited the disputed SCS as part of the *Queen Elizabeth* CSG. They completed their long-range mission by participating in the Bersama Gold 21 exercise with the other Five Powers Defence Arrangements partners — Singapore, Malaysia, the United Kingdom and Australia.

The first COVID-19-era international trips by New Zealand's Prime Minister and Foreign Minister highlighted Wellington's priorities. The PRC did not figure among them. It was all but inevitable Australia would be Mahuta's first stop on her November 2021 itinerary. She then continued to Singapore, Jakarta, the United Arab Emirates and Qatar, before visiting the Five Eyes capitals Washington and Ottawa. For her part, Prime Minister Ardern during her April 2022 first COVID-19-era travels visited Singapore and Tokyo. Her next trip, in May, took her to the United States and a meeting with President Joseph Biden.

The defence ministry's December 2021 *Defence Assessment*'s subtitle, 'a rough sea can still be navigated', poetically summarised another sombre official report on New Zealand's deteriorating security environment. It cited climate change and 'strategic competition' as the principal drivers of change.

Conclusion

As with so many other countries in and beyond the region, New Zealand's geopolitical shift was hardly inevitable. A less heavy-handed PRC could have achieved many of its goals without alarming such a diverse collection of states. AUKUS, for instance, arguably was a Chinese own goal, confirming the unnecessary squandering of the warm relations with London and Canberra of just a few years before. The shift in New Zealand policy may have been as significant, despite Wellington's still nuanced rhetoric. For Aotearoa, dependent on the China market and liable to take a rosy, popular view of its own security, a warier approach toward the PRC was neither inevitable nor desired.

There remains the question of how deeply rooted is Wellington's new geopolitical mindset. Senior New Zealand leaders have expressed unmistakable concerns about China but failed to place them in a clear strategic context. Ministry of Defence documents provide the most explicit treatment of PRC challenges to kiwi interests. Nonetheless, it is not clear how even those requiring Cabinet sign-off reflect the views of New Zealand's political leaders, whose comments on strategic and security concerns remain limited and coded.

There are exceptions. Prime Minister Ardern, for instance, characterised the Solomon Islands' April 2022 security agreement with Beijing as 'gravely concerning'. Her government's views on China were perhaps most explicit in her 31 May joint statement with President Biden. Confirming 'strategic competition' was, indeed, code for developments sparked by worrisome PRC behaviour, she joined Biden in using the term to characterise the China–Solomon Islands security agreement and in warning against the establishment of a Pacific military base by a country that did not 'share our values or security interests'. A paragraph on preserving the international rules-based order featured a shopping list of concerns about China, including freedom of navigation, unlawful maritime claims, Xinjiang, Hong Kong and, notably, peace and stability in the Taiwan Strait. The latter had been absent from New Zealand public declaratory policy for 20 years, despite Beijing's transformational military build-up and sharpening threats against Taipei.

Ardern's speeches later in mid-2022, however, retreated from this geopolitical candour. The Prime Minister's 30 June intervention at the NATO summit in Madrid sounded almost defensive for her being there in the first place. While condemning Russia's invasion of Ukraine, Prime Minister Ardern also urged the attendees to avoid a new nuclear arms race and not oversimplify a complex world. Her 2 July speech in London at Chatham House decried Russia's invasion of Ukraine and expressed concern about China's behaviour. The speech nonetheless substantially focused instead on international institutions, the Pacific and climate change. Emphasising New Zealand's identity as a Pacific nation, 'with a strong connection to a wider Indo[-]Pacific region', she laid out 'country[-]neutral' standards for appropriate engagement with the island countries. She defended China's right in principle to be there and implicitly faulted 'European and American partners' for letting China's contestation of the region, rather than respect for those standards, drive their increased interest in it.

These were politically safe speeches for a New Zealand Labour prime minster, perhaps reflecting post-Washington pressure from the traditional left (Young, 2022). Homeward bound from Europe, with an eye to a domestic audience and likely her Australian hosts, Prime Minister Ardern's 7 July speech at the Lowy Institute in Sydney continued along similar lines. Offering an extended meditation on maintaining a 'truly independent foreign policy' in a troubled world, she declared collectivism, values and Pacific identity to be New Zealand's guiding principles. The Prime Minister briefly grouped concerns about PRC behaviour along with other states' sins and reaffirmed a country-neutral declaration of standards for engagement in the Pacific. She again decried oversimplification of global challenges, rejecting Russia's Ukraine invasion as 'a demonstration of the inevitable trajectory in other areas of geostrategic contest'.

These speeches obscured rather than illuminated Wellington's response to the deteriorating Indo-Pacific geopolitical environment. Indeed, together they could easily be read as an assertion that kiwi foreign policy independence was founded on remaining above geopolitics entirely.

Realities are sharply different. Wellington's practical steps in recent years confirm New Zealand's deep concerns about Chinese behaviour. The Prime Minister may scold Europe and the United States for showing inadequate or inappropriate interest in the Pacific, but her government continues to work closely with them in response to PRC assertiveness. In the absence of a roll-back in co-operation with Australia, the United States, the United Kingdom and regional countries, there remains a substantial gap between Aotearoa's declaratory policy and its practical responses to the deteriorating geopolitical environment in which it finds itself.

This gap is not surprising, given New Zealand's history, society and luxurious geography. Wellington's security partners appear willing to accept it, appreciating the need to focus on what Aotearoa does more than on what it says. In geopolitical terms, New Zealand has come a very long way since Prime Minister Clark's 2001 celebration of the country's 'remarkably benign' strategic environment. As a geographically isolated, trade-dependent state less given than most to thinking of security in strategic terms, New Zealand's practical adaptation to these new realities has been a testament to strong leadership, ministerial responsibility and good kiwi common sense.

References

Brady, A.-M. (2017, September 18). Magic Weapons: China's political influence activities under Xi Jinping. *Wilson Center*. www.wilsoncenter.org/article/magic-weapons-chinas-political-influence-activities-under-xi-jinping.

Capie, D. (2018, July 9). Two audiences for the government's new defence policy. *Incline*. www.incline.org.nz/home/two-audience-for-the-governments-new-defence-policy.

Capie, D. (2021, August 5). New Zealand finds its voice on the South China Sea. But was anyone listening? *Incline*. www.incline.org.nz/home/new-zealand-finds-its-voice-on-the-south-china-sea-but-was-anyone-listening.

Galloway, A. (2021, February 22). What is driving the frostiness between Australia and New Zealand? *Sydney Morning Herald*. www.smh.com.au/politics/federal/what-is-driving-the-frostiness-between-australia-and-new-zealand-20210222-p574je.html.

Graham, E. (2019, September 12). Frigates for Venus. *Incline*. www.incline.org.nz/home/frigates-for-venus.

International Monetary Fund (2023). People's Republic of China. www.imf.org/en/Countries/CHN#data.

Jackson, V. (2018, July 12). The price of New Zealand's strategy — force mismatch. *Incline*. www.newsroom.co.nz/van-jackson-the-price-of-nzs-strategy-force-mismatch.

McClure, T. (2021, May 24). "A matter of time": New Zealand's foreign minister warns China "storm" could be coming. *The Guardian.* www.theguardian.com/world/2021/may/25/a-matter-of-time-new-zealands-foreign-minister-warns-china-storm-could-be-coming.

Nicita, A. & Razo, C. (2021, April 27). China: The rise of a trade titan. United Nations Conference on Trade and Development. unctad.org/news/china-rise-trade-titan.

Stockholm International Peace Research Institute (2023). SIPRI military expenditure database. milex.sipri.org/sipri.

Young, A. (2022, June 11). Helen Clark warns against "group think" by NZ in foreign relations. *New Zealand Herald.* https://www.nzherald.co.nz/nz/helen-clark-warns-against-groupthink-by-nz-in-foreign-relations/JF7CF6MOKOHMLPKMVDL5BJ6F5M/

Chapter 3

The Taniwha and the Dragon: New Zealand's Relationship with China under the Ardern Government at a Time of Growing Geopolitical Uncertainty

Nicholas Ross Smith

Introduction

New Zealand's relationship with China came under significant scrutiny during Jacinda Ardern's two terms as Prime Minister of New Zealand (2017–2020 and 2020–2023). Despite trade relations deepening to unprecedented levels, including the signing of an upgrade in 2022, the cooling of the Sino-American relationship, coupled with China's growing assertiveness abroad — not to mention numerous internal problems (Fallon & Smith, 2022) — has many hypothesising a future in which New Zealand is forced to abandon the China strategy it has followed hitherto. However, to date, Ardern has resisted following Australia and charting a future with the United States in favour of attempting to maintain a strong and progressive relationship with China (while also staying within the United States' strategic sphere). Such a decision is not only strategically difficult to manage but it has also elicited significant international and domestic criticism. Undeterred, however, the Ardern Government has engineered a 'mature relationship' between New Zealand and China — increasingly referred to as the '*taniwha*' (a mythical creature in Māori culture) and the 'dragon' (a mythical creature in Chinese culture) (Mahuta,

April 19, 2021) — that it hopes can survive the growing tension of the Indo-Pacific super-region.

This chapter begins with a historical overview of New Zealand's relationship with China, coupled with an appraisal of the relationship during Ardern's first term as Prime Minister. Thereafter, New Zealand's relationship with China will be theoretically assessed by examining the wider geopolitical dynamics found in the Indo-Pacific, with a specific utilisation of the Regional Security Complex Theory (RSCT). Following this, New Zealand's putative China policy under Ardern will be identified as an asymmetrical hedging strategy, and an examination of how New Zealand has tried to maintain this during Ardern's second term will be undertaken. Finally, a discussion of the future challenges and directions of New Zealand's relationship with China in light of the continued changing geopolitical dynamics of the Indo-Pacific will be offered.

Historical Background and the First Term of the Ardern Government

New Zealand and China formalised relations in 1972, although informal relations can be traced back to 1792 when sealskins were harvested in New Zealand for the Chinese market (Brady, 2008). In the first 150 years, there were significant waves of Chinese migration to New Zealand and, albeit much smaller, flows of (mainly) missionaries from New Zealand to China (and later, a wave of adventurers). After the Second World War and in the context of the emerging Cold War, New Zealand held off recognising the newly formed People's Republic of China in line with its ally, the United States, although this was a source of significant public debate in New Zealand (Brady, 2008). Subsequently, when the Sino-American rapprochement occurred in 1971, New Zealand was quick to seek a policy change, with the incoming Labour Government, under the leadership of Norman Kirk, choosing to formally recognise the People's Republic and derecognise the Republic of China in Taiwan (McCraw, 2002).

Relations were rather modest at first, particularly as China was in the midst of the Cultural Revolution and had somewhat retreated from the global stage (Barnouin & Yu, 1998). Trade, however, became an important consideration after New Zealand's top trade partner at the time, the United Kingdom, joined the European Economic Community in 1973. In the mid-1980s, New Zealand Prime Minister David Lange noted

(1984: p. 312): 'the realities of the Community mean that New Zealand has accepted the challenge to diversify and the drive has increasingly focused on the Pacific Rim nations Australia, USA and Canada; Japan, the ASEAN nations, China and Korea'. China's 'opening up' under the leadership of Deng Xiaoping, which began in 1978, undoubtedly set China and New Zealand on a trade convergence course, although hiccups did occur in the relationship, such as the fallout from the Tiananmen Square massacre in 1989 (Finnigan, 2019).

By the early 2000s, China had surpassed the United Kingdom as a destination for New Zealand's exports. In 2004, New Zealand and China opened negotiations on a Free Trade Agreement (FTA). Prime Minister Helen Clark remarked that New Zealand was 'the first developed country to conclude a bilateral market access agreement with China for its entry to the World Trade Organization; the first to recognise China's status as a market economy; and the first country to enter FTA negotiations with China' (Xinhua, 2005). The FTA came into force in 2008 and was 'upgraded' in 2022. Since 2008, China's trade importance to New Zealand has become unparalleled. By the time Ardern entered office as Prime Minister in late 2017, China was New Zealand's top destination for exports and its largest source of imports.

The Ardern Government entered into power with quite an ambitious strategy regarding China. Ardern's election occurred shortly before the 45th anniversary of official China–New Zealand relations, and on that occasion, the Foreign Minister, Winston Peters, remarked that the relationship in that period had evolved into something akin to a 'comprehensive strategic partnership' and that 'New Zealand and China have grown beyond the business and institutional contacts' (Peters, 2017). Thus, China was not simply seen as a country to which New Zealand could export, but rather as a partner and, even, a potential friend — forging friendships is a critical aspect of China's foreign policy under the leadership of Xi Jinping (Smith & Fallon, 2022).

With this development, the Ardern Government started playing with the idea that perhaps New Zealand's strong relationship with China could help it act as an 'honest broker' in helping soothe relations between China and the United States. In 2018, Trade Minister David Parker stated that New Zealand could be a 'bridge' between the United States and China (Hogan, 2018). Given that New Zealand signed a non-binding memorandum of understanding in 2018 with China to be part of its Belt and Road Initiative — the only member of Five Eyes to do so (Lin, 2018) — it appeared Wellington was flirting with the idea of cultivating a dual alignment with China and the United States. In other words, New Zealand was trying to have a firm foot in both camps.

However, the apparent dual alignment dream of the Ardern Government quickly ran into trouble. Firstly, the notion of New Zealand having the diplomatic capital to act as a bridge between China and the United States was widely ridiculed internally and failed to garner any attention in Washington or Beijing. Secondly, the trustworthiness of China remained an ongoing concern, especially given its increased assertiveness, which threatened the putative rules-based system New Zealand strongly adhered to (Mollman, 2018). The New Zealand Government's 2018 Strategic Defence Policy Statement noted that, despite China integrating 'into the international order, it has not consistently adopted the governance and values championed by the order's traditional leaders'.

Despite wobbles, New Zealand's relationship with China continued to deepen under the Ardern Government in its first term. In 2019, Ardern made her first official visit to China. While in Beijing, she met both Premier Li Keqiang and President Xi. Ardern remarked that she wanted to visit Beijing to 'underline the importance that we place on our relationship with China — it is one of our most important and far-reaching relationships' (Young, 2019). Although she raised the issues of Huawei and Xinjiang in these meetings, she was heavily criticised for refusing to divulge exactly what she talked about with regard to these issues. Furthermore, New Zealand agreed with China to upgrade the FTA, Ardern stating that 'our upgraded free trade agreement will remain the best that China has with any country' (Patterson, 2019).

The ongoing issues of Huawei (regarding cybersecurity and intellectual property), Xinjiang (regarding human rights) and, emerging later in 2019, the protests in Hong Kong, threatened the robustness of New Zealand's relationship with China, especially given the peer pressure emanating from many of New Zealand's longest friends to join in with public criticism of China (Brady, 2021). New Zealand did issue public criticisms at times, especially after clashes occurred over Hong Kong at the University of Auckland (Radio New Zealand, 2019). However, New Zealand typically attempted to avoid teaming up with its Western allies in jointly criticising China. The most glaring example of this was when New Zealand refused, despite a personal call from the Canadian Prime Minister Justin Trudeau, to join in the global condemnation of the imprisonment of two Canadian citizens in China (Small, 2019).

By the last year of Ardern's first term as Prime Minister, New Zealand had started to walk something of a tightrope between the United States and China. The onset of the COVID-19 pandemic, which began in Wuhan, China, was an obvious point of contention and helped cool China's relationships with numerous Western countries. However, as in the previous year, New Zealand — unlike Australia — avoided joining the international chorus for an investigation into China's handling of the initial outbreak, with Ardern stating she was 'not interested in blame or a witch hunt' (Andelane, 2020). Still, New Zealand did provoke the ire of the Chinese Embassy in Wellington when Foreign Minister Peters stated that he wanted Taiwan to rejoin the World Health Organization, resulting in a brief back-and-forth (Patterson, 2020, May 7). Later in 2020, Ardern was re-elected, and she began her second term with the assessment that New Zealand's relationship with China remained a net positive, stating 'there have been multiple times where there have been issues... that we have been able to raise, and we do while continuing, I think, a mature relationship' (Patterson, 2020, December 7).

Hedging and the Changing Geopolitics of New Zealand's Neighbourhood

New Zealand's China policy cannot be simply viewed in a bilateral bubble but, rather, needs to be contextualised with a focus on the regional setting in which both China and New Zealand reside. There is a significant body of International Relations (IR) literature about the role that regional geopolitical environments play in foreign policy making, led by the contributions of RSCT. Buzan and Wæver (2003: p. 44) argue that, increasingly, the most important security settings are regions that have developed security complexes: a 'set of units whose major processes of securitisation, desecuritisation, or both, are so interlinked that their security problems cannot reasonably be analyzed or resolved apart from one another'. While structurally focused IR approaches, such as neorealism and (most) neoclassical realist frameworks, place the global distribution of power as the prime factor in assessing international politics, it is posited here that the regional geopolitical environment a state resides in — especially for relatively smaller powers — is a more crucial systemic factor (Smith & Dawson, 2022). As Lake (2009: p. 35) asserts, regions are 'so interrelated in terms of their security that actions by any one member, and significant security-related developments inside any member, have a major impact on others'. Additionally, as the United States' international power position continues to decline relatively and the international system moves (albeit slowly) towards multipolarity, the challengers that are emerging will be chiefly 'regional' great powers to begin with (Smith, 2020).

There are various types of regional security complexes (RSCs), and only some are challenging for the smaller powers that reside in those regions. Particularly challenging are RSCs that are anarchic (i.e. they lack an agreed security architecture), have a bipolar or multipolar distribution of power, and experience increasing enmity among the larger powers (Buzan & Wæver, 2003). In these types of regional settings, relatively small powers are heavily restricted in their actions. As Korolev (2019: p. 419) argues, in more contentious regional settings, the number of policy options 'available to smaller states shrinks'. A notable recent example of a relatively small power getting embroiled in a 'great power' RSC was Ukraine during the early 2010s. Under the leadership of Viktor Yanukovych, it tried to find an advantageous middle ground between the West — notably the key institutions of the European Union and NATO — and Russia. However, although Ukraine's long-held 'multi-vectorism' (a kind of multi-alignment) was possible up until the mid-2000s when the eastern European security complex was less contested, the emergence of anarchy, bipolarity and enmity between the European Union and Russia led to Ukraine residing in an unstable and punishing regional setting (Smith, 2020, November).

Whether New Zealand currently resides in an RSC is debatable. It is geographically far away from the major 'Indo-Pacific' geopolitical flashpoints in the western Pacific and on the border of India and China. Notably, in Buzan's (2003) classification of RSCs in post-Cold War Asia (see Figure 1), New Zealand was conspicuously absent from the Asian supercomplex that he sketched out (this included a South Asian RSC, an East Asian RSC and a South East Asian subcomplex). Australia, on the other hand, was included in the supercomplex, as part of the East Asian RSC and the South East Asian subcomplex. Some have suggested that New Zealand might be part of a South Pacific RSC (Wallis *et al.*, 2023), which certainly complements its long-held foreign policy vision and goals, which are generally significantly Pacific-focused, exemplified by a strong involvement in regional bodies such as the Pacific Islands Forum (Mahuta, 2021, March). Since Buzan's initial conceptualisation, the idea of there being an Indo-Pacific 'super region' has become extremely popular and officially

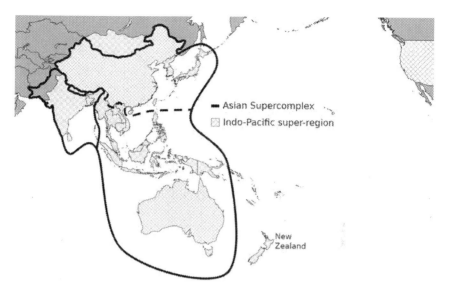

Figure 1. Buzan's Asian supercomplex compared to the United States' designation of the Indo-Pacific super-region.

pushed by the United States and its allies, replacing the previously used 'Asia-Pacific' moniker that remains China's preferred term (Medcalf, 2014). In most iterations of the Indo-Pacific, New Zealand is included as a member, along with the small states of the South Pacific. New Zealand's Ministry of Foreign Affairs and Trade (2021) also started using 'Indo-Pacific' instead of 'Asia-Pacific', most notably listing entrenching 'New Zealand as an active and integral partner in shaping an Indo-Pacific order' as one of its seven strategic goals.

The Indo-Pacific is arguably the area of the globe that has experienced the greatest geopolitical shift over the last decade (and it is likely to continue for the next decade too). Beginning with US President Barack Obama's decision to 'pivot to Asia' in 2011 — which was disrupted somewhat by events that occurred in Europe, most notably Russia's resurgence and the emergence of Islamic State in Syria and Iraq in 2013–2014 — it has become clear for some time that China and the United States have been on a collision course in the Asia-Pacific (Löfflmann, 2016). More recent security-focused efforts by the United States include resurrecting and strengthening the Quadrilateral Security Dialogue (colloquially known as the 'Quad') and the forming of AUKUS — a trilateral security pact between Australia, the United Kingdom, and the United States (Jackson, 2021). Economically, the United States also launched the Indo-Pacific Economic Framework in 2022 to solidify a 'commitment to a free, open, fair, inclusive, interconnected, resilient, secure, and prosperous Indo-Pacific region that has the potential to achieve sustainable and inclusive economic growth' (White House, 2022).

China too has sought to maximise its regional influence over the last decade, most notably through its flagship Belt and Road Initiative: a grand strategy that uses massive infrastructure investment to try and embed positive trade links between China and the rest of the world (Clarke, 2017). Furthermore, this has coincided with China adopting a far bolder stance under Xi — built off the back of a significant increase in military expenditure and capabilities — evident in more assertive action regarding territorial claims, such as in the South China Sea and on its border with India (Liu, 2020). Although New Zealand is far away from the major flashpoints of China's growing assertiveness — China's recent agreement with the Solomon Islands and its pursuit of a Pacific-wide pact has caused consternation, not only in Washington and Canberra but also in Wellington (Smith & McNeill, 2022).

At the very least, it appears that the Indo-Pacific super-region is an area where no agreed security architecture exists (thus, it is increasingly anarchic), in which there is increasing bipolarity (although the United States still has a significant power advantage over China), and growing levels of enmity (although Sino-American trade relations remain quite interdependent for the time being). This is a setting that is increasingly being referred to as the ground zero of a new Cold War (Hirsh, 2022) and while there are strong material and ideational reasons why that assertion is still quite hyperbolic, it is undeniable that psychologically, China and the United States are falling into the trap of seeing each other as unequivocal enemies (Smith, 2021). For the smaller powers that are caught in the middle, this is likely to create significant foreign policy headaches as well as shrink the room for hedging even further at a time when unprecedented global issues — such as the COVID-19 pandemic and the effects of climate change — have already created significant challenges.

New Zealand, like the majority of relatively small powers that have found themselves caught in the ripples of China's rise in the Indo-Pacific (Jackson, 2014; Medeiros, 2005), has been employing something of a hedging strategy in its foreign policymaking (Steff & Dodd-Parr, 2019;

Young, 2017). Hedging as a concept in IR is much like its use in the financial world, as these are strategies that aim to spread risk wide to mitigate potential calamity (Smith, 2018). Hedging is very much an umbrella term as a myriad of types of state behaviour — whether by greater or smaller powers — has been termed hedging by scholars in recent years. For smaller powers, however, hedging has generally been used to describe a strategy in which the smaller power attempts to 'cultivate a middle position that forestalls or avoids having to choose one side at the obvious expense of another' (Goh, 2005: p. 2). Indeed, such behaviour evokes the concepts of 'soft balancing' (Paul, 2005) or 'evasive balancing' (Rajagopalan, 2020), but this chapter retains the term 'hedging' as it is more of an umbrella concept involving different strategies that a smaller power can pursue to find a desirable middle ground.

While hedging is an alluring strategy for relatively small powers because, ostensibly, it appears as an optimal foreign policy grand strategy that enables them to avoid the trade-offs inherent in the more traditional options of balancing or bandwagoning, it is neither costless nor easy to execute (Lim & Cooper, 2015). This is particularly the case if the hedging state is residing in an unstable and competitive regional geopolitical environment. To this end, although numerous factors are important to the potential successfulness of a hedge — such as signalling (Lim & Cooper, 2015), capabilities (Vander Vennet & Salman, 2019), and domestic politics (Hiep, 2013) — it is argued here that the initial key factor a relatively small state needs to consider when devising a hedging strategy is the permissiveness of the regional geopolitical environment they reside in to hedging (Smith, 2020, November).

New Zealand's China Strategy as the Room for Hedging in the Indo-Pacific Shrinks

In practice, hedging strategies vary significantly from state to state. However, one aspect of smaller power hedging which can be more easily categorised is alignment, namely, what the underpinning alignment aim for the smaller power engaging the hedge is. The question of New Zealand's alignment between the United States and China has grabbed significant media attention and generated significant scholarly debate (Ayson, 2020; Köllner, 2021; Smith, 2022; Steff, 2021; Steff & Dodd-Parr, 2019; Young, 2017).

As alluded to earlier, the first term of Ardern's administration seemingly toyed with the idea of etching out a kind of dual alignment for New Zealand with both the United States and China. A dual alignment is a bold form of hedging because the smaller power aims to concurrently align with both sides of the regional great power competition they are caught between. In other words, rather than being a more passive player — such as in other forms of alignment — dual alignment entails a more active role by the smaller power in cultivating a 'win on both sides' middle ground between the competing larger powers (Smith, 2020, November).

However, New Zealand's putative dual alignment goal has become nothing more than a 'pipe dream', as Sino-American relations began to cool and the Indo-Pacific has become geopolitically tense. In lieu, New Zealand has had to maintain an asymmetrical alignment (Smith, 2022). An asymmetrical alignment is when the smaller power nominally (usually with regard to security) aligns with one great power but does so in a way that is not exclusive to having relations (usually trade) with the other great power (Lim & Cooper, 2015). This is a less ambitious strategy than dual-aligned hedging, but it is certainly more ambitious than a non-aligned hedge as the smaller power is still trying to forge a middle ground in which it reaps the benefits of alignment with one state but also the benefits of having cordial relations with the other. It also serves as a signal to China and the United States that it has a foot in both camps, albeit to different degrees.

New Zealand has been pursuing an asymmetrical alignment for at least the last decade and a half (Steff & Dodd-Parr, 2019). On the one side, New Zealand — although absent in recent initiatives like the Quad and AUKUS — is broadly aligned with several of Washington's security initiatives — such as contributing to its anti-Islamic State campaign in Iraq and supporting the Afghan state army and being a member in the Five Eyes intelligence alliance. Although New Zealand is still officially suspended from the ANZUS security treaty, relations have improved markedly since the signing of the Washington Declaration in 2012, and in mid-2022, US Deputy Secretary of State Wendy Sherman even hinted that New Zealand could be considered for membership of AUKUS (Radio New Zealand, 2022). But, on the other hand, New Zealand has continued to deepen trade ties with China, upgrading the 2008 FTA in early 2022. New Zealand's trade with China has, subsequently, increased significantly. In 2008, China, as a destination, accounted for a mere 5.8 per cent of New Zealand's exports, but by 2020 that had risen to 27.7 per cent. That total was only slightly less than combined exports to Australia, Japan and the United States, which accounted for 30.5 per cent (United Nations, 2021).

For Wellington, this 'asymmetrical' configuration now appears to be deemed the optimal one. The optimistic and idealistic tones of attempting to be a bridge between China and the United States that were present in Ardern's first year have ceased. However, New Zealand still clearly sees China as a significant part of its future, despite the increased tension between China and two of New Zealand's longest friends, Australia and the United States. In her first speech as New Zealand Foreign Minister, Nanaia Mahuta laid out a continuation of an asymmetrical alignment strategy, summarised by Thomas Manch (2021) as: 'China for trade, US for defence, and Pacific at the centre'.

Since Mahuta's maiden speech, New Zealand's tightrope act in trying to placate both sides of its asymmetrical alignment has become even more perilous. On the US-centric side, New Zealand, despite deciding not to join other Five Eyes members in criticising China, nor being part of initiatives like AUKUS or the Quad, has still chosen, on occasion, to join its allies in some activities designed to challenge China. These include sending a frigate to join the United Kingdom's 'Carrier Strike Group' on an exercise in the South China Sea and co-sponsoring a United Nations event on raising awareness of human rights abuses in Xinjiang. But, at the same time, New Zealand has maintained strong bilateral interactions with China and refused, on occasions, to publicly back its 'friends' (most notably Australia) that have become embroiled in disputes with China.

Mahuta (April 19, 2021) used the metaphor of a *taniwha* and a dragon to emphasise the maturity of the Sino-New Zealand relationship, stating: 'I see the Taniwha and the Dragon as symbols of the strength of our particular customs, traditions and values, that aren't always the same, but need to be maintained and respected'. But less than a month later, Mahuta also stated: 'We cannot ignore, obviously, what's happening in Australia with their relationship with China. And if they are close to an eye of the storm or in the eye of the storm, we've got to legitimately ask ourselves — it may only be a matter of time before the storm gets closer to us' (McClure, 2021).

What New Zealand appears to be practising is a form of constructive ambiguity (Miller, 2022). Constructive ambiguity is a critical aspect of effective hedging. As Darren Lim and Zack Cooper (2015: p. 709) argue, it is a case of:

> 'sending signals which generate ambiguity over the extent of their shared security interests with great powers, in effect eschewing clear-cut alignment with any great power, and in turn creating greater uncertainty regarding which side the secondary state would take in the event of a great power conflict.'

While New Zealand under Ardern has not been as brazen as the Philippines — especially by its former President Rodrigo Duterte (Wu, 2019) — in generating ambiguity, it is clear that Ardern and Mahuta, among other prominent individuals within the New Zealand foreign policy establishment, are using language which does not commit New Zealand to a specific stance — New Zealand does not fully share the world view of either the United States or China — and had a very firm intention to demonstrate its independent foreign policy, which got in the way of any clear messaging. However, there are costs to employing constructive ambiguity, and New Zealand's balancing act has drawn criticism from its allies, especially Australia and the United Kingdom, both of which have made unequivocal signals in their alignment. And although China has praised New Zealand for its independence, the times New Zealand has criticised China it has not gone unrebuked. There has been domestic criticism as well, as some fear New Zealand is hurting its long-term security outlook by alienating its trustworthy allies for the short-term benefits of maintaining trade with an untrustworthy China (Brady, 2021; Dunne, 2022). China is also increasingly seen as a threat by the general public in New Zealand (Craymer, 2021).

However, despite mounting criticism from all sides, New Zealand has remained resolute in continuing to undertake an asymmetrical alignment between the United States and China. In a speech in July 2021, Ardern seemingly doubled down on this strategy. After saying that New Zealand had adopted an 'Indo-Pacific outlook' — in line with the United States, the United Kingdom and Australia — she stressed that New Zealand was against the use of the Indo-Pacific concept 'as subtext, or a tool to exclude some nations [meaning China] from dialogue' and that 'our success will depend on working with the widest possible set of partners' (Ardern, 2021). China remained 'an engine of global growth and one of our most significant, but also one of our increasingly complex relationships' (Ardern, 2021).

Future Challenges and Directions

New Zealand's continued preference to maintain a 'mature relationship' with China will undoubtedly face growing external (and some internal) pressures. Indeed, if Sino-American relations deteriorate further and something akin to a Cold War emerges in the Indo-Pacific, then New Zealand will likely be forced to abandon its preferred asymmetrical alignment hedge and alter its current China strategy. The signing of a 'security pact' between China and the Solomon Islands in early 2022 led to Ardern noting China's 'growing assertiveness' in the region (Corlett & Hurst, 2022). However, as China has demonstrated in its recent interaction with Australia, when it feels slighted, it is not afraid to use economic statecraft to punish transgressions. China's growing assertiveness will put extra pressure on New Zealand's putative grand strategy because, ultimately, in an era of escalating great power rivalry (perhaps even a new Cold War) it will be likely impossible for New Zealand to maintain a security alignment with the United States and, at the same time, continue robust trade relations with China.

However, this does not necessarily mean New Zealand would be forced to abandon a hedging strategy and choose a side. Hedging would still be conceivable, albeit a more modest non-aligned style of a hedge (Smith, 2022). Non-aligned strategies became popular during the original Cold War for relatively small powers caught in regional settings beset by competition between the Soviet Union and the United States, two superpowers engaged in a global struggle for supremacy (Gaddis, 2006). Non-alignment should be considered the most modest type of hedge because although it still attempts to forge a middle ground between the larger powers to avoid having to choose a side, the relatively small power does not try actively force a win-on-both-sides outcome, like with more ambitious alignments (Fiori & Passeri, 2015). One historical example of the apparent successful implementation of a non-aligned hedge was that of Yugoslavia under the leadership of Josip Broz (Tito). Tito's apparent success was that through a policy of non-alignment, Yugoslavia was able to stay independent of Soviet control while also reaping the benefits of having relations with the more prosperous capitalist countries in the West (Kullaa, 2012).

New Zealand adopting a non-aligned strategy would entail breaking its 70-year strategic alignment with the United States, something which seems highly unlikely at the moment. Nevertheless, non-alignment might be attractive to New Zealand as avoiding being sucked into the increasing zero-sum tension of the Sino-American relationship appears to be a major goal of the Ardern Government, moving forward. Furthermore, as the Yugoslav experience demonstrates, forging friendships with other non-aligned countries is crucial to making it work (Smith & Fallon, 2022). In the Indo-Pacific, friends could potentially be found in two members of the 'official' non-aligned movement, Malaysia and Indonesia, who have jointly opposed the United States' increased efforts to counter China, fearing it could 'lead to tensions caused by an arms race and power projection' (Radio Free Asia, 2021). Given New Zealand's strong identification with pursuing a 'principled, independent foreign policy', it is plausible that non-alignment becomes a popular strategic option in Wellington if Sino-American relations deteriorate, as the Soviet-American relationship did in the late 1940s (New Zealand Ministry of Foreign Affairs and Trade, 2020).

However, if hedging is deemed too risky or becomes completely untenable, then New Zealand is likely to be forced to choose a side. This scenario evokes the classic neorealist view of international relations which holds that when a rising adversary threatens the status quo, a relatively small power has two main strategic options: to balance or bandwagon. Balancing entails a state solidifying its relationships with other powers against the revisionist power to preserve the status quo. Bandwagoning entails a state siding with the revisionist power to profit from their revisionism. Bandwagoning is generally much riskier than balancing as not only is it likely to upset those invested in maintaining the status quo, but also any material success for the bandwagoner relies on the revisionist power being successful. As Randall Schweller (1994: p. 74) argues, 'the aim of balancing is self-preservation and the protection of values already possessed, while the goal of bandwagoning is usually self-extension: to obtain values coveted'.

If New Zealand finds itself in a situation where it has to choose to balance with the United States or bandwagon with China, it is almost a certainty that New Zealand would follow Australia's footsteps and firmly align itself with the United States (Jung *et al.*, 2021). This is for good reason, as bandwagoning with China's rise would entail that New Zealand turns its back on its oldest friends and side with an increasingly totalitarian, defensively nationalistic, and internationally belligerent power (in China), all for maintaining the benefits of trade and inclusion in China's international initiatives. The costs simply massively outweigh the benefits. Of course, if New Zealand is forced to balance China by fully signing up to a US bloc, it would come with great economic costs too, especially as China is easily New Zealand's most important trading partner. But, perhaps as a contingency for this scenario, New Zealand has already set in motion efforts to diversify its trade to lessen its reliance on China. New Zealand was a founding member of the Comprehensive and Progressive Agreement for Trans-Pacific Partnership (CPTPP) and recently signed FTAs with the United Kingdom and the European Union. The urgency of trade diversification was evident in Ardern's 2022 schedule, which involved her leading 'trade delegations and trade-supporting visits into four key markets [in 2022] — Australia, Asia, the United States and Europe' (Manch, 2022).

Indeed, New Zealand might be eventually forced into choosing the United States at the expense of China, but, as it currently stands, it has arguably the most 'strategic wiggle room' of any state in the Indo-Pacific super-region (Smith, 2022). Compared to Australia, which has already clearly chosen to balance against China with the United States, New Zealand has a number of advantages that make pursuing a more independent foreign policy possible. New Zealand is small and non-threatening. It has earned a global reputation as being an 'honest broker'. New Zealand is also geographically isolated and is far away from the three largest powers involved in the Indo-Pacific: the United States (12,500 km), China (11,000 km), and India (12,000 km). Such factors allow New Zealand, for the moment, to continue pursuing a hedging strategy that keeps China as its most important trade partner. Furthermore, such a strategy complements New Zealand's dominant foreign policy strategic culture: a belief that it is a principled and independent international actor, self-evident in its anti-nuclear stance (Szöllősi-Cira, 2022). Therefore, despite the shrinking room for hedging in the Indo-Pacific, it is plausible that New Zealand — especially if Labour is re-elected in October 2023 — will continue to play its own game and seek to maintain a 'mature relationship' with China, rather than join the others that are conforming with the United States' Indo-Pacific strategy.

References

Andelane, L. (2020). Coronavirus: NZ "not interested in blame or a witch hunt" as country joins call for inquiry into COVID-19's origins — Ardern. *Newshub*. www.newshub.co.nz/home/politics/2020/05/coronavirus-nz-not-interested-in-blame-or-a-witch-hunt-as-country-joins-call-for-inquiry-into-covid-19-s-origins-ardern.html.

Ardern, J. (2021). Prime Minister's Speech to NZIIA Annual Conference. www.beehive.govt.nz/release/prime-ministers-speech-nziia-annual-conference.

Ayson, R. (2020). New Zealand and the great irresponsibles: Coping with Russia, China and the US. *Australian Journal of International Affairs*, *74*(4), 455–478.

Barnouin, B. & Yu, C. (1998). *Chinese Foreign Policy during the Cultural Revolution*. London: Kegan Paul International.

Brady, A.-M. (2008). New Zealand–China relations: Common points and differences. *New Zealand Journal of Asian Studies*, *10*(2), 1–20.

Brady, A.-M. (2021). Five Eyes: New Zealand avoids offending China, ends up offending closest partners. *Sydney Morning Herald*. www.smh.com.au/national/drawing-a-snake-and-adding-feet-new-zealand-avoids-offending-china-ends-up-offending-closest-partners-20210423-p57lzk.html.

Buzan, B. (2003). Security architecture in Asia: The interplay of regional and global levels. *Pacific Review*, *16*(2), 143–173.

Buzan, B. & Wæver, O. (2003). *Regions and Powers: The Structure of International Security*. Cambridge: Cambridge University Press.

Clarke, M. (2017). The belt and road initiative: China's new grand strategy? *Asia Policy*, *24*, 71–79.

Corlett, E. & Hurst, D. (2022). Jacinda Ardern questions motive for China–Solomons security pact. *The Guardian*. www.theguardian.com/world/2022/apr/21/jacinda-ardern-questions-motive-for-china-solomons-security-pact.

Craymer, L. (2021). New Zealanders increasingly see China as a threat. *Stuff*. www.stuff.co.nz/national/china-and-nz/125438932/new-zealanders-increasingly-see-china-as-a-threat.

Dunne, P. (2022). Fifty years of sycophancy to China have left NZ exposed. *Newsroom*. www.newsroom.co.nz/fifty-years-of-sycophancy-to-china-have-left-nz-more-exposed-than-protected.

Fallon, T. & Smith, N. R. (2022). The two-level game of China's public diplomacy efforts. In Zhang, X., & Schultz, C. (Eds.), *China's International Communication and Relationship Building*. Abingdon: Routledge.

Finnigan, L. (2019). A steady friendship. *New Zealand International Review*, *44*(6), 13–15.

Fiori, A. & Passeri, A. (2015). Hedging in search of a new age of non-alignment: Myanmar between China and the USA. *Pacific Review*, *28*(5), 679–702.

Gaddis, J. L. (2006). *The Cold War: A New History*. London: Penguin.

Goh, E. (2005). Meeting the China challenge: The US in Southeast Asian regional security strategies. *Policy Studies*, *16*, 82.

Hiep, L. H. (2013). Vietnam's hedging strategy against China since normalization. *Contemporary Southeast Asia*, *35*(3), 333–368.

Hirsh, M. (2022). We are now in a global cold war. *Foreign Policy*. foreignpolicy.com/2022/06/27/new-cold-war-nato-summit-united-states-russia-ukraine-china.

Hogan, F. (2018). NZ could be a "bridge" between US and China — David Parker. *Newshub*. www.newshub.co.nz/home/shows/2018/11/nz-could-be-a-bridge-between-us-and-china-david-parker.html.

Jackson, V. (2014). Power, trust, and network complexity: Three logics of hedging in Asian security. *International Relations of the Asia-Pacific, 14*(3), 331–356.

Jackson, V. (2021). America is turning Asia into a powder keg. *Foreign Affairs*. www.foreignaffairs.com/articles/asia/2021-10-22/america-turning-asia-powder-keg.

Jung, S. C., Lee, J., & Lee, J.-Y. (2021). The Indo-Pacific strategy and US alliance network expandability: Asian middle powers' positions on Sino–US geostrategic competition in Indo-Pacific region. *Journal of Contemporary China, 30*(127), 53–68.

Köllner, P. (2021). Australia and New Zealand recalibrate their China policies: Convergence and divergence. *The Pacific Review, 34*(3), 405–436.

Korolev, A. (2019). Shrinking room for hedging: System-unit dynamics and behavior of smaller powers. *International Relations of the Asia-Pacific, 19*(3), 419–452.

Kullaa, R. (2012). *Non-alignment and Its Origins in Cold War Europe: Yugoslavia, Finland and the Soviet Challenge*. London: I.B.Tauris.

Lake, D. A. (2009). Regional hierarchy: Authority and local international order. *Review of International Studies, 35*(S1), 35–58.

Lange, D. (1984). New Zealand: Changing directions. *Round Table, 73*(291), 311–315.

Lim, D. J., & Cooper, Z. (2015). Reassessing hedging: The logic of alignment in East Asia. *Security Studies, 24*(4), 696–727.

Lin, J. (2018). Small state, smart influence: China's belt and road extended to New Zealand. In Zhang, W., Alon, I., & Lattemann, C. (Eds.), *China's Belt and Road Initiative* (pp. 179–197). Cham: Palgrave Macmillan.

Liu, F. (2020). The recalibration of Chinese assertiveness: China's responses to the Indo-Pacific challenge. *International Affairs, 96*(1), 9–27.

Löfflmann, G. (2016). The pivot between containment, engagement, and restraint: President Obama's conflicted grand strategy in Asia. *Asian Security, 12*(2), 92–110.

Mahuta, N. (2021, March). A different approach. *New Zealand International Review, 46*(3), 2–5.

Mahuta, N. (2021, April 19). He Taniwha He Tipua, He Tipua He Taniwha — The Dragon and the Taniwha. www.beehive.govt.nz/speech/"he-taniwha-he-tipua-he-tipua-he-taniwha-dragon-and-taniwha".

Manch, T. (2021). Nanaia Mahuta lays out vision for NZ foreign policy: China for trade, US for defence, and Pacific at the centre. *Stuff*. www.stuff.co.nz/national/politics/124154902/nanaia-mahuta-lays-out-vision-for-nz-foreign-policy-china-for-trade-us-for-defence-and-pacific-at-the-centre.

Manch, T. (2022). Prime Minister Jacinda Ardern promises to travel to Europe, US, Asia, Australia in 2022. *Stuff*. www.stuff.co.nz/national/politics/127676201/prime-minister-jacinda-ardern-promises-to-travel-to-europe-us-asia-australia-in-2022.

McClure, T. (2021). "A matter of time": New Zealand's foreign minister warns China "storm" could be coming. *The Guardian*. www.theguardian.com/world/2021/may/25/a-matter-of-time-new-zealands-foreign-minister-warns-china-storm-could-be-coming.

McCraw, D. (2002). Norman Kirk, the Labour Party and New Zealand's recognition of the People's Republic of China. *New Zealand Journal of Asian Studies, 4*, 46–61.

Medcalf, R. (2014). In defence of the Indo-Pacific: Australia's new strategic map. *Australian Journal of International Affairs, 68*(4), 470–483.

Medeiros, E. S. (2005). Strategic hedging and the future of Asia–pacific stability. *Washington Quarterly, 29*(1), 145–167.

Miller, G. (2022). Ardern maintains ambiguity on China–New Zealand relations. *World Politics Review*. www.worldpoliticsreview.com/ardern-china-new-zealand-relations.

Ministry of Foreign Affairs and Trade, New Zealand. (2020). Briefing for Incoming Minister of Foreign Affairs. www.mfat.govt.nz/en/about-us/briefings-to-incoming-ministers.

Ministry of Foreign Affairs and Trade, New Zealand. (2021). Our Strategic Direction. www.mfat.govt.nz/en/about-us/our-strategic-direction.

Mollman, S. (2018). New Zealand risks becoming a "strategic nincompoop" as China woos tiny Pacific islands. *Quartz*. qz.com/1219925/new-zealand-risks-becoming-a-strategic-nincompoop-as-china-woos-tiny-pacific-islands.

New Zealand Government. (2018). Strategic Defence Policy Statement. www.defence.govt.nz/assets/Uploads/8958486b29/Strategic-Defence-Policy-Statement-2018.pdf.

Patterson, J. (2019). NZ Strikes Deal on China FTA Upgrade after Years of Talks. *Radio New Zealand*. www.rnz.co.nz/news/political/402505/nz-strikes-deal-on-china-fta-upgrade-after-years-of-talks.

Patterson, J. (2020, December 7). New Zealand, China in "a mature relationship", says Jacinda Ardern on row with Australia. *New Zealand Herald*. www.nzherald.co.nz/nz/new-zealand-china-in-a-mature-relationship-says-jacinda-ardern-on-row-with-australia/43KWM3WVOVB245I4OEEVGMREXY.

Patterson, J. (2020, May 7). Winston Peters Tells China's Ambassador to "Listen to Her Master". *Radio New Zealand*. www.rnz.co.nz/news/political/416128/winston-peters-tells-china-s-ambassador-to-listen-to-her-master.

Paul, T. V. (2005). Soft balancing in the age of U.S. primacy. *International Security, 30*(1), 46–71.

Peters, W. (2017). Anniversary of diplomatic relations with China. www.beehive.govt.nz/speech/anniversary-diplomatic-relations-china.

Radio Free Asia. (2021). Indonesia and Malaysia jointly amplify warning about AUKUS pact. *Radio Free Asia*. www.rfa.org/english/news/china/indonesia-malaysia-10182021172730.html.

Rajagopalan, R. (2020). Evasive balancing: India's unviable Indo-Pacific strategy. *International Affairs, 96*(1), 75–93.

Radio New Zealand (2019). Auckland University student cops abuse after dispute at Hong Kong protest. *RNZ News*. www.rnz.co.nz/news/national/395895/auckland-university-student-cops-abuse-after-dispute-at-hong-kong-protest.

Radio New Zealand (2022). NZ could eventually join AUKUS — US diplomat. *RNZ*. www.rnz.co.nz/national/programmes/morningreport/audio/2018852876/nz-could-eventually-join-aukus-us-diplomat.

Schweller, R. L. (1994). Bandwagoning for profit: Bringing the revisionist state back in. *International Security, 19*(1), 72–107.

Small, Z. (2019). China–Canada dispute: New Zealand's lukewarm response called out. *Newshub*. www.newshub.co.nz/home/politics/2019/04/china-canada-dispute-new-zealand-s-lukewarm-response-called-out.html.

Smith, N. R. (2018). Strategic hedging by smaller powers: What can neoclassical realism add? *Re-appraising Neoclassical Realism [workshop] London School of Economics, 29 November 2018*. eprints.nottingham.ac.uk/60852.

Smith, N. R. (2020). *A New Cold War? Assessing the Current US–Russia Relationship*. Cham: Palgrave.

Smith, N. R. (2020, November). When hedging goes wrong: Lessons from Ukraine's failed hedge of the EU and Russia. *Global Policy, 11*(5), 588–597.

Smith, N. R. (2021). US' distorted view of the China threat risks creating a cold war nightmare. *South China Morning Post*. www.scmp.com/comment/opinion/article/3130308/us-distorted-view-china-threat-risks-creating-cold-war-nightmare.

Smith, N. R. (2022). New Zealand's grand strategic options as the room for hedging continues to shrink. *Comparative Strategy, 41*(3), 314–327.

Smith, N. R., & Dawson, G. (2022). Mearsheimer, Realism, and the Ukraine War. *Analyse & Kritik, 44*(2), 175–200.

Smith, N. R., & Fallon, T. (2022). The importance of bona fide friendships to international politics: China's quest for friendships that matter. *Cambridge Review of International Affairs*, 1–22. https://doi.org/10.1080/09557571.2022.2044757.

Smith, N. R. & McNeill, H. (2022). Furore over Pacific nations' China deals puts focus on security instead of climate change. *South China Morning Post*. www.scmp.com/comment/opinion/article/3179809/furore-over-pacific-nations-china-deals-puts-focus-security-instead.

Steff, R. (2021). The Biden administration and New Zealand's strategic options: Asymmetric hedging, tight five eyes alignment, and armed neutrality. *National Security Journal, 3*(2), 1–22.

Steff, R. & Dodd-Parr, F. (2019). Examining the immanent dilemma of small states in the Asia-Pacific: The strategic triangle between New Zealand, the US and China. *Pacific Review, 32*(1), 90–112.

Szöllősi-Cira, L. (2022). *New Zealand's Global Responsibility: A Small State's Leading Role in Establishing Progressive Ideas*. Singapore: Springer Nature.

United Nations (2021). *Download Trade Data*. UN Comtrade Database. comtrade.un.org/data.

Vander Vennet, N. & Salman, M. (2019). Strategic hedging and changes in geopolitical capabilities for second-tier states. *Chinese Political Science Review, 4*(1), 86–134.

Wallis, J., McNeill, H., Batley, J., & Powles, A. (2023). Security cooperation in the Pacific Islands: architecture, complex, community, or something else? *International Relations of the Asia-Pacific, 23*(2), 263–296.

White House (2022). Statement on Indo-Pacific Economic Framework for Prosperity. www.whitehouse.gov/briefing-room/statements-releases/2022/05/23/statement-on-indo-pacific-economic-framework-for-prosperity.

Wu, C. C.-H. (2019). Why do states hedge in East Asia? An empirical study on hedging. *Asian Perspective, 43*(3), 557–584.

Xinhua (2005). New Zealand aims to conclude FTA talks with China first. *People's Daily Online*. en.people.cn/200505/31/eng20050531_187594.html.

Young, A. (2019). Ardern in China: Beijing "ready to strengthen relationship" with NZ. *New Zealand Herald*. www.nzherald.co.nz/nz/ardern-in-china-beijing-ready-to-strengthen-relationship-with-nz/UEAKRMZBVSG457ZRVRGVBNQZWI.

Young, J. (2017). Seeking ontological security through the rise of China: New Zealand as a small trading nation. *Pacific Review, 30*(4), 513–530.

© 2024 World Scientific Publishing Company
https://doi.org/10.1142/9789811285165_0004

Chapter 4

Trade Policy under the Ardern Government

Robert Scollay

Introduction: The Trade Environment for the Incoming Ardern Government

The external trade environment that the Ardern Government inherited in October 2017 contained several elements of continuity with the recent past, but also two emerging major disruptions. The domestic environment for trade policy also included an important element of unfinished business.

Continuity and Unfinished Business

Support for the World Trade Organization (WTO) as the guarantor of a rules-based multilateral trading system remained a cornerstone of New Zealand's trade policy. The market access commitments of its members together with its rules and dispute settlement system provided essential underpinnings for New Zealand's trade interests, especially in agricultural trade, and its negotiation process offered tantalising prospects for advancing those interests.

By 2017 however a stalemate appeared to have been reached in the 'Doha Round' of WTO trade negotiations, launched with much fanfare in 2001 during the term of New Zealand's Mike Moore as WTO Director-General, with an ambitious agenda for further far-reaching liberalisation of world trade, in which a succession of New Zealand ministers and officials had played major roles. A Trade Facilitation Agreement concluded in 2013 was finally ratified in early 2017, and a ministerial meeting in Nairobi in 2016 had finally reached agreement on the elimination of export subsidies, but negotiations remained deadlocked on the majority of the negotiating agenda, especially in the field of agricultural trade where New Zealand's principal objectives lay. Against a background of calls from major players like the United States for the Doha Round to be abandoned, a ministerial meeting was scheduled for the end of 2017 in Buenos Aires in a further attempt to make progress.

At the regional level, New Zealand had consistently supported the efforts of the 21 members of APEC (Asia-Pacific Economic Cooperation) towards a target known as the 'Bogor Goals' of achieving free trade and investment in the Asia-Pacific region by 2020, as part of an overall objective of achieving prosperity for people across the region through balanced, sustainable, inclusive and innovative growth. APEC is not a rule-making body; its members pursue consensus on a wide range of policy issues related to its objectives, through a network of working groups and leadership forums. Consensus on specific policy issues may be reflected in voluntary, non-binding commitments within APEC, or in negotiated agreements among groups of members. APEC's membership defines the Asia-Pacific region, comprising all economies of the 'Pacific Rim' with the exception of six Central American countries, and accounts for over a third of world population, almost half of world trade and over 60 per cent of world GDP.

In the absence of progress in the WTO, and given the voluntary, non-binding nature of APEC commitments, new binding commitments on trade for New Zealand, as for other countries, have been centred on Free Trade Agreements (FTAs) and other types of bilateral, plurilateral and regional trade agreements. In terms of continuity, New Zealand in 2017 was a partner in functioning trade agreements with Australia, China, the South East Asian nations of ASEAN (both as a group and individually with three members: Singapore, Thailand and Malaysia), Korea, Hong Kong and Taiwan. Negotiations had also been concluded in May 2017 for a PACER Plus trade agreement between New Zealand, Australia and nine independent island state members of the Pacific Islands Forum, although this agreement would not enter into force until December 2020. The members of these agreements accounted for 55 per cent of New Zealand exports in the year ended June 2017.

The arrangements with Australia had commenced with the signing in 1983 of the ANZCERTA (Australia–New Zealand Closer Economic Relations Trade Agreement) for trade in goods, and subsequently expanded to include agreements covering trade in services and a wide range of economic interactions, including a Trans-Tasman Mutual Recognition Agreement covering occupational standards and accreditation, a Trans-Tasman Travel Arrangement, an Investment Protocol, a Food Standards Treaty, and a Double Taxation Agreement. The parties are committed to eventual establishment of a Single Economic Market between the two countries.

The FTA with China had been celebrated in 2008 as the first between China and a developed country, and had facilitated a rapid increase in New Zealand's trade with China, establishing it as New Zealand's largest trading partner, accounting for over 20 per cent of its exports in the June 2017 year. In late 2016 John Key's Government had reached agreement with China to negotiate an upgrade to the FTA, aimed at updating and expanding its coverage and, from New Zealand's perspective, increasing market access to a level comparable to that provided in China's more recently concluded FTAs, notably with Australia. The agreements with Hong Kong and Taiwan were carefully crafted to avoid any suggestion of challenge to the 'One-China' policy. The agreement with Taiwan is formally known as the 'Agreement on Economic Cooperation with the Separate Customs Territory of Taiwan, Penghu, Kinmen and Matsu', and is mentioned separately from the list of New Zealand's FTAs featured on the website of the Ministry of Foreign Affairs and Trade (MFAT).

In South East Asia, relatively early FTAs with Singapore (entered into force 2001) and Thailand (entered into force 2005), and a later agreement with Malaysia (entered into force 2010) existed side by side with the ASEAN–Australia–New Zealand Free Trade Agreement (AANZFTA, concluded in 2008, fully operational by 2012). The FTA with Korea was signed and entered into force in 2015.

In the year ended June 2017, just before Jacinda Ardern's Government took office, East Asia accounted for 46 per cent, or almost half, of New Zealand exports. Exports to China accounted for 45 per cent of this figure, or 21 per cent of New Zealand exports. These shares compared with

17 per cent and 10 per cent respectively for Australia and the United States, and smaller shares for the European Union (7 per cent), United Kingdom (2 per cent) and India (1 per cent) (see Figure 1).

Two prospective 'mega-regional' agreements dominated the outlook for new trade agreements. The Trans-Pacific Partnership (TPP) Agreement between 12 members in East Asia, Oceania and the Americas was signed in 2016, but only a year later was challenged by the withdrawal of the United States, by far the most important economic power among its members, as described below; arrangements among the remaining 11 members to continue the agreement without the United States were moving toward their conclusion when the Ardern Government took office.

Negotiations had also been under way since 2013 for establishment of the second 'mega-regional' FTA, the Regional Comprehensive Economic Partnership (RCEP), aiming to bring together East Asia and Australasia together with India in a single trade agreement with a single set of trade rules; in October 2017 the 20th round of RCEP negotiations was held. Contrary to widespread belief, the RCEP negotiation process was led by ASEAN rather than China, although China was clearly the most significant economy in the group.

The leaders of APEC, in a 2014 'Roadmap', had identified the RCEP, along with the TPP, as 'building blocks' for an eventual Free Trade Area of the Asia–Pacific (FTAAP) covering all APEC members (APEC, 2014).

In the domestic environment for trade policy, government response to the Waitangi Tribunal's 2011 report *Ko Aotearoa Tēnei* (Waitangi Tribunal, 2011) on the Treaty of Waitangi claim known as Wai 262, originally lodged in 1991, constituted a key item of unfinished business in 2017. Wai 262, focused on Treaty rights and obligations in relation to *mātauranga Māori* (traditional knowledge) and taonga (treasures), was the tribunal's first 'whole of government' inquiry, ranging over the policy areas of more than 20 government departments. Both the claim itself and the tribunal's report extended to important implications for rights and obligations in relation to Māori participation in the negotiation and implementation of international conventions and agreements, including trade agreements. The tribunal concluded that the Treaty of Waitangi imposed obligations on the Crown to consult with Māori over negotiations that involved the assuming by New Zealand of new international obligations, including in international trade agreements, with the depth and nature of the required consultations depending on the extent and depth of Māori interests in the issues under negotiation. It emphasised its view that

'Māori are not just another interest group; Māori are the Crown's Treaty partner and their interests are always entitled to active protection, to the extent reasonable in all the circumstances'.

By 2017 there had been a number of stocktakes of government actions that could be interpreted as responses to the tribunal's recommendations on Wai 262, but no comprehensive 'whole of government' response had emerged (Houghton, 2021).

In the meantime a further trade-related claim, Wai 2522, had been lodged in 2016, seeking suspension of New Zealand's participation in the TPP Agreement, on the basis that both the consultation and negotiation processes followed by the New Zealand Government in the TPP negotiations had failed to respect the rights of Māori as Treaty partners, and that the so-called 'Treaty of Waitangi exception' article that the government had negotiated in the TPP (and that had been routinely included in some earlier agreements) did not adequately take account of Treaty obligations to recognise and protect Māori interests and Treaty rights.

In an initial report provided under urgency in the same year (due to the advanced stage of the TPP Agreement process) the tribunal expressed misgivings over the Treaty of Waitangi exception, and noted scope for improvement, but concluded that it provided 'reasonable protection' of Māori rights and interests. While also finding fault with the government's engagement with Māori over the TPP Agreement, it declined to recommend a suspension of New Zealand's process for ratifying the agreement. Several other issues in the Wai 2522 claim were held over to be addressed in a longer time frame. These included the key issue of Crown engagement with Māori in trade negotiations, and the problems for that engagement created by secrecy in trade negotiations, as well as Treaty-related issues arising in negotiations on e-commerce issues and on intellectual property provisions related to plant varieties (Waitangi Tribunal, 2021).

Emerging Disruptions

The first to appear of two major trade disruptions that would demand the attention of the Ardern Government had begun in June 2016 when a referendum in the United Kingdom produced a majority in favour of Brexit, the withdrawal of the United Kingdom from the European Union. Confirmation of the United Kingdom's determination to leave had followed soon after when it invoked Article 50 of the Treaty on European

Union, triggering a turbulent and often acrimonious process, at the end of which the United Kingdom formally left the European Union in January 2020, then completed the separation at the end of an agreed transition period in the final hour of December 2020 by withdrawing from the European Union's single market and customs union.

Brexit posed a significant trade challenge for countries like New Zealand, for whom access to the EU market for key exports, most often agricultural exports (in New Zealand's case, dairy products, beef and sheep meat), was provided in the form of tariff-rate quotas (TRQs), whereby exports of specified quantities of each product are admitted at a reduced or sometimes zero tariff. These TRQs were secured by legally binding EU commitments in the WTO.

The benefit to the exporting country of a TRQ comes in two parts: first, the volume of the permitted exports, and second, the opportunity (depending on how the TRQ is administered) to market that volume in the partner country at a price exceeding the price obtainable in other markets, by a margin reflecting the difference between the tariff rate applied under the TRQ (the in-quota tariff) and the tariff applied to non-TRQ imports: the higher return obtainable under the TRQ is known as the 'quota rent'. Allan Rae, Anna Strutt and Andrew Mead (2006) had shown that for selected products, EU TRQs enabled New Zealand exports to achieve a price exceeding the projected price attainable under unrestricted access by margins of between 26 per cent and 56 per cent. Under these conditions it is possible if not likely that the value to an exporting country of the quota rent might exceed the value of the increased export volumes that might be achieved under unrestricted market access (assuming of course that those additional volumes are readily saleable elsewhere at world market prices).

The exit of the United Kingdom from the European Union would clearly require adjustment to the European Union's TRQs that provided market access for their partners' exports. Logically the TRQs would need to be split in some way, and any split would inevitably be contentious. Quota-holding exporting countries would obviously be concerned that there be no diminution in the value of their market access to the combined market. Maintenance of both quota quantities and the difference between in-quota tariffs and non-quota tariffs that creates quota rents would both be crucial. On the other side, protected farmers in both markets would be equally determined to ensure that the outcome would not increase the competition they would face from quota imports. Splitting quotas on the basis of historic export performance faced the complication that quota holders had been able to utilise the fact that the quotas had hitherto been applied on a European Union-wide basis, to maximise their returns by varying the volumes they sold in the United Kingdom and the rest of the European Union, depending on changing market opportunities. They could reasonably also claim that loss of this flexibility in itself constituted an economic loss to themselves.

In New Zealand's case it would be well into the Ardern Government's second term before these issues were resolved.

The second disruption stemmed from the election in late 2016 of Donald Trump as President of the United States and the initiation of his promised 'America First' trade policy.

As his first trade policy action on becoming president in January 2017, Trump withdrew the United States from the TPP, which was awaiting ratification and entry into force after being signed in February 2016 following seven years of intense and controversial negotiations. The United States' withdrawal was devastating on at least two levels. For New Zealand, and for a number of other TPP participants that lacked any other free trade arrangement with the United States, notably Japan and Vietnam, its exit removed a major trade benefit that would not be available under any other trade agreement then existing or under negotiation. For the Asia–Pacific region as a whole, the plausibility of the proposal for an FTAAP was seriously damaged by this dramatic blow to one of its two intended 'building blocks'.

After considerable discussion, in which Japan played a leading part, the remaining 11 TPP members agreed in May 2017 to revive the agreement, to be renamed at Canada's insistence as the Comprehensive and Progressive Agreement for Trans-Pacific Partnership (CPTPP). Japan's hope was that American businesses, finding themselves disadvantaged relative to their CPTPP competitors in CPTPP markets, would pressurise their government to rejoin the agreement. As noted above, negotiations and discussion on the establishment of the CPTPP were at an advanced stage as the Ardern Government entered office.

Setting Directions

The Speech from the Throne (Reddy, 2017) at the opening parliament of the Ardern Government's first term contained only a brief paragraph on trade, beginning with an emphasis on continuity in the pursuit of 'high quality trade agreements'. This emphasis was immediately followed by an emphasis on 'protecting New Zealand's sovereignty' and always retaining 'the right to make laws in the public interest', an acknowledgement of public concerns that had been prominent in domestic controversy over the TPP negotiations. Further acknowledgement of those concerns followed in the statement of intent to 'renegotiate the Trans Pacific Partnership to exclude investor[–]state dispute mechanisms and avoid their inclusion in all future agreements'. Post-Brexit FTAs with the European Union and the United Kingdom were referenced as logical targets for new FTAs, preceded a little surprisingly by reference to a less obvious candidate in the form of an FTA with 'Russia and its Customs Union partners'; the latter was a nod toward an initiative strongly favoured by Deputy Prime Minister and coalition partner Winston Peters, which in the event would founder against strong opposition from Russia's customs union partner Belarus, motivated by concern over increased competition in the Russian dairy market.

Also included in the Speech from the Throne were extensive references to social inclusion priorities, and it soon became clear that the government intended these to be incorporated into its trade policy agendas as well, reflecting both the government's 'progressive' inclinations as well as recognition that the social licence for trade liberalising initiatives had been significantly dented by bruising domestic conflicts, over the TPP negotiations in particular.

Trade for All

Application to trade policy of the commitment to inclusiveness quickly followed, with the tabling at a Cabinet meeting early in 2018 of a paper on A New Progressive and Inclusive Trade Policy Agenda (NPITA), highlighting the need for dialogue with the public to address the level of scepticism toward trade that had been manifested during the TPP negotiations (Cabinet Business Committee, 2018). Cabinet approval was sought and given for a programme of public consultations aimed at the development of a NPITA that would encompass Zealand's traditional trade policy objectives together with consistency with climate change and health objectives, and a range of inclusiveness objectives, including the promotion of gender equity, labour rights, the rights of indigenous peoples, participation of small and medium enterprises in international markets, and the fostering of inclusive economic growth, poverty reduction and sustainable job creation across New Zealand's regions. The proposed NPITA also included a 'particular focus' on consultation with Māori, consistent with their rights as Treaty partner and the Crown's obligations under the Treaty.

The agenda quickly became known as the Trade for All Agenda. Its combination of 'traditional' and 'progressive' trade policy objectives was formalised as a set of key principles for the new agenda, which began to be reflected in negotiating mandates for ongoing and new trade negotiations, including those with the European Union and the United Kingdom.

Public consultation during 2018 on the 'Trade for All' agenda was followed at the end of the year by the appointment of a Trade for All Advisory Board, tasked with undertaking further public consultations on the new agenda. The board's report on its consultations, together with its recommendations, was released in late 2019 (Trade for All Advisory Board, 2019). Subsequently a new Trade for All Ministerial Advisory Group was established in June 2021 as successor to the advisory board.

Prior to the release of the Trade for All Advisory Board's report, the government had already begun to address issues relating to the connections between trade policy and Treaty rights and obligations, as part of a 'whole-of-government' response to issues raised in the Waitangi Tribunal's report on the Wai 262 claim.

Treaty of Waitangi Issues for Trade Policy

While consultation with Māori was included in the Trade for All agenda, the issues related to Māori interests in trade policy were in a fundamental way on a higher level than other issues in the Trade for All agenda, since they involved Treaty rights and obligations: the Treaty-based rights of Māori, Crown obligations to Māori, and the clarifications on these rights and obligations provided by the Waitangi Tribunal. Measures to address the unfinished business from the Wai 262 and Wai 2522 claims were developed in parallel to, but in important ways separately from, pursuit of the Trade for All agenda.

Unfinished business from the Wai 2522 claim included the crucial issue of the nature and level of Māori engagement and involvement in trade negotiation processes, and the implications of secrecy in trade negotiations for Māori Treaty rights, as well as more specific issues concerning the application of Treaty rights and obligations to issues raised by the intellectual property and e-commerce provisions of the TPP Agreement.

Government recognition that the Waitangi Tribunal's Wai 262 recommendations required a 'whole of government' response was reflected in the launching of the Te Pae Tawhiti initiative in September 2019, setting up a cross-agency governance structure and ministerial oversight groups focused on three broad sets of issues to drive cross-agency collaboration: systemic issues involving structural relationships through the law and other governance structures, domestic policy issues, and international policy issues, including trade. At the same time, the Te Taumata group of recognised leaders in Māori socioeconomic and cultural areas of development, chosen by Māori, was established as an independent body with its own terms of reference to engage with MFAT on trade policy and related matters.

The 'engagement' and 'secrecy' issues arising out of Wai 2522 were addressed in mediation between the Crown and Māori rather than in recommendations from the Waitangi Tribunal. The outcome was agreement announced in late 2020 between the claimants and the Crown on the establishment of a new Māori body, provisionally known as Ngā Toki Whakarururanga, to enable effective Māori influence on trade negotiations and trade policy, 'broadly defined'.

It was envisaged that the new body would be involved at various stages of decision making in negotiations for international trade and investment agreements, conducting or commissioning 'independent Tiriti [Treaty] impact assessments of proposed trade and investment agreements at various stages', and proactively identifying 'matters that potentially affect relationships with taonga and Tiriti/Treaty rights to enable their active and effective protection'.

In relation to the e-commerce issues outstanding under Wai 2522, the tribunal concluded that risks to Māori interests arising from the e-commerce provisions of the TPP Agreement were significant and that reliance on the exceptions and exclusions to mitigate that risk fell short of the Crown's duty of active protection. As a result, the Crown had breached Tiriti principles of partnership and active protection, failing to meet the Tiriti standard of active protection.

The tribunal chose however not to issue recommendations on the issues raised, observing that the appropriate level of protection of *mātauranga Māori* in international trade agreements, and in the governance of the digital domain more generally, together with any compromise or adjustments in the light of what is achievable in international negotiations, are matters for good-faith dialogue between the Crown and Māori.

Noting the evolution of relevant government policy, reflected in the whole-of-government response to the Wai 262 report under the Te Pae Tawhiti initiative, the successful resolution through mediation of the engagement and secrecy issues in Wai 2522, and the avenues for consultation and collaboration opened up by the establishment of Te Taumata and Ngā Toki Whakarururanga, the tribunal appeared to point to the utilisation of these processes in comprehensive reviews of relevant policy settings as essential preparation for future trade negotiations.

Completion of the CPTPP

An early and very delicate trade policy task for the Ardern Government was the completion of negotiations for the CPTPP, which were in their final stages when the government took office. Essentially the negotiations involved deciding which parts of the already-agreed TPP text would be modified in the CPTPP.

Attention was focused on provisions in the intellectual property chapter of the TPP that had been included at the insistence of the United States over the objections of other members. The solution adopted by the 11 CPTPP members was to 'suspend', but not delete, a number of provisions in the chapter. The suspended provisions related to patent terms, data protection for biologics, the term of copyright protection, the use of 'digital locks', and the legal liability of internet service providers. As a result, the CPTPP required little or no change to New Zealand's existing intellectual property settings.

The suspension of these provisions was expedient in avoiding what might have proved a lengthy and possibly contentious negotiation on how they might be modified, but it did also leave open the possibility that the suspension might be lifted in future, for example if the United States moved to rejoin the agreement. Many commentators and some governments viewed this as an incentive for the United States to rejoin the agreement, while others appeared content to leave it as an issue to be resolved if and when it arose.

There is reason to think that this could be a difficult issue if it does arise. While successive US Administrations have firmly ruled out 'rejoining' the CPTPP, US commentators advocating this course of action sometimes appear to assume that this would involve 'fixing' the CPTPP to align its terms more closely with US interests (Willems, 2023). Since the relevant

CPTPP provisions require that entry of new members be approved by all existing members, this could be a divisive issue among the existing members.

For the Ardern Government, the other key question was how to implement its commitment to 'renegotiate' the TPP to 'exclude investor[–]state dispute mechanisms' (ISDS). It did not prove possible to secure agreement on deleting ISDS provisions from the CPTPP. This forced New Zealand to adopt an alternative strategy of securing side agreements with as many CPTPP members as possible to exclude the use of compulsory ISDS in disputes between them. Side agreements to this effect were reached with five CPTPP members, while joint declarations were made with two further members to 'use ISDS responsibly'. In the event, the heat appeared to go out of this issue as international trade policy approaches moved against the use of ISDS in trade agreements.

The CPTPP negotiations concluded in January 2018, followed by signature and the entry into force of the agreement in March and December of the same year, respectively.

In practice Canada, Mexico and Peru are the only CPTPP members with whom New Zealand is not already linked in at least one other FTA. These three countries together accounted for less than 3 per cent of New Zealand's exports in the year ended June 2022 (see Figure 2). The CPTPP does however have importance as a magnet for potential new members, with the possibility of US re-entry to the agreement lurking, however remotely, in the background.

Conclusion of the Regional Comprehensive Economic Partnership

After seven years, 31 negotiating rounds and 11 ministerial meetings, the RCEP negotiations finally concluded in November 2020, and the agreement was signed in the following month. It entered into force in January 2022.

The RCEP covers 15 East Asian and Australasian countries: the three economic giants of north-east Asia (China, Japan and Korea), the ten ASEAN members in South East Asia, plus Australia and New Zealand. A sixteenth participant, India, had made a belated withdrawal from the negotiations in late 2019, citing incompatibility with its economic interests, much to the disappointment of the remaining 15. Nevertheless the remaining 15 members account for approximately 30 per cent of both world population and world GDP.

For New Zealand, India, which accounted for less than 1 per cent of New Zealand exports in the year ended June 2022, had been the only one of the original 16 participants with whom its trade was not covered by at least one existing FTA. Low volumes of trade with India, and its small share of New Zealand's exports, indicate an item of unfinished business in New Zealand's trade policy.

The significance for New Zealand of the RCEP however extended well beyond bilateral trade relations with its members. By filling in gaps in East Asia's FTA architecture, and making available to its members (including New Zealand) a single set of rules, crucially including rules of origin, it can support consolidation and expansion of trade within the region, underpinning ongoing economic growth within the region and offsetting threats from other developments in the global economy (Armstrong & Rizal Damuri, 2022). Investments by logistics providers in the region indicate expectations that expansion of trade and economic growth in East Asia is set to continue (Economist, 2023).

The importance for New Zealand of ongoing economic integration and resulting economic buoyancy in East Asian markets is underlined by noting that in the year ended June 2022 the region accounted for 56 per cent of New Zealand exports, up from 46 per cent in the year ended June 2017 (see Figure 1). Countries other than China accounted for just under half of these exports. Adding in Australia, RCEP members accounted for just over two-thirds of New Zealand exports in the same period (see Figure 2).

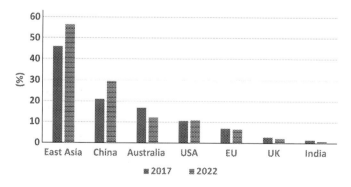

Figure 1. Shares of NZ total exports by region or country 2017 and 2022 (June years).
Note: East Asia includes China, Japan, Korea, Taiwan, Hong Kong and the 10 members of ASEAN.

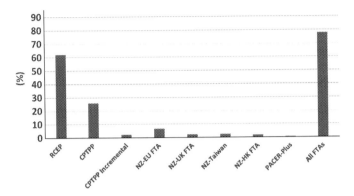

Figure 2. Share of New Zealand's total exports by membership of selected FTAs 2022 (June year).

Notes: (1) Membership of RCEP includes the members of AANZFTA, ANZCERTA, NZ–China FTA and NZ–Korea FTA. (2) CPTPP (Incremental) means Canada, Mexico and Peru (countries not included in another FTA with New Zealand).

Trump Tariffs and Trade Wars

While the United States' withdrawal from the TPP may not have had immediate direct effects on global trade flows, the avalanche of discriminatory tariffs and trade wars that President Trump, in his self-appointed capacity as 'tariff man', unleashed from 2018 in the name of his Make America Great Again mantra, certainly did. Discriminatory tariffs were imposed on imports of a range of products from various countries, most notably on steel and aluminium. These tariffs, imposed even on exports from US allies, were claimed to be necessary for national security reasons, and therefore legally permitted under the WTO's 'national security exception' set out in in GATT Article XXI, while target countries argued before WTO dispute panels that the tariffs failed to meet the conditions the article set out. When target countries retaliated, they were hit by WTO disputes launched against them by the United States, on the claimed grounds that retaliation was illegal since the tariffs subject to retaliatory action were themselves perfectly legal in that they were required for national security purposes. While these disputes could proceed at the panel stage, in December 2019 the United States rendered impossible the legal resolution of these disputes through the WTO dispute settlement process by effectively shutting down the WTO Appellate

Body that would be required to adjudicate on the inevitable appeals, by blocking the appointment of new members when the terms of existing members expired.

New Zealand joined 27 other WTO members, including Australia, China, the European Union and Japan, in agreeing to establish an alternative dispute mechanism, the Multi-Party Interim Appeal Arbitration Arrangement (MPIA), as a stop-gap tribunal to hear cases that could not be appealed to the Appellate Body while the latter was non-operational. Members wishing to utilise the MPIA were required to notify their willingness at the beginning of each dispute.

Although New Zealand was included among the targets of US steel tariffs, the effect on its trade was relatively minor. A much more serious threat resulted from the trade war that President Trump launched against China, which led to a rapidly escalating exchange of tit-for-tat tariffs between the two superpowers. A truce in the trade war was reached in early 2020 under an agreement whereby China undertook, among other things, to import specified substantial quantities of agricultural and other goods from the United States.

The problem with this 'managed trade' arrangement from the perspective of New Zealand and other agricultural exporting countries was that China could absorb the required imports from the United States only by cutting back substantially on imports from New Zealand and other agricultural exporters. Commenting on this situation, the prominent US trade expert Edward Alden opined that the world trading system was entering the world of Thucydides' Melian Dialogue, where 'the strong do what they can and the weak suffer what they must'; becoming a 'power-based' system, instead of 'rules-based'. In the event, the COVID-19 pandemic intervened, and the agreed increase in US exports to China did not materialise.

Responding to the Pandemic

The onset of the COVID-19 pandemic in late 2019 and early 2020 triggered an extraordinary challenge to trade policy in New Zealand, as elsewhere. Immediate concern at the rapid shutting down of international air services, which compromised both the import of high value medical supplies and the export of perishable agricultural commodities, was quickly followed by concern at the threats on the one hand of a 'domino effect' spreading export controls on essential medical supplies, including not only medicines but items like personal protective equipment and ventilators, and on the other hand a counterintuitive tendency for countries to impose import controls on the same items to stimulate production by their local industries.

The New Zealand Government reacted proactively to this situation, subsidising the maintenance of critical air transport links and reaching out to like-minded countries such as Singapore to build support for keeping borders open to trade during the pandemic. A joint declaration by New Zealand and Singapore launched an open plurilateral initiative, setting out a list of 120 products identified as essential goods in combating the COVID-19 pandemic, for which the participants would undertake to remove tariffs, not to impose export restrictions and to remove non-tariff barriers, as well as keeping supply chains open for these products. Subsequently the initiative was joined by ten further Asia-Pacific countries, including Australia, Canada and China (Parker, March 25, 2020).

A Trade Recovery Programme launched in 2020 emphasised the importance of keeping markets and supply chains open, as well as providing support to export businesses (Parker, June 8, 2020).

At the WTO, New Zealand joined other members in affirming support for the organisation's role in responding to COVID-19 and calling for government response measures to support rather than adversely affect trade in agriculture and food. New Zealand's ambassador to the WTO, David Walker, who had previously also been called upon to act as facilitator supporting (hitherto unsuccessful) efforts by WTO members to resolve their differences on the functioning of the Appellate Body, was selected by the WTO General Council Chair to lead WTO members in finding a multilateral and horizontal response to the COVID-19 pandemic. The WTO focused on disseminating information on COVID-19-related trade, trade-related measures, and support measures, and also endeavoured to reach agreement on a proposal for a waiver of COVID-19-related intellectual property rights, which was supported by New Zealand.

New Zealand also worked with other APEC members on building co-operation to ensure that efforts to counter COVID-19 are supported by continuity in Asia-Pacific trade and investment flows. As APEC host economy in 2021, New Zealand prioritised these efforts, pushing hard for the elimination of restrictive COVID-19-related trade measures by APEC economies.

Securing Post-Brexit Trade with Europe

Initial interaction between the Ardern Government and both the European Union and the United Kingdom on the subject of post-Brexit trade arrangements involved some difficult and at times acrimonious conversations, as New Zealand (along with other countries relying on quota access to the EU market) accused both Brexit parties of seeking to use Brexit as an opportunity to cut back their access to both markets. In the final year of the Ardern Government's first term the government was still finding it necessary adopt the defensive posture domestically of assuring exporters that it was 'leaving no stone unturned' to ensure that existing levels of market access were maintained.

The atmosphere appeared to change when the issues began to be considered within the context of proposed FTAs between New Zealand and both the European Union and the United Kingdom. Preliminary talks had been held on FTAs with both by the previous National Government, but New Zealand had been behind Australia in the queue for an FTA with the European Union, and the United Kingdom was unable to engage in FTA negotiations until it had formally left the European Union.

The European Union began FTA negotiations with both Australia and New Zealand in 2018, partly reflecting its new-found strategic interest in the Indo-Pacific, as well as its desire to burnish its pro-trade credentials in an era of increasing protectionism, especially in the United States under President Trump. Prime Minister Ardern made important visits to Paris and Berlin to secure support for New Zealand's FTA from French President Emmanuel Macron and German Chancellor Angela Merkel, having previously established a personal rapport with both leaders.

Negotiations with the United Kingdom began in June 2020, after its exit from the European Union was finalised, and proceeded remarkably quickly to completion of an FTA in early 2022, probably reflecting in part the United Kingdom's concern to quickly build its own post-Brexit trade connections. The United Kingdom–New Zealand FTA is remarkable for its comprehensiveness, with customs duties being eliminated on virtually all New Zealand exports to the United Kingdom once the agreement is fully implemented. Duties on the vast majority of exports are to be eliminated immediately, while duty-free and quota-free access for dairy products and beef and sheep meat are provided after five and 15 years respectively, after being subject to ongoing TRQs in the meantime. The eventual elimination of both duties and TRQs will be a benefit to UK consumers, while meaning that New Zealand trades off the loss of quota rents against the gaining of unrestricted duty-free market access.

The New Zealand–European Union FTA negotiations proceeded more slowly, with 12 negotiation rounds over a period of almost four years. The European Union may have been motivated to accord additional priority to the negotiations with New Zealand when its negotiations with Australia faltered due to a chilling of relationships following the abrupt cancellation by Australia of a contract to purchase French submarines, in deference to the AUKUS arrangement that it had concluded with the United States and the United Kingdom. A factor in New Zealand's favour would have been its willingness to include in the agreement provisions on sustainability issues that strongly reflected the European Union's emerging 'Green Deal', particularly the inclusion of sanctionable commitments to both parties' obligations under the Paris Accord on climate change.

Differently from the FTA with the United Kingdom, TRQs are not eliminated in the FTA with the European Union. Instead the size of the quotas are increased and the in-quota tariffs are reduced, potentially yielding substantial increases in quota rents, although this benefit was not acknowledged by New Zealand export interests.

In addition to market access, both FTAs tick a number of trade policy boxes for the Ardern Government, reflecting the Trade for All agenda with dedicated chapters on supporting Māori trade and economic interests, gender equity, trade and labour, participation of small and medium-sized enterprises, elimination of fossil fuel and fisheries subsidies, and anti-corruption. There is no ISDS provision in either FTA. A price paid by New Zealand for the FTA with the European Union is acceptance of provisions demanded by the European Union on protection of geographic indications.

In the year ended June 2022 the European Union and United Kingdom accounted respectively for 6.6 and 2.2 per cent of New Zealand exports (see Figures 1 and 2).

'Small States Trade Diplomacy': DEPA and ACCTS

The Ardern Government also reverted to a play book that New Zealand had followed in the early 2000s, in negotiating niche agreements with small economic partners that were intended as catalysts for larger agreements. In the 2000s New Zealand had joined with Singapore, Chile and

Brunei to establish the Trans-Pacific Strategic Economic Partnership (TPSEP), intended as the nucleus of a wider trans-Pacific trade agreement, at a time when APEC's trans-Pacific trade agenda was being overshadowed by East Asian regionalism. This strategic intent had borne fruit in 2008, when the United States decided to launch negotiations to establish the TPP on the foundations laid by the TPSEP.

In 2021 New Zealand again partnered with Singapore and Chile to sign the Digital Economy Partnership Agreement (DEPA), intended as an example of an international agreement on how to deal with digital trade and digital economy issues. The DEPA has attracted considerable international attention as a possible model for addressing these issues, and applications to join the DEPA have been received from China and Canada.

In 2019 New Zealand joined with Costa Rica, Fiji, Iceland, Norway and Switzerland to launch an initiative for an Agreement on Climate Change, Trade and Sustainability (ACCTS). According to MFAT's website, the ACCTS aims to bring together some of the interrelated elements of the climate change, trade and sustainable development agendas, possibly pointing the way to wider international agreement on these issues.

At meetings on the margins of COP 26 in Glasgow in 2021 and the WTO ministerial meeting in Geneva in 2022, the ACCTS participants reiterated their intention to highlight a possible path forward for multilateral action to increase the alignment and mutual responsiveness of trade and climate policy responses, and highlighted their commitment to conclude the ACCTS negotiations as swiftly as possible. At a further meeting convened by New Zealand's Minister for Climate Change James Shaw on the margins of COP 27 at Sharm El Sheikh, the ACCTS participants issued a more detailed statement on the need for the international community to ensure compatibility across actions to address climate change, trade and sustainability (Ministry of Foreign Affairs and Trade, 2022).

Stocktake of New Zealand's FTAs

With the conclusion of in 2022 of FTAs with the European Union and United Kingdom, the proportion of New Zealand's exports accounted for by FTA partners reached 78 per cent in the year ended June 2022, compared to 55 per cent of exports in the year ended June 2017. Of the 78 per cent, 61 per cent was accounted for by FTA relationships already in existence in June 2017, some of which have subsequently been deepened through the RCEP, CPTPP, and upgrades to the China–NZ FTA and AANZFTA, while 17 per cent was accounted for by the FTA relationships established after June 2017 (with the European Union, United Kingdom and Japan through the RCEP and CPTPP, Canada, Mexico and Peru through the CPTPP, and PACER Plus) (see Figure 2).

A glance at Figure 1 shows that the increase in the share of New Zealand exports attributable to pre-existing (in June 2017) FTA relationships reflected both a substantial increase of over 10 per cent in the share attributable to East Asian partners (from 46 to 56 per cent) and, perhaps surprisingly, a fall of almost 5 per cent in the share attributable to Australia, New Zealand's oldest FTA partner. Within East Asia, the share of China rose dramatically from 21 to almost 30 per cent, while the share of the rest of East Asia rose more modestly from 25 to 27 per cent. Perhaps also surprisingly, the share of both of New Zealand's most recent FTA partners (the European Union and United Kingdom) actually dropped slightly over the five years between 2017 and 2022.

The potential to further expand New Zealand's FTA portfolio is unclear. The biggest gap is of course the United States, which accounted for almost 11 per cent of New Zealand's exports in the year ended June 2017. New Zealand business interests continue to press the government to secure an FTA with the United States. At present however an FTA with the United States is ruled out by the clearly stated intention of the Biden Administration to avoid any new trade initiative that would require Congressional approval. It has accordingly declined to seek Trade Promotion Authority (TPA), which is a prerequisite for any new FTA negotiation.

The potential for expanding New Zealand's FTA portfolio in other directions is unclear. Negotiations for a FTA with the Pacific Alliance countries, effectively adding Colombia to New Zealand's existing portfolio of FTA partners, were launched with considerable enthusiasm in 2017, but subsequently stalled following a change of government in Colombia and the inclusion of the alliance's other three members (Mexico, Peru and Chile) in the CPTPP. In 2022 discussions began on the possibility of reviving FTA negotiations with the Gulf states, which were suspended in 2007 following a dispute with Saudi Arabia over live animal exports, and further precluded subsequently by a dispute between Qatar and Saudi Arabia. In the Pacific, Papua New Guinea and Fiji, by far the largest Pacific Island economies, are not members of PACER Plus, but it is unclear whether there is any likelihood that they will consider joining. The possibility of adding the relatively affluent French Pacific territories to PACER Plus could potentially be explored.

Concerns also began to be expressed at the potential vulnerability of a country like New Zealand arising from the concentration of its trade on a single region, and on a single country within that region.

Economic Outlook for East Asia

The International Monetary Fund (IMF)'s latest Regional Economic Outlook for Asia and the Pacific, issued in late October 2022, projects growth in the Asia-Pacific region (which includes India as well as China) to accelerate from 3.8 per cent in 2022 to 4.8 per cent in 2023, making it 'by far the most dynamic of the world's major regions and a bright spot in a slowing global economy'. The region's dynamism is driven by 'the region's emerging and developing economies, poised to expand by 5.3 percent' (Srinivasan *et al.*, 2023). China's projected growth was lower than this, at 4.4 per cent, as it emerges from its recent lockdowns, but a number of East Asia's smaller economies are projected to grow more rapidly (International Monetary Fund, 2023).

New Zealand appears well placed in having such a large part of its trade concentrated in the 'world's most dynamic region'. Conversely, new developments that disrupt that dynamism are likely to have significant negative flow-on effects for New Zealand's trade and economy.

Hosting APEC

New Zealand hosted APEC in 2021 at a critical time in APEC's life. The passing of the original target date of 2020 for the achievement of APEC's 'Bogor Goals', and the obvious reality that although much progress had been made toward their achievement, much also remained to be done, created a clear need for a 'refresh' of APEC's objectives, combined with a realistic time frame for their realisation.

As APEC hosts in 2020, Malaysia had made an important step toward meeting this need. After two successive years of disappointing APEC outcomes, for differing reasons, Malaysia had secured the agreement of APEC leaders to a 'Putrajaya Vision 2040'. The 'Vision' committed APEC to the ongoing pursuit of elements of its existing agenda over the years leading up to 2040, in particular the 'Bogor Goals' of free trade and investment — to be pursued within the context of a well-functioning multilateral trading system — together with an elevated emphasis on other elements of the agenda under the headings of Innovation and Digitalisation, and Strong, Balanced, Secure, Sustainable and Inclusive Growth. As APEC hosts in the following year, it fell to New Zealand to begin the process of translating the high-level objectives of the Putrajaya Vision into a working agenda.

A decision by New Zealand, in the light of ongoing risks related to the COVID-19 pandemic, to host the entire APEC year virtually meant that all meetings throughout the year, numbering over 350 and including ministerial and leaders' meetings, were held online rather than in person. As well as a major disappointment in relation to what had been billed as 'the most important international diplomatic event in New Zealand for many years', and a major technical and logistical challenge, this eliminated the scope for informal meetings on the margins of the official meetings that have often been found useful in building consensus. This unprecedented holding of an entire year of APEC meetings online was however widely regarded as a success, very much to the credit of the officials and others responsible.

The central outcome of the 2021 year was the Aotearoa Action Plan, mapping out an initial working agenda for the implementation of APEC's Putrajaya Vision, setting out a number of specific objectives in relation to each of the three headings of the Vision, and attaching to each objective the individual and collective actions committed by APEC economies, together with criteria for the evaluation of progress. In addition to renewed commitment to APEC's ongoing trade agenda, the Action Plan contains many action items that resonate with the New Zealand Government's Trade for All agenda, including for example women's economic empowerment; enabling MSME (micro-, small and medium enterprises) participation in international business; ensuring good quality and equitable health access and outcomes for all; ensuring lasting food security, food safety and improved nutrition for all; accelerating progress towards the 2030 target of doubling the share of renewable energy in the APEC energy mix, including in power generation, from 2010 levels by 2030; phasing out fossil fuel subsidies; and many others (APEC, 2021).

New Zealand took particular satisfaction from securing a place for the interests of indigenous peoples on APEC's agenda, and also in the acceptance and implementation by APEC members of commitments to refrain from trade policy actions that would impede responses to the pandemic across the region.

Asia-Pacific and Indo-Pacific

In the meantime, the United States had begun to look for alternative architectures that could serve as vehicles for its growing determination to push back against China, the unfolding of which may potentially have outsize implications for New Zealand trade and trade policy.

The first step was the revival in 2017 of the Quadrilateral Security Dialogue (the 'Quad'), originally a Japanese initiative, with Japan, the United States, Australia and India as members, which operated from 2007 to 2010, and was widely viewed as a response to growing Chinese economic and military power, prompting a formal protest from China at the establishment of an 'Asian NATO'. The revival of the Quad in 2017 was linked to a 'shared vision' among the members of a 'Free and Open Indo-Pacific' (FOIP, also a concept that originated with Japan) and the perceived need to counter Chinese maritime claims, especially in the South China Sea. From about 2019 the United States embraced the FOIP concept, and US Government representatives and officials, taking a lead from President Trump at the 2019 APEC leaders' meeting, began to routinely substitute 'Indo-Pacific' for 'Asia-Pacific' in spoken and written communications where they would previously have referred to the latter.

Because of the origins and circumstances of the recent adoption of the term 'Indo-Pacific', choices by countries to follow the United States in substituting it for 'Asia-Pacific' came to be seen as signifying a desire for closer alignment with the United States, as a counterweight or even an ally against China. ASEAN sought to avoid the 'for/against' element of the choice by stating that it was prepared to support FOIP provided it was an inclusive concept, that is, not excluding China. All this happened at a time when the pros and cons of the United States economically decoupling from China were being actively debated inside the United States.

Pressure to take sides began to intensify when the Biden Administration made clear its determination to confront China, and set out to build alliances to support this effort. By mid-2021 the New Zealand Government had decided to make the change in nomenclature to 'Indo-Pacific', from one perspective a bizarre change to make in a year that New Zealand was hosting APEC, the pre-eminent Asia-Pacific institution. A personal call from President Biden to Prime Minister Ardern expressing appreciation for the change removed any doubt that this was regarded in the United States as an important symbolic change. At the same time the wording of the New Zealand announcement of the change appeared carefully worded to convey to Beijing that its policy toward China remained unchanged. Nevertheless MFAT subsequently decided that wherever possible its officials should use the term 'Indo-Pacific' rather than 'Asia-Pacific' in all official communications. It was notable that these decisions were never discussed with stakeholders, nor aired in public, before being made.

Indo-Pacific Economic Framework

Having withdrawn from the TPP, the United States lacked a vehicle for engagement with countries in the region. In late 2021 US Secretary of Commerce Gina Raimondo had announced that the United States would not rejoin the CPTPP but would instead create a new trade framework to 'surpass the CPTPP' in nearly the whole Indo-Pacific region. President Biden launched the Indo-Pacific Economic Framework (IPEF) in May 2022. The framework consists of four pillars: trade; supply chains; clean energy, decarbonization and infrastructure; and tax and anti-corruption. According to the United States launch announcement, the 'framework will offer tangible benefits that fuel economic activity and investment, promote sustainable and inclusive economic growth, and benefit workers and consumers across the region'.

In reality, the structure of the framework is carefully designed to fit US priorities and political constraints. The Biden Administration's 'trade policy for the middle class' is squarely focused on bringing jobs back to the United States and ensuring that they are protected, leaving no room for providing any new market access to trading partners. In addition, given the toxic politics of trade in the United States, the administration is determined to avoid any initiatives that may require Congressional approval. Thus the trade pillar will not involve the provision of any new market access to IPEF partners. US rhetoric on supply chain resilience emphasises eliminating China from supply chains where possible, and encouraging transfer of supply chain production to locations within US spheres of influence, either within the United States itself ('re-shoring'), in ready proximity to the United States ('near-shoring') or in countries deemed friendly to the United States ('friend-shoring'). Against this background, it may be difficult for IPEF members to identify significant benefits to themselves from the framework that might match the commitments they will be required to make.

New Zealand is participating in the IPEF, along with Australia, Japan, Korea, most ASEAN members and Fiji. The participants, including New Zealand, appear to be mainly motivated by a desire to ensure that the United States remains involved in the region, and a hope that some useful initiatives may emerge from at least some of the IPEF pillars.

Potential CPTPP Expansion

Under the terms of the CPTPP agreement, accession of a new member must be agreed unanimously by all members. In 2019 the process for accession of new members was established by the CPTPP Commission, the decision-making body whose membership comprises ministers and senior officials of all member economies, and a Chair rotating among the members on an annual basis. Under the agreed process, an applicant for accession is encouraged to first engage informally with all CPTPP members before submitting a formal request for accession to New Zealand, as the depository for the CPTPP. A decision is then made by the commission on whether to commence negotiations with the applicant country, with a positive decision being followed by establishment of an Accession Working Group comprising representatives of each member to negotiate the accession.

The applicant must then demonstrate how its domestic laws and regulations, including any changes that it is making or planning to make, are compliant with the obligations of a CPTPP member, followed by submission of its market access offers to the existing members. If the working group agrees that the material submitted meets the benchmarks for new members set by the CPTPP members, they will in turn submit their market access offers to the applicant, leading to the negotiation of terms and conditions for the applicant's accession. The negotiated terms and conditions are then submitted to the CPTPP Commission for a decision by consensus on whether to approve them. If approval is given, the applicant's CPTPP membership becomes effective when both the existing members and the applicant have completed their respective required legal procedures covering the accession. The process is thus in many ways similar to that for a WTO accession.

In addition to its responsibilities as depositary for the CPTPP, New Zealand is also, by rotation, the chair of the CPTPP Commission for 2023, and in that capacity will host a meeting of the Commission in mid-2023.

In 2021 a series of applications was lodged to begin negotiations for CPTPP membership. The United Kingdom lodged an application in February of that year, followed by near simultaneous applications from China and Taiwan in September. The Commission proceeded quickly to move to accession negotiations with the United Kingdom, but no such decision has yet been made in relation to the applications from China and Taiwan. There are obviously sensitive issues related to the 'One-China' policy, as well as contentious issues between China and some CPTPP members, notably Australia, Canada and Japan. China and Taiwan could also be concerned that if their entry to the CPTPP is not simultaneous, the earlier entrant of the two could use its membership position to block the application of the other. For Canada and Mexico there is also the issue of the 'poison pill' inserted by the United States into the USMCA (United States–Mexico–Canada) Agreement (the agreement negotiated to replace CPTPP at the insistence of President Trump), whereby entering into an FTA with China by either country can trigger withdrawal of all preferential treatment accorded to that country by the United States.

In 2022 further applications for membership were received, from Ecuador, Costa Rica, Paraguay and Uruguay. Korea and Thailand have also been reported as close to submitting applications.

At the WTO: Limited Progress and Ongoing Crisis

Over the two terms of the Ardern Government, the WTO essentially lowered its ambition to the level of the 'politics of the possible' among its members, while at the same time the behaviour of its most important member continued to undermine the WTO's ability to perform its most important functions in ensuring the effective operation of the multilateral trading system.

The WTO Ministerial Conference in Buenos Aires in the early months of the Ardern Government failed to make significant progress. Perhaps prompted by frustration with the 'tyranny of unanimity' that was blamed for this failure, there followed a proliferation of plurilateral initiatives, some aimed at establishing new rules, for example on e-commerce, investment facilitation and trade in environmental goods, and others aimed at reaching consensus on best practice for addressing issues like services domestic regulation, trade and gender, and fossil fuel subsidy reform. The initiative on the latter was developed by New Zealand and 11 other WTO members, and was aimed at developing an ambitious statement on effective disciplines on fossil fuel subsidies to be delivered at the next WTO ministerial meeting. While progress has been variable across these initiatives, some of the plurilaterals have achieved substantive outcomes. During the pandemic the WTO took an active role in documenting and endeavouring to co-ordinate the trade response of members, as described above.

After several postponements, the next WTO ministerial meeting was held in Geneva in mid- 2022. Although outcomes were limited, some important steps were taken (World Trade Organization, 2022). Members decided to adopt the TRIPs (Trade-Related Aspects of Intellectual Property Rights) waiver for vaccines that New Zealand and other members had supported. They also agreed to extend the moratorium on placing customs duties on electronic transmissions and to refrain from restricting exports to the World Food Programme. Pleasingly for New Zealand, they agreed to take 'concrete steps' to facilitate agricultural products, and to work towards necessary reforms of the WTO to improve its functioning, including holding discussions so as to restore full functioning of the WTO dispute settlement system within four years. An agreement was reached on fisheries subsidies, an issue of major interest for New Zealand and its Pacific Island neighbours, but the agreement left out the elimination of subsidies leading to the creation of excess fishing capacity, arguably the most important type of fisheries subsidy. The parties agreed to allow four years to resolve this issue, after which time the agreement as a whole would lapse if the issue had not yet been resolved. On fossil fuel subsidies, New Zealand reports that the sponsors of the initiative would now work towards elaborating concrete options for presentation at the next WTO ministerial meeting,

In late 2022, a WTO dispute panel released its ruling on the steel and aluminium tariffs that the United States had imposed earlier on national security grounds, holding that the tariffs breached the United States' WTO obligations. The United States very quickly rejected the ruling, stating categorically that it would not remove these or any other tariffs that it had imposed on national security grounds, and rejecting the right of the WTO to require it to do so. Observers were shocked by the bluntness of the US rejection of the WTO ruling, making clear that WTO members could not expect protection from the WTO rules against any similar action by the United States. Effectively the United States was confirming its adoption in relation to international trade of the principle set out in Thucydides'

Melian Dialogue, that 'the strong do what they can and the weak suffer what they must'.

Navigating Trade Risk and Geopolitical Tensions

Arguably the most demanding challenges facing the Ardern Government's trade policy revolved around managing relations with New Zealand's largest trading partner, in parallel with rising geopolitical tensions surrounding that partner. It faced these challenges from the starting point of the strong positive relationship with China that had been assiduously cultivated by the former John Key/Bill English Government. It endeavoured early on to assert an independent foreign policy as the foundation of its approach to China-related international tensions, combined with a stated intention to speak out on specific issues where New Zealand's 'values' required this.

This approach was soon put to the test by the handling of responses to pro-democracy demonstrations in Hong Kong, and growing international awareness of China's policies toward the Uyghur community in its Xinjiang Province. The Ardern Government registered the critical response to these developments based on New Zealand's 'values' that domestic public opinion demanded. China's representatives retorted that these were matters of internal Chinese policies, in relation to which external interference could not be accepted. Similar exchanges occurred more than once, with the flavour of 'set pieces'. New Zealand did not however experience the type of punitive trade action, or even threat of such action, that China took against Australia.

As Australia's relationship with China rapidly deteriorated in the later years of Scott Morrison's Government, New Zealand came under increasing pressure from Australia to adopt a more forceful stance against China. Increasing pressure also came from the United States for support of its Indo-Pacific initiatives. An accelerating downward spiral in United States–China relations through 2022 raised worrying questions for countries like New Zealand and a number of countries in South East Asia that had been determined to avoid choosing sides between the United States and China, and for whom their economic relations with China were a crucial factor in their economic prosperity, while they welcomed the US presence as a 'balancing' factor against China. For New Zealand in particular, the establishment of a 'no-limits' partnership between China and Russia immediately before the outbreak of the Ukraine War, and China's ill-fated push for influence in the Pacific Islands, were sobering developments, although a level of understanding was eventually reached between China and New Zealand on the latter.

As these developments unfolded, language in MFAT communications began to hint at concerns over the future of the China–New Zealand relationship. The 'Trade Recovery Strategy 2.0' contained references to the importance of export diversification and ensuring supply chain resilience that were easily understood signals in the prevailing external policy climate, as were increasingly frequent references by senior government figures and officials to the benefits of partnering with countries that 'share our values'.

In mid-2022 Prime Minister Ardern led a successful trade mission to the United States in support of the post-Covid opening-up of New Zealand to the outside world, at the end of which she secured a successful meeting with President Biden. The success of that meeting was an important signal to domestic constituencies that the relationship with the United States remained strong, but the reiteration in the post-meeting communique of a number of US complaints against China (White House, 2022) raised questions as to whether New Zealand was abandoning its independent foreign policy. The Prime Minister pushed back strongly against those suggestions in a speech to the Lowy Institute in Sydney (Ardern, 2022), and at end of the year was able to hold a successful meeting with President Xi Jinping at the APEC Summit in China, at which the two leaders acknowledged historically determined differences in 'values' between their two countries, effectively reconfirming the 'agree to disagree' approach that had been implicitly followed earlier in the relationship (Trevett, 2022).

Concerns had also been widely expressed by observers over the future health of the Chinese economy following its lengthy COVID-19 lockdown. These concerns however quickly diminished as the Chinese economy rebounded from the lockdown at the end of 2022, with 2023 growth rates of 4.4 and 5 per cent respectively being projected by the IMF and the Chinese Government.

As 2022 drew to a close, New Zealand's trade relationships, trade policy and independent foreign policy all appeared to be in good shape. A major remaining threat, arising from the Ukraine War, and potentially devastating in its consequences, was however lurking in the background.

Trade Implications of the Ukraine War

As is well-known, the Ukraine War has had significant effects on world trade, most notably in raising world prices for grains, fertiliser and energy. These effects have had an indirect, if not direct, effect on prices for these products in New Zealand. Sanctions imposed on Russia have had mixed effects on Russia's trade, but little effect on New Zealand's because trade with Russia was already at a very low level.

The significant risk to New Zealand is that China, in the name of its 'no-limits' partnership with Russia, might intervene in the war to the extent of supplying lethal weapons to Russia, potentially prompting the United States to unleash sanctions on China. China has repeatedly denied any intention to do this, and its businesses have reportedly been careful to respect existing sanctions. US officials and politicians have however already been quoted as expressing frustration that the Ukraine War has distracted the United States from pursuing its main strategic objective of confronting and pushing back against China. Reports from the United States quoting CIA and FBI leaders as citing undisclosed evidence that China is preparing to supply lethal weapons to Russia (*BBC*, 2023) could suggest that the United States may be building a case for the launching of sanctions against China.

The launching of sanctions against China would potentially have at least three economic effects on New Zealand. First, to the extent that they are successful in their intended effect of damaging the Chinese economy, they will reduce the potential of China as an export market and possibly also as a supplier of competitive imports. Second, sanctions that successfully damage the Chinese economy will also have negative effects on the world economy that are hard to predict in advance but are likely to be substantial given China's position as a major trading partner for many countries and a major contributor to global economic growth. These effects are likely to be especially serious on the East Asian countries that are closely interconnected economically with China and that also loom large in New Zealand's trade. Negative effects on the United States itself would also be likely. These indirect effects on New Zealand would likely be substantial. Thirdly, it is likely that the United States would insist on participation in sanctions on China by the countries such as New Zealand that are already participating in the sanctions on Russia, and might also endeavour to enforce this demand extraterritorially, by using or threatening to use the status of the US dollar as the world's reserve currency to shut sanction-breakers out of the world payments system, as it has done in the case of earlier sanctions on other countries. Fourthly, China might retaliate by shutting down any remaining trade with New Zealand and other sanctioning countries. The likely overall consequence of the first three effects would in any case be likely to largely shut down New Zealand's trade with China, as happened years earlier with its (much smaller) trade with Iran.

China might endeavour to avoid US-imposed sanctions by setting up a separate international payments system using its own currency, the renminbi, probably in digital form, and it is known to be working on developing the capability to do this. The feasibility of such a response is untested, but it would likely be a poor substitute for the existing world payments system, and if appearing to be successful would probably trigger ever more stringent countermeasures by the United States.

The preceding scenarios can be considered as (perhaps extreme) illustrations of the possible end results of today's trend towards the ever-increasing weaponisation of trade for security and geopolitical strategy purposes, in the absence of a well-functioning multilateral trading system.

References

Alden, E. (2020, February 9). Smaller countries lose in the US–China trade deal. *East Asia Forum*. www.eastasiaforum.org/2020/02/09/smaller-countries-lose-in-the-us-china-trade-deal.

APEC (2014, November 11). The Beijing roadmap for APEC's contribution to the realization of the FTAAP (Annex A to the 22nd APEC Economic Leaders' Declaration Beijing, China). mddb.apec.org/Documents/2014/AELM/AELM/14_aelm_dec_1_anxa.pdf.

APEC (2021). Aotearoa action plan: Annex to 2021 APEC leaders' declaration. www.apec.org/meeting-papers/leaders-declarations/2021/2021-leaders-declaration/annex-aotearoa-plan-of-action.

Ardern, J. (2022, July 7). A Pacific springboard to engage the world: New Zealand's independent foreign policy. www.beehive.govt.nz/speech/pacific-springboard-engage-world-new-zealand%E2%80%99s-independent-foreign-policy.

Armstrong, S. & Rizal Damuri, J. (2022, April 19). Going above and beyond RCEP's negotiated agreement. *East Asia Forum*. www.eastasiaforum.org/2022/04/19/going-above-and-beyond-rceps-negotiated-agreement.

BBC (2023). Ukraine war: Blinken says China might give weapons to Russia. www.bbc.com/news/world-us-canada-64695042.

Cabinet Business Committee (2018, February 18). A new progressive and inclusive trade agenda. Document CBC-18-MIN-0026, www.mfat.govt.nz/assets/Trade-General/Trade-policy/A-New-Progressive-and-Inclusive-Trade-Agenda-redacted-doc.pdf.

Economist (2023, January 14). Investments in ports foretell the future of global commerce: It will be more Hi-Tech — and more Asian. www.economist.com/interactive/business/2023/01/14/investments-in-ports-foretell-the-future-of-global-commerce.

Houghton, J. (2021). The New Zealand government's response to the Wai 262 report: The first ten years. *International Journal of Human Rights*, 25(5), 870–893.

International Monetary Fund (2023, May). Regional economic outlook for Asia and Pacific: Recovery unabated amid uncertainty. www.imf.org/en/Publications/REO/APAC/Issues/2023/04/11/regional-economic-outlook-for-asia-and-pacific-april-2023.

Ministry of Foreign Affairs and Trade, New Zealand (2022, November 16). Agreement on Climate Change, Trade and Sustainability (ACCTS): Ministers issue a joint statement in the margins of COP27, Egypt. www.mfat.govt.nz/en/media-and-resources/agreement-on-climate-change-trade-and-sustainability-accts-ministers-issue-a-joint-statement-in-the-margins-of-cop27-egypt.

Parker, D. (2020, March 25). Canada, Australia, Chile, Brunei and Myanmar join NZ and Singapore in committing to keeping supply and trade links open. www.beehive.govt.nz/release/canada-australia-chile-brunei-and-myanmar-join-nz-and-singapore-committing-keeping-supply.

Parker, D. (2020, June 8). Trade strategy for the recovery from the impacts of Covid-19. www.beehive.govt.nz/speech/trade-strategy-recovery-impacts-covid-19.

Rae, A., Strutt, A., & Mead, A. (2006, September). New Zealand's agricultural exports to quota markets. Agricultural Policy Discussion Paper No. 21, Centre for Applied Economic and Policy Studies, Massey University, Palmerston North. www.researchgate.net/publication/242141792_New_Zealand%27s_Agricultural_Exports_to_Quota_Markets.

Reddy, P. (2017, November 8). Speech from the Throne ... on the occasion of the State Opening of Parliament. www.beehive.govt.nz/speech/speech-throne-2017.

Srinivasan, K., Helbling, T., & Peiris, S. J. (2023, February 20). Asia's easing economic headwinds make way for stronger recovery. *IMF Blog*, www.imf.org/en/Blogs/Articles/2023/02/20/asias-easing-economic-headwinds-make-way-for-stronger-recovery#:~:text=The%20region%27s%20emerging%20and%20developing,and%20the%20service%20sector%20booms.

Trade for All Advisory Board (2019, November). Report of the Trade for All Advisory Board. www.mfat.govt.nz/assets/Trade-General/Trade-policy/Trade-for-All-report.pdf.

Trevett, C. (2022, November 19). PM Jacinda Ardern meets China's President Xi Jinping, asks for Xi to use influence in "testing times". *New Zealand Herald.* www.nzherald.co.nz/nz/pm-jacinda-ardern-meets-chinas-president-xi-jinping-china-sees-nz-as-important-partner-and-friend/ZMPLPMK6HRBQ5ESQUSNGWG2IBY.

Waitangi Tribunal (2011). Ko Aotearoa Tēnei: Report on the Wai 262 claim released. waitangitribunal.govt.nz/news/ko-aotearoa-tenei-report-on-the-wai-262-claim-released.

Waitangi Tribunal (2021). The report on the comprehensive and progressive agreement for trans-pacific partnership (Wai 2522. Waitangi Tribunal Report 2023). forms.justice.govt.nz/search/Documents/WT/wt_DOC_195473606/Report%20on%20the%20CPTPP%20W.pdf.

White House (2022). United States — Aotearoa New Zealand joint statement, 31 May 2022. www.whitehouse.gov/briefing-room/statements-releases/2022/05/31/united-states-aotearoa-new-zealand-joint-statement.

Willems, C. (2023, February 7). How to get the US back into the TPP. *Hinrich Foundation,* www.hinrichfoundation.com/research/article/us-china/how-to-get-the-us-back-into-the-tpp.

World Trade Organization (2022). MC12 "Geneva package" — in brief. www.wto.org/english/thewto_e/minist_e/mc12_e/geneva_package_e.htm#:~:text=The%20MC12%20outcome%20package%20on,from%20export%20prohibitions%20or%20restrictions.

Part III

The Promise and Possibilities of Ardern's COVID-19 Pandemic Stance

© 2024 World Scientific Publishing Company
https://doi.org/10.1142/9789811285165_0005

Chapter 5

The New Zealand Public Health Response to COVID-19 and International Implications for Managing Future Pandemic Threats

Philip C. Hill

Introduction

As of 30 June 2022, New Zealand had incurred 1473 deaths in people within 28 days of being diagnosed with COVID-19, equating to 286 deaths per million people. This compares to over 3000 deaths per million in the United States, over 2600 per million in the United Kingdom and over 1800 per million in Sweden. It even compares favourably to other Asia-Pacific countries, such as Australia (385 per million), South Korea (480 per million) and Taiwan (280 per million) (Our World in Data, 2022). By the end of the first quarter of 2022, 95 per cent of the eligible New Zealand population over 12 years of age were estimated to have received at least two doses of an mRNA vaccine from a single manufacturer. In the first half of 2022, New Zealand progressively opened its borders and the hospitals and intensive care units were not overwhelmed by severe cases of COVID-19.

By these measures of death, vaccination coverage and pressure on the health system, New Zealand's experience in dealing with COVID-19 can rightly be considered an overall success story. However, as in all countries, New Zealand's public health response to COVID-19 has been a mix of successes and failures, and the pandemic is not over. In this chapter, a basic summary of the epidemiology of COVID-19 is provided, followed by a description of key aspects of the public health response. This is then followed by a description of specific initiatives undertaken in the New Zealand public health response that are of some significance. Finally, the local and international implications for managing future pandemic threats are discussed.

Epidemiology

New Zealand's COVID-19 experience has been characterised by distinct phases. In the first phase, from January to June 2020, outbreaks were dominated by travellers and their contact networks. Low initial laboratory capacity limited testing to those connected to the border with a combination of symptoms. The cases tended to be aged 20–34 years, mainly of European ethnicity, and had relatively high socioeconomic status (Jefferies *et al.*, 2020). Case numbers reached a peak of 80 per day, then rapidly decreased during a stringent lockdown and then slowly tapered to zero (Figure 1). The SARS-CoV-2 strains reflected the genomic diversity

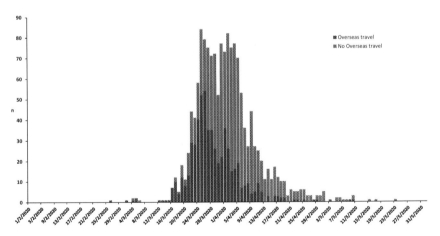

Figure 1. Number of new cases of COVID-19 in New Zealand from 1 February to 1 June 2020, according to travel status.

Source: Ministry of Health.

of the virus across the globe, and only a fifth of virus introductions led to more cases (Geoghegan et al., 2020).

In the second phase, from early June 2020 to January 2022, New Zealand maintained a policy of elimination and responded aggressively to outbreaks in the community, which arose from the border. During this period, there were a number of incursions of the virus into the population. Two significant community outbreaks, commencing in August 2020 and August 2021, were extinguished (Table 1). Community cases were predominantly in border workers or had some link to the border workforce. Pacific people in South Auckland were the dominant ethnic group.

In August 2021, the government moved the country into temporary lockdown in response to one new community case of COVID-19 in Auckland, correctly assuming it was due to the more dangerous SARS-CoV-2 Delta variant. The number of cases detected rapidly expanded and the virus found its way into a marginalised urban population with relatively uncontrolled spread. Māori and Pacific cases predominated. The cumulative number of cases reached over 10,000 by late December and

Table 1. Details of two significant outbreaks that were extinguished during New Zealand's phase of COVID-19 elimination (Hill & Ryan, 2021).

Outbreak time period	Description
Detection of first cases: 11 August 2020 Detection of final case: 27 September 2020	Four cases were reported in South Auckland initially. The index case worked at a cool store with border workers who are required to be tested regularly. However, this individual was not required to be tested. There were 179 cases identified, of whom 75 per cent were of Pacific Island ethnicity. The former Cook Islands Prime Minister Joe Williams died of COVID-19 during the outbreak.
Detection of first cases: 14 February 2021 Detection of final case: 27 February 2021	Three cases within a family in South Auckland were reported initially. One visited the doctor three times with symptoms but was not tested because of the testing criteria at the time. There were 15 cases identified, but through adjusted contact criteria with a new 'early aggressive' approach, over 2200 close contacts and 3775 casual contacts were identified and managed. There were a similar number of contacts managed as in the August 2020 outbreak. Several cases were associated with a high school.

20 people had died with COVID-19 during the outbreak. However, with rapidly escalating vaccination coverage, and continuing isolation of cases and quarantine of household contacts, the number of cases per day dropped to close to zero in January 2022.

In the third phase, from January 2022 onwards, as New Zealand progressively reduced restrictions and opened its borders, the 'Omicron wave' took over and was very similar to that found in other countries, with a very steep rise in cases, peaking in the tens of thousands per day, followed by a prolonged period of many months of cases in the several thousands per day, and associated deaths.

Of 1410 deaths in the 28 days after a COVID-19 diagnosis, with details reported up until 27 June 2022, three-quarters were in those of European or other ethnicity, as opposed to 13 per cent in those who self-reported as being Māori, 10 per cent in Pacific peoples and 3.9 per cent in Asians (Table 2). However, in those under 60 years of age, Māori accounted for 40 per cent of the deaths despite being only 14.4 per cent of the population. Māori were also over-represented across other age groups with respect to death. Pacific people were also over-represented among the deaths.

A study of excess mortality covering the period from the beginning of 2020 to the middle of 2021 found that New Zealand was one of only a handful of countries that had had fewer deaths than expected, based on those that had occurred pre-pandemic (Karlinsky & Kobak, 2021).

Public Health Response

It was hoped that New Zealand's recently updated influenza pandemic plan (Ministry of Health, 2017) would provide an adequate framework for COVID-19 pandemic responsiveness (Murdoch & French, 2020). However, a 2019 Global Health Security Index ranked New Zealand 35th in the world for pandemic preparedness (Cameron *et al.*, 2019). Further, the health system had significant vulnerabilities. For example, New Zealand was estimated to have only 3.6 intensive care unit (ICU) beds per 100,000 people, compared to a median of 10 per 100,000 across 23 selected OECD countries (OECD, 2020). Furthermore, the public health units were estimated to be only able to cope with contact tracing less than approximately 50 cases per day (Verall, 2020).

Table 2. Age and ethnicity of deaths in New Zealand within 28 days of being reported as a COVID-19 case, up to 30 June 2022 (Ministry of Health, June 27, 2022). Percentages of the New Zealand population were obtained from Stats NZ (2022).

Age group (years)	Māori deaths n (%)	Māori percentage of NZ population	Pacific peoples deaths n (%)	Pacific percentage of NZ population	Asian deaths n (%)	Asian percentage of NZ population	European/ other deaths n (%)	European/ other percentage of NZ population	Total deaths
0–59	57 (39.9)	14.4	23 (16.1)	10.8	8 (5.6)	22.6	55 (38.5)	52.2	143
60–69	40 (29.0)	8.7	22 (15.9)	5.2	8 (5.8)	15.6	67 (48.6)	80.3	138
70–79	43 (14.2)	6.0	26 (8.6)	4.0	15 (5.0)	10.8	219 (72.2)	79.1	303
80–89	31 (6.6)	4.3	47 (10.0)	2.8	14 (3.0)	9.1	378 (80.3)	83.8	471
90+	13 (3.7)	2.2	17 (4.8)	1.9	10 (2.8)	5.0	315 (88.7)	90.1	355
Total	184 (13.0)	13.1	135 (9.6)	9.7	55 (3.9)	20.9	1034 (73.3)	56.3	1410

Modelling by Imperial College London in early 2020 suggested that COVID-19 epidemics could easily overwhelm the best hospital services in the world (Adam, 2020). However, a report from the World Health Organization (WHO) visit to China in February 2020 showed that the virus was being contained there. Furthermore, many of New Zealand's other main regional trading partners (e.g. Taiwan, South Korea and Singapore) were doing the same. It was reasonable for there to be an expectation internally and externally for New Zealand to follow suit. Indeed, in March 2020, public health specialists and epidemiologists strongly exhorted the government to consider adjusting its approach to the possibility that COVID-19 could be contained (University of Otago, 2020; Hill, 2020), citing the relevance of its relatively long incubation period to case contact management (Hill & Usher, 2020).

New Zealand's response to COVID-19 was relatively slow initially, but then escalated quite quickly (Figure 2). Flights from China were banned in early February 2020, and then those from Iran. On 14 March, with just six cases, the Prime Minister announced further border restrictions, mandatory self-isolation for those entering the country, and foreshadowed economic support measures and policies regarding mass gatherings. The overall stated intention was that New Zealand intended to 'go hard, and go early' with a strategy to 'flatten the curve'.

An alert level system with four levels was introduced (Table 3). Each step up was associated with increasingly tight restrictions in

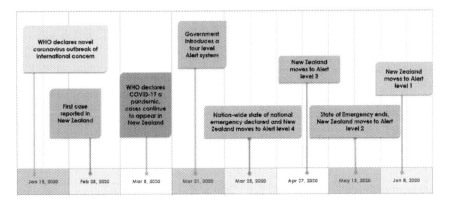

Figure 2. Key moments in New Zealand's early response to the COVID-19 pandemic, 2020.

Table 3. The Alert level system in New Zealand.

Alert level	Situation
1 (Prepare)	COVID-19 was contained domestically but uncontrolled elsewhere
2 (Reduce)	While it was contained, the risk of community transmission of COVID-19 existed
3 (Restrict)	There was a high risk that the disease was not contained
4 (Lockdown)	The disease was not contained

movement, social contact and economic activity. On 25 March, New Zealand moved to Alert Level 4 and a national state of emergency was declared. On 31 March, at the virtual Epidemic Response Committee (see below), the leading epidemiologist, Professor Sir David Skegg challenged New Zealand to try and eliminate COVID-19 from the country. A few days later, a policy of elimination was formally adopted by the government. Other epidemiologists, now convinced that COVID-19 could be eliminated, helped shape and formalise the strategy (Baker et al., 2020a).

The implementation of a nationwide Alert Level 4 lockdown, tailing off over several weeks through the lower alert levels, had a number of outstanding features that led to successful elimination. These included the following: the natural advantages of an island nation with a low population density; border restrictions; the realisation of a need to act drastically because of limited preparedness; a rigorous lockdown; excellent communications; a government that acted upon scientific advice; a constructive and informative news media; exceptional support from and to the community, with buy-in; and good fortune in relation to virus incursions (Skegg, 2021).

During the lockdown period, New Zealand built its capacities to combat the virus. A whole-of-government approach to leading and managing the COVID-19 pandemic response evolved and was facilitated by the Department of the Prime Minister and Cabinet (DPMC), with the Ministry of Health as the lead agency. Public health tools were strengthened to enable outbreaks to be extinguished. However, there was ongoing scepticism in the Ministry of Health in particular about the efficacy of masks outside of healthcare settings (Gray et al., 2020). Despite early exhortations (Kvalsvig et al., 2020), their mandatory use was not introduced until

November 2021. Mathematical models were created to answer key questions related to the transition out of the first lockdown (James *et al.*, 2021), and to provide risk estimates associated with different planning scenarios (Plank *et al.*, 2021).

Initially, in February 2020, repatriated New Zealanders from Wuhan stayed at a temporary isolation facility. By early April, all people entering New Zealand by air were ordered to enter managed isolation and quarantine (MIQ) and the first of 18 facilities was opened. By August, there were 31 facilities in four cities, with increasingly improved systems. By early October, weekly staff testing at MIQ was introduced, and by early November, a voucher system to obtain a space in MIQ was established. In January 2021, pre-departure and arrival tests were introduced, along with the 'cohorting' of people from the same flights to avoid mixing of people at different stages of their quarantine period. At that time, quarantine-free travel from the Cook Islands was introduced and Pacific seasonal workers were brought in. Vaccination of MIQ workers commenced in February 2021.

In April 2021, in a bold but widely supported move, quarantine-free travel with Australia commenced, only to be suspended in July in response to new outbreaks in Australia. A 'virtual lobby' was introduced to manage returnee demand in September 2021, and in November, the length of an MIQ stay was reduced to seven days, followed by seven days home isolation. By March 2022, vaccinated New Zealanders and other eligible travellers were able to enter New Zealand without self-isolating, and MIQ facilities were progressively closing, the last being closed in August.

In 2020, the New Zealand Government was aware of likely vaccine supply issues and the global implications (Polack *et al.*, 2020). Agreements from direct negotiations with several vaccine developers were put in place. After efficacy trial results were published, New Zealand focused on the Pfizer–BioNTech mRNA vaccine. A pathway was mapped out to deliver vaccines in parallel with supply. In addition, Vaccine Alliance Aotearoa New Zealand was created (Malaghan Institute, n.d.), a public–private partnership to support vaccine development and establish an mRNA vaccine development platform for New Zealand for the future. The government contributed 9.7 million doses of vaccines and over $30 million to the WHO-led COVAX initiative (World Health Organization, n.d.), provided vaccines and roll-out support to the Cook Islands, Tokelau and Niue, and donated vaccines and various support to Samoa, Tonga and

Fiji. As host of the APEC 2021 summit, New Zealand set an agenda focused on policies to manage the economic and health effects of COVID-19 and to help communities recover. The declaration from the November virtual summit focused on committing to efforts to improve global vaccine equity (APEC, 2021).

In August 2021, the government mapped out its Reconnecting New Zealanders to the World plan to cautiously open the border after high vaccine coverage was reached in early 2022. At the same time, vaccination coverage was accelerated (Figure 3). Extra purchases of vaccines were made from other countries. Vaccine mandates were introduced, with modelling suggesting that the risk profile to the country would change dramatically from vaccine coverage of 70 per cent to over 90 per cent. Studies estimated that only 5 per cent of the population would never get vaccinated, and 20 per cent were in the 'can't be bothered' category (Kaine *et al.*, 2022). There were differences by ethnicity too, with Māori and Pacific people more likely to be hesitant (Thaker & Floyd, 2021). Vaccine mandates were eventually reduced on advice from the Strategic COVID-19 Public Health Ministerial Advisory Group (Skegg *et al.*, 2022).

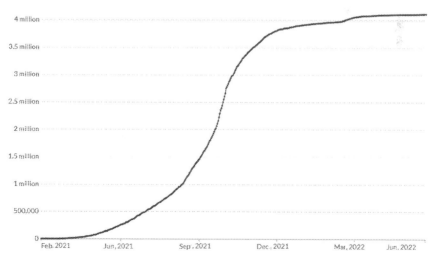

Figure 3. Number of people in New Zealand who received two doses of a COVID-19 vaccine over time.

Source: www.worldometers.info.

Table 4. The 'traffic light' system when New Zealand opened its borders in late 2021.

Colour	Situation
Green	There were some COVID-19 cases in the community but hospitalisations were at a manageable level
Orange	There was increasing community transmission that was putting pressure on the health system
Red	Action was needed to protect people at risk and to protect the health system

Preparations for border reopening continued across a broad array of sectors. The New Zealand Government's social licence for continuing its vigorous response began to erode as the Delta outbreak continued, while vaccination coverage accelerated quickly. On 22 October 2021, the Prime Minister announced a plan to move to the COVID-19 Protection Framework (CPF) (Ardern, 2021). On the advice of the Strategic COVID-19 Public Health Ministerial Advisory Group, the stated goal was to 'Minimise and Protect' — to keep the spread of COVID-19 as low as possible, and actively protect people with vaccination and a managed response, similar to a 'tight suppression' strategy (Baker et al., 2021). There was a debate as to whether this was a step forward or a retreat from elimination (Dyer, 2021), but this was largely academic.

Central to the framework were three levels: green, orange and red, commonly referred to as the 'traffic light' system (Table 4). For each level, expectations of the public were presented for gatherings, visiting others, travel, businesses and workplaces, hospitality, shopping, events, education and recreation. The Prime Minister announced the introduction of vaccine certificates (certifying at least two doses of a COVID-19 vaccine), required at entry to public places, mainly hospitality services and events. The goal was to shift to the new system when there was 90 per cent vaccination coverage; the shift occurred on 3 December 2021.

Notable Features of the New Zealand Public Health Response

A number of components were incorporated in New Zealand's COVID-19 response, with variable levels of success and failure. Examples are summarised as follows:

1. The 'Bubble'

The term 'bubble' was used to describe mandatory household arrangements when the government instructed people to limit physical contact to their own households or 'bubbles', setting out who they could isolate and socialise with during lockdowns. Dr Tristram Ingham, an epidemiologist of Māori descent, Chairperson of Muscular Dystrophy New Zealand, informed by this and his own experience of disability, coined this term as a way to empower all people to keep themselves safe (Kearns *et al.*, 2021). Ingram said that the term captures the idea of the bubble being 'a fragile yet beautiful structure that has to be nurtured and preserved' (Quince, 2021). The concept became a way to apply public health case contact principles to real life, portraying vulnerability but also mutual protection within and beyond households to contact networks, based on risk and intimacy. It had its own legal framework and was applied in other countries beyond New Zealand (Trotter, 2021).

2. Outstanding Communication

The leadership of the government of Prime Minister Jacinda Ardern in 2020 received widespread acclaim (Cousins, 2020), with several key features noted, including the following: engaging expertise, effective coordination of multiple agencies, and the strategic ability to enable coping (Wilson, 2020). The Prime Minister was selected by *Nature* as one of the top ten people who helped shape science in 2020 (Cyranoski *et al.*, 2020). High-quality communication was a feature, and a case study analysis of Prime Minister Ardern's daily press briefings with Director-General of Health Ashley Bloomfield identified three key themes: (1) open, honest and straightforward communication; (2) distinctive and motivational language; and (3) expressions of care (Beattie & Priestley, 2021). The briefings built trust in the lockdown as an urgent, collective and meaningful cause. The phrase adopted by the Prime Minister, 'the team of five million', resonated with New Zealanders in 2020, who reported higher trust in science, politicians and the police, and higher levels of patriotism, but also higher rates of mental distress compared to the pre-lockdown period (Sibley *et al.*, 2020).

3. An Epidemic Response Committee

With the lockdown affecting the normal functions of parliament, the government accepted that the work of the Opposition in holding the government to account was hindered. The 11-member Epidemic Response

Committee was established on 25 March 2020, to last for two months, chaired by the leader of the opposition, Simon Bridges. It had representation from each of the political parties in parliament. The committee met remotely via video conference three mornings a week and meetings were live-streamed. It scrutinised contact tracing, border measures, impacts on society and the post-Covid outlook. It also examined urgent pieces of legislation and suggested amendments. With the population mainly staying at home, there was considerable national interest in and high visibility for the committee's deliberations.

4. *The Elimination Strategy*

New Zealand's formal adoption of a COVID-19 elimination strategy, up until late 2021, served the country well. It was recommended to other countries (Baker *et al.*, 2020c) as requiring the absence of community transmission from a defined location for at least 28 days, adequate surveillance to reliably confirm the absence of transmission, and specific exemptions. A pragmatic definition was proposed as the 'achievement of a situation in which outbreaks of COVID-19 are extinguished eventually, with no continuing widespread transmission' (Skegg & Hill, 2021). Separate outbreaks could overlap in time, maintaining elimination without necessarily having zero cases. In mid-2021, a study found that five countries, including New Zealand, that had adopted this approach had experienced much lower deaths per million people, less negative change to gross domestic product, and lower strictness of lockdowns over time than other countries (Oliu-Barton *et al.*, 2021).

5. *Contributions from the Health Research Community*

New Zealand researchers built a body of evidence around the impact of the pandemic and the response on a variety of health measures, along with possible solutions. The following are examples of their findings:

- There were no seasonal influenza epidemics in 2020 and 2021 (Hills *et al.*, 2021) and there were markedly reduced incidences of other viral respiratory illnesses (Huang *et al.*, 2021).
- During lockdown, patients avoided healthcare facilities, downplayed symptoms and feared going out, non-essential care was put on hold, and allied services were reduced (Wilson *et al.*, 2021a).
- Health communication interventions to prevent COVID-19 furthered the marginalisation of communities already at the margins (Elers *et al.*, 2021).

- People across all demographic groups with less severe symptoms avoided presenting at hospitals with myocardial infarctions during lockdown (Chan *et al.*, 2020).
- There was a 40 per cent decline in cancer registrations during lockdown, but this returned to pre-shutdown levels over subsequent months (Gurney *et al.*, 2021). Results of long-term studies are awaited.
- Healthcare and other essential workers were at increased risk of anxiety and poor well-being compared to non-essential workers (Bell *et al.*, 2021).
- Hospital emergency departments experienced sustained increases in demand above historical norms (McBride *et al.*, 2021).
- Telehealth was greatly expanded (Goodyear-Smith, 2021) and overall patient satisfaction with telephone consultations was high (Curtis *et al.*, 2021).
- People increased their use of 'comforting' recipes during lockdown, scoring more highly in relation to unhealthy dietary pattern measures (Roy *et al.*, 2021).
- People (particularly women) reported increased job losses following the initial lockdown. Women also experienced an increase in family troubles when restrictions eased, and reported increased negative lifestyle changes (Howard *et al.*, 2022).
- A quarter of online gamblers increased their gambling during lockdown, especially their use of overseas gambling sites, instant scratch cards and Lotto (Bellringer & Garrett, 2021).

6. *The Potential and Practice of the Response for Māori*

Under Te Tiriti o Waitangi (the Treaty of Waitangi), the indigenous Māori people of New Zealand should be in partnership with the Crown in all aspects of society. In reality, the pandemic response was mixed in this regard, despite the increased relative risk of hospitalisation and death for Māori (Steyn *et al.*, 2021). It was suggested that central aspects of Māori understanding of well-being could have added significantly to the country's pandemic response as a whole. Māori-led responses to the pandemic were swift and innovative, with several examples of *tino rangatiratanga* (self-determination) and tikanga Māori (values) used to develop successful responses (Te One & Clifford, 2021). During the 2020 lockdown, Māori cultural values and practices offered individuals, families and communities a digital–social space of safety and hope, aligned to *Whiti te Raā*'s six dimensions of relational well-being (Waitoki & McLachlan, 2022).

In March 2021, the Crown's COVID-19 Māori Vaccine and Immunisation Plan (Ministry of Health, 2021) made many important statements about governance, targeted vaccination, provider support, and communications. However, in practice, the vaccination coverage of Māori lagged well behind that of other ethnic groups. It became clear that the implementation of the policies was problematic, including the way in which Māori providers were empowered and funded. The Waitangi Tribunal found that the Crown did not collect sufficient data to inform the roll-out of the vaccine for Māori and that two key Cabinet decisions were inappropriate: to reject advice to adopt an age adjustment for Māori in the age-based vaccine roll-out and to transition to the CPF without vaccination thresholds having been reached for Māori (Waitangi Tribunal, 2021).

7. The Potential and Practice of the Response for Pacific People in New Zealand

Pacific people were at increased risk of hospitalisation and death from COVID-19 (Steyn *et al.*, 2021) and outbreaks were dominated by Pacific COVID-19 cases. Pacific leaders pointed out that the fundamental collective world view of Pacific communities needed to be reflected in the pandemic response (Ioane *et al.*, 2021). Six key priorities were proposed: utilising Pacific knowledge, practice and protocols while enabling safe face-to-face engagement; prioritising basic needs with a goal of self-determination; education using an array of appropriate tools; testing, including mobile testing clinics; partnership with the community; and culturally appropriate and long-lasting solutions. However, the design and capabilities of the early pandemic response did not fully meet the needs of the affected Pacific communities.

In 2021, the government invested heavily in enabling Pacific providers to manage the response for their own people, alongside public health unit leaders. One provider developed a successful 'village model' approach to the Delta outbreak (Hill *et al.*, 2021a), based on seven critical elements: understanding and communicating the 'rules of the system' appropriately for the community; providing culturally appropriate support; adopting an ethos of service and comprehensive care; hosting leadership groups; forming established, trusted relationships; involving community village fono (assemblies); and connecting dozens of partners (churches, sports clubs, health providers and social service organisations). The interconnectedness of Pacific communities turned from a facilitator of virus transmission into a strength, once engaged and empowered optimally.

8. The Evolution of Rapid Case Contact Management

Rapid case contact management relates to diagnosing and isolating cases, and identifying and quarantining their contacts as quickly as possible. The systems to achieve this evolved to have a number of key components (Figure 4), including an enabling environment, molecular testing, and the integration of an array of tools in practice. A performance indicator-based approach (Hill *et al.*, 2011) was applied (Verrall, 2020). This informed WHO guidelines on case contact management for countries' responses to COVID-19 (World Health Organization, 2021).

An application was developed, and Bluetooth and QR code scanning functionality was introduced late in 2020. The majority of cellphone users downloaded the application. However, the number of activated devices and scanning activity was low (Parkin *et al.*, 2021), even during community outbreaks, though mandating its use increased activity (Howell & Potgieter, 2022). Mathematical modelling supported the policy of early as opposed to late aggressive responses to outbreaks (Binny *et al.*, 2021). As new variants of SARS-CoV-2 emerged, modelling provided information to guide alert-level decisions.

The use of whole-genome sequencing (Geoghegan *et al.*, 2021) received international acclaim (Watson, 2020). Genomic data identified links between cases and distinguished simultaneously occurring, but separate, outbreaks to avoid the prolongation of lockdowns, and provided

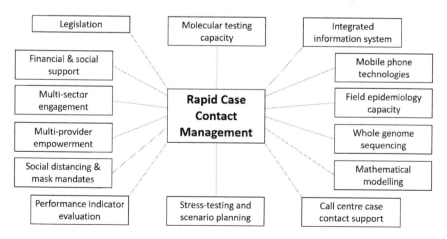

Figure 4. Components of New Zealand's rapid case contact management response to COVID-19.

evidence of airborne transmission in MIQ (Fox-Lewis *et al.*, 2022). Wastewater polymerase chain reaction (PCR) testing detected SARS-CoV-2, although it lacked sensitivity (Hewitt *et al.*, 2022) and could not distinguish viable from unviable viruses.

The integration of social support into case contact management, at its best, promptly provided households with essential support, and electronic data entry could trigger social support engagement in real time.

A number of issues arose with respect to the leadership, planning and operational aspects of responses to outbreaks. Examples included the following:

- In between outbreaks, limited stress-testing and scenario planning exercises resulted in suboptimal system performance under pressure during outbreaks. Over-complicated processes led to confusion in messaging and in practice.
- Insufficient capacity was built to cope with a large outbreak. It was not entirely clear whether this was due to a lack of belief in the need for such capacity, financial issues, staff availability, planning issues, or a combination of these.
- A number of innovations took too long to develop. For example, leading technology providers offered to help develop digital technologies as early as March 2020, including developing a 'Covid card' for electronic contact tracing, which showed promise (Chambers & Anglemyer, 2023).
- Information provided by the application was utilised only variably by the public health specialists who were leading outbreak responses, especially in high-pressure situations.
- While capacity to meet the needs of the Māori and Pacific populations was increased over the course of the pandemic, it was not adequate to match the need.
- Lack of properly integrated information systems hampered the Ministry of Health's ability to provide reliable and timely reporting.

9. *Protection at the Border*

The border protection system in New Zealand had a number of components added over time (Figure 5), collectively referred to as a 'Swiss cheese' model, whereby multiple layers with different gaps together provide an effective block. A modelling study based on real data in Australia and New Zealand (Wilson *et al.*, 2021b) found that multi-layered

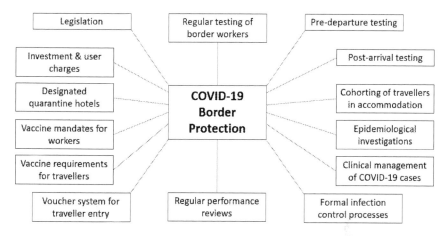

Figure 5. Components of New Zealand's border protection system against COVID-19.

interventions can markedly reduce the risk of importing the pandemic virus via air travel, including pre-flight testing, 14 days of quarantine, and testing during the quarantine period. However, there was evidence that the New Zealand MIQ system was not as good as it could be with respect to virus incursions through the border. One study analysed 22 Australian New Zealand MIQ system failures. The risk was estimated to be 5.0 failures per 100,000 travellers passing through quarantine and 6.1 (95 per cent CI, 4.0–8.3) failures per 1000 SARS-CoV-2-positive travellers. The risk per 1000 SARS-CoV-2-positive travellers was higher in New Zealand than in Australia (relative risk, 2.0; 95 per cent CI, 1.0–4.2) (Grout et al., 2021).

10. The Introduction of New Testing Tools

From mid-January 2020, planning started for the implementation of molecular diagnostic testing for SARS-CoV-2 through genuine collaboration between routine and university laboratory scientists and government agencies (Lawley et al., 2021). A variety of testing platforms were developed to conduct PCR on nasopharyngeal samples, avoiding vulnerability to supply chain issues. Capacity was expanded steadily, including through the pooling of samples.

It became increasingly clear that the Ministry of Health did not have adequate expertise or systems in place during 2020 and 2021 to make timely important decisions in relation to new testing tools. An ad hoc testing technical advisory group review in 2021 recommended better planning and strategies for future scenarios, clearer processes for the accreditation and adoption of new tests, and better engagement with innovators (COVID-19 Testing Technical Advisory Group, 2021).

The report confirmed that the Ministry of Health was too slow to adopt saliva testing. An earlier COVID-19 Surveillance Plan and Testing Strategy Ministerial Advisory Committee (Advisory Committee, 2020) had observed that other settings, such as Hong Kong, had transitioned away from the more invasive nasopharyngeal sampling to saliva sampling in 2020, while sustaining an elimination approach. Studies showed little difference in sensitivity between the two sampling methods (Bastos *et al.*, 2021), while there was evidence of increased uptake with saliva testing. However, the Ministry of Health did not establish widespread saliva testing in New Zealand, despite receiving significant funding to do so.

11. *Organisation of the Pandemic Response*

The 'all-of-government' response to COVID-19 that was facilitated by the DPMC was a complex structure organisationally, but one which ultimately delivered an outstanding result for New Zealand. There were certainly issues that arose. Some felt that the pandemic response could have been less reactive (Murdoch *et al.*, 2021), with better anticipation (Mazey & Richardson, 2020), while being more adaptive and agile (Gorman & Horn, 2021). It was also felt that the alert level system could have been more flexible in response to unintended inequities in its effects across the population (Kvalsvig *et al.*, 2021). Business leaders felt that more innovation would have led to ways to allow them to operate more freely at higher alert levels. Some felt that the Ministry of Health, which is mainly focused on policy, had too much operational responsibility (Gorman & Horn, 2020b). There were certainly shortcomings operationally at times, such as the following:

- An early Auditor-General's office report found that there were problems with the decentralised procurement model for personal protective equipment, which led to a more centralised approach being put in place (Fenton, 2020).
- Hospital and primary care treatment options were slow to be optimised for the change to more open borders and reliance on protection from vaccination.

- Estimated ICU capacity had grown to a total, including 'on-call' surge capacity, of no more than six ICU beds per 100,000 people in 2021 (Young *et al.*, 2021).
- The virtual lobby system for travellers to obtain an MIQ voucher was criticised as being unfair and inflexible in practice, although the primary problem was MIQ capacity.

Whether a different organisational structure would have been better is a moot point. There was debate about whether a pandemic response agency should be in place and how independent the pandemic response leadership and functions should be, financially and politically (Murdoch *et al.*, 2021). It was even suggested during the pandemic that political leadership should be bi-partisan (Gorman & Horn, 2020a), which seems unrealistic given the primary responsibilities of elected government ministers in a national emergency.

12. *Vaccine Coverage, Mandates and Certificates*

The acceleration of vaccine coverage in late 2021 was probably due to a number of factors including the following: urgency in the presence of an uncontained Delta outbreak; an increased vaccine supply, including from one-off purchases from other countries; the better engagement of Māori and Pacific health providers; a rapid increase in vaccine delivery by pharmacies; and the introduction of vaccine mandates and certificates.

Estimation of vaccine coverage was based on health utilisation data. This led to overestimates, especially for Māori and Pacific people. Indeed, for Māori, the overestimation of vaccine coverage was thought to be 5–12 per cent (Anglemyer *et al.*, 2022). Priority populations with the most pressing need were subject to inequitable distribution and inequitable access, for cultural and social reasons (Whitehead *et al.*, 2022).

The government required certain occupational groups to be vaccinated in order that they could continue working (Skegg *et al.*, 2022). Apart from the health and disability sector, two-dose vaccine orders were applied to at least some workers at the borders and in education, corrections (prisons), fire and emergency, the police, and the defence force. The government also provided a tool for employers to assess whether it was reasonable to require that workers be vaccinated. Under the CPF, there was a legal requirement for businesses to use vaccine passes in order to operate with fewer restrictions, and there were limits on the numbers of those who could attend hospitality venues or gatherings, depending on whether or not vaccination certificates were used.

13. *Advisory Committees*
During the pandemic response, there were two main types of advisory committees employed. Firstly, ministry advisory committees were mainly technical advisory groups for specific components of the response. Several specific reviews of components of the system were commissioned by both the Ministry of Health and other ministries to support ongoing improvement activities.

Secondly, ministerial advisory committees provided ministers with advice and assurance about the response. A Contact Tracing Assurance Committee produced a report in 2020 with a number of recommendations to improve contact tracing (Contact Tracing Assurance Committee, 2020). A COVID-19 Surveillance Plan and Testing Strategy Ministerial Advisory Committee reviewed the implementation of the government's testing policies and made substantial recommendations for changes (Advisory Committee, 2020). Three other ministerial advisory committees were established in 2021 and met regularly to review aspects of the pandemic response and provide advice to ministers: the COVID-19 Independent Continuous Review, Improvement and Advice Group; the Strategic Public Health Advisory Group; and a Community Panel (Unite against COVID-19, n.d.).

14. *Engagement in the Global Pandemic Response*
During the pandemic, New Zealand Government ministers and ministries maintained formal and informal interactions with global institutions and jurisdictions in relation to COVID-19, most obviously in relation to vaccines, vaccine passes and certificates (APEC, 2021). Beyond the issue of global vaccine equity, where the catch-cry 'none of us is safe until we are all safe' was used frequently, there is little evidence that the New Zealand Government strategically sought to influence the global pandemic response. Rather, the government saw their role as primarily to protect the people of New Zealand. Perhaps more significant have been key roles New Zealanders outside of government have played internationally. Some examples are as follows: former Prime Minister Helen Clark co-chaired the key WHO-commissioned panel that produced a report on the early global response to SARS-CoV-2, making recommendations to address immediate global issues and future preparedness (Independent Panel, n.d.);

Professors Sir Peter Gluckman and Sir David Skegg led a major International Science Council initiative (Skegg *et al.*, 2021), resulting in a report with key recommendations relating to possible scenarios for the pandemic going forward (International Science Council, 2022); Professor Chris Bullen played a leadership role on the Lancet COVID-19 Commission task force on public health measures to suppress the pandemic (Lee *et al.*, 2021); and Professor Michael Baker represented New Zealand's response on numerous interviews with the media in Europe, North America and other places, along with key articles in the scientific literature (Baker *et al.*, 2020b). There was certainly considerable international interest in the strategy adopted by New Zealand and its outcomes.

International Implications for Managing Future Pandemics

1. *An Early Pandemic Response Capability to Avoid Lockdown*
In Asia, SARS-CoV-2 was contained early in populations that had experienced SARS-CoV-1 in 2003 (Singh *et al.*, 2021). For example, Taiwan contained COVID-19 until vaccination roll-out without employing hard national lockdowns (Wang *et al.*, 2020). On 31 December 2019, Taiwanese officials began to board aircraft and assess their passengers on direct flights arriving from Wuhan. Surveillance and quarantine procedures were quickly established, a Central Epidemic Command Center was activated, and all inter-agency relationships and systems needed were put in place. Innovation was incorporated early across the response, with integration of big data, QR code scanning and specialised text messaging linked to careful risk profiling. The government provided food, frequent health checks, and mental health support. Rapid case contact management operated at high quality and capacity. Pandemic preparedness, at least for a virus with similar properties to SARS-CoV-2, should be regarded as a failure if a country requires a lockdown in the first six months.

2. *Leadership*
Leadership is crucial in a response to any national emergency. A highly capable pandemic virus will expose failure in both leadership and systems. Proactivity, anticipation, agility and accountability are crucial. These issues come into sharp focus during outbreaks, the response to

which should be led by experienced public health specialists who are empowered to make strategic decisions under pressure and at pace, in an enabling and responsive multi-agency environment.

3. *Equity*

In New Zealand, equity was repeatedly identified as a core issue in key documents from the start of the pandemic, but inequitable outcomes persisted. Māori and Pacific people in particular have suffered the most from COVID-19 illness and death. They have also been more adversely affected by the downside of measures that have been taken to combat the virus and had less effective access to vaccination in an otherwise successful roll-out. Data systems created 'on the fly' performed reasonably well but often did not facilitate equity-based decision-making in real time, and there were ongoing problems with numerators and denominators. Genuine involvement that includes design by Māori and Pacific people, and not just consultation, is crucial and would have enriched the response.

4. *Piloting and Testing Tools before the 'Heat Comes On'*

It is important to have tools 'at the ready' for the heat of the battle with a capable pathogen. Ministerial committee reports and other reviews showed repeatedly that the Ministry of Health did not test new tools optimally before they were used in outbreaks. A systems approach to optimising pandemic response capabilities is necessary (Murdoch *et al.*, 2021). The engineering approach of systems design could provide a structured development process, focused on defining the need early, documenting requirements, then proceeding with design synthesis and system validation (Rasmussen, 2003).

5. *Modernisation of Training for Public Health Practice*

The necessary evolution of rapid case contact management in New Zealand exposed a lack of familiarity with tools that had been utilised in many Asian countries for several years, and a reluctance to integrate their full capability into practice. It also exposed weaknesses in the information systems of public health practices, being disjointed and outdated. All countries should make sure that public health trainees engage with developing new technologies, develop an understanding of how these can be evaluated properly and applied in practice, and have experience in using them in real outbreak situations under pressure.

6. *National Vaccine Discovery and Production*
It was felt that small countries such as New Zealand should not prioritise the development of vaccines for potential pandemic viruses. However, with increased connectivity across the world, many countries have researchers who have trained in the laboratories that produced COVID-19 vaccines. With global supply constraints and injustices in relation to COVID-19 vaccines, it is important for each country to consider whether it is possible to establish capabilities to design, produce and trial a pandemic vaccine (Ussher *et al.*, 2020).

Conclusion

New Zealand made an unlikely move from the position of being a poorly rated pandemic 'underdog' to mounting a public health response to COVID-19 that received worldwide acclaim for its ability to contain the virus before the completion of vaccine roll-out. Inspired to be members of a 'team of five million', people across the country sought to make a meaningful contribution to the cause. While under-resourced, in finance and capability, the Ministry of Health was complemented by other government entities to orchestrate the response. But it is the wider team, across the population, that also stands out as having enabled success. Some played major international roles. There are many lessons to learn from the successes and failures along the way. Not the least of these is the possibility that Māori and Pacific lenses and paradigms might be applied centrally in the future, with the potential to transform population-wide pandemic planning and practice. New Zealand is well placed to contribute constructively to efforts to prepare for a more integrated global response to the next pandemic.

Acknowledgements

I thank Professor Sir David Skegg, Dr Debbie Ryan, Dr Susan McAllister, and the editors for their very helpful comments on late drafts of this manuscript.

Conflict of Interest Statement

Philip Hill served on four Ministerial Advisory Committees during the New Zealand COVID-19 response. He was also a Crown expert witness in the Grounded Kiwis Group Incorporated v Minister of Health High Court case in 2022. For these activities, the Centre for International Health at the University of Otago received payment from the government, in keeping with the amount of his time spent. This income was used to support the activities of the centre.

References

Adam, D. (2020). Special report: The simulations driving the world's response to COVID-19. *Nature, 580*(7803), 316–318.

Advisory Committee, New Zealand. (2020, September 28). Report of Advisory Committee to Oversee the Implementation of the New Zealand COVID-19 Surveillance Plan and Testing Strategy. covid19.govt.nz/assets/Proactive-Releases/proactive-release/Draft-report-on-the-implementation-of-the-NZ-COVID-19-surveillance-plan-and-testing-strategy.pdf.

Anglemyer, A., Grey, C., Tukuitonga, C., Sporle, A., & Sonder, G. J. B. (2022). Assessment of ethnic inequities and subpopulation estimates in COVID-19 vaccination in New Zealand. *JAMA Network Open, 5*(6), e2217653.

APEC. (2021, November 12). 2021 Leaders' Declaration. www.apec.org/meeting-papers/leaders-declarations/2021/2021-leaders-declaration.

Ardern, J. (2021, October 22). COVID-19 Protection Framework. www.beehive.govt.nz/speech/covid-19-protection-framework.

Baker, M. G., Kvalsvig, A., Verrall, A. J., Telfar-Barnard, L., & Wilson, N. (2020a). New Zealand's elimination strategy for the COVID-19 pandemic and what is required to make it work. *New Zealand Medical Journal, 133*(1512), 10–14.

Baker, M. G., Wilson, N., & Anglemyer, A. (2020b). Successful elimination of Covid-19 transmission in New Zealand. *New England Journal of Medicine, 383*(8), e56.

Baker, M. G., Wilson, N., & Blakely, T. (2020c). Elimination could be the optimal response strategy for COVID-19 and other emerging pandemic diseases. *BMJ, 371*, m4907.

Baker, M. G., Kvalsvig, A., Crengle, S., Harwood, M., Tukuitonga, C., Betty, B., et al. (2021). The next phase in Aotearoa New Zealand's COVID-19 response: A tight suppression strategy may be the best option. *New Zealand Medical Journal, 134*(1547), 135.

Bastos, M. L., Perlman-Arrow, S., Menzies, D., & Campbell, J. R. (2021). The sensitivity and costs of testing for SARS-CoV-2 infection with saliva versus nasopharyngeal swabs: A systematic review and meta-analysis. *Annals of Internal Medicine, 174*(4), 501–510.

Beattie, A. & Priestley, R. (2021). Fighting COVID-19 with the team of 5 million: Aotearoa New Zealand government communication during the 2020 lockdown. *Social Sciences & Humanities Open, 4*(1), 100209.

Bell, C., Williman, J., Beaglehole, B., Stanley, J., Jenkins, M., Gendall, P., et al. (2021). Challenges facing essential workers: A cross-sectional survey of the subjective mental health and well-being of New Zealand healthcare and "other" essential workers during the COVID-19 lockdown. *BMJ Open, 11*(7), e048107.

Bellringer, M. E. & Garrett, N. (2021). Risk factors for increased online gambling during COVID-19 lockdowns in New Zealand: A longitudinal study. *International Journal of Environmental Research and Public Health, 18*(24), 12946.

Binny, R. N., Baker, M. G., Hendy, S. C., James, A., Lustig, A., Plank, M. J., et al. (2021). Early intervention is the key to success in COVID-19 control. *Royal Society Open Science, 8*(11), 210488.

Cameron, E. E., Nuzzo, J. B., & Bell, J. A. (2019, October). Global Health Security Index: Building Collective Action and Accountability. Nuclear Threat Initiative and Johns Hopkins Bloomberg School of Public Health. www.ghsindex.org/wp-content/uploads/2020/04/2019-Global-Health-Security-Index.pdf.

Chambers, T. & Anglemyer, A. (2023, June 14). Pilot of a digital contact tracing card in a hospital setting in New Zealand, 2020. *Journal of Public Health, 45*(2), e171–e174.

Chan, D. Z., Stewart, R. A., Kerr, A. J., Dicker, B., Kyle, C. V., Adamson, P. D., et al. (2020). The impact of a national COVID-19 lockdown on acute coronary syndrome hospitalisations in New Zealand (ANZACS-QI 55). *Lancet Regional Health – Western Pacific, 5*, 100056.

Contact Tracing Assurance Committee (2020, July 16). Final Report on the Contact Tracing System. www.health.govt.nz/system/files/documents/pages/final-contact-tracing-assurance-committee-report-2020.pdf.

Cousins, S. (2020). New Zealand eliminates COVID-19. *Lancet, 395*(10235), 1474.

COVID-19 Testing Technical Advisory Group, New Zealand (2021, October 4). A Rapid Review of COVID-19 Testing in Aotearoa New Zealand. www.beehive.govt.nz/sites/default/files/2021-10/COVID-19%20Testing%20Rapid%20Review%20Report.pdf.

Curtis, M., Duncan, R., Jing, M., Kim, A., Lu, V. T., Redshaw, J., et al. (2021). "Not a perfect situation, but …" A single-practice survey of patient experience of phone consultations during COVID-19 alert level 4 in New Zealand. *New Zealand Medical Journal, 134*(1544), 35–48.

Cyranoski, D., Dolgin, E., Gaind, N., Hall, S., Ledford, H., Lewis, D., et al. (2020). Nature's 10: Ten people who helped shape science in 2020. *Nature, 588*(7839), 563–576.

Dyer, O. (2021). Covid-19: Is New Zealand's switch in policy a step forward or a retreat? *BMJ, 375*, n2476.

Elers, C., Jayan, P., Elers, P., & Dutta, M. J. (2021). Negotiating health amidst COVID-19 lockdown in low-income communities in Aotearoa New Zealand. *Health Communication, 36*(1), 109–115.

Fenton, E. (2020). Management of personal protective equipment in New Zealand during the COVID-19 pandemic: Report from the auditor-general. *New Zealand Medical Journal, 133*(1522), 144–148.

Fox-Lewis, A., Williamson, F., Harrower, J., Ren, X., Sonder, G. J. B., McNeill, A., et al. (2022). Airborne transmission of SARS-CoV-2 delta variant within tightly monitored isolation facility, New Zealand (Aotearoa). *Emerging Infectious Diseases, 28*(3), 501–509.

Geoghegan, J. L., Douglas, J., Ren, X., Storey, M., Hadfield, J., Silander, O. K., et al. (2021). Use of genomics to track coronavirus disease outbreaks, New Zealand. *Emerging Infectious Diseases, 27*(5), 1317–1322.

Geoghegan, J. L., Ren, X., Storey, M., Hadfield, J., Jelley, L., Jefferies, S., et al. (2020). Genomic epidemiology reveals transmission patterns and dynamics of SARS-CoV-2 in Aotearoa New Zealand. *Nature Communications, 11*(1), 6351.

Goodyear-Smith, F. (2021). Editorial: Challenge and resilience: Primary care in a COVID-19 world. *Primary Health Care Research & Development, 22*, e76.

Gorman, D. & Horn, M. (2020a). On New Zealand's weak, strong and muddled management of a COVID-19 epidemic. *Internal Medicine Journal, 50*(8), 901–904.

Gorman, D. & Horn, M. (2020b). Time for a sea change in our COVID-19 management. *New Zealand Medical Journal, 133*(1520), 12–14.

Gorman, D. & Horn, M. (2021). COVID-19: What comes after elimination? *New Zealand Medical Journal, 134*(1543), 8–11.

Gray, L., MacDonald, C., Tassell-Matamua, N., Stanley, J., Kvalsvig, A., Zhang, J., et al. (2020). Wearing one for the team: Views and attitudes to face covering in New Zealand/Aotearoa during COVID-19 alert level 4 lockdown. *Journal of Primary Health Care, 12*(3), 199–206.

Grout, L., Katar, A., Ait Ouakrim, D., Summers, J. A., Kvalsvig, A., Baker, M. G., et al. (2021). Failures of quarantine systems for preventing COVID-19 outbreaks in Australia and New Zealand. *Medical Journal of Australia, 215*(7), 320–324.

Gurney, J. K., Millar, E., Dunn, A., Pirie, R., Mako, M., Manderson, J., et al. (2021). The impact of the COVID-19 pandemic on cancer diagnosis and service access in New Zealand — A country pursuing COVID-19 elimination. *Lancet Regional Health — Western Pacific, 10*, 100127.

Hewitt, J., Trowsdale, S., Armstrong, B. A., Chapman, J. R., Carter, K. M., Croucher, D. M., et al. (2022). Sensitivity of wastewater-based epidemiology for detection of SARS-CoV-2 RNA in a low prevalence setting. *Water Research, 211*, 118032.

Hill, P. C., Rutherford, M. E., Audas, R., van Crevel, R., & Graham, S. M. (2011). Closing the policy–practice gap in the management of child contacts of tuberculosis cases in developing countries. *PLoS Medicine, 8*(10), e1001105.

Hill, P. (2020, July 17). NZ's Covid-19 Public Health Response Must Be Aggressive. www.newsroom.co.nz/ideasroom/why-the-covid-19-public-health-response-must-be-aggressive.

Hill, P. & Ussher, J. (2020, March 18). Simple, common factor in success against Covid-19 in Asia. *Newsroom.* www.newsroom.co.nz/ideasroom/simple-common-factor-in-success-against-covid-19-inasia.

Hill, P. & Ryan, D. (2021, June 4). Review of the Auckland February 2021 COVID-19 Outbreak and New Zealand's Current COVID-19 Outbreak Response Capability. https://covid19.govt.nz/assets/reports/Independent-Advisory-Groups/IAG3-Review-of-the-Auckland-February-2021-COVID-19-Outbreak-and-New-Zealands-current-COVID-19-Outbreak-Response-Capability.pdf.

Hill, P., Vaisola-Sefo, L. S., Ryan, D., & Percival, T. (2021a, November 29). Why we should adopt a village model Covid-19 response. *Ideasroom.* www.newsroom.co.nz/ideasroom/why-we-should-adopt-a-village-model-covid-19-response.

Hills, T., Hatter, L., Kearns, N., Bruce, P., & Beasley, R. (2021b). COVID-19 border controls prevent a 2021 seasonal influenza epidemic in New Zealand. *Public Health, 200*, e6–e7.

Howard, C., Overall, N. C., & Sibley, C. G. (2022). Monthly trends in the life events reported in the prior year and first year of the COVID-19 pandemic in New Zealand. *Frontiers in Psychology, 13*, 829643.

Howell, B. E. & Potgieter, P. H. (2022). COVID-19 contact-tracing smartphone application usage — The New Zealand COVID tracer experience. *Telecomm Policy*, 102386.

Huang, Q. S., Wood, T., Jelley, L., Jennings, T., Jefferies, S., Daniells, K., et al. (2021). Impact of the COVID-19 nonpharmaceutical interventions on influenza and other respiratory viral infections in New Zealand. *Nature Communications, 12*(1), 1001.

Independent Panel for Pandemic Preparedness & Response (n.d.). COVID-19: Make it the last pandemic. theindependentpanel.org/wp-content/uploads/2021/05/COVID-19-Make-it-the-Last-Pandemic_final.pdf.

International Science Council (2022). Unprecedented and Unfinished: COVID-19 and Implications for National and Global Policy. council.science/wp-content/uploads/2020/06/UnprecedentedAndUnfinished-OnlineVersion.pdf.

Ioane, J., Percival, T., Laban, W., & Lambie, I. (2021). All-of-community by all-of-government: Reaching Pacific people in Aotearoa New Zealand during the COVID-19 pandemic. *New Zealand Medical Journal*, *134*(1533), 96–103.

James, A., Plank, M. J., Binny, R. N., Lustig, A., Hannah, K., Hendy, S. C., et al. (2021). A structured model for COVID-19 spread: Modelling age and healthcare inequities. *Mathematical Medicine and Biology*, *38*(3), 299–313.

Jefferies, S., French, N., Gilkison, C., Graham, G., Hope, V., Marshall, J., et al. (2020). COVID-19 in New Zealand and the impact of the national response: A descriptive epidemiological study. *Lancet Public Health*, *5*(11), e612–e623.

Kaine, G., Wright, V., & Greenhalgh, S. (2022). Predicting willingness to be vaccinated for Covid-19: Evidence from New Zealand. *PLoS One*, *17*(4), e0266485.

Karlinsky, A. & Kobak, D. (2021). Tracking excess mortality across countries during the COVID-19 pandemic with the World Mortality Dataset. *Elife*, *10*, e69336.

Kearns, N., Shortt, N., Kearns, C., Eathorne, A., Holliday, M., Mackle, D., et al. (2021). How big is your bubble? Characteristics of self-isolating household units ("bubbles") during the COVID-19 alert level 4 period in New Zealand: A cross-sectional survey. *BMJ Open*, *11*(1), e042464.

Kvalsvig, A., Wilson, N., Chan, L., Febery, S., Roberts, S., Betty, B., et al. (2020). Mass masking: An alternative to a second lockdown in Aotearoa. *New Zealand Medical Journal*, *133*(1517), 8–13.

Kvalsvig, A., Wilson, N., Davies, C., Timu-Parata, C., Signal, V., & Baker, M. G. (2021). Expansion of a national Covid-19 alert level system to improve population health and uphold the values of Indigenous peoples. *Lancet Regional Health — Western Pacific*, *12*, 100206.

Lawley, B., Grant, J., Harfoot, R., Treece, J. M., Day, R., Hernandez, L. C., et al. (2021). Rapid response to SARS-CoV-2 in Aotearoa New Zealand: Implementation of a diagnostic test and characterization of the first COVID-19 cases in the South Island. *Viruses*, *13*(11), 2222.

Lee, J. K., Bullen, C., Ben Amor, Y., Bush, S. R., Colombo, F., Gaviria, A., et al. (2021). Institutional and behaviour-change interventions to support COVID-19 public health measures: A review by the Lancet Commission Task Force on public health measures to suppress the pandemic. *International Health*, *13*(5), 399–409.

Malaghan Institute of Medical Research (n.d.). Our Research. COVID-19. www.malaghan.org.nz/our-research/covid-19.

Mazey, S. & Richardson, J. (2020). Lesson-drawing from New Zealand and Covid-19: The need for anticipatory policy making. *Political Quarterly*, *91*(3), 561–570.

McBride, P., Hoang, T., Hamblin, R., Li, Y., Shuker, C., Wilson, J., et al. (2021). Using REACH, a new modelling and forecasting tool, to understand the delay and backlog effects of COVID-19 on New Zealand's health system. *New Zealand Medical Journal*, *134*(1544), 159–168.

Ministry of Health, New Zealand (2017). New Zealand Influenza Pandemic Plan: A framework for action. www.health.govt.nz/system/files/documents/publications/influenza-pandemic-plan-framework-action-2nd-edn-aug17.pdf.

Ministry of Health, New Zealand (2021, March). COVID-19 Māori Vaccine and Immunisation Plan Supplementary to the Updated COVID-19 Māori Health Response Plan. www.health.govt.nz/system/files/documents/publications/covid-19_maori_vaccine_and_immunisation_plan_-_supplementary_to_the_updated_covid-19_maori_health_response_plan.pdf.

Ministry of Health, New Zealand (2022, June 27). COVID-19: Case demographies. www.health.govt.nz/covid-19-novel-coronavirus/covid-19-data-and-statistics/covid-19-case-demographics#deaths.

Murdoch, D. R., Crengle, S., Frame, B., French, N. P., & Priest, P. C. (2021). "We have been warned" — Preparing now to prevent the next pandemic. *New Zealand Medical Journal*, *134*(1536), 8–11.

Murdoch, D. R. & French, N. P. (2020). COVID-19: Another infectious disease emerging at the animal–human interface. *New Zealand Medical Journal*, *133*(1510), 12–15.

OECD (2020, April 20). Intensive Care Beds Capacity. OECD Data Insights. www.oecd.org/coronavirus/en/data-insights/intensive-care-bedscapacity.

Oliu-Barton, M., Pradelski, B. S. R., Aghion, P., Artus, P., Kickbusch, I., Lazarus, J. V., et al. (2021). SARS-CoV-2 elimination, not mitigation, creates best outcomes for health, the economy, and civil liberties. *Lancet*, *397*(10291), 2234–2236.

Our World in Data. (2022, June 30). Coronavirus (COVID-19) Deaths. ourworldindata.org/covid-deaths.

Parkin, L., Singh, A., Seddon, E., Hall, Y., Bridgman, F., Saunders, K., et al. (2021). Audit of NZ COVID Tracer QR poster display and use in Dunedin. *New Zealand Medical Journal*, *134*(1531), 67–76.

Plank, M. J., Binny, R. N., Hendy, S. C., Lustig, A., & Ridings, K. (2021). Vaccination and testing of the border workforce for COVID-19 and risk of community outbreaks: A modelling study. *Royal Society Open Science*, *8*(9), 210686.

Polack, F. P., Thomas, S. J., Kitchin, N., Absalon, J., Gurtman, A., Lockhart, S., et al. (2020). Safety and efficacy of the BNT162b2 mRNA Covid-19 vaccine. *New England Journal of Medicine*, *383*(27), 2603–2615.

Quince, K. (2021, December 25). It's been a challenging year in any language. *Stuff*. www.stuff.co.nz/opinion/127379145/its-been-a-challenging-year-in-any-language.

Rasmussen, J. (2003). Systems design. In H. Bidgoli (Ed.), *Encyclopedia of Information Systems* (pp. 361–377). Amsterdam: Elsevier.

Roy, R., de Castro, T. G., Haszard, J., Egli, V., Te Morenga, L., Teunissen, L., et al. (2021). Who we seek and what we eat? Sources of food choice inspirations and their associations with adult dietary patterns before and during the COVID-19 lockdown in New Zealand. *Nutrients, 13*(11), 12946.

Sibley, C. G., Greaves, L. M., Satherley, N., Wilson, M. S., Overall, N. C., Lee, C. H. J., et al. (2020). Effects of the COVID-19 pandemic and nationwide lockdown on trust, attitudes toward government, and well-being. *American Psychologist, 75*(5), 618–630.

Singh, S., McNab, C., Olson, R. M., Bristol, N., Nolan, C., Bergstrom, E., et al. (2021). How an outbreak became a pandemic: A chronological analysis of crucial junctures and international obligations in the early months of the COVID-19 pandemic. *Lancet, 398*(10316), 2109–2124.

Skegg, D., Gluckman, P., Boulton, G., Hackmann, H., Karim, S. S. A., Piot, P., et al. (2021). Future scenarios for the COVID-19 pandemic. *Lancet, 397*(10276), 777–778.

Skegg, D. C. (2021). The Covid-19 pandemic: Lessons for our future. *Policy Quarterly, 17*(1), 3–10.

Skegg, D. C., & Hill, P. C. (2021). Defining covid-19 elimination. *BMJ, 374*, n1794.

Skegg, D. C. G., Brewerton, M., Hill, P. C., Iosua, E., Murdoch, D. R., & Turner, N. (2022). Vaccine mandates in the time of Omicron. *New Zealand Medical Journal, 135*, 11–15.

Stats NZ (2022). NZ.Stat. nzdotstat.stats.govt.nz/wbos/Index.aspx?DataSet Code=TABLECODE7994&_ga=2.203254551.726782005.1656295086-1811306828.1651721090#.

Steyn, N., Binny, R. N., Hannah, K., Hendy, S. C., James, A., Lustig, A., et al. (2021). Māori and Pacific people in New Zealand have a higher risk of hospitalisation for COVID-19. *New Zealand Medical Journal, 134*(1538), 28–43.

Te One, A. & Clifford, C. (2021). Tino Rangatiratanga and well-being: Māori self determination in the face of Covid-19. *Frontiers in Sociology, 6*, 613340.

Thaker, J. & Floyd, B. (2021). Shifting COVID-19 vaccine intentions in New Zealand: Next steps in the vaccination campaign. *Lancet Regional Health – Western Pacific, 15*, 100278.

Trotter, S. (2021). Ways of being together during the COVID-19 pandemic: Support bubbles and the legal construction of relationships. *Frontiers in Sociology, 6*, 730216.

Unite Against COVID-19 (n.d.). Independent Advisory Groups. covid19.govt.nz/about-our-covid-19-response/independent-advisory-groups.

University of Otago (2020, March 24). NZ Must Urgently build contact tracing for COVID-19 to make nationwide lockdown worthwhile, infectious diseases expert says. www.otago.ac.nz/news/news/otago734116.html.

Ussher, J. E., Le Gros, G., Quinones-Mateu, M. E., Gulab, S. A., & Yiannoutsos, M. (2020). The case for New Zealand to have its own COVID-19 vaccine programme. *New Zealand Medical Journal*, *133*(1513), 112–115.

Verrall, A. (2020, April 10). Rapid Audit of Contact Tracing for Covid-19 in New Zealand. www.health.govt.nz/system/files/documents/publications/contact_tracing_report_verrall.pdf.

Waitangi Tribunal (2021). *Haumaru: The COVID-19 Priority Report*. Wellington: Waitangi Tribunal.

Waitoki, W. & McLachlan, A. (2022). Indigenous Māori responses to COVID-19: He waka eke noa? [We are all in this together]. *International Journal of Psychology*, *57*(5), 567–576.

Wang, C. J., Ng, C. Y., & Brook, R. H. (2020). Response to COVID-19 in Taiwan: Big Data analytics, new technology, and proactive testing. *JAMA*, *323*(14), 1341–1342.

Watson, C. (2020). How countries are using genomics to help avoid a second coronavirus wave. *Nature*, *582*(7810), 19.

Whitehead, J., Atatoa Carr, P., Scott, N., & Lawrenson, R. (2022). Structural disadvantage for priority populations: The spatial inequity of COVID-19 vaccination services in Aotearoa. *New Zealand Medical Journal*, *135*(1551), 54–67.

Wilson, G., Windner, Z., Dowell, A., Toop, L., Savage, R., & Hudson, B. (2021a). Navigating the health system during COVID-19: Primary care perspectives on delayed patient care. *New Zealand Medical Journal*, *134*(1546), 17–27.

Wilson, N., Baker, M. G., Blakely, T., & Eichner, M. (2021b). Estimating the impact of control measures to prevent outbreaks of COVID-19 associated with air travel into a COVID-19-free country. *Scientific Reports*, *11*(1), 10766.

Wilson, S. (2020). Pandemic leadership; lessons from New Zealand's approach to COVID-19. *Leadership*, *16*(3), 279–293.

World Health Organization (n.d.). COVAX: Working for global equitable access to COVID-19 vaccines. www.who.int/initiatives/act-accelerator/covax.

World Health Organization (2021, February 1). Contact Tracing in the Context of COVID-19: Interim Guidance. apps.who.int/iris/handle/10665/339128.

Young, P. J., Psirides, A., & Streat, S. (2021). New Zealand's staffed ICU bed capacity and COVID-19 surge capacity. *New Zealand Medical Journal*, *134*(1545), 8–10.

© 2024 World Scientific Publishing Company
https://doi.org/10.1142/9789811285165_0006

Chapter 6

Climate Considerations[*]

Alice C. Hill

This chapter draws lessons from the COVID-19 pandemic that the world can use today to prepare for the damaging impacts of climate change. As catastrophic risks, both pandemics and climate change have the capacity to cause widespread harm — a phenomenon communities across the globe experienced throughout 2020 and 2021.

Pandemics have plagued the entire arc of human history. In the fourteenth century, the Black Death killed one third of the world's population. In 1918, fifty million lost their lives in the Spanish influenza pandemic. As a result of hundreds of years of experience with pandemics, humans, in theory, know a lot about what to do to prepare. On the other hand, climate change impacts, including greater temperature extremes, bigger and hotter wildfires, rising sea levels and more, are often unfamiliar threats. In the summer of 2021, Canadian citizens and residents of the US Pacific Northwest suffered temperatures more like those of the hottest areas of the Middle East, reaching 49.6 °C in some areas. In Portland, Oregon, which normally remains very cool with temperate weather, melting power cables and surging electricity demand forced the suspension of light rail and streetcar services. Road surfaces expanded due to the heat, causing them to buckle and forcing lane closures. Workers used tanker trucks to douse drawbridges with water because they were afraid the steel

---

[*] This chapter draws on lectures given by the author in 2021, including to the University of Otago Foreign Policy School in July.

would expand so much that it would break the operating mechanisms. And deaths soared as people in many places unaccustomed to hot temperatures lack air conditioning. These events make clear that humans can no longer rely on the fundamental assumption that has guided every design choice about all of our systems for the entire stretch of human history. That is, the assumption that the past can serve as an accurate guide for the future.

The changes happening now mean that countries must plan for a future that is unfamiliar and for a climate that is no longer stable. And this unfamiliarity and instability leaves humanity deeply unprepared. In Hawaii, the Mauna Loa Observatory sits about 3,400 m above sea level. In 1958, the year scientists at that laboratory began tracking the accumulation of carbon in the atmosphere, the amount of carbon dioxide reached 315 parts per million (ppm). This represented an increase from an estimated concentration of 280 ppm during the pre-industrial era. As carbon emissions from human activity accumulate, they form a kind of blanket around the globe that retains heat. Over time, as the concentration of emissions in the atmosphere grows, the earth's temperature rises. In June 1988 in Washington, DC, the warnings of a climate scientist about the consequences of rising greenhouse gas emissions finally landed centre stage in the United States. That day, the scientist James Hansen told the US Congress that he was 99 per cent certain that the year's record temperature increases resulted from the growing atmospheric concentration of greenhouse gases rather than natural variation. By then, atmospheric levels of carbon at Mauna Loa had climbed to 353 ppm.

Two decades later, in 2008, I was a judge on the Los Angeles Superior Court in California, after serving as a federal prosecutor. Shortly after the election of President Barack Obama in November of that year, my telephone rang. On the other end, one of my friends from law school, Janet Napolitano, asked: 'How would you like to come to Washington?' President Obama had recruited Napolitano to become secretary of the Department of Homeland Security (DHS), the third largest agency in the US Federal Government behind the Departments of Defense and Veterans Affairs.

The DHS was born in the aftermath of the terrorist attacks on 11 September 2001, which spurred the largest government reorganisation since the formation of the Department of Defense after the Second World War. In addition to a strong anti-terrorism focus, the DHS shoulders broad security responsibilities across nearly two dozen agencies. These agencies include the Federal Emergency Management Agency, which handles disaster preparedness and response, in addition to Immigration and Customs Enforcement, which administers US borders, and the Coast Guard, which is responsible for the protection of American waterways. In 2009, President Obama issued one of his first executive orders on climate change. The order required all federal agencies not only to find ways to cut their carbon emissions but also to begin to plan for the impact of climate change. By the time I received this climate assignment, Mauna Loa scientists had detected carbon concentrations of 384 ppm.

At that time, in 2009, it wasn't clear what the DHS needed to do, or even if it needed to prepare itself for climate impacts. To find the answer, I assembled a task force to ask the basic question: 'Should the US Department of Homeland Security, with all of its other responsibilities, care about the impacts of climate change?' This inquiry was essential to inform ourselves whether and how we should tackle this assignment in the face of persistent scepticism about the reality and science of climate change. Interviews with dozens of scientists from NASA and officials from the Department of Defense, in addition to planners and security experts, delivered the answer. As we learned about the projected climate-worsened storms, wildfires, flooding and droughts that could pummel the entire globe, the task force had a clear response: the DHS should care deeply about climate change. Climate change would affect virtually all of the department's missions and all of the systems upon which human civilisation relies.

Then-Secretary Napolitano also asked me to head the DHS leadership group on biological threats. The DHS had the responsibility of co-ordinating federal efforts with those of state, local, territorial and tribal governments in preparing for and responding to biological threats ranging from an influenza pandemic to an aerosolised anthrax attack. It was because of this work and my time on the National Security Council staff as special assistant to the president and senior director for resilience policy that I realised the profound similarities climate change and pandemics bear.

Both climate change and pandemics are 'when', not 'if', problems. They both carry deep uncertainty as to their precise timing and scope, but not as to whether they will occur. Fighting pandemics and climate change requires the use of science to inform decision-making, and both risks are 'borderless disasters', meaning they do not honour the jurisdictional boundaries humans have crafted over the centuries. Because they cross borders freely, efforts to address the threats must cross borders as well.

With pandemics and climate change, it is the most vulnerable among us, including people with disabilities, women and girls, older people and marginalised communities, that pay the highest price. Any programmes developed to counter these threats must account for the vastly disproportionate impacts inflicted on different sectors of society. And climate impacts and pandemics act as threat multipliers, increasing vulnerability to horrors like economic impoverishment, famine and criminal activity. Once the threats materialise, they undermine critical systems, including finance, public health, transportation, communication, and national and human security.

The pandemic revealed that failed, weak or sluggish responses in the immediate aftermath of disaster provide opportunities for bad actors to use humanitarian aid to recruit members and expand their territory. For example, as COVID-19 began to spread, members of the Sinaloa Cartel delivered hand sanitiser and other pandemic supplies in boxes stamped with the picture of a leader of the cartel, while a mayor in Italy complained about the Mafia using the pandemic to make criminal inroads. And perhaps most important of all, the COVID-19 experience demonstrated how greater preparation and early action can buffer the damage caused by both climate change and pandemics. But success in combating these two risks requires both public support and political leadership. Without adequate preparedness and leadership, the consequences can ripple throughout societies, causing losses of lives and livelihoods.

At the same time as the pandemic swept across the globe in 2020 and 2021, climate disasters ravaged the planet, proving that climate change was no longer a threat just for the distant future. The danger had arrived firmly in the present. In Australia, devastating wildfires raged on an unprecedented scale during the 2019–2020 bushfire season, decimating 42 million acres (17 million ha) of land and releasing 715 million tonnes of carbon dioxide into the atmosphere (Mallapaty, 2021). The strongest cyclone ever to make landfall hit the Philippines with record-breaking sustained wind speeds of 314 km/h (195 mph). In the Horn of Africa, 200 billion locusts flew in voracious swarms twenty times the size of Paris and devoured 50 to 80 per cent of crops in the fields. That is an estimated eight thousand times more locusts than would appear in the absence of climate change, and the equivalent of 25 for every person on the planet (Khan, 2020). Temperatures soared to the highest ever recorded in the Arctic Circle, 38 °C, as well as the highest ever recorded on Earth, 54 °C, in the aptly named Death Valley in California in 2020. And these records were broken once again when temperatures surged to 54.4 °C in Death Valley in July 2021, which became the world's hottest month in recorded history up to that time (Masters, 2021).

The string of record-breaking events also carried record-breaking invoices for damage. According to the global reinsurance company Munich Re, the economic losses from natural disasters jumped from US$116 billion in 2019 to US$210 billion in 2020, and to US$280 billion in 2021, and many of those disasters were influenced by climate change (Munich Re, 2021).

In 2020, New Zealand's Climate Change Commission published a report to advise the country's government how to deliver on climate action. The report made a number of recommendations, including ensuring inclusivity in planning for mitigation and adaptation. In this case, this would involve partnering with Māori leaders in line with the Treaty of Waitangi to ensure a just transition where no one is left behind. The report also found that greater climate financing is needed at home and abroad, particularly in developing countries. Increasing finance to help nations mitigate and adapt in advance of climate-fuelled disasters reaps substantial benefits. The World Bank has found that US$1 billion invested in early warning systems and other preparedness measures in developing countries can create benefits worth between US$4 billion and US$36 billion (Hallegatte, 2012).

Still, funding for adaptation lags far behind that for mitigation. As the chair of the Adaptation Committee of the UK Climate Change Committee described it, adaptation is 'under-resourced, underfunded, and often ignored' (Gabbattis & McSweeney, 2021). The damage of climate change is already here. The world is beyond the point at which mitigation alone can address the climate crisis. In fact, even if global emissions dropped to zero tomorrow, the world's population could suffer worsening impacts for some period because of the delay in heating.

So, what can policymakers do?

New Zealand has already begun to take serious steps forward. The country adopted building codes to ensure structures last for at least 50 years. Additionally, it became the first country to introduce mandatory climate-related risk disclosure and to require banks to report on the climate change impacts of their operations and investments. Nations across the globe can learn from New Zealand's progress. However, much work remains to be done, particularly when it comes to adaptation.

One of the most basic adaptation steps is to prompt earlier action, and that requires planning. Direction from the central government is important to clarify roles, prioritise investments, including in disaster risk reduction, and prevent poor choices that lock communities into hazardous circumstances. Planning is a universally recognised way to improve disaster response. It could drive the creation of stockpiles of necessary provisions. The benefit of these reserves was observed during the pandemic. Planning can also drive investments in innovation and scientific research. It can improve emergency response, ensuring sufficient resources to respond to multiple consecutive or simultaneous disasters, and it can work to reinforce supply chains to prevent abrupt breaks that cause extensive harm to dispersed populations.

Tackling climate change requires collective action among international governments, local communities, NGOs, the private sector, business leaders and others. A national adaptation plan can increase the co-ordination among these groups by identifying the roles that each can play. Nations across the globe have heeded the call to create national adaptation strategies. For instance, China unveiled its strategy in 2013, as did Russia in 2019. The Room for the River programme in the Netherlands, which has had a national adaptation plan since 2007, succeeded in substantially reducing flood risk, and the government now plans for the one-in-10,000 year flood.

Unfortunately, the United States currently lacks a national climate adaptation plan. Without a national adaptation plan, the United States tends to wait for disasters to happen before it addresses the risk. When disaster does strike, often causing lengthy breaks in critical supply chains like food and medicine, the response is costly. Still, research shows that spending before disaster strikes saves up to US$15 in recovery costs for every dollar invested in risk reduction. And each dollar used to make infrastructure climate-resilient saves US$4 in post-disaster reconstruction (UN Office for Disaster Risk Reduction, 2021).

It will take multiple co-ordinated efforts across geopolitical borders to confront the challenges of climate change and pandemics, and this preparation must reflect the uncertainty of the unfamiliar and unprecedented extremes that will occur in the future. It is going to take increased efforts in both mitigation and adaptation to meet the crisis caused by current and future warming. The time is now, not only for mitigation but also for an increased focus on adaptation.

Regardless of your aptitude for maths, there's one problem set worth remembering: the lily pads on the pond. Suppose you take a walk by a pond with a single lily pad at its edge, and suppose that every day you go by the number of lily pads has doubled. On the first day, one lily pad sits on the pond. On the second day, two lily pads float on the surface. On the third day, there are four lily pads. On the fourth day there are eight, and so on. If the pond is covered entirely on the thirtieth day, when was it covered halfway? The right answer is on the twenty-ninth day. If you didn't get that right, you are not alone. In fact, after two weeks, observers would hardly notice the lily pads since they would cover only a small fraction of the pond. Because exponential growth is almost imperceptible at first, it is easy to ignore the spread of the lily pads for a very long time (McArdle, 2020). That is, until they smother the pond.

The world's failure to appreciate the exponential growth of climate change and its impacts has left the global population increasingly vulnerable. In May 2021, atmospheric carbon dioxide measured at Mauna Loa peaked at a monthly average of 419 ppm, the highest level since scientists started recording accurate measurements over six decades ago, and likely to be the highest measurement in about three million years. This is an 'all-hands-on-deck' problem. Confronting the challenge requires the work of everyone to find ways not just to cut harmful greenhouse emissions but also to prepare for the impacts that will continue to arrive for the foreseeable future. The past is no longer a safe guide for the future when it comes to catastrophic risks. And the question for each of us is: What do we dare to do about it?

References

Gabbattis, J. & McSweeney, R. (2021, June 16). CCC: Adaptation to climate risks 'underfunded and ignored' by UK government. *Carbon Brief.* www.carbonbrief.org/ccc-adaptation-to-climate-risks-underfunded-and-ignored-by-uk-government.

Hallegatte, S. (2012). *A Cost Effective Solution to Reduce Disaster Losses in Developing Countries: Hydro-Meteorological Services, Early Warning, and Evacuation.* Washington, DC: World Bank.

Khan, R. S. (2020, July 14). Record locust swarms hint at what's to come with climate change. *Eos.* eos.org/articles/record-locust-swarms-hint-at-whats-to-come-with-climate-change.

McArdle, M. (2020, March 10). Opinion: When a danger is growing exponentially, everything looks fine until it doesn't. *Washington Post.* www.washingtonpost.com/opinions/2020/03/10/coronavirus-what-matters-isnt-what-you-can-see-what-you-cant/.

Mallapaty, S. (2021). Australian bush fires belched out immense quantity of carbon. *Nature 597*, 459–469.

Masters, J. (2021, August 13). July 2021 was Earth's warmest month in recorded history, says NOAA. *Yale Climate Connections.* yaleclimateconnections. org/2021/08/july-2021-was-earths-warmest-month-in-recorded-history-says-noaa/#:~:text=on%20the%20Storm-,July%202021%20was%20 Earth's%20warmest%20month%20in%20recorded%20history%2C%20 says,)%20at%20Death%20Valley%2C%20California.

Munich Re (2021, January 7). Record hurricane season and major wildfires — The natural disaster figures for 2020. www.munichre.com/en/company/ media-relations/media-information-and-corporate-news/media-information/ 2021/2020-natural-disasters-balance.html.

United Nations Office for Disaster Risk Reduction (2021). Funding. www.undrr. org/about-undrr/funding.

© 2024 World Scientific Publishing Company
https://doi.org/10.1142/9789811285165_0007

Chapter 7

Climate Policy in Jacinda Ardern's New Zealand: A Ngāi Tahu Perspective

Lisa Tumahai

Introduction

It was the evening of 1 August 2017 — two years before the world would learn of a coronavirus known to scientists as SARS-CoV-2.

Jacinda Ardern arrived at a town hall meeting in Auckland to accept the mantle of the Labour Party leadership — the centre-left party of Aotearoa, or New Zealand — which had been occupying the opposition benches for nine years.

Some 54 days later, a closely fought election would make this relatively unheard-of politician the nation's 40th Prime Minister. Ardern, aged 37, became the youngest elected female leader in the world.

In a rousing acceptance speech, the soon-to-be-leader used a phrase which has been often repeated. She referred to climate change as 'my generation's nuclear-free moment' (Newshub, 2017), a statement which name-checked a pivotal period of foreign policy in Aotearoa.

When Jacinda Ardern spoke of her generation's 'nuclear-free moment', she referenced the actions of a previous Labour administration from the 1980s, a controversial ban on nuclear warship visits from the United States and all other nuclear powers.

The political scientist Amy L. Catalinac from Harvard University conceptualised this dispute (the so-called ANZUS dispute) as 'a case of intra-alliance opposition by a small state toward its stronger ally' (Catalinac, 2010).

'As a developed, but ultimately small island nation, it can be argued that New Zealanders perceive themselves as the "underdog" as a small country on the world stage' (Ibbetson, 2017).

'This means that New Zealand often sees itself as competing on an asymmetric world stage, which is why it describes itself through the national slogan, even used by the [former] Prime Minister [John Key], "punching above our weight"' (Hurley, 2017; quoted by Ibbetson, 2017).

Ardern neatly linked her climate change aspirations with a historical piece of 'underdog' foreign policy which had raised Aotearoa to the international stage.

The Prime Minister-to-be was setting a high bar. Climate policies had run through previous governments and would undoubtedly be an important part of future policy, but Ardern was drawing something of a line in the sand. The clear implication was that Aotearoa would become a climate action beacon for the world.

Ardern was adamant in her words and intentions:

'There will always be those who say it's too difficult. There will be those who say we are too small, and that pollution and climate change are the price of progress. They are wrong' (Newshub, 2017).

The ambitious environmental pledge made by Ardern was cautiously welcomed at the time by our *iwi* (tribe) Ngāi Tahu, which had already recognised climate change as a major challenge to our people.

By 2017, Ngāi Tahu was several years into designing a climate strategy, to be published the following year, based on the underlying core values of our people and their relationship with *te taiao* (the natural environment).

Watching Ardern's *whaikōrero* (speech), there was some concern among Ngāi Tahu that the speed of policy action indicated by such a bold call to action, in its haste to meet an oncoming crisis, might cause unintentional consequences for *tangata whenua* (Māori people).

Jacinda Ardern concluded her nuclear-free comment with a determination 'to tackle it [climate change] head on' (Newshub, 2017).

For this 'generational moment' of Ardern's to succeed in practice there were some underlying structural aspects which could not be ignored if climate change was to be confronted.

Our people's experience of COVID-19 and the poor outcomes from decisions made during the height of the pandemic are a salutary lesson in hasty policymaking, highlighting a failure to sufficiently engage the indigenous population in the decision-making process.

Research has shown that Māori were 2.5 times more likely to be admitted to hospital from COVID-19 than non-Māori, and 50 per cent more likely to die (Meggat, 2022).

It is plain that climate action needs to be prioritised and policies enacted with a high degree of urgency — however, equal weight and immediacy must be given to partnership with *tangata whenua*.

A Māori-centred climate policy will help ensure a lasting societal shift that does not inflict detrimental effects on the most vulnerable.

I am optimistic that this important *mahi* (work) can be carried out contiguously in a way that will lead to a harmonious and equitable transition to a more resilient, economically sound, and climatically viable Aotearoa.

Pepeha (Personal Introduction)

Before we dive into an examination of climate policy in the COVID-19 era in Aotearoa, it is customary for me to tell you something about myself and where I come from.

Tēnā koutou katoa,
Ko Tuhua te maunga   Tuhua is my mountain
Ko Arahura te awa   The Arahura is my river
Ko Ngāi Tahu te iwi   Ngāi Tahu is my tribe
Ko Ngāti Waewae te hapū   Ngāti Waewae is my sub-tribe
Ko Lisa Tumahai ahau   I am Lisa Tumahai

I am the *Kaiwhakahaere* or Chair of *Te Rūnanga o Ngāi Tahu*, the tribal council of the *iwi* of Ngāi Tahu.

We are one of the largest Māori tribes in New Zealand. Our tribal territory covers approximately 80 per cent of the land mass of Te Waipounamu (the South Island). At present, we have more than 75,000 *whānau* (extended family) members.

As Ngāi Tahu, we made our home in Te Waipounamu more than 800 years ago. Our *tīpuna* (ancestors) were the first long-distance seafarers in the Pacific, riding the ocean currents and navigating by stars on voyaging waka (canoes) from Hawaiki. They populated the islands of the South Pacific, eventually making their way to Aotearoa and Te Waipounamu.

Ngāi Tahu means the 'people of Tahu', linking us to our eponymous ancestor Tahu Pōtiki. *Waitaha*, the first people of Te Waipounamu, journeyed on the *Uruao* waka and settled in *Kā Pākihi Whakatekateka o*

Waitaha — the Canterbury Plains. Ngāti Māmoe and then Ngāi Tahu followed. Through warfare, intermarriage and political alliances a common allegiance to Ngāi Tahu was forged.

I also wear a second *pōtae* (hat), as Deputy Chair of *He Pou a Rangi* (the New Zealand Climate Change Commission). This is a Crown entity and it is our job to provide independent, evidence-based advice to the government to help Aotearoa transition to a climate-resilient and low-emissions future.

On the Front Line

Since our *tīpuna* landed on these shores in the thirteenth century, our people have faced their fair share of existential challenges. In the wake of European arrival in the nineteenth century, Ngāi Tahu were forced into being a people almost devoid of land, depleted by disease and divorced from the growing economy. Our language was stripped from us, our cultural identity almost lost forever in the process.

The climate crisis is one of the most pressing threats of our current epoch. Overcoming this emergency demands a united effort from all inhabitants of Earth. We are all affected, and we must play our part. But even if all the world's citizens were equally determined to resolve this existential challenge, there remains the uncomfortable fact that some communities will be more greatly afflicted than others.

'Although there might only be "one Earth", resilience and vulnerability to environmental change differs widely at national to household levels, reflecting a variety of factors including age, class, gender, ethnicity, income, and livelihood, among others. As the environmental scientist Jesse Ribot cautions, vulnerability does not "fall from the sky;" it is socially constructed' (Ford *et al.*, 2020).

Climate change can be seen as a global issue, experienced locally. In this part of the world, our Pacific cousins are experiencing some of the most intense manifestations of the climate emergency, with atolls among the most vulnerable places on Earth (Amores *et al.*, 2022).

In Aotearoa, the indigenous people, *iwi* like our own, are also on the front line. As the UN Department of Economic and Social Affairs states:

'Indigenous peoples are among the first to face the direct adverse consequences of climate change, due to their dependence upon, and close relationship with the environment and its resources' (UN Department of Economic and Social Affairs, n.d.).

For Ngāi Tahu, geography plays a key role. The vast majority of traditional *marae* (settlements) across our *takiwā* (territory) are coastal-based, so many *urupā* (sacred burial sites), *wharenui* (meeting houses) and other buildings are exposed to rising sea levels.

Shifts in climatic patterns, extreme weather events, sea temperature changes and ocean acidification also threaten to deplete stocks of *mahinga kai* (traditional foods gathered in a customary manner).

Our people continue to live off the land and practice *mahinga kai*, but as is becoming all too familiar, these traditional practices, like many others, are increasingly under threat. The sustainable management of the environment and its natural resources has become a priority now more than ever before.

In Aotearoa, patterns of settlement by Pākehā (non-Māori) also show a distinct coastal distribution. Many owners of properties by the sea, and the insurance companies they pay for protection, are rapidly reassessing the risks of sea level change, flooding and storm surges.

'According to the government, the scale of the problem is enormous: 675,000 people — one in seven New Zealanders — live in areas prone to flooding ... another 72,065 live in areas projected to be subject to extreme sea level rise' (McClure, 2022).

A draft national adaption plan is presently asking for public input on a 'managed retreat' — abandoning areas where it is not possible or financially viable to live any longer (Ministry for the Environment, 2022).

For our people, it is not quite as simple as moving bricks and mortar, wood or corrugated iron. There is another layer of nuance. Our attachment to *whenua* (the land) is spiritual. This is particularly true for our *urupā* and *wāhi tapu* — the burial grounds of our *tīpuna* and sites of cultural significance that are sacred to *mana whenua*.

Besides buildings, there are climate impacts on our food gathering sites situated in waterways and wetlands, and on tiny offshore islands. Ancient gardens, healing places, *rongoā* crops (medicinal plants) and other culturally important sites are located alongside rivers and coastlines prone to flooding and inundation.

According to the results of a newly released five-year research project, the sea level in some parts of Aotearoa is rising twice as fast as previously thought, significantly reducing the amount of time we have left to respond (Cardwell, 2022).

James D. Ford *et al*. hold that strong connections to the 'land' bring unique considerations for understanding and responding to environmental change: 'the indirect effects of environmental change on interpersonal and environmental relationships, life experience, spiritual considerations, family, kinship, and oral history are often as important as, if not more so, the more direct impacts of change' (Ford et al., 2020).

The following case study demonstrates the complex nature of climate adaption and rising sea levels in a Ngāi Tahu context:

At Te Rūnanga o Moeraki on the east coast, their sacred sites are at great risk. The *urupā* which contain *tīpuna* are subject to extreme coastal erosion and sea level rise.

The following comes from a biography of one of our *rangatira* (leaders), Te Rūnanga o Moeraki *Upoko* David Higgins:

> 'Moeraki Marae is located well above sea level, so it's not at risk of climate change. But our historic pā sites, our archaeological sites, and our urupā (cemeteries) of our tīpuna are all directly in line with the predicted future sea level. Some of our pā sites are located right on the beach and our tīpuna are buried in the sand dunes. Others are located very close to present sea levels. The sad reality is over the next few decades or so we will lose a lot of those burial sites and they will be washed away over time.
>
> One of the most influential tribal leaders in the history of Kāi Tahu whānui is buried at Moeraki. Matiaha Tiramōrehu made the first formal statement of Kāi Tahu grievances against the Crown regarding South Island land purchases on 22 October 1849. In 1837 he led the migration of our people from Kaiapoi pā south in a convoy of canoes to settle near a whaling station at Port Moeraki.
>
> I am one of the kaitiaki with the responsibility to care for Matiaha's final resting place, which is at risk of climate change and erosion in the future. As a wider whānau, we have considered the exhumation of the contents of our urupā, with the goal of relocating our tīpuna such as Matiaha, to a site that isn't at risk of climate change. However, some of our whānau are more than happy for the ocean to claim our urupā.
>
> Our ancestors migrated to Niu Tīreni (New Zealand) across Te Moana-nui-a-Kiwa, and in this way our tīpuna would return to the sea. So, we have some difficult decisions to make in the future' (Ngāi Tahu, n.d.).

Though short on specifics, it is heartening to see that the draft national adaption plan has included proposals for protecting important cultural sites such as coastal marae. There is also acknowledgement of our people's particular sensitivity to climate for 'social, economic, cultural and spiritual reasons' (Ministry for the Environment, 2022).

Across our *takiwā*, the challenges from climate change are varied and require differing responses. The last Intergovernmental Panel on Climate Change predicted dry areas in the north and east of Aotearoa will get much drier, while the south and west will be far wetter, with more floods, amplified by vapour corridors in the sky called 'atmospheric rivers' (Intergovernmental Panel on Climate Change, 2021).

During 2022–2023, communities around Aotearoa have been repeatedly hit by devastating flooding. In March 2023, Tairawhiti (Gisborne) in the North Island was struck with its second destructive flood in less than a year, another so-called 'one in a hundred-year event'.

In Te Waipounamu, flooding in Westport, 140 km north of my own marae, left 450 houses unlivable or damaged in October 2021. That is a significant number of family homes in a town of just 4280 people. The West Coast is a narrow strip of coastline running alongside Kā Tiritiri-o-te-moana (the Southern Alps). Inundation is a clear and present danger for those who live where I come from.

As James Renwick, the New Zealand climate scientist described similar flooding in 2022, 'We are gradually pushing the odds of a heavy rainfall event up, it is more likely we will get events like this in the future' (*Radio New Zealand*, 2021).

Meanwhile, on the other side of the Alps, on the Canterbury Plains, just a couple of hundred kilometres east, our people will face the increasing likelihood of drought.

The Ministry for Primary Industries has been predicting for some time that '[s]ecurity of water supply is likely to be the greatest issue for Canterbury in the future, even if the worst effects of climate change are not realised. Drier average conditions during the summer months, together with increased demand for water, [are] likely to place pressure on resources' (Ministry of Agriculture and Forestry, 2010). This brings into sharp relief legal efforts to reclaim *rangatiratanga* (stewardship) over freshwater in our *takiwā* from the Crown, an ongoing struggle for our people as the present government seeks a historic overhaul of the management of this precious resource.

'There is perhaps no issue in New Zealand today more contentious than water rights. The Crown claims that no one owns water, but its use, irrigation and treatment are controlled by local governments empowered by the Crown. Since the 1990s resource consents for the taking of water, in Canterbury and Southland especially, have increased dramatically and the environmental situation is reaching a breaking point' (Tau, 2017).

An Equitable Climate Path

In the same 2017 speech in which Ardern made a generational pledge about climate change, she also promised a 'government of transformation' to tackle poverty and inequality.

The campaign promises were delivered in a leafy suburb of Tamaki Makaurau (Auckland), the largest city of Aotearoa, where the average house price is $2.2 million — twice the national average.

I think of my father and mother who live on the West Coast (average house price $269,000), a region which has traditionally provided Aotearoa with much of its coal. I managed to shift them into heating their home with electricity three years ago, only to find that after I had been gone for a week for my *mahi*, my mother had lit the fire again. Her monthly power bill had arrived, and it was NZ$600 (US$380). That is one of the challenges we face with trying to transform our communities to a different way of living when, actually, it is structurally unaffordable.

How do you shift 'Coasters' behaviour as they suffer through a winter of power cuts when they can get a trailer-load of coal for 80 bucks? My parents would tell you it will last three weeks, and the heat stays in longer. It is one thing to talk boldly about individual action on climate when you have enough money to buy a Tesla, another when you are struggling to pay the bills. Climate action needs to be buttressed with social justice.

Climate justice 'insists on a shift from a discourse on greenhouse gases and melting ice caps into a civil rights movement with the people and communities most vulnerable to climate impacts at its heart', according to Mary Robinson, former President of Ireland, talking on the UN sustainable development goals (United Nations, 2019).

As Leslie Solomonian and Erica Di Ruggiero argue:

'The global crises of ecological degradation and social injustice are mutually reinforcing products of the same flawed systems. Dominant human culture is morally obliged to challenge and reconstruct these systems in order to mitigate future planetary harm. We argue for the moral necessity of a socially just approach to the ecological crisis ... The forces that have contributed to and continue to perpetuate the devastation of the biosphere are the very ones that have caused deep harm to and stark inequities among humans' (Solomonian & Ruggiero, 2021).

Like many indigenous peoples, Māori experience ongoing societal inequities within wider communities. Māori have a lower average income than Pākehā and tend to represent poorly in other socioeconomic indicators such as health and education. Hence they will bear the brunt of challenges presented by climate change and the necessary mitigations which face the population as a whole.

For generations, our *tīpuna* relied on the plentiful natural resources to survive, developing a duty of care to sustain the environment that in turn sustained them. Policy-wise these traditional relationships must be balanced, in the modern context, against the very real needs of our people to thrive in a Pākehā-dominated world where money is the measure of wealth.

Climate mitigation measures in communities like my own carry the double-edged sword of removing income-generating industries and imposing extra household costs on low-income families.

Land ownership is another key factor which impacts our people. Much of the land that was originally allocated to Māori by the Crown is extremely marginal. Also, it tends to be shared among large numbers of *whānau*. Land use change may be something which is demanded by climate policy but it is not remunerated. This may have a disproportionate effect on Māori landowners, who are restricted by a complicated ownership structure and an inability to secure investment.

In many cases, the land they jointly own may represent their only major investment, and they have limited opportunities to diversify into long-term climate-positive uses such as regenerating native forests.

Economically, Māori are strongly represented in sectors such as farming, fishing, forestry, transport, and energy, all of which will be heavily affected by climate change or the transition of the country to a zero-emissions future.

Benefits of a Māori-Centred Climate Policy

There are other compelling reasons, aside from climate justice, for putting Māori at the centre of climate policy.

Māori share a strong relationship with the natural world, to the extent that many of our traditional narratives and mythologies suggest that we descend from the mountains and the waterways of our tribal territory.

As Māori, and as Ngāi Tahu, we are deeply connected with *te taiao*. This connection forms the basis of our cultural identity, language, practices and value systems regarding who we are and where we come from.

Much like other indigenous cultures, our own *mātauranga* Māori, or knowledge, is passed down intergenerationally and draws from our holistic relationship with the natural environment. It embodies an intangible connection to all its ecosystems and spiritual beings, as well as other living entities that we share the environment with.

At a time when governments and corporations are looking to produce values-led systems to guide us into a zero-carbon future, as Ngāi Tahu, these principles are second nature to us. Fulfilling this obligation enables the *mana*, or dignity and integrity, of the natural environment.

We rely on values established by our people over hundreds of years, based upon a close relationship with the environment:

- *Whānaungatanga*: Fostering relationships among our own and within our communities.
- *Manaakitanga*: Respecting and taking care of each other and those within our *takiwā*.
- *Tohungatanga*: Growing the expertise and knowledge we need to strengthen ourselves.
- *Kaitiakitanga*: This role of guardianship is a responsibility and derives from our *whakapapa* (genealogy) and connection to place. We will work actively to protect the people, natural environment, knowledge, culture, language and resources important to Ngāi Tahu for future generations.
- *Tikanga*: This is defined as appropriate action; we have a responsibility to ensure that the norms defined by our culture and people underpin our decision-making and approach.
- *Rangatiratanga*: We will strive to be leaders; we will strive to give our people the tools to live lives defined by choice, not by necessity. Self-determination is an aspiration we hold dear in all aspects of tribal activity.

It is important to note that our holistic relationship creates an obligation, in that we must care for, protect, restore and respect our natural environment as though it is a living entity, as if it were yourself, or one of your own *whānau* or family members.

A *whakataukī* (proverb) that encapsulates this view has been derived from our Wanganui River *whānaunga* (cousins) in the North Island, which states: 'Ko au te awa, ko te awa ko au' (I am the river; the river is me). This Māori world view underpins why sustainability is imperative to us as indigenous people.

From a Ngāi Tahu perspective, this world view is what drives our decision-making, in terms of what we strive to do as an *iwi*. The holistic relationship and the connections we hold with the natural environment, its ecosystems and all living entities are also of particular importance, in the sense that we aim to maintain and improve the mauri and *mana* of these entities.

Mauri refers to the vitality of an entity and its life-supporting capacity. A relationship that maintains the *mauri* is one that involves us, humans, engaging with the environment in a way that maintains and increases its capacity to support life.

Ford *et al.* (2020) argue that '[a]s stewards and guardians of lands that intersect with about 40% of all terrestrial protected areas and ecologically intact landscapes, Indigenous peoples also have a central role in detecting and managing change'.

Our knowledge of the natural environment, handed down over generations, and the values that place its well-being at the heart of everything we do mean that we can provide invaluable input to environmental policy and climate action.

Te Waihora (Lake Ellesmere) is a lake in Canterbury on the east coast. Ngāi Tahu first notified the New Zealand Government about the destruction of this body of water in the late 1800s. It is well documented. We raised issues about the pollution going into Te Waihora and that our lake was going to die.

Successive chiefs since that time continued to bring the matter of the degradation of that lake up with the government. That lake has nearly died, but at least now there is a significant restoration project in place. It is going to take decades to turn around the damage that has been done to Te Waihora, but the alarm bells were ringing more than a hundred years ago.

Ki uta ki tai (from the mountains to the sea) is another philosophy which we implement regarding our obligations and responsibilities to the natural environment. It is a traditional concept representing *kaitiakitanga*, or guardianship, using a whole-systems approach.

Kaitiakitanga reflects the special relationship that we have with the environment and, as noted above, it is fundamental to our cultural identity. *Ki uta ki tai* encapsulates the need to recognise and manage the interconnectedness of the natural environment.

One of the international experts we called on to help us with our climate implementation plan was Will Steffen, an American-born Australian chemist. In his ground-breaking work he determined nine planetary boundaries which characterise the Holocene, the workable operating zone for humans (Steffen, 2015).

This meshes with our need to look at all things that affect *Hau Ora Te Ao* (the health of our world). In the planetary boundaries model, first published in 2009, besides climate change there are eight other crucial pressure points for Earth. 'The planetary boundaries framework provides a systemic, long-term view of environmental modification, degradation and resource use. It delineates a precautionary "safe operating space" for multi-generational sustainable development' (Anderson *et al.*, 2020).

The Stockholm Resilience Centre's assessment describes Aotearoa as in breach of six planetary boundaries, including climate change, where it exceeds its national share. The other boundary breaches are in freshwater consumption, land system change, biogeochemical flows (Phosphorus and Nitrogen) and biodiversity loss (Anderson *et al.*, 2020).

As our ancestors have always taught us, environmental health is a complex web, and many of these planetary boundaries are interrelated. It would be naive to think that if we just solved our climate issues, then our place in the world would be completely safeguarded.

The long-term nature of the climate threat is another aspect of the climate crisis which can benefit from *te ao Māori* (the Māori world view). It is a strong antidote to the *ad interim* thinking which is arguably responsible for the position we find ourselves in, a place where 'short-term thinking and long-term consequences collide' (Paulson, 2015).

'Antecedents related to short-termism and uncertainty avoidance reinforce each other at three levels — individual, organizational, and institutional — and result in organizational inaction on climate change' (Slawinski, 2017).

At Ngāi Tahu, our planning horizon lasts not ten or twenty years, but one hundred or two hundred. Long-term thinking is baked in. Like many indigenous communities, we view everything through an intergenerational lens. In this way we are honouring our descendants and aiming to become the best ancestors we can be.

Our *whakataukī* that guides all our decisions and our operation is *Mō tātou, ā, mō kā uri ā muri ake nei* (for us and our children after us). We must ensure that we are not making decisions today that will impact the well-being of our future generations. In the context of a changing climate, this means that we have a responsibility to set the foundations for the future that our children and our grandchildren will inherit.

We want the future to be safe and prosperous, and we want them to have the freedom of choice to thrive in a climate-resilient community. That is why Ngāi Tahu developed our own climate strategy and why we have always considered it essential that Māori are empowered to stand alongside the New Zealand Government as we meet the challenges of our changing environment and the opportunities of a post-carbon economy.

Partnership and co-governance are provided for in the country's founding document, *Te Tiriti o Waitangi* (the Treaty of Waitangi). Under *Te Tiriti*, our *tīpuna* entered contracts with the Crown to sell some of our land, with the promise of the creation of reserves sufficient for our people to thrive, as well as the provision of key social infrastructure, including schools and hospitals.

As history shows, the Crown did not honour its side of the bargain. Following that breach of contract, *Te Kerēme* — the Ngāi Tahu Claim was born. Over seven generations, Ngāi Tahu carried its quest for justice, led and inspired by an intergenerational philosophy and approach.

This culminated in the Ngāi Tahu Settlement of 1998 which, through the transfer of a range of resources and tools, forged the next stage of our tribal journey to preserve our tribal identity and begin to create a prosperous future for our people.

In the settlement, we received $170 million from the Crown. Many would say that represented a drop in the bucket of what we were entitled to, but this was enough to ensure that through wise investments in a diverse range of areas, including seafood, tourism, property and farming, we have been able to grow that *pūtea* (fund) to a tribal asset base of over $1.5 billion. Along the way, we have invested approximately $600 million into well-being initiatives to create better outcomes for *whānau*.

The *iwi* now faces a challenge which could be seen as a microcosm of the government's own. The investments which previously brought a degree of financial security are now producing greenhouse gases which fuel climate change, a trade-off between short-term benefits and long-term consequences. We must negotiate the dilemma of saving future generations from the climate crisis without saddling them with poverty.

That is why the recently agreed climate implementation plan aims to mitigate our contributions to climate change. We are trialling regenerative practices in our farming business, electrifying jet boats for tourism and looking to find alternatives to diesel in our transport division.

We are about to push 'go' on a suite of 88 different actions to protect the environment, cut emissions, keep our *whānau* and marae safe from the worst effects of climate change and help them to co-create a better future, taking advantage of all the opportunities which will come from a low emissions economy.

How COVID-19 and Climate Collided

So how, from a Ngāi Tahu perspective, has this government performed on climate?

Its pre-pandemic initiatives included the following:

- A commitment to generate all electricity from renewable sources by 2035.
- A determination to reduce national carbon emissions to zero by 2050 (the Climate Change Response (Zero Carbon) Amendment Act of 2019).
- In April 2018, the government also announced that it would not grant any new offshore oil and gas exploration permits in New Zealand territorial waters.
- The establishment of a Climate Change Commission in 2019.

Aotearoa is one of the few countries to have a legislated goal of net zero emissions by 2050. However, the government's short-term policies do not yet synchronise with that ambition.

Some 48 per cent of greenhouse gas emissions come from the farming sector, and the government has forestalled the entry of agriculture into the Emissions Trading Scheme (the greenhouse gas pricing mechanism) to allow the industry to come up with its own method for cutting emissions.

According to one respected scientific measure, Aotearoa is well short of its greenhouse gas emissions targets (Nationally Determined Contributions) agreed to internationally.

The Climate Action Tracker (CAT) is an independent scientific analysis produced by two research organisations that have been tracking climate action since 2009. It tracks progress towards the globally agreed aim of holding global warming well below 2°C, and pursuing efforts to limit it to 1.5°C.

In 2017, the year Ardern was elected, CAT classified the climate policies of Aotearoa as 'insufficient' to meet its international treaty obligations: 'We rate New Zealand's Nationally Determined Contribution (NDC) target of a 30% reduction from 2005 levels by 2030 as 'insufficient,' meaning that it is not consistent with holding warming to below 2°C, let alone limiting it to 1.5°C as required under the Paris Agreement, and is instead consistent with warming between 2°C and 3°C' (Climate Action Tracker, 2017). In the latest report, released on 15 September 2021, Aotearoa had slipped to a lower rating of 'highly insufficient' (Climate Action Tracker 2021).

It is impossible to know what might have happened without the advent of a global pandemic, but arguably, by international standards, New Zealand appears to be a long way off meeting the climate challenge 'head-on'.

As it turned out, the scale and pace of government policies were to prove generally disheartening to those hoping that Aotearoa might 'punch above its weight' on climate action. Certainly, members of Ngāi Tahu were disappointed that climate policy did not go far enough. Guided by the concept of *kaitiakitanga*, looking after the environment is a priority for us.

The pandemic played a major role in this outcome. It also underlined a very important aspect of any new, sweeping public policy in Aotearoa — the authentic engagement of the indigenous population.

Our people's experience with COVID-19 was not easy to bear. Our leaders had hoped for an equitable response, but the government was seemingly slow to prioritise those who needed the most help, and as a result, Māori were disproportionately affected.

COVID-19 has emerged as the deadliest respiratory disease pandemic since 1918, when the influenza outbreak killed an estimated 50 million people.

The 'Great Flu' epidemic was devastating for the indigenous population in Aotearoa. Deaths recorded for Māori were more than seven times the European rate (Wilson *et al.*, 2012).

During the most recent pandemic, our people still had a hospitalisation rate more than twice that of Pākehā. As the *British Medical Journal* saw it, 'New Zealand's COVID-19 strategy failed Māori' (Meggat, 2022).

'Te Pūnaha Matatini (the New Zealand Centre of Research Excellence for complex systems) research shows the risk of hospital admission from COVID-19 for a 40-year-old Māori and a 35-year-old Pasifika is approximately equivalent to the risk of hospital admission for a 60-year-old European' says Polly Atatoa Carr, a public health physician and Associate Professor of population health at the University of Waikato in Hamilton (Kirikiriroa).

'With COVID-19, in early November [2021], more than 70 per cent of cases and more than 70 per cent of hospital admissions were from Māori and Pasifika communities. By mid-December, following a vaccine drive and a drop in COVID-19 cases coinciding with summer, these figures were closer to 50 per cent. The youngest New Zealander to die with COVID-19 was a Māori boy under the age of 10' (Meggat, 2022).

It can be argued that the government's policy response to COVID-19 and the inequitable outcomes experienced by the Māori population are important lessons for the careful introduction of a dynamic climate policy which is just and fair.

Inequitable outcomes for Māori, both historical and contemporary, lend heavy weight to the notion that any fast-tracked policies to adapt to and mitigate the effects of climate change need to give careful consideration as to their impact on *tangata whenua*.

So where does the Climate Change Commission come in?

The commission provides direction on policy. However, it is up to the government and the agencies to write policy. While the commission can recommend that the government ensures they are giving effect to the treaty partnership in consideration of the impacts for *iwi* Māori, the Public Service Act puts the onus on government agencies to ensure they support the Crown and its relationships with Māori under *Te Tiriti*.

Climate legislation requires the government to consider *Te Tiriti*. More specifically, the Climate Change Response Act 2002 requires the commission to consider the Crown–Māori relationship, *te ao Māori* and specific effects on *iwi* and Māori in all advice given to the government.

The act also requires the government to include strategies that recognise and mitigate the impacts on *iwi* and Māori of the effects of climate change. The government must consider the economic, social, health, environmental, ecological and cultural effects of climate change on *iwi* Māori. Those requirements created strong expectations from *iwi* Māori regarding what the government's approach will be to articulating the Māori world view in future policy and how the Māori voice will come through.

There is an expectation from Ngāi Tahu that effective partnership means not just ensuring the co-design of policy that will impact on *iwi* Māori, but creating opportunities for protection, partnership and participation.

It is fairly plain that *iwi* and Māori policy advisors need to be actively engaged in partnership with government agencies. Climate action involves several ministries such as the Ministry for Primary Industries and the Ministry for the Environment. There are several Māori academics with a comprehensive understanding of *mātauranga* Māori, but right now there is no co-ordinated approach. We hope that the recently announced Māori platform will be a better way forward.

Ngāi Tahu is pleased with where the commission's final report has landed. As an *iwi*, we are looking for guidance for ministers so that they can interpret the report and create policy and legislation. The report has gone to the government And we now, as an *iwi*, expect to see them pick up those recommendations.

As I have described, Māori are likely to be disproportionately impacted by the effects of climate change. It is important to ensure that Māori are part of the conversation and the decision-making — that Māori initiatives are actively explored. *Iwi* have their own solutions; we are also part of the wider solution. The government must ensure we are part of the decision-making; if not we will see familiar patterns of inequity.

In both of my jobs, I am there to ensure *te ao Māori, mātauranga* and *tikanga* Māori are considered and demonstrated in the work — alongside the obligations of *Te Tiriti o Waitangi*.

From a Ngāi Tahu point of view, the ambitious starting point of the Ardern Government needs to be backed up with a high degree of Māori engagement. It is fantastic to have big, bold aspirations, but we have to have big, bold climate action too. We cannot hide the fact that the COVID-19 response has resulted in inequitable outcomes.

To neglect the Māori engagement aspect of climate action would exacerbate existing inequities, to the detriment of our people. It would also miss an important opportunity to shape and code policy with a strong *te ao Māori* value system. A set of principles that carries a profound affinity with the environment, emphasising long-term thinking and intergenerational responsibilities — centuries-old precepts which have starkly relevant modern applications.

As we say round here, what is good for Ngāi Tahu is good for Aotearoa.

References

Amores, A., et al. (2022). Coastal flooding and mean sea-level rise allowances in atoll island. *Nature*, *12*(1281).

Andersen, L., et al. (2020). A safe operating space for New Zealand/Aotearoa: Translating the planetary boundaries framework. Potsdam: Potsdam Institute for Climate Impact Research; Stockholm: Stockholm Resilience Centre, Stockholm University; Berlin: Mercator Research Institute on Global Commons and Climate Change. www.stockholmresilience.org/download/1.66e0efc517643c2b810218e/1612341172295/Updated%20PBNZ-Report-Design-v6.0.pdf.

Cardwell, H. (2022, May 1). Sea levels rising twice as fast as thought in New Zealand. *Radio New Zealand*. www.rnz.co.nz/news/national/466262/sea-levels-rising-twice-as-fast-as-thought-in-new-zealand.

Catalinac, A. (2010). Why New Zealand took itself out of ANZUS: Observing "opposition for autonomy" in asymmetric alliances. *Foreign Policy Analysis*, *6*(4), 317–338.

Climate Action Tracker (2017, November 6). New Zealand — Climate Action Tracker. climateactiontracker.org/media/documents/2018/4/CAT_2017-11-06_CountryAssessment_NewZealand.pdf.

Climate Action Tracker (2021, September 15). New Zealand — Climate Action Tracker. climateactiontracker.org/countries/new-zealand.

Ford, J., et al. (2020). The resilience of indigenous peoples to environmental change. *One Earth*, *2*(6), 532–543.

Hurley, E. (2017, March 21). John key's legacy: A confident New Zealand. *Newshub*. www.newshub.co.nz/home/politics/2017/03/john-key-s-legacy-a-confident-new-zealand.html.

Ibbetson, O. (2017). Punching above our weight: How a small island nation navigates the world of global strategy. Master's dissertation, Victoria University of Wellington. VUW Archive. researcharchive.vuw.ac.nz/xmlui/bitstream/handle/10063/6947/thesis_access.pdf.

Intergovernmental Panel on Climate Change (2021). Sixth Assessment Report. Working Group 1: The Physical Science Basis. Atlas Chapter: 1985–1991. www.ipcc.ch/report/ar6/wg1.

McClure, T. (2022, April 27). New Zealand unveils plan to tackle climate crisis by adapting cities to survive rising seas. *The Guardian*. www.theguardian.com/world/2022/apr/27/new-zealand-unveils-plan-to-tackle-climate-crisis-by-adapting-cities-to-survive-rising-seas.

Meggat, K. (2022). How New Zealand's Covid-19 Strategy Failed Māori People. *BMJ*, *376*, o180.

Ministry for the Environment, New Zealand (2022). Draft National Adaption Plan. Wellington: Ministry for the Environment. environment.govt.nz/assets/publications/Draft-national-adaptation-plan.pdf.

Ministry of Agriculture and Forestry, New Zealand (2010). Climate change: A guide for land managers. Ministry for Primary Industries. www.mpi.govt. nz/dmsdocument/27031-effects-and-impacts-canterbury-regional-summary.
Ngāi Tahu (n.d.). Our People: David Higgins. Ngāi Tahu: Kā Huru Manu. www.kahurumanu.co.nz/our-people/david-higgins/david-higgins.
Newshub (2017, August 1). Jacinda Ardern — Climate change is my generation's nuclear-free moment. *Newshub*. www.newshub.co.nz/home/election/2017/08/jacinda-ardern-climate-change-is-my-generation-s-nuclear-free-moment.html.
New Zealand Herald (2015, November 30). NZ wins first "Fossil" award at Paris talks. *New Zealand Herald*. www.nzherald.co.nz/nz/nz-wins-first-fossil-award-at-paris-talks/XFX2W7HZJOWRCTJUODUS3VBU4U/#.
Paulson, H. (n.d.). Short-termism and the threat from climate change. www.mckinsey.com/business-functions/strategy-and-corporate-finance/our-insights/short-termism-and-the-threat-from-climate-change#:~:text=Climate%20 change%20is%20where%20short,consequences%20of%20failure%20 are%20irreversible.
Radio New Zealand (2021, July 22). Climate change and recent flooding: What you need to know. *Radio New Zealand*. www.rnz.co.nz/news/what-you-need-to-know/447378/climate-change-and-recent-flooding-what-you-need-to-know.
Slawinski, N., et al. (2017). The role of short-termism and uncertainty avoidance in organizational inaction on climate change: A multi-level framework. *Business and Society, 56*(2), 253–282.
Solomonian, L. & Ruggiero, E. (2021). The critical intersection of environmental and social justice: A commentary. *Globalization and Health, 17*(30), 1–4.
Steffen, W., et al. (2015). Planetary boundaries: Guiding human development on a changing planet. *Science, 347*(6223), 736–746.
Tau, T. (2017). Water Rights for Ngāi Tahu: A Discussion Paper. Christchurch: Canterbury University Press and Ngāi Tahu Research Centre.
United Nations (2019, May 31). Climate Justice. United Nations: Sustainable Development Goals. www.un.org/sustainabledevelopment/blog/2019/05/climate-justice.
UN Department of Economic and Social Affairs. Indigenous Peoples (n.d.). Climate Change: The Effects of Climate Change on Indigenous Peoples. www.un.org/development/desa/indigenouspeoples/climate-change.html.
Wilson, N., et al. (2012). Differential mortality rates by ethnicity in 3 influenza pandemics over a century, New Zealand. *Emerging Infectious Diseases, 18*(1), 71–77.

© 2024 World Scientific Publishing Company
https://doi.org/10.1142/9789811285165_0008

Chapter 8

Big Global Issues and Soft Power: New Zealand and the Pacific

Marion Crawshaw

This chapter is based on a presentation to the 2021 Otago Foreign Policy School that addressed the question 'How should New Zealand use its soft power in the Pacific Region to address the big global issues?' Since then, big global issues have pressed in on the Pacific, even more so than at the time the original paper was written. In particular, geopolitical manoeuvring in the Pacific has intensified and COVID-19 has arrived across the Pacific, placing health impacts on top of the economic effects created by the now largely lifted COVID-19 lockdowns. The Pacific's most pressing concern, climate change, continues to impact Pacific states, but focused attention now has to be shared with a proliferation of other global challenges. The global multilateral system is under pressure, as is Pacific regional multilateralism, with a serious split, as yet unresolved, in the Pacific's peak regional body, the Pacific Forum. The Pacific is also in a period of internal political intensity and potentially one of change, with a difficult change of government having taken place in Samoa, a contested referendum on independence in New Caledonia and elections forthcoming at the time of writing in Papua New Guinea (PNG), Fiji and Australia.

Personal relationships are at the heart of soft power. COVID-19 protocols in both New Zealand and in Pacific countries have severely restricted people's movement. This has had a significant impact on New Zealand's ability to utilise its soft power instruments, especially the building and maintenance of face-to-face personal relationships in the Pacific nations.

Changes to the construction of New Zealand's Government in 2020 brought new personalities into the mix, which means that the work of rebuilding strong personal relationships across the Pacific is all the more important. The lifting of COVID-19 restrictions in both New Zealand and the Pacific provides the opportunity to travel again and reconnect.

The perspective expressed here is consciously that of a foreign policy practitioner, not an academic. Academic work and theory help shape policy development and implementation, but practitioners balance different tactical and strategic considerations to those of academics.

Soft Power

Soft power entails influence and persuasion and is based on respect, not coercion. It starts at home and rests on perceptions of our values and the ways in which we implement them domestically as much as we do offshore. New Zealanders are increasingly defining themselves as the independent state of Aotearoa/New Zealand based in the South Pacific. It helps us assert a distinctive identity offshore and it supports our Pacific relationships. But we cannot assume that Pacific Islanders will necessarily perceive our Pacific identity in the way we do. They are also conscious of our strong colonial inheritance and connections to other settler societies.

Offshore actions are seen and judged in the context of our own domestic actions and results. At home, we need to consider the Pacific dimensions of policy decisions that are primarily domestic, or we risk diluting our relationships with the Pacific. The decisions taken on immigration policy for example, especially as it affects the Pacific, resonate with our reputation and our soft power in the Pacific.

New Zealand also draws on its significant Polynesian population for its claim to a Pacific identity, sometimes without the consciousness that 'Pacific' does not mean just 'Polynesia' and that the Pacific is inhabited by many other peoples. There are complicated relationships among the peoples of the Pacific, and while New Zealand is geographically and historically close to the Polynesian states to our north, effective soft power in the Pacific needs to be inclusive across the entire ocean. With COVID-19 restrictions in place, this has not always been evident in the last couple of years, but it is time to renew a cohesive approach across the Pacific.

The practise of soft power relies on the successful deployment of diplomatic tools over long periods of time. Engagements, activities and people that build and sustain relationships are central. Listening is key.

In 2018, the Minister of Foreign Affairs Winston Peters announced a Pacific Reset to 're-energize' New Zealand's approach to the Pacific, based on New Zealand values and increased technical and financial support to the Pacific: 'A re-energised approach also based on greater co-ordination of effort by all New Zealand stakeholders with an interest in the Pacific, with Pacific governments and people, and with key partners near and far' (Peters, 2018). While the Pacific Reset increased development funds for the Pacific, it sought to go beyond tactical development funding and put relationships at the heart of our approach to the Pacific. This included resources to support more systematic relationships between the government sector in New Zealand and their Pacific counterparts, and to provide more people in our Pacific diplomatic posts.

Minister of Foreign Affairs Nanaia Mahuta has refined the expression of New Zealand's values in a way that links them more closely to the definition of ourselves as the independent state of Aotearoa/New Zealand based in the South Pacific. It supports a post-colonial identity for Aotearoa/New Zealand that blends the different strands of our heritage. She has also moved beyond the Pacific Reset of her predecessor to a strategy that focuses on resilience in the Pacific as the objective of our engagement.

The values the minister defined include *manaaki* (kindness or the reciprocity of goodwill); *whanaunga* (our connectedness or shared sense of humanity); *mahi tahi* and *kotahitanga* (collective benefits and shared aspiration); and *kaitiaki* (protection and stewardship of our intergenerational well-being) (Mahuta, 2021). 'Shared' and 'reciprocal' have strong places in the definitions of these values.

There is more work to be done on just how the implementation of these values can be embedded in the practice and implementation of New Zealand's foreign policy, especially when difficult choices have to be made, including in the region itself. As we move towards a more indigenous identity, based on these values, questions arise, for example as to how we balance our interests in the relationships with France, which is an important global partner for New Zealand, and with the Kanaks in New Caledonia in their struggle for independence. Similar issues arise in the relationship with Indonesia and the Melanesian people of its West Papua provinces.

Maintenance of relationships needs face-to-face contacts. While many COVID-19 restrictions have been lifted, travel remains more complicated than it was pre-pandemic. This means that the presence and spread of New Zealand's diplomatic posts throughout the Pacific remain as important as ever. Posts can help provide a deeper understanding of how COVID-19 and closed borders have already changed, in some cases irreversibly, the political, social and economic environments in the Pacific. COVID-19 restrictions have reshaped the context and opportunities for the use of our diplomatic tools in the Pacific. Closed borders and the absence of face-to-face contacts, from high level visits to technical expert visits to non-governmental organisation contacts, meant that it was more difficult to project our identity and make our Pacific relationships distinctively of Aotearoa/New Zealand. Distant nations engaged in ways that are much more similar to us than previously. Development activities have had to rely more on in-country expertise.

In that period diplomatic posts became even more important, but with restrictions lifting, we need to recharge in-person contacts, in both directions. This is especially the case where ministers and senior officials are concerned. Restarting a consistent programme of high level and other visits should be a priority. There is also a need to rebuild personal contacts between those involved in developing policy and implementing particular activities in both New Zealand and the Pacific. New Zealand has a wide range of such personal contacts in Polynesia, but to be an effective Pacific partner, we need to ensure that we also have a breadth of personal contacts right across the Pacific.

The use of soft power in the Pacific is sometimes seen almost exclusively through the lens of visits, development co-operation activities and, to some extent, sport. It would enrich our Pacific relationships if we were to address more consistently the implications of policy decisions for our Pacific relationships. We could also extend to the Pacific more of the public diplomacy tools that we use with developed countries, especially more mutual engagement in cultural activities.

Big Global Issues and the Blue Pacific Region

'Big global issues' increasingly dominate foreign policy discourse. Today's list includes not only changing global strategic security and economic balances but also broader challenges across the policy spectrum: challenges to democracy, multilateralism, climate and health. For the Blue Pacific, defined by the ocean, the health of oceans and ocean resources is a primary global concern. Other important issues on the global agenda include gender and diversity, movement of people, whether through labour mobility or as refugees, indigenous rights, transnational crime and the increasing connectedness of everything, driven by digitalisation.

Pacific nations have demonstrated the ability to place themselves at the centre of global debate and negotiations on issues that impact on them most closely, especially on climate change, oceans and fish management. Pacific nations have been active in the whole range of international negotiations that bear on these issues, from the UN Convention on the Law of the Sea to the Western and Central Pacific Fisheries Agreement, to the success of the Pacific Islands Forum Fisheries Agency.

Climate change is an existential issue for small island states, who see their very existence threatened by rising seas and more destructive and unpredictable weather patterns. Their concerns have driven action by the United Nations. The health of oceans and the sustainable harvest of fish, especially tuna, is also central to nations that are larger in terms of their waters than land.

In these issues, the Pacific nations have shown how countries that are small in population and land area but are coherent, serious and united in their voice can play a significant role globally. In these circumstances New Zealand's voice most effectively supports the voice and agency of our Pacific partners. In this regard the recent split in the Pacific Forum is a tragedy that needs to be resolved soon to ensure that the Pacific retains a strong and united voice at the global level.

In the last couple of years, the global COVID-19 pandemic has brought health to the top of international agendas. With fast and strict lockdowns, Pacific nations initially largely avoided COVID-19, but the Omicron variant has changed that and all Pacific nations now have COVID-19 in their populations. Vaccination rates have been inconsistent. Polynesia generally is far more highly vaccinated than Melanesia. Vaccination rates in PNG and the Solomon Islands in particular have been very low, apparently driven more by social media anti-vaccination disinformation than the availability of vaccines. This is a grave concern. It is not yet clear what the long-term impact of COVID-19 on the delicate health systems and on the populations themselves of these nations will be.

The Pacific Forum has been a central force bringing together diverse Pacific views on global issues in which the Pacific holds serious interests, and promoting them internationally. The split in the Forum over the appointment of the Secretary General has led to a quieter and diminished Pacific voice, which is clearly marked by its absence. It is of particular concern that this diminution of a united Pacific voice has occurred at a time when a contested global environment means that collegiality and a common voice are needed more than ever.

Some global issues resonate in the Pacific but can appear to be of greater concern to Pacific nations' partners than to the leadership of the nations themselves. Pacific nations still struggle with gender issues, including political representation and violence, although there is increasing recognition that they are important not only for some partners and groups of their own citizens but also for the overall health of their societies. Diversity is not a highly visible issue, although how to peacefully integrate different groups within Pacific societies still bubbles away under the surface in some Pacific nations.

The global place of China, including in the Pacific, economically and strategically, is a visible issue regarding which Pacific nations have been treading their own careful way through the global minefield, as has New Zealand. China has been an important and respected partner of most Pacific nations for many years. It is a key trade partner for many, and generally China has been careful to cultivate respectful relationships with those Pacific counties that recognise it, despite the disparities in size and influence.

How China's engagement in the Pacific over the last 20 years has changed is more complex than the present security-focused debate allows for. Many Pacific nations switched recognition from Taiwan to the People's Republic of China at the same time as much of the rest of the world. However, the Pacific retained a proportionally larger number of nations recognising Taiwan than most other regions. While Taiwan has been vigorous in its efforts to retain its partners, the competition between Taiwan and China has ebbed and flowed over the years. China's engagement in the region has changed over time. It became the largest trade partner for many. Immigration from China greatly increased across the region in the early 'noughties' but appears to have levelled off in recent years. The increase in Chinese immigration left the small grocery shop sector largely in Chinese hands in many Pacific counties, which has raised resentments. Chinese infrastructure companies entered the Pacific in strength, competing on price with existing Australian and New Zealand businesses, although questions have been raised about quality. All of this means that the relationships between China and Pacific nations are more complex, more long-standing and more embedded than the geopolitical security-focused debate allows for.

Geopolitically, the Pacific is more contested by more global players than it has been for many years. This discomforts Pacific nations, who resent their implied lack of agency in their own space. On the one hand, Solomon Islands and Kiribati's switch in recognition from Taiwan to China has received intense focus, all the more so in the light of the recently signed security agreement between China and Solomon Islands. On the other, numbers of other non-Pacific nations have also indicated their intention to strengthen their Pacific relationships. Britain has reopened its Pacific embassies; the United States has announced its intention to do so also, along with various other initiatives. Countries such as Indonesia and India, who have particular interests in the Pacific, have also announced their intentions to strengthen ties. The multiplying threads of debate regarding China and its interests in the Pacific are not easily reconciled. Some media commentary appears to be based on intelligence that has found its way into the public domain, but the information itself is not easily available. We need a better open understanding of the depth and breadth of the interactions between China and the Pacific nations in order to reach analytical conclusions about the drivers of these relationships and policy conclusions as to our responses.

New Zealand lacks an organisation providing independent analysis, policy recommendations and advocacy on behalf of the Pacific. This is an obvious gap, particularly when, for example, New Zealand media go to Australian institutions for commentary and analysis of Pacific happenings. An organisation playing the role for the Pacific that the Asia New Zealand Foundation plays on behalf of New Zealand–Asia relationships does not exist. We should fill that gap.

How Should New Zealand Use Its Soft Power in the Pacific?

There are two ways to read the question of how New Zealand should use its soft power in the Pacific. The first is: 'How should we use our influence in the Pacific itself?' The second is: 'How should we use our Pacific influence in forums outside the Pacific for both our benefit and the benefit of the Pacific?'

It is in New Zealand's interest as much as in the interests of the Pacific nations themselves that they be sustainable, socially, culturally and economically. We are a part of the Blue Pacific and what occurs in one part of its waters impacts on all of us that share the ocean.

The obvious answer to the first question is that we should be using our influence in the Pacific to build and maintain mutually supportive relationships that support sustainable development both in the Pacific and in New Zealand. Relationships are at the centre of soft power. Our aid programme funds many activities, but alongside the tactical implementation of projects, we should seek to build supportive and consistent relationships between our peoples, whether through direct engagements or with the various arms of governments and civil society organisations. It is difficult to know how much of this day-to-day engagement has been disrupted by two years of COVID-19, but it is time to pick it up again. It is essential that personal contacts and senior-level visits start to be programmed again.

New Zealand shares the interests of the Pacific nations in many areas of the global agenda and welcomes the agency they demonstrate to promote and defend their own interests. New Zealand's exercise of any soft power in relation to many of these issues is therefore mainly in terms of a mutually supportive relationship where we connect and support Pacific nations, for example on issues of climate change and oceans.

New Zealand is an active participant in many global discussions in which our national interests are at stake but in which Pacific Island nations have a less direct interest or engagement. Soft power in these instances looks more like the usual diplomatic engagement that takes place with any partner whose support we are trying to gain. New Zealand cannot, and does not, take the support of Pacific Island countries for granted.

In other areas, New Zealand's interactions are focused more on support through development assistance, which has been heavily impacted by COVID-19.

Development Assistance in the Age of COVID-19

Development assistance is a key tool of New Zealand's soft power in the Pacific. It supports development while also providing avenues for engagements. It is difficult to determine from the outside the precise impact of COVID-19 and COVID-19 restrictions on the nature and operation of aid programmes. It is even more difficult to determine what the long-term changes to development assistance might look like, but we can make some observations and ask some questions.

In terms of aid, New Zealand's funding in this year's budget is similar to previous years. What the funds are being spent on now is however somewhat opaque. It is difficult to easily find a plain-language description of the activities that are being funded in the Pacific. From official announcements, it is clear to see that work is clearly continuing on some long-term projects. Examples include support to policing in Bougainville and Solomon Islands; in the latter work is continuing on airport runway upgrades, and a recent announcement has been made taking forward long-term work to establish a second fish processing plant; support has been provided to Fijian elections, and so on.

A key issue for many Pacific countries has been the COVID-19-induced drop in government revenues, especially those that were heavily dependent on tourism. These include Fiji, the Cook Islands and Samoa. PNG was already experiencing fiscal difficulties, and COVID-19 has exacerbated these.

New Zealand provided an initial NZ$50 million support package to help the Pacific countries to prepare their health systems and address wider health, economic, governance and social challenges arising from the effects of the pandemic. The funding has also helped ensure medicines, food and other vital supplies have continued to move to where they are needed.

In addition to the initial funding package, New Zealand has continued to support especially those Pacific counties experiencing COVID-19 outbreaks with vaccines, personal protective equipment and medical support.

Although New Zealand has been quick to provide funding, including directly supporting Pacific budgets, the need is enormous and will be protracted.

What Next?

During the height of COVID-19, as appropriate and necessary, New Zealand's development funding was quickly turned to immediate needs to address the pandemic and its impacts. Borders are now largely open, which means that relationship-supporting activities can resume, but COVID-19 impacts remain, both in the islands themselves and in the broader global community. Development funding needs to return to longer-term and more strategic development support, but there are ongoing impacts of COVID-19 that still need attention. This is especially the case for the health systems and the economic situation of many Pacific countries, both of which are quite fragile in the normal run of events. There are more questions than answers as to what this support might look like.

It is difficult to determine what the level of COVID-19 threat will be going into the future. More transmissible but milder variants appear likely to be the case. But with vaccination rates still low, particularly in Melanesia, even so-called mild variants are likely to continue to put strains on health systems.

Border closures and isolation may mean that Pacific nations have become more accustomed to self-reliance. Development partners sometimes under-rate the human capacity that exists in the Pacific. It is a pre-Covid example, but the agency that Pacific Island countries demonstrated in the establishment of the Parties to the Nauru Agreement Vessel Day Scheme, which preserves fish stocks by limiting the period fishing vessels can operate, is a stunning example. We need more analysis of this impact of closed borders.

Pre-Covid, Pacific leaders, both government and non-government, spent significant time travelling abroad. COVID-19 has required them to spend more time at home, and the more complicated nature of travel post-Covid reopenings means than the extent of overseas travel is unlikely to quickly return to pre-Covid levels. It would be interesting to understand the impacts on ministers and senior officials of simply having more time at home to govern.

Another consideration is that economic management is changing in developed countries. Large spending debt-funded budgets have been acceptable in a way that would not have been the case pre-Covid. Even with the resulting relatively high inflation, economic structural reform programmes are taking a back seat in developed countries. Development partners tend to transfer their economic approaches into their development programmes. Economic reform programmes have been the backbone of our economic support programmes in Pacific nations. What impact on development programmes will there be of an approach at home that is more relaxed about higher levels of debt funding and places much less emphasis on structural reform programmes? What will take the place of these programmes?

It was already the case pre-Covid that Pacific countries were looking for partner support beyond simply funding projects in-country. It is likely that, with the demand for supportive interventions that require relationships and engagements with the donor country, not just funding for the recipient, relationships will grow. Sectors where there is a demand for this two-way engagement include trade, investment, health, immigration and governance initiatives.

The demand for Recognised Seasonal Employer (RSE) schemes was already growing, and in circumstances of hugely increased unemployment in many Pacific countries, this demand is now exploding. For New Zealand, this demand came up hard against not only closed borders and limited numbers of places in Managed Isolation and Quarantine facilities, but also against new approaches towards immigration that sought to place responsibility for New Zealand's low productivity on migrant labour.

This debate placed heavy emphasis on the (capped) 14,400 Pacific RSE workers undertaking only horticultural work. There was little to no comparable focus in the pre-Covid period on the more than 70,000 young people in New Zealand on Working Holiday Scheme visas. Their numbers are mostly uncapped and they undertake unskilled work, including in horticulture. While the question of entry to New Zealand for RSE workers has now largely been resolved, broader immigration policy is changing and appears likely to be more restrictive than it was pre-Covid. Some immigration initiatives for specific sectors have been announced, and RSE workers are returning. It is worth noting, however, that Australia permits Pacific seasonal workers to undertake work in a wide range of sectors, while New Zealand's scheme is limited to seasonal horticultural work. As New Zealand's immigration policy evolves, appropriate priority must be given to our Pacific relationships and to how the values we espouse are represented in decisions about migrant labour.

We need to be innovative in our thinking about policy interventions and relationships that support both Pacific Island countries and New Zealand's capability. The RSE scheme is one of these, but we need to think more broadly about how we can support the development of Pacific expertise, and use it to raise productivity in both New Zealand and the Pacific, rather than seeing them as being in competition.

New Zealand has a good history of support for education, especially basic education. We should double down on support for education at all levels, but at the same time recognise that in many Pacific nations there are simply not enough jobs for educated people. Can we develop solutions that support young people in the Pacific to contribute at home and potentially in New Zealand too?

For many Pacific nations, we may need to consider direct budget support for a significant period of time. Tourism may take time to revive, and may never return to previous levels. For those countries reliant on tourism, COVID-19 has exposed the extent of their economic dependence on a single sector. Economic diversification is very difficult, as New Zealand itself knows, but we need to support Pacific countries in taking a fresh look at their economic opportunities. We need to do that taking a true partnership approach that also reflects New Zealand interests and values.

Conclusion

New Zealand's soft power in the Pacific only works if our relationships are strong, our values are evident at home and offshore, and we are seen as a trusted partner. Our aid programme is a solid basis, but close and engaged people-to-people relationships are even more important. Increasingly complicated global and regional politics mean it is more difficult than it has ever been to balance our interests in the Pacific with our broader global interests. We need strong relationships to fall back on when that balance is difficult to sustain. We need to work harder to develop shared relationships with the Pacific in particular sectors, especially those of greatest concern to the Pacific. Developing local capacity is important, but we may need to find ways to implement support that go beyond an assumption that training local capacity should be able to meet all needs. Long-term subsidies for some functions in small island states may need to be considered.

To help develop all of this, we need an independent, Pacific-focused organisation in New Zealand with strong Pacific links and engagement that provides analysis, visibility and advocacy for New Zealand's Pacific relationships and supports policy development.

References

Mahuta, N. (2021, February 4). Inaugural foreign policy speech to diplomatic corps. www.beehive.govt.nz/speech/inaugural-foreign-policy-speech-diplomatic-corps.

Peters, W. (2018, March 1). Shifting the dial. www.beehive.govt.nz/speech/shifting-dial.

Part IV

Security and Foreign Policy Directions for New Zealand during the COVID-19 Era

Chapter 9

National Security, COVID-19 and New Zealand Foreign Policy

Bethan Greener

COVID-19 is a time-stamped phenomenon that has indelibly left its imprint on the world. Not only has the pandemic been responsible for more than six million deaths, but it has either directly generated or more indirectly exacerbated national security and foreign policy concerns too. For example, the last few years have seen an increased awareness of the use of different forms of pandemic diplomacy, the fragility of economic and supply chains, and the power of misinformation and its impacts on social cohesion. Here in New Zealand these pandemic-related issues have presented unprecedented challenges to officials charged with keeping New Zealand and New Zealanders safe and navigating the foreign policy arena. This chapter outlines the nature of New Zealand's pandemic response before considering key subsequent security developments, noting the ways in which the pandemic has either exacerbated known concerns or created new ones, as well as recognising that COVID-19 *itself* has not been overly securitised in the New Zealand context. But while New Zealand officials have, by and large, managed to minimise the myriad effects of the pandemic, some security issues seeded or amplified by the pandemic may well require careful handling in future years. Indeed, the overall effects of the pandemic — both direct and indirect — have reinforced the argument that national security is an ever-evolving and slippery concept (Baldwin, 1997).

Early Responses

In response to the emergence and spread of COVID-19, the New Zealand Government activated its National Security System on 27 January 2020, setting up a National Health Coordination Centre shortly after. New Zealand's first active case of COVID-19 was identified on 28 February 2020. Officials swiftly initiated a 'go hard and go early' approach. On 10 March, a National Crisis Management Centre (NCMC) was activated, augmented by an Operational Command Centre. Key actors at this initial stage included the Director General of Health, the Commissioner of Police, and representatives from the Ministry of Civil Defence and Emergency Management (Kitteridge et al., 2020). As a result of its 'go hard and go early' approach to the pandemic, the New Zealand Government closed the country's borders on 19 March; introduced an alert level system on 21 March that ranged from Level 1 (no restrictions) to Level 4 (strict restrictions on movement — or full lockdown); initiated a national State of Emergency on 23 March; and put the country into Level 4 lockdown at 11.59 p.m. on 25 March 2020. The legal justification for these executive decisions drew on the Civil Defence Emergency Management Act 2002 and the Health Act 1956 (McLean et al., 2020). Later, on 13 May, the COVID-19 Public Health Response Act 2020 was passed by the New Zealand Parliament to further buttress the government's response.

The early phases of the pandemic response saw the Ministry of Health and the NCMC take the lead, but this was wound down such that the lead agency role was handed to the Ministry of Business, Innovation and Employment (MBIE) in mid-2020, and the NCMC was replaced by an ongoing working group established within the Department of the Prime Minister and Cabinet (DPMC). The ongoing nature of the pandemic thus required the creation of a specific co-ordinating capacity. The membership of the National Response Leadership Team was established and comprised the Chief Executive of the DPMC, the Director-General of Health, the Secretary to the Treasury, the Commissioner of Police, the Chief Executive of the National Emergency Management Agency, and the Deputy Chief Executive of the COVID-19 All-of-Government Response Group, in the DPMC. When the initial-response-capacity NCMC was deactivated on 30 June 2020, the government then created a COVID-19 Group within the DPMC to continue the co-ordination of government efforts. Although the group does not have any statutory responsibilities, it provides advice to the government, seeks to mitigate risks, and takes the lead on public communication strategies, amongst other things (COVID Briefing to Incoming Ministers, 2020, p. 11).

It is important to emphasise the fact that prior to the pandemic the Labour–New Zealand First coalition government had earned broad social approval for its sensitive handling of the 15 March 2019 Christchurch mosque attacks and the December 2019 White Island volcanic eruption. When the pandemic occurred, official narratives drew heavily on this social licence to emphasise the need to pull together again as a 'team of five million', with exhortations to 'Be Kind'. Public approval of the Jacinda Ardern-led government's approach to managing the pandemic was confirmed by the results of the September 2020 election. This election delivered a majority Labour Government: a highly unusual situation in a mixed-member proportional democracy where coalition governments are the norm. Social cohesion was apparently at a high. But this was not to last.

As the pandemic developed and as the Delta variant emerged in 2021, the government shifted to emphasise vaccination and proactive management. By the end of 2021 the Alert Level system was replaced with a new 'traffic light' system that restricted gatherings and required masking and signing in, but which also allowed more freedoms for those who had attained full vaccination status. Public dissatisfaction about perceived discrimination against 'unvaxxed' citizens and unfair mandates grew. This dissatisfaction was accentuated by misinformation and external influence, as well as by frustration about other government decisions, such as the controversial Three Waters campaign.[1] This dissatisfaction resulted in Convoy 2022 NZ, an umbrella protest movement that incorporated a wide range of groups that coalesced in the grounds of the New Zealand Parliament. This encampment, and smaller protests that sprang up in Auckland, Christchurch, Dunedin, Whangārei, Tauranga, Rotorua, New

---

[1] 'Three Waters' refers to the government's plan to reform the delivery of drinking water, waste water and storm water. The aim is to bring these 'three waters' under the control of new, geographically based, Water Service Entities. This reform is controversial in part because it removes some of the control that local councils have over water delivery, but the controversy is predominantly related to the incorporation of a form of 'co-governance' with local Māori authorities via those *mana whenua* (indigenous people) having equal voting rights to local government.

Plymouth and Nelson, were eventually forcibly removed by the police, though elements of frustration remained and continued to drive occasional protest marches or occupations.

In many ways, these protests were overtaken by events as vaccination rates increased and the Omicron variant made controlling the virus more difficult, requiring a change of approach. The New Zealand Government thus moved more quickly than anticipated to do away with some of the controls that had been implemented to help tackle the virus. By the end of March 2022 most measures had been relaxed, signalling a return to more 'normal' life. By mid-April, New Zealand moved to remove most limitations on gatherings, vaccine pass requirements and masking. But the events of 2019–2022 had irrevocably shaped the security and foreign policy landscape in subtle and not-so-subtle ways.

COVID-19, Security Risks and Foreign Policy Concerns

The advent of the pandemic highlighted certain security risks and foreign policy conundrums. But it also highlighted some enduring themes in New Zealand's approach to security overall. In an early commentary, for example, concerning the impact of COVID-19 on New Zealand's national security, it was pointed out that Prime Minister Ardern's 'human-centred' approach to leadership was part of a broader historical pattern in New Zealand's foreign and security policy, one in which New Zealand's approach to security policy 'has been geared toward soft security issues' (Burton, 2020).

It is also important to emphasise the fact that the government's approach to managing the pandemic largely avoided securitising the issue. In this vein, no 'war on COVID was declared' (Burton, 2020). Even the way in which the military was brought in to support the pandemic response reinforced this civilianised, public health-oriented approach. Hence, although Operation Protect came to be the largest deployment for the New Zealand Defence Force (NZDF) since Timor-Leste in the early 2000s, with 800 or so personnel at any one time being rotated into pandemic support roles from mid-2020 to early 2022, all their efforts were undertaken in a clear supporting role. Military leads, for example, were seconded to MBIE whilst organising the NZDF effort, and only very specific and limited powers were granted for personnel to enter certain locations and to request information of civilians (Greener, 2022).

This pandemic response was thus framed more as a public health issue than a security one per se. This is despite the National Security Framework emphasising an 'all hazards — all risk' approach to defining what constitutes a national security issue, suggesting a broad understanding of security such that pandemics are in fact officially included alongside state and armed conflicts or terrorist attacks as constituting national security concerns. In this case, however, the pandemic was handled as an urgent public health issue that required a degree of border control, and control over the movement of people to stem the spread of the disease. The pandemic did not result in a highly securitised or militarised response, unlike in some other countries. Yet some observers have suggested that there were other, 'harder' security issues to be found with regard to the pandemic's broader impacts, and concerns have been raised as to the ability of a democratic government to enforce restrictions on the movement of people.

In a paper authored in mid-2020, for example, political scientist Anne-Marie Brady suggested that the outbreak had strengthened China and Russia and weakened the United States and the European Union (2020, p. 1). Brady noted the use of conditional assistance and misinformation by both China and Russia, as well as pointing out the economic risks that the pandemic presented to New Zealand. Although it is impossible to ascertain how the pandemic, as a single identifiable variable, has affected the relative power of key states, some of the issues raised by Brady and others are worthy of further attention.

The first is the fact that COVID-19 has, in diplomatic terms, brought a security-via-influence-or-soft-power dynamic to the fore. The second is that the pandemic has raised concerns about possible risks to New Zealand's economic security. Finally, the power of misinformation has had international and domestic consequences — including assertions that the Ardern Labour-led Government was behaving in an authoritarian or tyrannical manner in its management of the pandemic response. These three issues — pandemic diplomacy and strategic manoeuvring, economic security and social cohesion — have presented specific challenges to New Zealand officials working in the security and foreign policy fields, and these are explored in more depth below.

Risks and Concerns

1. *Pandemic Diplomacy*

The pandemic has provided a range of soft power opportunities. As well as facilitating vaccine diplomacy and strategic engagement, the pandemic has also impacted on both the nature of diplomacy itself (with mobility limitations requiring online or hybrid diplomacy to come to the fore) and the success or failure of certain management strategies, which have implications for a state's prestige domestically and internationally.

The first of these issues relates to the delivery of aid and assistance. The New Zealand Government's plans for the delivery of more than 2.4 million vaccines focused on recipients in the Indo-Pacific, with more than half of the first tranche of vaccines headed to Indonesia as one of the countries worst hit in the region (Strang, 2021). In keeping with its stated diplomatic and security priorities, and due to concerns about economic as well as health repercussions, the government also focused on delivering vaccines across the South Pacific, announcing in May 2021 that it would donate vaccines to immunise an estimated 1.2 million people in the South Pacific over the coming year, with priority going to the Cook Islands, Niue and Tokelau, then Samoa, Tuvalu, Tonga and Fiji (Craymer, 2021). This entailed not only delivery via the usual means such as air freight, but also a concerted maritime effort which saw New Zealand naval ships and NZDF personnel delivering vaccines directly to isolated islands (Keogh, 2021). Some contributions were also arranged through the COVAX scheme (the COVID-19 Vaccines Global Access facility), an international alliance seeking to deliver vaccines to poorer countries. Indeed, in addition to delivering the vaccines themselves, more than NZ$26 million in funds was donated by New Zealanders to support further government vaccination efforts via the scheme (Strang, 2021).

As noted above by Brady (2020), there are strategic as well as humanitarian dimensions to such pandemic diplomacy. Medical diplomacy is not new — the eradication of smallpox was hurried along by Cold War competition — and nor are the strategic intentions with which countries engage in that diplomacy. It has been notable that China has made a concerted effort to deliver pandemic aid in the Pacific in the form of financial support, the delivery of vaccines and personal protective equipment (PPE), information sharing, efforts by Chinese communities and medical teams, and the publicising of such efforts (Zhang, 2020). This adds another layer to concerns about strategic competition between those great powers active in the region. Such diplomacy, it is presumably calculated, can buy influence, with the example of the Brazilian Government changing its stance on allowing Huawei to bid for telecommunications contracts after the delivery of vaccines from China being noted as a case in point (Craymer, 2021).

The practice of pandemic diplomacy has thus been caught up in concerns about strategic manoeuvring and the ways in which donor states might seek to use their pandemic responses to exercise political leverage. Clashing vaccine delivery efforts in Papua New Guinea between China and Australia highlighted this issue, with the former Australian Prime Minister Scott Morrison directly asserting that Australia's vaccination efforts in the Pacific had prevented an 'incursion' by Beijing into the region (cited in *Reuters*, 2022). However, although for New Zealand the delivery of vaccines may have had some strategic intent, as suggested by the security studies specialist Anna Powles, amongst others, it is more likely that the government would have prioritised this effort for humanitarian reasons (cited in Craymer, 2021). Vaccine or pandemic or medical diplomacy thus adds another dimension to 'soft' and public diplomacy efforts.

Yet it is also important to recognise the nature of diplomacy itself has also had to adapt to the constraints imposed by governmental responses to COVID-19. New Zealand's approach to managing the pandemic effectively stopped travel, even at a ministerial level, which impacted relationships and left commentators to suggest that this inability to travel would 'cost' New Zealand dearly as 'diplomacy is as much about building trust and personal relationships on the sidelines as it is about tackling formal agendas' (Miller, 2021). Indeed, in 2019, the Soft Power 30 Index had noted Prime Minister Ardern's handling of the events of 15 March 2019 and the subsequent Christchurch Call (an initiative which sought to encourage stronger regulation of harmful online activity), as increasing New Zealand's soft power across the globe (Soft Power 30, 2019). By 2022, the authors of the index noted that the New Zealand Government's pandemic track record 'continues to be recognised as exemplary, but the decline of the nation's mental and physical availability around the world has caused its score to fall in other areas' (cited in Ensor, 2022).

Although Zoom diplomacy was widely utilised as an attempt to substitute for face-to-face engagements, including New Zealand's hosting of the Asia-Pacific Economic Cooperation (APEC) Summit in 2021, it is widely recognised that digital diplomacy is a 'mixed bag'. Although some have noted that it avoids some of the costs of travel (in economic, health and environmental terms) and thus broadens the range of those who may be able to attend, increasing reach and democratisation (Ray, 2022), it is also clear that the inability to effectively address sensitive issues in an online environment is a significant shortcoming. Moreover, it is well known that it is the informal opportunities to engage around formal talks that can be their most stimulating or rewarding aspect, and they are also useful for building trust. Hence the return to international travel in April 2022 was generally welcomed as a necessary step in combating rising perceptions in the region that New Zealand was 'isolated and unfamiliar' (Draper, 2022).

Finally, we can also note how the pandemic has impacted upon perceptions of effective leadership. Leaders in countries that managed to blunt the effects of the virus experienced increases in popularity and gained recognition abroad for doing so. In the case of New Zealand, for example, the early success of the elimination strategy brought increased credibility and status for the Ardern Government on the international stage. Moreover, the differences in the approaches of various leaders towards handling the pandemic — to 'flatten the curve' or to seek 'herd immunity' by adopting a 'hands-off approach' — initiated discussions about the possibility of strengthening connections with states that had handled the pandemic in similar ways. Yet as the pandemic evolved and as the virus mutated, the lack of a standardisation of approach across the globe to managing the virus has become, in a sense, less important in influencing the state of interstate relations. What has become of more importance is recognition of the various economic risks generated by the pandemic and subsequent responses.

Some issues straddle concerns about pandemic diplomacy and economic security. In the early months of the pandemic, for example, the New Zealand authorities worked hard to diversify sources of PPE due to concerns about the reliability of ongoing supply from China (Strang, 2020). Due to this diligence, New Zealand went from being totally dependent on China for all PPE supplies to accessing supplies from Spain and Taiwan within a few months (Brady, 2020, p. 4). The New Zealand authorities were similarly conscientious in attempts to secure vaccines, negotiating four independent purchasing agreements with pharmaceutical companies. A recent review of the vaccine procurement strategy by the Auditor-General has since confirmed that 'a clear strategy was developed and implemented', and that these agreements had deliberately included commitments to purchase more vaccines than strictly necessary in order to hedge against any 'uncertainty about if and when the vaccines would be supplied' (Controller and Auditor General, 2021, p. 17).

The pandemic thus brought very real concerns about the possibility of other countries stockpiling PPE and vaccines to the detriment of New Zealand. These concerns were directly pandemic-related and sit at the nexus of diplomatic and security concerns, but other more general concerns about economic security were also intensified by the advent of COVID-19.

2. *Economic Security*

COVID-19 has raised awareness of economic security risks, such as sites of over-reliance, supply chain issues or particularly vulnerable commodities. Certain activities were curtailed as ports became clogged and the movement of goods slowed. Economic sectors such as tourism and hospitality suffered significant losses during lockdowns, whilst these economic pressures, combined with rising inflation, have helped feed rising levels of discontent, discussed in more detail below.

Supply chain issues began to emerge soon after the pandemic picked up pace. By May 2020, New Zealand officials were seeking to shore up supply chain resilience in the region, working alongside Australia, Canada, Singapore and South Korea to better 'facilitate the flow of goods and services as well as the essential movement of people' (Parker, 2020). New Zealand was a keen signatory of a range of joint statements made via trade institutions such as the World Trade Organization and APEC in efforts to try to keep trade moving.

Despite these efforts, certain goods did become scarcer or more difficult to source. The shortage of timber and plasterboard during a time of increasing demand for building in New Zealand — fuelled by an apparent shortage of housing — has been among the more visible of these, but there are many more impacts of the pandemic on global supply lines that are less easy to identify. The semiconductor industry has faced a computer chip shortage since 2021, whilst logistic and transport costs have risen steeply because of distribution pressures and energy cost increases, impacting everything from vehicles to fuel, clothing, processed foods and manufacturing materials (according to Sen & Srivastava, 2022, Mainfreight, a logistics and transport company, has been forced to add between 20 and 30 days to normal shipping times for deliveries). Some laboratory work and other scientific activities, too, have been curtailed by the inability to guarantee the delivery of specimens in a timely manner. But in addition to the disruption of trade or the movement of commodities and people, perhaps of greater import is the fact that the pandemic has also increased economic security concerns.

'Sustaining economic prosperity' is one of New Zealand's seven key security objectives (DPMC, 2016, p. 8). Major disruptions and price shocks have been identified as two potential impediments to that objective (DPMC, 2016, p. 9). Clearly the pandemic has generated such disruptions and shocks. But it has also occurred at a time of New Zealand Government concerns about growing United States–China strategic competition and an over-reliance, or a form of trade dependency, on China.

Concerns about economic security have thus been specifically noted with reference to New Zealand's trade dependency on China. As Brady (2020, p. 3) notes, the normal definition of a trade dependence is a state being 50 per cent or more reliant on a sole market, and by 2020, 50 per cent of New Zealand's imports were from China. With China the epicentre of the pandemic storm, and as geopolitical issues have become more pressing, New Zealand's concerns about its perceived trade dependence on China loomed large.

Efforts to increase trade diversification have picked up pace. Notably, and ironically, given that New Zealand was heavily trade dependent on the United Kingdom in the post-Second World War era and was poorly served by the United Kingdom's entry into the European Economic Community in 1973, a significant new trade deal with the United Kingdom was signed into being in late 2021. In May 2022, too, the Ardern Government, along with twelve other states, signed up to the initiative of an Indo-Pacific Economic Framework for Prosperity. The Four Pillars of this framework are: trade; supply chain resilience; clean energy, decarbonisation and infrastructure; and tax and anti-corruption (Ministry of Foreign Affairs and Trade, 2022). Some commentators have further noted the possible relevance to New Zealand of developments such as the trilateral Supply Chain Resilience Initiative (SCRI) mooted in late 2020 and brought into being in early 2021 between Australia, Japan and India. The SCRI aims to identify vulnerable sectors and seeks to improve their resilience but also, perhaps more notably, provides a pathway for disengaging strategic supply chains (such as semiconductors and telecommunications) from China, hence enabling a broader decoupling (Palit, 2020). Notably, too, some regional partners have also initiated a more obviously securitised approach to economic issues. The Japanese Government, for example, recently introduced legislation aimed at buttressing economic security by a range of measures such as increasing its capacity for producing semiconductors whilst expressing concerns about alleged intellectual property theft, technology leakage and economic espionage by Beijing (Akimoto, 2021).

Notwithstanding some industries such as tourism and hospitality bearing the brunt of mobility restrictions, the New Zealand economy has, overall, remained robust since the outbreak of the pandemic. The OECD asserts this is due to 'effective virus containment, measures to protect jobs and incomes and highly expansionary macroeconomic policies' (OECD, 2022). In late 2021, in responding to news that the economy had fared better than expected through the pandemic, the Minister of Finance Grant Robertson suggested that this showed that 'our actions since the start of the pandemic to protect lives and livelihoods are working and has been the best economic response' (Robertson, 2021). However, the pandemic did exacerbate the gender pay gap and the disparity of health outcomes for different groups whilst laying bare the dire nature of New Zealand's housing crisis. Economists also note that the pandemic is at least partly responsible for steep rises in inflation, with 'pandemic-induced money-printing campaigns designed to stimulate economies' a major driver (Brettkelly, 2022). High rates of inflation have since increased the cost of living to a 'crisis' level where a third of New Zealand households are finding themselves unable to cope (Stock, 2022). These economic pressures have in turn helped to feed rising levels of dissatisfaction and social unrest.

3. *Social Cohesion*

On 23 March 2022, the New Zealand Government began to dismantle many of its pandemic control efforts. At that point, just over 200 people had died from COVID-19 or from complications caused by the virus intersecting with co-morbidity factors. In terms of the security of people's well-being, or in terms of threat to life, the New Zealand Government could therefore be said to have competently secured New Zealand citizens. For many, the decisions that were taken over the course of 2019–2022 directly saved lives and prevented indirect loss of life by protecting the health system from the almost impossible pressures observed overseas. Morale was damaged over time by the rolling in and out of different lockdown levels, and by the impacts of these efforts on business, schooling, sports and general lifestyles, but many still supported the general direction of the government's pandemic strategy. Some, however, became disenchanted.

Convoy 2022 NZ was a patchwork of individuals and groups with various causes coming together in their disapproval of the Ardern Government. Ostensibly motivated by opposition to the vaccine mandate system, those in the convoy or taking part in the subsequent occupation of the parliamentary grounds were often also mobilised by a variety of other issues. Many focused on the issue of 'freedom' more generally, some were concerned about the requirement to wear masks, others about the inability to open their businesses to the unvaccinated, but many believed that the government had become tyrannical in some way. A number of protestors therefore had other related concerns, voicing discontent about the 'Maorification' of government, or espousing conspiracy theories about the 'true' nature of the vaccine as involving tracking and controlling nanotechnology. Of significant concern was violence threatened at individual leaders such as Prime Minister Ardern, Minister of Health Andrew Little or Director-General of Health Ashley Bloomfield, with some protestors calling for trials, including the possibility of execution (Mitchell, 2022). Salient concerns were thus raised about the security (and health) threats posed by mis-, dis- or mal-information about the pandemic (Philips, 2022).

Convoy 2022 NZ highlighted a number of troubling developments — some of which are particularly relevant to New Zealand security and foreign policy. In fact, many of the ideas expressed by different members of the group had their origins in movements based overseas. The use of certain phrases (such as 'sovereign citizen') and acronyms (such as 'MSM' for 'mainstream media'), as well as the dissemination of misinformation about the nature of the vaccine (such as the suggestion that it makes the skin magnetic), were recycled from North America. Even groups that have appeared guileless, such as the 'mumfluencer' Voices for Freedom movement have been criticised for being 'cult-like' and linked to overseas interests (Johnston, 2022). Notably, too, the protest in Wellington was also apparently linked to similar and concurrent protests in Ottawa. Investigative journalism, such as that provided by the Stuff documentary 'Fire and Fury: Disinformation in New Zealand' (August 2022), and the work of think tanks such as the Disinformation Project have since confirmed patterns of external influence.

What this means is that, although these developments have increased security concerns about potential violent domestic extremism or threats to democratic stability, these developments have a strong international dimension too, bringing us to the concept of a grey zone conflict. 'Grey zone conflict' is a broad term that refers to aggressive practices below the official threshold of war (Dowse & Bachman, 2019). Seeding social unrest is an effective tactic for overseas countries or entities interested in weakening governments and societies from within (Carment, 2018). Part of the narrative of the Convoy 2022 NZ protestors about the overall situation emphasised a lack of trust in the 'mainstream media' or 'MSM', with some suggesting that the media have been complicit in enabling unwanted government policy to emerge (Mitchell, 2022), and hence alternative narratives were deployed on Telegram or other communication applications, as well as via live streaming from the protest itself. As democracies rely on an informed public, especially when that public is making election choices, the availability of balanced and credible information, and public trust in journalism as democracy's 'fourth estate', is paramount. In the European Union, for example, it is stressed that voters have the right to vote in elections free from coercion or manipulation (Colomina *et al.*, 2021). Mis-, dis-, and mal-information thus present a direct challenge to the workings of a democratic state.

In this case, moreover, mainstream media reporting about the protests in Wellington included both highly critical and supportive/understanding reports (*Radio New Zealand*, 2022). The majority of New Zealanders still express trust in the media, in public institutions and in the health system (Philipps, 2022). There thus remain some strong indicators of persistent social cohesion in the New Zealand context, but this question of a lack of trust in government or mainstream media narratives could be an issue that will re-emerge with increasing seriousness in future — particularly as such protest movements generate counter-protests (Williams & Killick, 2022).

Future Issues

In thinking about any enduring legacies of COVID-19, it is possible that such pandemics may well become a more regular occurrence. The apparent failure of the World Health Organization to generate a collective response to the crisis means that the absence of effective global public health infrastructure increases the likelihood of unchecked contagion. Although the New Zealand authorities will undoubtedly also work to support global or regional health and pandemic initiatives, it is national-level planning for border and population movement control, robust health services and strong strategic communication capabilities that will be most important for successfully tackling future events as they unfold. Managing more indirect concerns, such as threats posed to economic prosperity and security, means continuing with policies supporting the diversification of trade, decreasing reliance on overseas supplies in critical sectors, such as oil or pharmaceuticals, and shoring up options regarding supply chains.

However, it is in the field of information that more original initiatives will need to be developed. Increasing understanding about the creation and dissemination of misinformation, as well as 'pre-bunking' rather than reactively 'debunking' such information will be key (Roy, 2022) — as will increasing forensic capacities to trace and reveal inflows and the uptake of information coming from international sources. Notably, these efforts will be important for managing relationships between states as well as between populations within and across state borders. Much future effort will thus need to focus on developing new capacities and new skill sets.

However, Russia's invasion of Ukraine has also reminded the world that a more traditional form of physical, armed, interstate conflict is not unthinkable. This attack has also prompted further discussions about China's relationship with Taiwan, with some commentators suggesting possible parallels to the situation in Europe. Concerns about the state of geopolitics in the Indo-Pacific region have thus been exacerbated further. This adds pressure to governments seeking to balance the rise of complex problems requiring a broad array of response options with more traditional diplomacy and defence expenditures. More than ever, it seems, the New Zealand authorities will need to be masters of balance — balancing health and security, diplomacy and deterrence, and economic prosperity and support for desirable state behaviour. It is the exacerbation and broadening of the range of pressures on foreign policy and security practitioners that will be COVID-19's legacy.

Conclusion

Despite at face value looking like simply a public health issue, the COVID-19 pandemic has presented or exacerbated challenges to both national security and foreign policy. Governments around the world have responded to the various challenges birthed by COVID-19 in different ways. Indeed, in the earlier days of the pandemic it seemed as if the manner of response — from free-for-all to highly managed lockdowns — might create new alignments within foreign relations. As the pandemic has rolled on and new variants have emerged, however, the relevance of this has eased. Instead, certain diplomatic lines of effort have emerged in the pursuit of vaccine diplomacy and in the development of various economic security measures. New Zealand authorities have sidestepped some of these measures, avoiding diplomatic stand-offs in the delivery of vaccines into the Pacific, for example. At home, however, the pressures wrought both directly and indirectly by the pandemic have strained social cohesion. Economic security and domestic cohesion will need to be enduring foci for future governments, as will a readiness to face the possibility of another pandemic. Perhaps most importantly, this experience has demonstrated that such pandemics will have not just health dimensions but will also necessarily involve significant national security and foreign policy concerns, and that security remains an ever-evolving and 'essentially contested' topic.

References

Akimoto, D. (2021). What to expect from Japan's economic security legislation. *The Diplomat.* thediplomat.com/2021/12/what-to-expect-from-japans-economic-security-legislation.

Baldwin. D. (1997). The concept of security. *Review of International Studies, 23*(1), 5–26.

Brady, A. M. (2020, June 8). Brave new world: New Zealand foreign policy in the Covid-19 era. *Small States and the New Security Environment. Research Project Policy Briefs.* www.canterbury.ac.nz/media/documents/oexp-arts/research-centres/ssanse/Brave-new-world---New-Zealand-foreign-policy-in-the-COVID-19-era.pdf.

Brettkelly, S. (2022, March 17). The recipe for a cost of living crisis. *Radio New Zealand.* www.rnz.co.nz/programmes/the-detail/story/2018834447/the-recipe-for-a-cost-of-living-crisis.

Burton, J. (2020, August 24). "Go Hard, Go Early": Human security, economic security and New Zealand's response to COVID-19. *Centre for International Governance Innovation.* www.cigionline.org/articles/go-hard-go-early-human-security-economic-security-and-new-zealands-response-covid-19.

Carment, D. (2018). *War's Future: The Risks and Rewards of Grey-Zone Conflict and Hybrid Warfare.* Calgary: Canadian Global Affairs Institute.

Colomina, C., Sanchez Margalef, H., & Youngs, R. (2021). *The Impact of Disinformation on Democratic Processes and Human Rights in the World.* Report for the EU Parliament, www.europarl.europa.eu/RegData/etudes/

STUD/2021/653635/EXPO_STU(2021)653635_EN.pdf. Brussels: European Union.

Controller and Auditor-General, New Zealand (2021, May). Preparations for the nation-wide roll-out of the COVID-19 vaccine. oag.parliament.nz/2021/vaccines/docs/vaccines-roll-out.pdf.

Department of the Prime Minister and Cabinet, New Zealand (2020, November 2). Briefing to Incoming Ministers. COVID-19 overview. www.beehive.govt.nz/sites/default/files/2020-12/COVID-19%20Overview.pdf.

Craymer, L. (2021, September 21). Covid-19 vaccine diplomacy swings in Pacific nations' favour. *Stuff Online*. www.stuff.co.nz/national/politics/126350699/covid19-vaccine-diplomacy-swings-in-pacific-nations-favour.

Dowse, A. & Bachman, S.-D. (2019, June 17). Explainer: What is "hybrid warfare" and what is meant by the "grey zone"? *The Conversation*. theconversation.com/explainer-what-is-hybrid-warfare-and-what-is-meant-by-the-grey-zone-118841.

Draper, S. (2022, April 5). The importance of rebuilding New Zealand's "soft power" overseas. *Stuff Online*. www.stuff.co.nz/business/opinion-analysis/300570752/the-importance-of-rebuilding-new-zealands-soft-power-overseas.

Ensor, J. (2022, March 16). New Zealand falls in "soft power" nation rankings due to "COVID isolation policies" but still "punching above weight". *Newshub*. www.newshub.co.nz/home/politics/2022/03/new-zealand-falls-in-soft-power-nation-rankings-due-to-covid-isolation-policies-but-still-punching-above-weight.html.

Greener, B. K. (2022, January). The role of the military in New Zealand's response to COVID. *Kingston Consortium on International Security Insights*, 2(2). www.thekcis.org/publications/insights/insight-22.

Jack, M. & Corich, K., on behalf of MBIE (2021, April 9). *Rapid Assessment of MIQ: Final Report*. www.miq.govt.nz/assets/MIQ-documents/rapid-assessment-miq-final-report.pdf.

Johnston, K. (2022, February 22). "It's like a cult": How anti-vaccine "mumfluencers" are fuelling the Parliament occupation. *Stuff Online*. www.stuff.co.nz/national/health/coronavirus/300520631/its-like-a-cult-how-antivaccine-mumfluencers-are-fuelling-the-parliament-occupation.

Keogh, B. (2021, September 8). Covid-19: How some of the world's most remote islands achieved the best vaccination rates. *Stuff Online*. www.stuff.co.nz/national/health/coronavirus/126262881/covid19-how-some-of-the-worlds-most-remote-islands-achieved-the-best-vaccination-rates.

Kitteridge, R, Valines, O., Holland, S., & Carter, R. (2020, October). Second rapid review of the COVID-19 all-of-government response. Wellington: New Zealand Government, covid19.govt.nz/assets/resources/22-Mar-21-

Proactive-Release/Second-rapid-review-of-the-COVID-19-all-of-goverment-response.pdf.

McLean, J, Rosen, A., Roughan, N., & Wall, J. (2021). Legality in times of emergency: Assessing NZ's response to Covid-19. *Journal of the Royal Society of New Zealand, 51*(1), 197–213.

Ministry of Foreign Affairs and Trade, New Zealand (2022). Indo-Pacific economic framework for prosperity. www.mfat.govt.nz/en/trade/free-trade-agreements/free-trade-agreements-under-negotiation/indo-pacific-economic-framework-for-prosperity.

Miller, G. (2021, September 3). COVID-19 continues to impact New Zealand's diplomacy. *The Diplomat*, thediplomat.com/2021/09/covid-19-continues-to-impact-new-zealands-diplomacy.

Mitchell, C. (2022, February 12). Inside the disorienting, contradictory swirl of the convoy, as seen through its media mouthpiece. *Stuff Online*, www.stuff.co.nz/national/health/coronavirus/127741171/inside-the-disorienting-contradictory-swirl-of-the-convoy-as-seen-through-its-media-mouthpiece.

OECD (2022, January). *New Zealand Economic Snapshot: Economic Survey of New Zealand*. www.oecd.org/economy/new-zealand-economic-snapshot.

Philips, J. (2022, May). The threat we all face? Mis/dis/malinformation on social media in NZ and beyond. Video Presentation for *Democracy, Social Media and Security in Aotearoa. Massey University Online Conference*, 2–5 May. digitalculturelab.co.nz/?page_id=175.

Radio New Zealand Mediawatch (2022, February 20). Mad, bad or mostly moderate? Media's mixed message on protest. *Asia Pacific Report*. asiapacificreport.nz/2022/02/20/mad-bad-or-mostly-moderate-medias-mixed-message-on-protest.

Ray, S. (2022, January 20). The art of diplomacy gets a tech makeover, looking beyond coffee and corridors to a post-pandemic world. *Microsoft New Zealand News Centre*. news.microsoft.com/en-nz/2022/01/20/the-art-of-diplomacy-gets-a-tech-makeover-looking-beyond-coffee-and-corridors-to-a-post-pandemic-world.

Reuters (2022, March 13). Australia's vaccine diplomacy in Pacific Islands wards off Beijing: PM Morrison. *The Straits Times*. www.straitstimes.com/asia/australianz/australias-vaccine-diplomacy-in-pacific-islands-wards-off-beijing-pm-morrison.

Robertson, G. (2021, December 16). NZ economy's resilience shown despite COVID impacts. *Press Release*. www.beehive.govt.nz/release/nz-economy%E2%80%99s-resilience-shown-despite-covid-impacts#:~:text=GDP%20declined%20a%20less%20than,Year%20Economic%20and%20Fiscal%20Update.

Roy, R. (2022, May). Going down the rabbit hole: Analysing the narratives and techniques of COVID misinformation and denialism in Aotearoa New Zealand. Video Presentation for *Democracy, Social Media and Security in Aotearoa.*

Massey University Online Conference, 2–5 May. digitalculturelab.co.nz/?page_id=175.

Sen, R. & Srivastava, S. (2022, February 18). The pandemic exposes New Zealand's supply chain vulnerability — be ready for more inflation in the year ahead. *The Conversation.* theconversation.com/the-pandemic-exposes-nzs-supply-chain-vulnerability-be-ready-for-more-inflation-in-the-year-ahead-176232.

Soft Power 30 (2019). New Zealand 2019 overview. softpower30.com/country/new-zealand.

Stock, R. (2022, April 8). A third of households not coping with cost of living crisis and women carry the worry load — Westpac. *Stuff Online.* www.stuff.co.nz/business/128295298/a-third-of-households-not-coping-with-cost-of-living-crisis-and-women-carry-the-worry-load--westpac.

Strang, B. (2020, April 17). "It feels like China will turn off tap soon": Fears over PPE importation. *Radio New Zealand.* www.rnz.co.nz/news/national/414466/it-feels-like-china-will-turn-off-tap-soon-fears-over-ppe-importation.

Strang, B. (2021, December 21). New Zealand donates 1.2m doses of vaccine to Pacific, Asia. *Stuff Online.* www.stuff.co.nz/national/health/coronavirus/127249083/new-zealand-donates-12m-doses-of-vaccine-to-pacific-asia.

Williams, C. & Killick, J. (2022, August 6). Tensions between rival groups at anti-government protest in Auckland Domain. *Stuff.* www.stuff.co.nz/national/300655526/tensions-between-rival-groups-at-antigovernment-protest-in-auckland-domain.

Zhang, D. (2020). China's Coronavirus 'COVID-19 Diplomacy' in the Pacific. *In Brief 2020/10.* Department of Pacific Affairs, Australian National University, dpa.bellschool.anu.edu.au/sites/default/files/publications/attachments/2020-04/ib_2020_10_zhang_final_0.pdf.

© 2024 World Scientific Publishing Company
https://doi.org/10.1142/9789811285165_0010

Chapter 10

The Ardern Government's Independent Foreign Policy at a Time of Great Power Competition and Australia–China Tensions

Reuben Steff

The principles of openness and inclusivity are especially key for New Zealand. Often language and geographic 'frames' are used as subtext, or a tool to exclude some nations from dialogue. Our success will depend on working with the widest possible set of partners.
 — Prime Minister Jacinda Ardern's speech to the New Zealand Institute of International Affairs Annual Conference, 14 July 2021 (Ardern, 2021).

Outcomes will be stronger and more enduring if they are built through dialogue, shared understanding, and taking account of a range of diverse perspectives.
 — Nanaia Mahuta, New Zealand Minister of Foreign Affairs, 4 February 2021 (Mahuta, 2021).

Introduction

In recent years, deteriorating ties between Australia and China have mirrored, in many ways, the worsening of United States–China relations over the same period. This has led to a debate over whether a new 'Cold War' is under way and if a bipolar or multipolar system is emerging that signals the end of US global pre-eminence and the onset of a more competitive and dangerous world (Kaplan, 2019; Zhao, 2019; Christensen, 2021; Coats, 2020; Gladstone, 2020; Goldstein, 2020; Zakaria, 2020; Kupchan, 2021; Shuyong & Boran, 2021; Xing & Bernal-Meza, 2021). Clearly, in military affairs (as discussed in the next section) there are some hallmarks of Cold War-style military balancing and counterbalancing taking place but, especially in economic affairs, there is a breadth and depth of United States–China economic interchange (outside of the sensitive high-tech sector, where the United States has gone some way to decoupling from China (Bateman, 2022) — as well as China's key position in the global economic system — that sets the current contest apart from the United States–Soviet Cold War. Furthermore, the globalised nature of the current international system, as well as the geographic locations of the United States and China (and the limited willingness or inability, so far, of the latter to create a US-style extended alliance system), ensure that the Washington–Beijing competition will likely, in many key respects, be distinct from the United States–Soviet tussle.

In terms of polarity, it should be recognised that, according to material power metrics, the United States and China are the only two states that could be considered as superpowers today — they are ahead of everyone else by a decent margin and there are no near-term major competitors to their positions (Kupchan, 2021; Bekkevold & Tunsjø, 2022). Therefore, on a material level, the overall balance of power is arguably bipolar, even as many regional balances are considered multipolar. This exists even as we must recognise the current international system is more complex and states are more economically interdependent today than at any prior time in human history, and potentially material metrics may equate to less global influence than they did in the decades and centuries before 1991.

Irrespective of how we interpret the new competition, United States–China competition appears to be *a new structural reality for international relations* and diplomacy. It is not hyperbole to say that grappling with it should be the highest priority for New Zealand's foreign and defence policymakers. As part of the new equation, Washington and Canberra are portraying China as both a military and ideological threat to democracy, and to their preferred concept of the international liberal, rules-based order — an order that has been immensely beneficial to New Zealand.

The shifting relationships and balance of power in the Indo-Pacific (and sub-regions like the South Pacific) has seemingly created a dilemma for New Zealand, given its close security ties on the one hand to Australia (its sole military ally) and the United States (a close military partner), and high levels of trade with China on the other. Wellington, therefore, has sought to balance relations between the two sides and prefers to take a relatively nuanced approach over differences with China compared to Canberra and Washington.

But the deterioration of relations between the United States and Australia, on the one hand, and Beijing, on the other, threatens to upend Wellington's balancing act, and great power conflict is no longer inconceivable — in 12 of 16 cases over the last 500 years, rapid shifts in power between rising nations and declining ones resulted in war (Allison, 2015). Indeed, notable voices are claiming that a number of trends suggest the prospects of a conflict between the United States and China may very well peak during this decade (Brands & Beckley, 2022; Foreign Affairs, 2022). Meanwhile, functionally, Canberra has seemingly dispensed with any notion of hedging or seeking balance between the United States and China, putting its cards 'all in' on the side of the United States. It indicated this when it joined the Australia, United Kingdom, United States (AUKUS) trilateral security arrangement with the United States and United Kingdom on 15 September 2021 (addressed in more detail as follows).

To address these rising tensions, some commentators have suggested New Zealand should act as an intermediary, leveraging its independent credentials and reputation for pragmatism and fair-mindedness (Tan, 2021). Yet these appeals rarely include a broader conceptual framework for such a role. To fill the gap, this chapter outlines what might be called *strategic liberalism* — a set of ideas consistent with New Zealand's aspirations (Steff, 2016). These ideas offer a foundation to guide Wellington's response to tensions between the United States/Australia and China.

As part of this, Wellington could make a conscious political decision to frame its objectives as more far-reaching than appears currently plausible. Ultimately, the intention would be to foster an inclusive and sustainable peace that contributes toward an emerging world order founded on great, medium and small power co-operation. The prospects for this can be improved if we credibly address — and shift the conception — as to the most effective way states can ensure their self-preservation in a 'self-help' world where there is no international sovereign to settle disputes. Historically, this has contributed to a cycle of suspicion, uncertainty and tit-for-tat cycles of behaviour that resulted in destructive great power wars (and costly competition short of war). To do this, it is suggested that a harmony of interests prevails in the existing interdependent international system where self-preservation and prosperity is maximised via co-operation and commitment to a rules-based order.

This chapter builds its case in four stages. First, it outlines the new competition in the Indo-Pacific region. Second, it discusses the implications of this for New Zealand's interests, and how it threatens New Zealand's current hedging strategy. Third, this chapter provides an overview of strategic liberalism and its key principles, and fourth, it puts forward a four-point Action Plan. It concludes that the stakes involved in the spiral of escalation in the Indo-Pacific are high and, while there are risks in New Zealand adopting a more proactive posture, the present trajectory of great power relations is already threatening to undermine the foundation of Wellington's hedging strategy.

A New Era of Indo-Pacific Competition

A multi-dimensional process of competition and interconnectedness is under way across the Indo-Pacific. It comprises military balancing and counterbalancing, economic competition, new institutional arrangements, territorial disputes, coercive diplomacy and a dash for military–technological advantage.

Washington, under the Trump Administration (2017–2021), portrayed China to be a 'revisionist power' that was undermining the international order, and officially elevated great power competition to the forefront of US grand strategy (Trump White House, 2017, p. 25; US Department of Defense, 2018; Pompeo, 2020).

A hard policy turn against China took place. This included a trade war; partial decoupling from China in high technology areas; tightening visa rules for Chinese Communist Party members; and launching investigations into Chinese efforts to acquire research by scientists employed by US universities and research institutes. Additionally, the Pacific Deterrence Initiative (Shelbourne, 2021) — a plan designed, according to US officials, to 'maintain a credible balance of military power' vis-à-vis China's expanding military to 'reassure US allies and partners, and send a strong signal to the Chinese Communist Party that the American people are committed to defending US interests in the Indo-Pacific') — was announced, and ties between India, Japan and Australia, the four members of the Quadrilateral Security Dialogue (Indo-Pacific Quad), were reinvigorated (Akita & Sugiura, 2020). Furthermore, countries across Europe, from

Britain to France, Germany and Russia are all increasing their respective interests in the region, producing their own Indo-Pacific strategies and dispatching naval forces for manoeuvres (Wintour, 2021). Rather than the Pacific living up to its name, the possibility, if not probability, of increased militarisation of the region beckons.

The arrival of the Biden Administration did not change the fundamental trajectory of United States–China relations, with its *Interim National Security Strategic Guidance* declaring China to be 'the only competitor potentially capable of combining its economic, diplomatic, military, and technological power to mount a sustained challenge to a stable and open international system' (White House, March 2021, p. 8). As such, the Biden Administration seeks to enact domestic and foreign policies to allow the United States to 'prevail in strategic competition with China' (White House, March 2021, p. 20). Relative to its predecessor, the Biden Administration has elevated ideological differences with Beijing in its strategy, believing this will clarify the difference between the US and Chinese world view and rally more nations to its side. Yet while tactics shifted, the emphasis on competition has remained a hallmark of the Biden Administration's policy, and no breakthrough in United States–China relations has been forthcoming.

Meanwhile, Wellington's sole military ally by treaty, Australia, became engaged in a heated back-and-forth spat with Beijing in 2016 over the nature and extent of Chinese influence in Australian politics, society and economy, and China's maritime claims and activities in the South China Sea. In July 2020, Canberra took significant steps in the military sphere with China in mind by announcing a plan to spend A$270 billion over the next decade to strengthen its industrial defence infrastructure and extend the reach and power of its military forces. Many of the new capabilities it entails are designed for deterring Beijing and imposing costs in the event of a conflict (including new Long-Range Anti-Ship Missiles purchased from the US Navy; research and development into high-speed, long-range weapons, including hypersonic missiles, an underwater surveillance system, and improving Australia's cyber, information and space warfare capabilities; and potentially US missile defence systems) (Australian Government, 2020).

Canberra and Washington argue that their concern is Chinese expansionism on a number of levels. This includes Beijing's military activities in the South China Sea and naval build-up; institutionally, Beijing's new economic groupings and initiatives (such as the Asian Infrastructure

Investment Bank and the Belt and Road Initiative); diplomatically, its 'wolf warrior' diplomacy that has cast Washington as a declining and irresponsible superpower (with China positioned to take its place); and ideologically, Beijing's challenge to liberal values through its behaviour toward Hong Kong and Taiwan, and in Xinjiang.

The Chinese leadership did little to reassure its critics in the United States and Australia, declaring it is 'building a socialism that is superior to capitalism, and laying the foundation for a future where we will win the initiative and have the dominant position' (Xi, 2019). Meanwhile, the Chinese Communist Party domestically characterises its efforts as inevitable and natural; having been a great power for much of its history, China is rightfully returning to a position of global prominence that was waylaid by a 'century of humiliation' between 1839 and 1949 as Western powers, Russia and Japan intervened and subjugated China.

The outbreak of COVID-19 (and concerns about Beijing's transparency and management of the outbreak) compounded matters. It derailed a potential breakthrough, the United States–China 'Phase I' trade deal signed in January 2019, as Washington and Beijing politicised COVID-19 with officials on both sides launching a disinformation war that blamed the other as the source of the outbreak. By the end of President Trump's tenure, United States–China relations were at their worst point since 1991, with Chinese Foreign Minister Wang Yi declaring in May 2020 that relations had been pushed 'to the brink of a new Cold War' (Deutsche Welle, 2020).

The AUKUS Trilateral Security Pact

Nevertheless, until the outbreak of the COVID-19 pandemic it still appeared that Canberra (like Wellington) had sought to avoid having to clearly 'pick a side' between the Washington and Beijing (Köllner, 2021). But then Sino-Australia relations went into free fall after the Scott Morrison Government in Australia called for an independent investigation into COVID-19's outbreak in China in May 2020. This almost immediately resulted in Beijing banning a range of Australian imports (beer, wine, barley, cotton, lobsters and wood, and by December 2020 the ban extended to coal imports). Amidst further threats of trade bans, in April 2021 the State of Victoria cancelled its participation in China's Belt and Road Initiative.

The Sino-Australia spat culminated in the announcement of AUKUS on 15 September 2021 via a joint, and public, virtual teleconference that included US President Biden, Australian Prime Minister Morrison and UK Prime Minister Boris Johnson (White House, September 15, 2021). This new trilateral security pact surprised and shocked the region. If all remains on track, AUKUS will see Australia acquire US and UK technology to build eight new nuclear-powered submarines to be deployed in the late 2030s (Australia may lease and pilot US submarines of the same type prior to this). These new capabilities will extend the range, endurance and firepower of Canberra's submarine fleet. AUKUS also commits its members to pool resources, technical know-how and forge co-operation on cutting-edge emerging technologies (such as cyber, artificial intelligence (AI), quantum computing and hypersonic missiles) and integrate the related supply chains for science and industry. It will also lead to a greater presence of US air, naval and sea assets and personnel at Australian bases and ports, more rotation of US forces through Australia, and refurbishment of major military platforms.

The deal was considered a 'stab in the back' by France since AUKUS involved Canberra withdrawing from a deal (worth a reported A$90 billion) for French-made diesel-fuelled submarines (Vock, 2021). A Chinese foreign ministry spokesperson, Zhao Lijian, for his part, spoke against the pact, saying AUKUS 'intensified' the regional arms race and reflected a 'Cold War zero-sum mentality' (Geiger, 2021).

It was lost on no one that AUKUS reflected a further tilt by Canberra to align Australia alongside the United States and to join Washington in confronting and containing China's growing naval power. Indeed, the new nuclear-armed submarines cement Canberra as a key player in any potential future United States–China war due to the level of investment it will take, the long-term and sustained levels of co-operation it requires (along multiple economic–military–defence–industrial–diplomatic–technological dimensions), and the fact that, relative to French-built diesel-powered submarines, the new submarines will allow Canberra's submarine fleet to be at sea for longer periods of time, retain stealth, have more formidable strike capabilities, and operate over long distances to patrol the Indian and Pacific Oceans, including into the South China Sea (Pfeifer, Sevastopulo, Gross, 2021; Sadler, 2021). Robert Ayson made things plain, saying 'Any nuclear-powered submarines based in Australia, whether leased or owned by Canberra, will be an intrinsic part of a United States-led order of battle for missions focused on China's People's Liberation Army' (Ayson, 2021).

It is also telling that Canberra has publicly committed to joining the United States should Washington take military action to defend Taiwan against a future Chinese invasion (*Radio New Zealand*, 2021).

New Zealand's View

There was a wide range of responses to AUKUS in New Zealand. Prime Minister Jacinda Ardern adopted a middle position, saying that while she welcomed increased UK and US engagement in the region, the new submarines could not enter New Zealand waters due to its nuclear-free policy (Ayson, 2021). Yet this 'in no way changes our security and intelligence ties with these three countries' (Young, 2021). Nor is it expected to alter levels of naval co-operation, a potentially sensitive area for Beijing given these, at times, take place in and/or around the South China Sea. Indeed, New Zealand has long joined exercises in South East Asian waters through the Five Power Defence Arrangements (a grouping established in 1971 of Singapore, Malaysia, New Zealand, Australia and the United Kingdom), participation in RIMPAC (Rim of the Pacific) exercises (begun in 1971, they are the world's largest annual multilateral naval exercises comprising up to 22 nations) (Royal Navy, 2022) and, following the announcement of AUKUS, New Zealand's naval frigate *Te Kaha* and tanker *Aotearoa* exercised and trained alongside the UK Carrier Strike Group led by the (conventionally powered) HMS *Queen Elizabeth* and with US carrier battle groups led by the nuclear-propelled USS *Ronald Reagan* and USS *Carl Vinson* (Ayson, 2021). Given the expected increase in rotation and basing of US and UK military forces in Australia in coming years, there will be more opportunities for New Zealand to join military exercises throughout the Indo-Pacific and likely an expectation from Canberra, Washington and London that Wellington will do so.

Most non-government commentators in New Zealand (and some elsewhere) criticised or issued concerns over AUKUS. They fear it contributes to the heightening levels of militarisation in the region, undermines nuclear non-proliferation efforts (discussed below), dismisses the concerns of South Pacific island nations, and could place pressure on New Zealand to increase military spending to purchase additional military hardware to remain interoperable with the Australian, US and UK militaries (Blades, 2021; Edwards, 2021; Turnbull, 2021; Sukma, 2021; Laksmana, 2021; Ogilvie-White & Gower, 2021; Geiger, 2021). Some suggested that the fall-out from AUKUS actually presents new opportunities for New Zealand to deepen partnerships, particularly in the economic sphere, with countries that seek a middle path between the United States and China (this includes a number of European Union, South East Asian and South Pacific nations, and Canada). With these nations New Zealand has generally shared the desire to pursue a less confrontational approach to Beijing (Miller, 2021).

AUKUS and the Nuclear Equation

An issue that should greatly concern Wellington, given its nuclear-free policy and support for the multilateral nuclear non-proliferation agenda, is the potential damage AUKUS could do in this area in the medium to long term. As James Acton explains, this is because Australia's nuclear submarines will lead it to become the 'first non-nuclear-weapon state to exercise a loophole to remove nuclear material from the International Atomic Energy Agency (IAEA) inspection system. Other states in the future could opt to do the same — seeking a nuclear submarine programme to exercise the same loophole to acquire nuclear arms, and pointing to Australia as a precedent' (Acton, 2021). Nations with pro-nuclear weapon lobbies include South Korea, Japan and Saudi Arabia. They, no doubt, have taken note of AUKUS. It may also lead to nuclear submarine proliferation by China and Russia who, in 'tit-for-tat' fashion, seek to balance the trilateral pact.

AUKUS may very well turn Australia into a potential nuclear-weapon state. Given that Canberra lacks intercontinental ballistic missiles, a logical alternative, should they ever seek a nuclear strike capability, would be to acquire nuclear weapons for their submarines. This is not to say that a covert intention lies behind Australia's submarine programme but, rather, that the programme could in principle provide this should Australia feel the need to shift towards that direction. Given little is certain in international affairs and past Australian Governments' flirtation (from 1956 to 1972) with acquiring nuclear arms (Walsh, 1997), we cannot rule out that a dramatic shift in the regional strategic environment would compel Canberra to consider them once again.

Uncomfortable Realities

It is worth plainly recognising a few uncomfortable realities. In the South China Sea region, the military balance of power may have shifted in China's favour — and Washington and its allies appear unwilling to start a war to remove China's presence. AUKUS, from Washington and Canberra's view, may be viewed as a way to counterbalance China's growing maritime power, but it will take years (even perhaps decades) to manifest and on its own will not compel Beijing to withdraw its military infrastructure from across the sea; Beijing will likely strengthen it.

To be glib — for the moment, China appears to have established a predominant position in the South China Sea while ignoring international law and without firing a shot. This is, in effect, a challenge to the rules-based international system that New Zealand regularly affirms is critical to its long-term security (Ministry of Defence, 2021). China is also increasing its presence and influence in the South Pacific through greater levels of diplomacy, trade, aid and loans, infrastructure development (with dual-use utility — for example, ports can be used for both trade activity and military operations) and increasing security and military co-operation (Zhang, 2020; Pryke, 2020). The New Zealand Government's 2021 *Defence Assessment* was forthright on this, declaring of the 'establishment of a military base or dual-use facility in the Pacific by a state that does not share New Zealand's values and security interests: Such a development would fundamentally alter the strategic balance of the region' (Ministry of Defence, 2021, p. 23). Indeed, the recent announcement of an agreement to expand security co-operation between China and the Solomon Islands (notably, an agreement between Australia and the Solomons already exists), followed by a tour of the South Pacific by Chinese Foreign Minister Wang, which led to further agreements with Pacific nations but which failed to secure Beijing's objective of forging a regional trade and security agreement, suggests the balance of influence in the region is slowly shifting and that China's navy may eventually secure a permanent base or naval access (CNBC, 2022; O'Brien, 2022).

Ultimately, public recrimination does not change the reality that unless someone wants to open Pandora's box and head into a military confrontation with China, the nations of the Indo-Pacific need to learn to live with an emboldened Beijing. And New Zealand, Canberra and Washington need to deal with a new superpower that has different values and a markedly different political system to their own.

Implications for New Zealand

The interconnected global system means the consequences of crises and conflicts in distant regions do not stay localised — they cascade outwards to affect New Zealand and other geographically distant actors. The events in Ukraine since February/March 2014 — after Russia annexed Crimea — and since 24 February 2022 — when Russia launched a full-scale invasion of Ukraine — have been a sharp reminder of this. As a result of the former, tit-for-tat sanctions between Russia and the European Union resulted in a glut of dairy products on the international market for a time. This significantly decreased dairy prices, reduced New Zealand's export income, and torpedoed a once-promising economic relationship between Wellington and Moscow by forcing New Zealand to put a free trade agreement with Russia on hold indefinitely (*Radio New Zealand*, 2014; Duver, 2019). Furthermore, the latter has resulted in higher fuel and food prices in New Zealand, increased the value of the New Zealand dollar, exacerbated ongoing global supply chain disruptions and increased the chance of a global recession (Anthony, 2022; Rogoff, 2022).

The implications for New Zealand's interests as a result of a conflict between the United States and China would be far worse. Consider that a third of the world's shipping, carrying over $3.4 trillion in trade each year, passes through the South China Sea (Congressional Research Office, 2022). A crisis or conflict over the multiplying number of disputes between Canberra, Washington and Beijing would immediately compromise New Zealand's shipborne trade to China, and the security of our citizens in the region would be placed at risk. If the Cold War taught us anything, it is that crises — and 'accidents' — between competing superpowers *will* occur, and actors on either side can lose control. US House Speaker Nancy Pelosi's trip to Taiwan on 2–3 August 2022, was predictably viewed by Beijing as a provocation, leading to the largest military manoeuvres by Beijing around the island in decades and what some are now calling the fourth Taiwan Strait crisis (ChinaPower, 2022). It also, apparently, took place against the wishes of the White House and Pentagon, revealing how crises can occur despite the desires of leaders on either side (Wilkie, 2022). Miscalculations and unintended escalation were avoided in this instance but there is no guarantee they will not occur during future events.

Meanwhile, the Biden Administration's quest to get allies and friends to align with Washington's strategy vis-a-vis China is, on the one hand, welcome news in Wellington. It suggests greater engagement by Washington in the affairs of the Indo-Pacific, an effort Prime Minister Ardern has already endorsed. But Washington is signalling it expects more in return out of its allies to challenge China. This will include New Zealand, given its status in the 2017 *National Security Strategy* as a key US partner 'contributing to peace and security across the [Indo-Pacific] region' (Trump White House, p. 46), its designation as a Major non-NATO Ally (Department of State, 2021), and its involvement in the Five Eyes intelligence arrangement. Australia also seeks a greater contribution from New Zealand to US/Australian activities and will be lobbying for it to step up its game, especially in the military realm.

In short, Wellington will be invited to provide (so far undefined) contributions to assist in the containment of China's rise as a military power. Furthermore, we need to recognise that, in the event of a future military clash in the Indo-Pacific, Washington could ask New Zealand to provide a military contribution to a US/Australian-led effort.

China, for its part, seems to have immense economic leverage over New Zealand that it could choose to exercise were Wellington to align too closely with Canberra and Washington or join a more robust response to counter its expanding influence. After all, Beijing has already dished out considerable economic pain to Australia (costing Australian exporters A$5–6 billion) in response to what Beijing said was Australia's 'rash participation in the US Administration's attempts to contain China', and damaged South Korea's tourism industry in 2017 when Beijing limited travel to Korea in protest at Seoul allowing a US missile defence system on its territory (*BBC News*, 2017; Handley, 2020). While China has taken a nuanced approach to the behaviour of liberal democracies, distinguishing between the behaviour of Canberra and Wellington, it is not impossible that New Zealand — were it to act in a way or say something that Beijing finds especially objectionable — could be subject to similar economic coercion in the future.

Managing Relations

To balance its relations, New Zealand has adopted an asymmetric hedging strategy, aligning with traditional partners like Australia and the United States on some aspects of security and military co-operation, while maintaining a margin of difference through both the use of a messaging strategy that stresses New Zealand's independent foreign policy credentials and the absence of a working security treaty with Washington (Steff & Dodd-Parr, 2019; Ross Smith, 2020). The former signals ambiguity to Beijing over how tight the alignment is, allowing room for New Zealand to work at ensuring the continuance of high levels of trade with China.

It is, in good times, an optimal strategy, allowing Wellington to benefit from ties with all parties so long as neither imposes serious costs on it for sustaining positive ties with the other. But the decline in Australia–China and United States–China relations threatens the foundation beneath Wellington's hedging strategy — it raises the prospects that either side will try compel New Zealand to take steps that are viewed as undermining the other power's interests.

Ultimately, it is clear that New Zealand has an interest in a stable and secure Indo-Pacific region. Intensifying Indo-Pacific competition is at odds with this; it threatens the foundation of New Zealand's strategy. Diplomacy to address the escalation of tensions would clearly be preferable to New Zealand than a continuation of existing trends. Unfortunately, working against this it appears that an air of fatalism and inevitability has taken hold among commentators and governing elites, especially in the United States. There is a sense at times that some relish a new great power confrontation, as a perceived common threat from China provides some Western leaders with a mission to rally democracies into a countervailing force. Yet, no future is set in stone — countries, even small ones, have agency and can seize opportunities to push for change, especially as military solutions to disputes with China in the Indo-Pacific are exceedingly unattractive on a whole variety of grounds. This chapter now turns to strategic liberalism as a framework that could guide New Zealand's approach to Australia/United States–China competition.

What is Strategic Liberalism?

The two words that comprise the phrase strategic liberalism are not a contradiction in terms. Its prescriptions are strategic in that they improve the security position of states, and liberal in that they require co-operation between them. It incorporates the idea that states have a harmony of interests (Owen, 1994), based upon the twin objectives of ensuring self-preservation and prosperity, with the two going hand in hand given it is practically impossible for a state to ensure its self-preservation in the modern global economy without ensuring the prosperity of its people. This, in turn, is maximised by liberal policies that reduce barriers to trade and guarantee the rights of all states to sovereignty and self-determination. As such, many illiberal states (until recently this included China for much of the post-1971 period) have recognised the value to their interests of the liberal, rules-based order. However, intensified great power competition (and war in the worst-case scenario) characterised by military balancing and counterbalancing could decisively cripple the very trade that is necessary for prosperity and for achieving the realist emphasis on self-preservation in the contemporary international system.

This strategic liberalisms core principles are outlined as follows:

Strategic liberalism: Core principles and objectives

- *Anti-determinism*: The continued decline of relations between the United States/Australia and China, for example, is not inevitable, given active diplomacy.
- *Recognising and creating a harmony of interests*: Interdependence means states have a common interest via recognising the interrelationship between self-preservation and prosperity in a globalised economy. In this, states should strive for ambitious goals that maximise common interests.
- Open multilateral organisations and architectures in which states practise and encourage transparency while sharing knowledge and expertise/best practices.
- *Diplomacy and rapprochement*: As discussed below, pathways exist towards assisting states in overcoming security dilemmas through diplomatic spirals of confidence-building activities comprising signalling and reciprocation.

Recognising that overall security is reduced when states take unilateral decisions in the realm of strategic–military affairs, strategic liberalism opens space for a new co-operative approach: one in which states can seek security without intentionally decreasing the security of others. This approach is consistent with the principles espoused in the inaugural speech of New Zealand Foreign Minister, Nanaia Mahuta, to the Wellington diplomatic corps in February 2021. Amongst other things, Mahuta said: 'outcomes will be stronger and more enduring if they are built through dialogue, shared understanding, and taking account of a range of diverse perspectives'; New Zealand 'can offer a mature approach to dialogue aimed at progressing regional and global priorities', and Wellington has 'a deep stake in the wider Indo-Pacific region's stability. We share the common ambition of Peace and Prosperity for the region' (Mahuta, 2021).

The vision of strategic liberalism is also consistent with Prime Minister Ardern's speech to the New Zealand Institute of International Affairs Annual Conference in July 2021. Noting that 'the Indo-Pacific is to some degree at an inflection point', she declared the following principles should guide New Zealand's foreign policy:

> '*Openness:* that the region is open for trade, investment, and the movement of people to support prosperity and open supply chains ... *Inclusivity:* that all countries in the region can participate ... That sovereignty is upheld and respected ... *Transparency:* that states are honest about their foreign policy objectives and initiatives beyond their borders ... In our view, the Indo-Pacific region will need to conduct its affairs in accordance with these principles if it is to successfully address common challenges' (Ardern, 2021).

Her speech also connected to the non-exclusionary objective of strategic liberalism, as she said 'the principles of openness and inclusivity are especially key for New Zealand. Often language and geographic 'frames' are used as subtext, or a tool to exclude some nations from dialogue. Our success will depend on working with the widest possible set of partners' (Ardern, 2021). This is a point that would not be lost on Chinese decision makers, given their concern over the alignments and alliances the United States is developing throughout the Indo-Pacific.

In short, strategic liberalism embodies the view that greater security requires states to work together and envisions a wellspring of new thinking to contribute to regional security and transcend security dilemmas.

Strategic Liberalism and New Zealand

Strategic liberalism assumes that strategic futures are inherently indeterminate and that we need not repeat the tragic mistakes of the past; a reinvigorated twenty-first-century great power rivalry, with the attendant risks and instability it will produce, is not inevitable. With determined diplomacy and ambition, alternative outcomes are possible.

It encourages New Zealand to emphasise *open polylateralism*: commitment to partnerships based on core interests and values in international affairs and open multilateral architectures that do not exclude other states or non-state actors. This is an important point: closed multilateral and security architectures generate feelings of insecurity amongst others, generating pressure to form countervailing alliances.

Overcoming what realist observers call security dilemmas in international relations is a key objective of strategic liberalism, and the United States/Australia–China competition has all the hallmarks of this dynamic (Jervis, 1976; Jervis, 1978; Glaser, 1997; Taliaferro, 2000–2001; Tang, 2009; Steff & Khoo, 2014; Johnson, 2018; Ekmektsioglou & Lee, 2022). This is a dynamic where states have defensive intentions but, nonetheless, perceive their opponents to be aggressive and offensive. To defend themselves, they are compelled to enhance and expand their military forces, acquire territory, and forge and deepen alliances. In short, they engage in activities that are practically indistinguishable from a state bent on conquest. A tit-for-tat spiral of action and reaction commences, heightening tensions and increasing the chances of conflict even though no state desires it. Fears and mistrust intensify on both sides and a net decrease in security occurs.

Security dilemmas are fundamentally tragic and self-defeating. This is especially the case in an increasingly interdependent international system where security is indivisible — unilateral military actions in recent years and decades have rarely redounded to the aggressor by delivering significant gains or, in their wake, benefited other states in the region or beyond it. As such, it seems evident that states can best improve their positions by working with one another. If both sides can acknowledge their joint predicament, the principles and assumptions of strategic liberalism offer the potential to change the equation through programmatic steps to reassure one another and transform each states' view of the other's intentions. Through ambitious diplomacy, strategic liberalism can open up new avenues to build confidence, blunting the fears held on both sides and dampening the cycle of negative tit-for-tat behaviour.

A Path Forward

A significant change in the global and regional balance of power is taking place in the Indo-Pacific as China rises, and it is the thousands of small decisions and changes in interpretation of the other state's intention that will determine the future stability of the Indo-Pacific region as to whether a co-operative or aggressively competitive mode of behaviour prevails.

Therefore, as it relates to Australia/United States–China tensions, a maximalist objective via the framework of strategic liberalism is for New Zealand to adopt a facilitator or 'circuit breaker' role in diplomacy to disrupt the spiralling security dilemma. To this end, a four-pronged Action Plan is contained in the table below. Each prong is intended to be mutually complementary but they need not be pursued as a full set — pursuing just some of them may deliver a positive pay-off, and surely at least considering and debating them does no harm. I recognise that some will critique the plan below for being naive (I would hope the analysis and characterisation of the regional state of affairs in this chapter would dispel a sense that this writer is naive), but if New Zealand fears that it cannot promote the cause of peace and diplomacy in the Indo-Pacific, then the world will truly have entered a bleak period.

Point 1 would require time to develop and embed. New intellectual and material investment would be required, and relevant research, training and teaching capacity developed. The objective would be to create a New Zealand-based, specialised Centre of Excellence able to work with other existing expertise at academic and government institutions in New Zealand working on different aspects of Indo-Pacific geopolitics and economics.[1]

The institution would seek to train New Zealand Government staff about geopolitics (broadly defined to include salient aspects of strategic studies and international relations for practitioners), and the emerging dynamics of the contemporary Australia/United States–China confrontation. This could include residential or full-day training sessions as part of its ambit.

Point 2 has already been suggested by a number of commentators, but it is worth briefly elaborating: the objective of such talks would be to move the region toward a reassurance programme that includes incremental efforts in both military and non-military realms, centred on reciprocal restraint, trust-building, and creating a cycle of co-operation. A meaningful regional security multilateral architecture is necessary. Ultimately, a non-aggression and non-interference pact between Australia/United States and China could be proposed.

---

[1] Existing centres of research and teaching in New Zealand address some aspects of Indo-Pacific geopolitics and economics include the Asia New Zealand Foundation in, as well as the China Contemporary Studies Centre and the Centre for Strategic Studies (the latter two at Victoria University of Wellington).

> **Action Plan: Addressing Australia/United States–China Competition**
>
> 1. Fund a new institution in New Zealand to 1. facilitate co-operation in the Indo-Pacific based on the principles of strategic liberalism; 2. up-skill New Zealand Government staff as well as personnel from relevant non-government organisations on great power competition; 3. direct attention to researching New Zealand's greatest strategic vulnerabilities (given the intensifying array of negative international trends) and the domestic state-building capacities required to address them.
> 2. Offer to provide a neutral location for Australia/United States–China confidence-building discussions over the South China Sea and other security-related issues. This could include an offer to host a United States–China high level summit at the Waitangi Trust National Treaty Grounds, supported by Royal New Zealand Navy (RNZN) ships off Waitangi and other New Zealand Defence Force assets in support.
> 3. Seek RNZN observer or associate status in the Indo-Pacific Quad grouping and the MALABAR series of maritime exercises in the Indo-Pacific theatre. Relatedly, Wellington should pursue an arrangement with AUKUS to access and participate in new and emerging technologies.
> 4. A call to evolve and direct the suite of international institutions towards the cause of international unity. This would begin by leveraging the COVID-19 pandemic into calls for a global public health-care system. This would be complemented by a global tax system to fund it; and an international crisis-management and quick-response system to global crises.

Admittedly, there are risks with this aspect of the Action Plan. A well-meaning diplomatic effort, but one that leaves New Zealand looking incompetent, insensitive and misguided, could harm Wellington's brand and interests. It would, therefore, be remiss if it made such an effort without adequate preparation and careful preparatory diplomacy.

Point 3 may appear to be at odds with the strategic liberalism agenda, but it is included to address one of the strategic realities of the region. New Zealand's security ultimately rests upon free and open access at sea, and is facilitated by the ability of navies to work with each other. Military co-operation, as evidenced by the MALABAR series of naval exercises, helps to build confidence, as well as contributing to regional peace and security.

It would be in New Zealand's immediate security interests to seek associate or observer status in both the Quad arrangements between the United States, India, Japan and Australia and the MALABAR series of naval exercises in the Indo-Pacific region (Gillespie, 2021). In time, China could also be invited to observe these exercises to reduce the possibility of miscalculation and misinterpretation.

Pursuing an arrangement with AUKUS to access and participate in new and emerging technologies is also essential for New Zealand to ensure it does not miss out on technologies that will prove pivotal to the Fourth Industrial Revolution. Despite surprising growth in New Zealand's digital sector since the outbreak of COVID-19 (according to New Zealand's Technology Investment Network, the country's technology exports in their entirety brought in $12.7 billion in 2020 — up 10 per cent from 2019 — and the sector aims to be the nation's largest export sector by 2030 (Steff, 2021)), New Zealand economically remains overly dependent on agricultural exports — an industry beholden to international price fluctuations and geopolitical shocks.

For those hesitant to seriously push for Wellington to engage with AUKUS, they should bear in mind New Zealand High Commissioner to Australia Annette King's statement in October 2021 that, while Wellington would never co-operate on the nuclear aspects of AUKUS, it could be interested in joining the agreement to collaborate on 'other parts of the architecture', such as the development of cyber technologies, AI and quantum computing (Galloway, 2021). Furthermore, in December 2021 New Zealand Defence Minister Peeni Henare said there was potential to 'leverage' off the opportunity of the 'technology gains' AUKUS may create. This line of thought has not just come from the New Zealand side, as acting US Deputy Secretary of State Wendy Sherman, during a visit to Wellington on 9 August 2022, said there could be 'scope for others to join' (presumably New Zealand) when the 'other emerging technologies' involved in AUKUS were considered (Miller, 2022; US Mission New Zealand, 2022).

New Zealand could balance this co-operation by encouraging AUKUS members to mitigate the proliferation risks of the agreement, drawing upon the recommendations of Acton (Acton, 2021). Furthermore, it would be wise to weigh up the potential diplomatic (and material) fall-out of pursuing an 'AUKUS-lite' relationship. Some preliminary diplomatic outreach to see how ASEAN states and China would view Wellington heading in this direction before committing would be prudent.

Point 4 is the most idealistic of all the recommendations, yet it is clear that the wellspring of liberal ideas underpinning the 'international community' needs active promotion and invigoration. A moment, like right now, where military-centric responses to the rise of China and Russia's invasion of Ukraine is precisely the time for thinkers to articulate an ambitious international liberal agenda. International institutions must become more effective, broader and deeper, and reach into a wider array of activities. Here, I suggest New Zealand do nothing less than articulate an agenda to create a global public health-care system, a global tax system to fund it, and an international crisis-management and quick-response system for global crises.

With respect to Points 1 and 2, Wellington could draw on the international relations specialist Charles Kupchan's ideas on great power reassurance, where initial signals act as feelers and require a corresponding reaction to induce further steps (Kupchan, 2010). The most significant signals involve a state opting to unilaterally decrease or reassign its forces and engage in joint arms control efforts to modify military postures and capabilities in a way that decreases the ability of states to challenge the status quo (Montgomery, 2006).

Charles Kupchan's Ideas on Great Power Reassurance

1. States should take steps to initiate cycles of positive action–reaction processes.
2. Arms control and modifying military postures and capabilities can send signals of peaceful intent and a desire for mutual accommodation.
3. Withholding power and influence where a state has a preponderance of power (foregoing short-term gains of primacy) is an investment in stability over the long term.
4. Stronger parties are capable of making initial openings and concessions, given their relative strength, and provide some insulation should weaker parties not reciprocate.
5. Mutual deterrence is an indirect form of relationship management; it creates a stable basis for accommodation and rapprochement to take place.
6. States seek *security* rather than conquest. As such, states can overcome hostility, mutual distrust and security dilemmas through rapprochement programmes aimed at reducing fear and facilitating co-operation.

Arguably, the power of Australia, the United States and China affords them the capacity to offer concessions in specific areas where they have a relative advantage compared to the other, and historical cases of successful rapprochement show that it is usually the stronger party that is most capable of making the initial opening that can lead to better relations (Bull, 1977; Boulding, 1978; Rock, 1989; Deutsch, 1998; Cronin, 1999; Buzan & Little, 2000; Kacowicz *et al.*, 2000; Buzan, 2004). This suggests that in an area like the South China Sea, the onus is on Beijing to bring something forward to accommodate the interests of the various other parties in the region.

A strategic liberalism framework would help facilitate an 'outside-the-box' and 'no-issues-off-the-table' conceptual approach. This is critical. Conceptual alignment between states over the make-up of the future multilateral and institutional architecture in the region is required — and it is currently lacking.

An inclusive and sustainable peace that contributes toward an emerging world order founded on great power co-operation between Australia/the United States and China is the ultimate goal. If New Zealand can play any small part in this, it should seek to do so. Here, a caveat is in order: while getting diplomacy under way is the central cog to a broader regional peace, it is imperative that it eventually evolves into a broader regional process. An outcome where Australia/the United States and China 'solve' their most significant clashes of interest but shunt aside or ignore the interests of other states is at odds with New Zealand's interests. It is critical to avoid a return to atavistic great power 'spheres of influence' — it would be seen as an abandonment of any intention of creating an inclusive and stable order in the region, leaving smaller powers to go it alone and pursue their interests in increasingly tense and competitive sub-regions.

Importantly, Kupchan recognises that co-operation between democracies and non-democracies is possible. He holds that assuming otherwise not only reduces the chance for immediate collaboration but 'discourages non-democracies from remaining open to mutual accommodation and the exchange of concessions — steps critical to advancing reconciliation and programmatic cooperation' (Kupchan, 2010, p. 408). An approach to Australia/United States–China relations that emphasises ideological differences all but guarantees that deep forms of co-operation will remain out of reach.

Point 4 may come across as fantastical *but* so were, once upon a time, the notions of international institutions like the United Nations, World

Health Organization, World Bank and World Trade Organization. Furthermore, some of the most pernicious effects of international anarchy (the lack of an international sovereign or world government) have moderated over time, as revealed by the political scientist Shiping Tang. In his social evolutionary approach, Tang has shown that the international system has been transformed from one comprised primarily of offensive and aggressive states to one comprised chiefly of defensively motivated ones (Tang, 2010). Co-operation is the most successful grand strategic paradigm for the contemporary international system, as a majority of states have been socialised into perceiving the use of military force to settle most disputes as illegitimate. When force has been used in recent times (for example the US invasions of Iraq and Afghanistan, and the Russian invasion of Ukraine in early 2022), the costs have outweighed the benefits. Tang's thesis is supported by the fact that general deterrence between states, rather than conflict, has become internalised, while nuclear weapons and economic interdependencies have reduced the chances of great-power wars breaking out (Freedman, 2004). In contrast, offensive approaches, which call for a self-conscious effort to contain rising powers — such as China and Russia — would prove costly and likely create a self-fulfilling prophecy of confrontation (Kirshner, 2010). Unfortunately, this is being borne out in reality right now, while the emergence of 'security communities' in many regions is a direct challenge to assumptions that competition and conflict are endemic; if the modern system privileged offence and aggression, security communities would never emerge (Jervis, 2011).

Conclusion

The negative trajectory of United States–China relations should be of immense concern to New Zealand, and even though President Biden suggests the United States and China 'need not have a conflict', he admits there is likely to be 'extreme competition' (Macias, 2021). This reflects a bipartisan position in US politics (Herb et al., 2021).

As such, United States–China competition is a new structural reality of international relations. No state, no matter how geographically remote, is free from its implications. The stakes involved are high. In an interdependent world, New Zealand's interests will be affected in the event of a serious conflict or crisis between the two Pacific superpowers. But, short of that, the trajectory toward ever more intense levels of competition makes New Zealand's hedging strategy more difficult to sustain; we are likely to find ourselves pulled toward both greater economic dependency with China and more co-operation on security issues with the United States in the Indo-Pacific.

At some point, the balance could tip too far in one direction, or distant events force New Zealand to make decisions in favour of one party that hurts its relations with others. It is recognised that a direct military confrontation could embroil us in a coalition or UN-organised response.

This chapter has made the case that the principles of strategic liberalism offer a conceptual foundation to guide New Zealand foreign policy going forward, and a four-pronged approach to enhancing our contribution to peace and stability in a new era of United States–China great power competition has been offered.

But even short of major diplomatic breakthroughs, these efforts could at least slow the speed at which United States–China ties are deteriorating and create new stabilising mechanisms to underpin them. It is also essential to recognise that rapprochement is often a long-term and iterative process. Progress could be slow and halting, and it could take a decades-long effort to move the region toward a more normal state of stability, but it is a goal New Zealand should do its utmost to support.

References

Acton, J. M. (2021). Why the AUKUS submarine deal is bad for nonproliferation — And what to do about it. *Carnegie Endowment for International Peace.* carnegieendowment.org/2021/09/21/why-aukus-submarine-deal-is-bad-for-nonproliferation-and-what-to-do-about-it-pub-85399.

Adler, E. & Barnett, M. (eds.) (1998). *Security Communities.* Cambridge: Cambridge University Press.

Akita, H. & Sugiura, E. (2020). Pompeo aims to "institutionalize" Quad ties to counter China. *Nikkei Asia.* asia.nikkei.com/Editor-s-Picks/Interview/Pompeo-aims-to-institutionalize-Quad-ties-to-counter-China.

Allison, G. (2015). The thucydides trap: Are the U.S. and China headed for war? *The Atlantic.* www.theatlantic.com/international/archive/2015/09/united-states-china-war-thucydides-trap/406756.

Anthony, J. (2022). War in Ukraine having immediate impact on NZ businesses, with ongoing fall out expected. www.stuff.co.nz/business/the-monitor/128027235/war-in-ukraine-having-immediate-impact-on-nz-businesses-with-ongoing-fall-out-expected.

Ardern, J. (2021). *Speech to the New Zealand Institute of International Affairs (NZIIA) Annual Conference.* www.beehive.govt.nz/release/prime-ministers-speech-nziia-annual-conference.

Australian Government (2020). *2020 Defence Strategic Update and 2020 Force Structure Plan.* www1.defence.gov.au/strategy-policy/strategic-update-2020.

Ayson, R. (2021). PacNet #48 — New Zealand and AUKUS: Affected without being included. *Pacific Forum.* pacforum.org/publication/pacnet-48-new-zealand-and-aukus-affected-without-being-included.

Bateman, J. (2022). U.S.–China technological "decoupling": A strategy and policy framework. *Carnegie Endowment for International Peace.* carnegieendowment.org/2022/04/25/u.s.-china-technological-decoupling-strategy-and-policy-framework-pub-86897.

BBC News (2017). South Korea tourism hit by China ban. www.bbc.com/news/business-40565119.

Bekkevold, J. I. & Tunsjø, Ø. (2022). The geopolitical foundations for U.S. strategy in a new U.S.–China bipolar system. *China International Strategy Review*, 4(1), 39–54.

Blades, J. (2021). Aukus pact strikes at heart of Pacific regionalism. *RNZ,* www.rnz.co.nz/international/pacific-news/451715/aukus-pact-strikes-at-heart-of-pacific-regionalism.

Boulding, K. (1978). *Stable Peace.* Austin: University of Texas Press.

Brands, H. & Beckley, M. (2022). *Danger Zone: The Coming Conflict with China.* New York: W.W. Norton.

Buzan, B. (2004). *From International to World Society? English School Theory and the Social Structure of Globalisation.* Cambridge: Cambridge University Press.

Buzan, B. & Little, R. (2000). *International Systems in World History: Remaking the Study of International Relations.* Cambridge: Cambridge University Press.

Bull, H. (1977). *The Anarchical Society.* London: Macmillan.

ChinaPower (2022, August 19). Tracking the fourth Taiwan strait crisis. chinapower.csis.org/tracking-the-fourth-taiwan-strait-crisis/

Christensen, T. J. (2021, March 24). There will not be a New Cold War: The limits of U.S.–Chinese competition. *Foreign Affairs.* www.foreignaffairs.com/articles/united-states/2021-03-24/there-will-not-be-new-cold-war.

CNBC (2022). China and Pacific islands unable to reach consensus on security pact. www.cnbc.com/2022/05/30/china-and-pacific-islands-unable-to-reach-consensus-on-security-pact.html.

Coats, D. (2020). There's no Cold War with China — and if there were, we couldn't win. *Washington Post.* www.washingtonpost.com/opinions/2020/07/28/new-cold-war-between-us-china-is-dangerous-myth.

Congressional Research Office (2021). U.S.–China strategic competition in South and East China Seas: Background and issues for Congress. fas.org/sgp/crs/row/R42784.pdf.

Cronin, B. (1999). *Community Under Anarchy: Transnational Identity and the Evolution of Cooperation*. New York: Columbia University Press.

Duver, A. (2019). Dairy: June Quarter 2019. search.informit.org/doi/epdf/10.3316/informit.512636010072185

Deutsche Welle (2020, May 24). China diplomat warns U.S. against pushing to "Brink of a New Cold War". www.dw.com/en/beijing-says-us-is-pushing-china-to-brink-of-a-new-cold-war/a-53550524.

Department of State, US. Bureau of Political–Military Affairs (2021, January 20). Major Non-NATO ally status. www.state.gov/major-non-nato-ally-status.

Edwards, B. (2021, September 22). Political roundup — Why Australia's nuclear-sub defence plans are unpopular in NZ. *Democracy Project*. democracyproject.nz/2021/09/22/bryce-edwards-political-roundup-why-australias-nuclear-sub-defence-plans-are-unpopular-in-nz.

Ekmektsioglou, E. & Lee, J.-Y. (2022). North Korea, missile defense, and U.S.–China security dilemma. *Pacific Review*, 35(4), 587–616.

Foreign Affairs (2022). Is China changing how it sees the world? Interview with Kevin Rudd. foreignaffairsmagazine.podbean.com/e/is-china-changing-how-it-sees-the-world.

Freedman, F. (2004). *Deterrence*. Boston, MA: Polity Press.

Galloway, A. (2021). New Zealand could join AUKUS security pact to boost cyber technologies. *Sydney Morning Herald*. www.smh.com.au/politics/federal/new-zealand-could-join-aukus-security-pact-to-boost-cyber-technologies-20211025-p592tr.html.

Geiger, J. (2021). AUKUS: Recalling legacies of Anglo-Saxonism and muffling the voices of Island Nations. www.e-ir.info/2021/09/25/aukus-recalling-legacies-of-anglo-saxonism-and-muffling-the-voices-of-island-nations/

Gillespie, A. (2021). Without evidence of real progress, NZ's foreign policy towards China looks increasingly empty. *The Conversation*. theconversation.com/without-evidence-of-real-progress-nzs-foreign-policy-towards-china-looks-increasingly-empty-158946.

Gladstone, R. (2020, July 22). How the Cold War between China and U.S. is intensifying. *New York Times*. www.nytimes.com/2020/07/22/world/asia/us-china-cold-war.html.

Glaser, C. L. (1997). The security dilemma revisited. *World Politics*, 50(1), 171–20.

Goldstein, A. (2020). US–China Rivalry in the twenty-first century: Déjà vu and Cold War II. *China International Strategy Review*, 4(1), 48–62.

Handley, E. (2020). China warns Australian economy could "suffer further pain" after reported export ban. *ABC News*. www.abc.net.au/news/2020-11-06/china-daily-warns-australia-economic-pain-export-ban/12857988.

Herb, J., Fox, L., & Mattingly, P. (2021). Republicans and Democrats have found one thing they can all rally around: Curbing China's influence. *CNN politics*.

edition.cnn.com/2021/03/24/politics/congress-china-economic-influence-bipartisanship/index.html.
Jervis, R. (1976). *Perception and Misperception in International Politics*. Princeton, NJ: Princeton University Press.
Jervis, R. (1978). Cooperation under the security dilemma. *World Politics, 30*(2), 167–74.
Jervis, R. (2011). Force in our times. *International Relations, 25*(4), 403–25.
Johnson, J. (2018). *The US–China Military and Defense Relationship during the Obama Presidency*. Cham: Springer International.
Kacowicz, A., Bar-Siman-Tov, Y., Elgström, O., & Jerneck, M. (eds.) (2000). *Stable Peace Among Nations*. Lanham, MD: Rowman & Littlefield.
Kaplan, R. (2019, January 7). A New Cold War has begun. *Foreign Policy*, foreignpolicy.com/2019/01/07/a-new-cold-war-has-begun.
Khoo, N. & Steff, R. (2014). "This program will not be a threat to them": Ballistic Missile Defense and US relations with Russia and China. *Defense & Security Analysis, 30*(1), 17–28.
Kirshner, J. (2010). The tragedy of offensive realism: Classical realism and the rise of China. *European Journal of International Relations, 18*(1), 1–23.
Köllner, P. (2021) Australia and New Zealand recalibrate their China policies: Convergence and divergence. *Pacific Review, 34*(3), 405–436.
Kupchan, C. A. (2010). *How Enemies Become Friends: The Sources of Stable Peace*. Princeton, NJ: Princeton University Press.
Kupchan, C. (2021). Bipolarity is back: Why it matters. *Washington Quarterly, 44*(4), 123–139.
Laksmana, E. A. (2021, October 17). AUKUS mixed reception a symptom of strategic fault-lines in Southeast Asia. *East Asia Forum*. www.eastasiaforum.org/2021/10/17/aukus-mixed-reception-a-symptom-of-strategic-fault-lines-in-southeast-asia.
Macias, A. (2021, February 7). Biden says there will be "extreme competition" with China, but won't take Trump approach. *CNBC*. www.cnbc.com/2021/02/07/biden-will-compete-with-china-but-wont-take-trump-approach.html.
Mahuta, N. (2021). Inaugural foreign policy speech to the Diplomatic Corps. www.beehive.govt.nz/speech/inaugural-foreign-policy-speech-diplomatic-corps.
Miller, G. (2022). AUKUS Door Held Ajar for New Zealand: Could nuclear-free New Zealand join an alliance centered on nuclear submarines? *The Diplomat*. thediplomat.com/2022/08/aukus-door-held-ajar-for-new-zealand.
Miller, G. (2021, September 20). New Zealand could be the big winner of Aukus fallout. *RNZ*. www.rnz.co.nz/news/on-the-inside/451895/geoffrey-miller-new-zealand-could-be-the-big-winner-of-aukus-fallout.
Ministry of Defence, New Zealand (2021). He moana pukupuke e ekengia e te waka: A rough sea can still be navigated. *Defence Assessment 2021*. www.defence.govt.nz/assets/publication/file/Defence-Assessment-2021.pdf.

Montgomery, E. B. (2006). Breaking out of the security dilemma: Realism, reassurance, and the problem of uncertainty. *International Security*, *31*(2), 151–185.

O'Brien, P. (2022, April 5). The China–Solomon islands security deal changes everything. *The Diplomat.* thediplomat.com/2022/04/the-china-solomon-islands-security-deal-changes-everything.

Ogilvie-White, T. & Gower, J. A. (2021, October 5). Deeper dive into AUKUS: Risks and benefits for the Asia-Pacific. www.apln.network/analysis/special-report/a-deeper-dive-into-aukus-risks-and-benefits-for-the-asia-pacific.

Owen, J. M. (1994). How liberalism produces democratic peace. *International Security*, *19*(2), 87–125.

Pfeifer, S. Sevastopulo, D. & Gross, A. (2021). The nuclear technology behind Australia's Aukus submarine deal. *Financial Times.* www.ft.com/content/aa5c9fd5-891b-4680-b3c7-5a55d03f673c.

Pompeo, M. R. (2020, July 23). Communist China and the free world's future. *U.S. Embassy in Georgia.* ge.usembassy.gov/communist-china-and-the-free-worlds-future-july-23.

Pryke, J. (2020). The risks of China's ambitions in the South Pacific. *Brookings.* www.brookings.edu/articles/the-risks-of-chinas-ambitions-in-the-south-pacific.

Radio New Zealand (2014, March 4). PM says not right time to sign deal with Russia. *RNZ Politics.* www.rnz.co.nz/news/political/237803/pm-says-not-right-time-to-sign-deal-with-russia.

Radio New Zealand (2021, November 13). "Inconceivable" Australia would not join US to defend Taiwan — defence minister. *RNZ World Politics.* www.rnz.co.nz/news/world/455630/inconceivable-australia-would-not-join-us-to-defend-taiwan-defence-minister.

Rock, S. R. (1989). *Why Peace Breaks Out: Great Power Rapprochement in Historical Perspective.* Chapel Hill, NC: University of North Carolina Press.

Rogoff, K. (2022, April 26). The growing threat of global recession. *Project Syndicate.* www.project-syndicate.org/commentary/economic-recession-risk-in-china-united-states-europe-by-kenneth-rogoff-2022-04.

Royal Navy (2022). Rim of the Pacific. www.royalnavy.mod.uk/news-and-latest-activity/operations/pacific/rimpac.

Sadler, B. D. (2021). AUKUS: U.S. Navy nuclear-powered forward presence key Australian nuclear submarine and China deterrence. *Heritage Foundation.* www.heritage.org/sites/default/files/2021-10/BG3662.pdf.

Shelbourne, M. (2021). U.S. Indo-Pacific command wants $4.68B for new Pacific deterrence initiative. *USNI News.* news.usni.org/2021/03/02/u-s-indo-pacific-command-wants-4-68b-for-new-pacific-deterrence-initiative.

Shuyong G. & Boran, L. (2020). The myth of the New Cold War. *Chinese Journal of International Review*, *2*(2), 1–16.

Smith, N. R. (2020). When hedging goes wrong: Lessons from Ukraine's failed hedge of the EU and Russia. *Global Policy, 11*(5), 588–597.

Steff, R. & Dodd-Parr, F. (2019). Examining the immanent dilemma of small states in the Asia-Pacific: The strategic triangle between New Zealand, the US and China. *Pacific Review, 32*(1), 90–112.

Steff, R. (2021). The great disconnect? US–China technology decoupling and it's [sic] implications for New Zealand. *NZUS Council*. www.nzuscouncil.org/the-great-disconnect-us-china-technology-decoupling-and-its-implications-for-new-zealand.

Steff, R. (2016). Strategic Liberalism and Kiwi maximalism. *New Zealand International Review, 41*(2), 14–17.

Sukma, R. (2021, October 1). Is AUKUS a problem or blessing for ASEAN? *Jakarta Post*. www.thejakartapost.com/academia/2021/09/30/is-aukus-a-problem-or-blessing-for-asean.html.

Taliaferro, J. (2000–2001). Security seeking under anarchy: Defensive realism revisited. *International Security, 25*(3), 128–161.

Tan, S. (2021). Could New Zealand serve as an "honest broker" to repair ties between China and the West? *South China Morning Post*. www.scmp.com/economy/china-economy/article/3120096/could-new-zealand-serve-honest-broker-repair-ties-between.

Tang, S. (2009). The security dilemma: A conceptual analysis. *Security Studies, 18*(3), 587–623.

Trump White House (2017). *National Security Strategy*. trumpwhitehouse.archives.gov/wp-content/uploads/2017/12/NSS-Final-12-18-2017-0905.pdf.

Tunsjø, Ø. (2018). *The Return of Bipolarity in World Politics*. New York: Columbia University Press.

Turnbull, M. (2021). Address to the National Press Club. www.malcolmturnbull.com.au/media/address-to-the-national-press-club-september-2021.

US Mission New Zealand (2022). U.S. Deputy Sherman in New Zealand. nz.usembassy.gov/deputy-secretary-sherman-in-new-zealand.

US Department of Defense (2018). *National Defense Strategy of the United States*. dod.defense.gov/Portals/1/Documents/pubs/2018-National-Defense-Strategy-Summary.pdf.

Vock, I. (2021, September 16). "Stab in the back": How the new Aukus pact sparked French outrage. *New Statesman*. www.newstatesman.com/security/2021/09/stab-in-the-back-how-the-new-aukus-pact-sparked-french-outrage.

Walsh, J. (1997). Surprise down under: The secret history of Australia's nuclear ambitions. *Nonproliferation Review, 5*(1), 1–20.

White House (2021, March). Interim national security strategic guidance. www.whitehouse.gov/wp-content/uploads/2021/03/NSC-1v2.pdf.

White House (2021, September 15). Joint leaders statement on AUKUS. www.whitehouse.gov/briefing-room/statements-releases/2021/09/15/joint-leaders-statement-on-aukus.

Wilkie, C. (2022). Pelosi's Taiwan trip is a new headache for Biden, increases tension with China. *CNBC*. www.cnbc.com/2022/08/02/white-house-struggles-to-insulate-bidens-china-policy-from-pelosis-taiwan-trip.html.

Wintour, P. (2021, March 15). Why Britain is tilting to the Indo-Pacific region. *The Guardian*, www.theguardian.com/politics/2021/mar/15/why-britain-is-tilting-to-the-indo-pacific-region?CMP=Share_iOSApp_Other.

Xi Jinping (2019, May 31). Uphold and Develop Socialism with Chinese Characteristics. Speech to the CCP Central Committee. In Greer, T. (trans.), Xi Jinping in translation: China's guiding ideology. *Palladium*. palladiummag.com/2019/05/31/xi-jinping-in-translation-chinas-guiding-ideology.

Xing, L. & Bernal-Meza, R. (2021). China–US rivalry: A new Cold War or capitalism's intra-core competition? *Revista Brasileira de Política Internacional*, *64*(1), 1–20.

Young, A. (2021, September 16). New AUKUS security pact: Jacinda Ardern says no change to relationships. *NZ Herald*, www.nzherald.co.nz/nz/new-aukus-security-pact-jacinda-ardern-says-no-change-to-relationships/4MBOHQV5MXANHTVD5XBLDW3CPE.

Zakaria, F. (2020, December 6). The New China scare: Why America shouldn't panic about its latest challenger. *Foreign Affairs*. www.foreignaffairs.com/articles/china/2019-12-06/new-china-scare.

Zhang, D. (2020). China's military engagement with Pacific Island countries. *Policy Forum*. www.policyforum.net/chinas-military-engagement-with-pacific-island-countries.

Zhao, M. (2019). Is a New Cold War inevitable? Chinese perspectives on US–China strategic competition. *Chinese Journal of International Politics*, *12*(3), 371–394.

Chapter 11

New Zealand's Asia Story: The Curious Case of New Zealand–India Relations

Suzannah Jessep

That is what learning is. You suddenly understand something you've understood all your life, but in a new way.

— Doris Lessing.

Growing and formalising trade between New Zealand and India has been one of the long-standing goals held by successive New Zealand Governments, including the Labour Government led by Jacinda Ardern. Like many other trading nations, New Zealand has tended to see India's greatest value proposition as being its market of 1.4 billion consumers, with a growing middle class and appetite for the kinds of products that countries such as New Zealand can produce. It is a trade-focused model of engagement that has worked well for New Zealand across most parts of Asia, but not India.

This chapter explores the development of New Zealand's relations with South Asia, and India in particular. It looks at the factors that have helped and hindered the growth of the relationship and shines a light on the opportunities that exist to rejuvenate the bilateral partnership based on deepening knowledge, growing targeted people-to-people connections and changing the lens through which New Zealand has become accustomed to viewing India.

This chapter starts with a look at how New Zealanders conceptualise 'Asia' and how the rise and dominance of North Asia — particularly

China — has shaped the way the New Zealand Government engages with and allocates resources to bilateral partnerships across Asia. It then looks at how relations with South Asia have evolved over time, from the arrival of the very first immigrants from the Indian subcontinent through to the development of a whole-of-government 'NZ Inc' India strategy positioning India as a priority 'lift country' for New Zealand in the Indo-Pacific. It concludes by reflecting on the historic but notably low-key visit to New Zealand by the Indian Minister of External Affairs, Subrahmanyam Jaishankar, in October 2022, just three months before the resignation of Ardern as Prime Minister.

'Getting Asia': New Zealand in the Early 2000s

In 2003, when the Asia New Zealand Foundation hosted a major forum looking at New Zealand's relationship with Asia, one of the key findings was that New Zealanders tended to think of and talk about Asia as a single entity. New Zealanders spoke about 'Asia' when they identified opportunities for New Zealand offshore, and when they highlighted trends that their fellow New Zealanders should be alert to. Policy papers and media headlines alike typically grouped Asia and Asians together, despite the cultural, religious and ethnic diversity across the region and the vast geographical distances between Asian countries.

At the time of the 2003 forum, it was clear that the Asia region was going to be consequential to New Zealand's future prosperity and security. The growth and economic development of the so-called Asian tiger economies of Singapore, Hong Kong, South Korea and Taiwan (Huang & Wang, 2011), alongside the growth of other high-performing economies such as China, Indonesia, Malaysia and Thailand, had had a marked impact on New Zealand's economic fortunes (Page *et al.*, 1993). Immigration and the rapid growth of New Zealand's international education services had transformed the country's social fabric, turning Auckland into one of the most ethnically diverse cities in the world (Seiler, 1997). Equally, the Asian financial crisis of 1997 and outbreak of SARS (Severe Acute Respiratory Syndrome) in 2003 served as a reminder of shared vulnerabilities and the need to work together, in partnership with countries across Asia, if New Zealand was to respond effectively to global economic and security challenges (Osisanya, n.d.).

The Rise and Dominance of North Asia

Research conducted by the Asia New Zealand Foundation shows that while New Zealanders' knowledge of Asia has been improving over time, it is North Asia — principally China — that now dominates their understanding and perceptions of Asia. In survey findings released in 2022, over 70 per cent of New Zealanders said they considered North Asia to be the most important region for New Zealand's future. Asked which country New Zealanders most closely associate with Asia, the vast majority said China (Asia New Zealand Foundation, June 16, 2021). When asked which countries in Asia New Zealanders consider to be friendliest or most threatening towards New Zealand, Japan and North Korea are consistently ranked number one respectively (Asia New Zealand Foundation, June 2021, p. 34).

New Zealand's leaning toward North Asia is not a product of geographic proximity or a cultural likeness, but rather of the decisions that have been taken by North Asian governments that have propelled them onto the world stage. It was China's determination to integrate into the global economy that saw it grow to become the largest trading partner of the majority of countries, including New Zealand (Sundell, 2022). It was Japan's decision to utilise its soft power as a key pillar of its foreign policy that has seen it rise to become one of the most recognisable Asian cultures in New Zealand (Asia New Zealand Foundation, 2020). And it has been North Korea's military build-up and recurrent missile tests — just under a hundred launched in 2022 alone — that has positioned it as a threat in the minds of New Zealanders.

The rise and expansion of China has also created complex security challenges that have demanded New Zealand Government time and resources to manage, and that have dominated media headlines — further reinforcing the centrality of North Asia in the minds of New Zealanders and effectively rendering invisible the other countries of Asia whose activities have not demanded equal levels of government or public attention (Jorgensen, 2020). Consequently, much of New Zealand's diplomacy under Ardern's five-year tenure as Prime Minister was orientated towards managing the 'China balance' and endeavouring to stabilise trade opportunities against security risks.

As North Asia has grown in prominence in New Zealand, other Asian regions have effectively slipped from the radar, despite positive and long-standing people-to-people connections, a broad alignment of democratic systems, and their having many shared interests. There can be no clearer example of this than South Asia, and India in particular. As India has grown and sought to develop its foreign relations across the Indo-Pacific, and as other countries have significantly scaled up their bilateral partnerships in response, New Zealand's effort has remained notably static. To understand why this is, and the factors that have led New Zealand to value and invest in certain Asian partners over others, it is helpful to look back at the evolution of relations between New Zealand and India, where trade and security have waxed and waned as the central driving forces of the relationship.

The Brief History of New Zealand–South Asia Relations

New Zealand's relations with South Asia — encompassing India, Nepal, Bhutan, Bangladesh, Sri Lanka, the Maldives and Pakistan — date back many years, from around the sixteenth century when South Asians were employed as seamen on British ships, through to later voyages for gold exploration, timber trade, sealing and settlement (Bandyopadhyay, 2010). By the mid-1800s, settlers from India were establishing themselves within New Zealand communities and making their mark on New Zealand's towns and cities, with the 'Cashmere Estate' (Kashmir) in Christchurch, the suburb of Khandallah in Wellington, and the Bombay Hills in Auckland.

Unlike immigrants of Chinese heritage who were almost exclusively male and concentrated around the goldfields, the 905 Indian and Sri Lankan settlers recorded in the 1878 census were spread throughout New Zealand and were a mix of both men and women (Didham, 2010). Early records show how Sikh immigrants from India's Punjab Province in the nineteenth century started small businesses and, over time, married and lived among Māori communities in the North Island (*Indian newslink*, 2014). In other areas, Indian immigrants started small stores and delivered other community services. This diverse gender and geographic distribution meant South Asian immigrants settled and assimilated into local communities much faster than other early immigrants — and in doing so, laid the groundwork for a community of New Zealanders of South Asian heritage who are today well integrated and represented across New Zealand's regions.

During the First and Second World Wars, large numbers of soldiers from both South Asia and New Zealand fought alongside one another as part of an allied campaign against the Central and Axis Powers. In 1951, after the end of the Second World War, government-led arrangements such as the Colombo Plan for Cooperative Economic Development in Asia and the Pacific were spearheaded by Commonwealth partners including New Zealand, and that helped to grow positive connections between member states. The year after the Colombo Plan was agreed, New Zealand moved to establish formal diplomatic relations with several South Asian countries, starting with India in 1952, followed by Sri Lanka in 1955, Nepal in 1961 (eight years after Edmund Hillary and Tenzing Norgay summited Mount Everest in 1953), Pakistan in 1971, Bangladesh in 1972 and the Maldives in 1974.

The Early Years of Formal India–New Zealand Relations

The early years of the New Zealand–India relationship were shaped by the two countries' experiences as British colonies and subsequently as members of the Commonwealth, newly independent from colonial Britain. For India, the transition from colony to independence had been quick and brutal, resulting in the division of subcontinental India into two countries (India and Pakistan) and the division of the nation along religious lines.

New Zealand's transition to independence, formalised just three months after India, could not have been more different. Led by a government dominated by settlers of British heritage who were anxious to maintain rather than sever New Zealand's economic and security ties with Britain, the transition had been gradual and even somewhat reluctant. Although the Statute of Westminster granted full sovereign status to New Zealand in 1931, it was not until November 1947 that New Zealand formally adopted the statute, ending Britain's rights to override the decisions of the New Zealand Parliament (McDowell & Webb, 1998, pp. 107–108).

Despite their very different experiences achieving independence, New Zealand and India formed a robust bond in the Commonwealth. An early sign of the friendship that would grow between the two countries came in the form of New Zealand's support for India's admission to the grouping in 1947:

> 'Figures like Churchill and Robert Menzies, though both in opposition, were concerned over the effect of an alien India entering their 'club' ... Yet, unlike them, [New Zealand Prime Minister Peter] Fraser enthusiastically stated to the New Zealand people on the day independence was announced that India was warmly welcomed into a 'free and powerful association' that was based on 'mutual confidence and cooperation in the full respect of the independence, sovereignty, and individuality of each member.' (Ministry of Foreign Affairs, 1972, pp. 137–138).

Prime Minister Fraser (1940–1949) saw India as a country that had shown fortitude and resilience, and as 'an example which had been an inspiration to the world' (Kumarasingham, 2010). The two countries had fought alongside each other, both suffering disproportionately heavy casualties, and now were looking to each other to repair and rebuild in the post-war period. This sense of shared heritage and partnership shaped relations over the decades that followed, driven at first by close people-to-people relations and development needs, but over time becoming more exclusively focused on trade.

After the Second World War: Developing Relations through Aid and Trade

Over the following years, New Zealand and India worked to slowly grow and diversify their relationship as two independent countries, each grappling with their own internal challenges and regional priorities. As the smaller of the two, much of New Zealand's focus went to maintaining relations with the United Kingdom as its major trading partner and continuing to develop relations with other Commonwealth members. For India, after hundreds of years of colonial rule and with a 15,000 km land border shared with a number of adjoining states, much of its attention went to strengthening its defences as an independent nation and distancing itself — through the establishment of the 'non-aligned movement' — from major powers who might seek once again to draw down on its resources (Laskar, 2004).

In 1950, India declared itself a sovereign, democratic and republican state. It needed to lift millions — a seventh of the world's population at the time — out of acute poverty, the majority of whom relied on subsistence agriculture. Literacy and life expectancy stood at 14 per cent and 32 years respectively (Adhia, 2015). In short, Britain had left India asset-stripped and in a state of disrepair, with a low trust in foreign powers and a very important, highly sensitive agriculture sector.

Unsurprisingly, early bilateral engagement between India and New Zealand focused on India's immediate development needs (see Figure 1). It included New Zealand's support for the establishment of an Amul milk pasteurisation plant in Bombay (modern-day Mumbai) and monetary assistance for the establishment of the All India Institute of Medical Sciences in New Delhi. In the 1950s, India's Verghese Kurien studied at New Zealand's Massey University and would go on to become the founder of India's successful dairy co-operative industry (Waters, 2020).

During the 1970s, India experienced war with Pakistan, domestic uprisings, student protests, soaring inflation, and in 1975 a governing crisis when Prime Minister Indira Gandhi declared a state of emergency and suspended the constitution and democratic rights for a period of two years. At the same time, New Zealand experienced its own modest ructions: Britain joined the European Economic Community, effectively

Figure 1. The first Prime Minister of independent India, Jawaharlal Nehru (left) with New Zealand Prime Minister Sidney Holland (centre), probably at the Commonwealth Prime Ministers' Conference in London in 1956.

Source: McGibbon, 2016.

ending New Zealand's preferential access to Britain's market and in doing so upending a large share of New Zealand's exports.

New Zealand's deteriorating economic position prompted a programme of radical reforms throughout the 1980s, including deregulating the financial market, removing foreign exchange controls and eliminating tariff protections. For New Zealand, these changes had two significant consequences that would later impact its relations with India. Firstly, they accelerated New Zealand's integration into global markets and secondly, they cemented New Zealand's foreign policy around the pursuit of market access. As Prime Minister Robert Muldoon declared, 'our foreign policy is trade. We are not interested in the normal foreign policy matters to any great extent. We are interested in trade' (Round, 1980).

In the decades that followed, New Zealand dedicated much of its diplomacy to market integration and trade liberalisation, signing trade deals with Japan, South Korea, China and the so-called dynamic tiger economies of Singapore, Taiwan and Hong Kong. In the case of India, which had shown reluctance to join the movement, New Zealand officials judged that it was just a matter of doubling down on their efforts and making it clear that a trade agreement was a top bilateral priority for New Zealand. While India's nuclear weapons test in 1998 cooled relations for a period, by 2007 Wellington and New Delhi agreed to undertake a joint study on the feasibility of negotiating a bilateral Free Trade Agreement (FTA). That study found that an agreement could be of mutual benefit, and so formal trade negotiations commenced in 2010 (Rolls, 2016).

As part of New Zealand's expanding trade agenda, New Zealand's Official Development Assistance also transitioned toward a more overt focus on trade and economic development (Spratt & Wood, 2018). Under the government of Prime Minister John Key (2008–2016), New Zealand aid was to be directly linked to New Zealand's commercial and geostrategic interests, of which the most important element was 'to align aid policy with trade policy' (Spratt & Wood, 2018; McCully, 2009). India, too, was changing its trade and aid policies. Under the National Democratic Alliance Government led by Atal Bihari Vajpayee (during his 1999–2004 term), India decided to stop accepting aid from foreign sources, including New Zealand. Rather than have development objectives set by others, India wished to demonstrate its own economic empowerment and self-sufficiency and — importantly — show it was now in a position to come to the aid of others (*Economic Times*, 2003).

Getting Strategic: Formalising New Zealand–India Relations

In 2011, without an FTA agreed, the New Zealand Government set about formally declaring India a priority country in its 'Opening Doors to India' policy which, as Prime Minister Key said during its announcement, 'has a strong trade and economic focus' (Key, 2011). The strategy set out six priority actions. The first four were to grow merchandise exports to at least NZ$2 billion by 2015; grow the services trade with India by an average of 20 per cent per year; improve the bilateral investment framework and facilitate growth in the investment relationship; and to attract and retain skilled migrants from India who could make an effective contribution to New Zealand's economic base.

The fifth and sixth goals were to build a strategic framework around the trade-centred relationship and included engaging 'more deeply with India on regional and global issues that will impact on New Zealand's future prosperity and security', and secondly, raising 'the profile of New Zealand's value proposition in India through a series of conscious steps, from enhanced cricket diplomacy to increased political contact with India' (New Zealand Trade and Enterprise, 2011). By this stage, trade in services — predominantly education — was also starting to ramp up, with large numbers of Indian students travelling to New Zealand each year for study, which was for many, a pathway to residency.

With the election of Narendra Modi's Bharatiya Janata Party (BJP) in 2014, however, India started a process of reviewing all of its FTAs, including with Singapore (signed 2005), South Korea (2010), ASEAN (2010), Malaysia (2011) and Japan (2011). The review proposed a number of changes to India's negotiating strategy with trading partners such as New Zealand, including the decision to move away from goods-focused negotiations and to focus instead on gaining ground in the area of services and investment (*India Today*, 2016). In practical terms, this put India–New Zealand trade negotiations, and arguably the relationship more generally, on the back burner.

Shifting Emphasis: From Trade to Security

By 2016, New Zealand and India had completed approximately seven rounds of FTA negotiations but had made little meaningful progress.

With trade as the centrepiece of New Zealand diplomacy in Asia, and India focused on services trade and attracting foreign direct investment, the bilateral relationship appeared from the outside to have plateaued. From the inside, the relationship appeared to be full of unrealised potential but marred by the experience of New Zealand officials who had become jaded by rounds of unsuccessful trade negotiations and irked by ongoing nuclear-related issues. Co-operation in the wider defence and security sector was, however, starting to pick up momentum.

That same year Prime Minister Key undertook his second visit to India, after his first in 2011. During their joint press conference, Prime Minister Modi sought to reassure New Zealand on trade, noting: 'Trade and Investment ties have been one of the key areas of our conversation. We both recognized the need for greater economic engagement in order to effectively respond to the growing uncertainties in global economy and, agreed that expanding business and commercial ties should continue to be one of the priority items of our partnership' (*Indian Express*, 2016).

Prime Minister Key reiterated New Zealand's long-standing interests in growing trade but started to drive the conversation toward areas that were seeing greater tangible progress: in defence, security and regional co-operation. He noted: 'It is important we work together with likeminded countries to enhance regional prosperity and stability and working more closely with India, which is playing an increasingly important role in global and regional affairs, [and we] will build on our efforts to do this.' He went on to note: 'We also agreed to new cooperation in areas such as cyber security, counter-terrorism, customs, education and food safety as well as for our leaders and officials to meet more regularly, reflecting the broadening of our relationship' (Key, 2016).

The Election of Prime Minister Ardern: From Trade to Security

With the formation of Prime Minister Ardern's Labour-led coalition in 2017, trade continued to play a major role in New Zealand's international agenda with the transition of the Trans-Pacific Partnership (TPP) trade deal to the Comprehensive and Progressive Agreement for Trans-Pacific Partnership (CPTPP), and continuing negotiations for the Regional Comprehensive Economic Partnership (RCEP) which included India.

Two events in 2019 began to turn that agenda around. The first was the Christchurch terrorist attack which drew the government's attention towards countering violent extremism and related online content. The second was India's withdrawal from RCEP — putting paid to any hope that New Zealand and India might be able to get past their bilateral FTA impasse. The emergence of the COVID-19 pandemic in early 2020 drove a major swing toward the protection of New Zealanders and security of New Zealand's borders.

China's growth and increasing assertiveness had also fomented a range of complex domestic and regional challenges, including concerns over foreign interference, economic coercion, the control of sensitive and critical technology, the fate of Hong Kong and of the Uyghurs in Xinjiang, the protection of sovereignty and the liberal, rules-based order, and — in 2022 — concerns over the Chinese military presence in the South Pacific.

In early 2020, at the end of Prime Minister Ardern's first term in office, the New Zealand Government released a refreshed and revitalised India Strategy. Titled *India–New Zealand 2025: Investing in the Relationship*, the strategy aimed to formally rebalance New Zealand's engagement with India, by reprioritising new areas of co-operation in the defence and security sector; openly acknowledging that more work was needed at the New Zealand end to build and deepen knowledge of India beyond trade; and highlighting the two countries' shared strategic interests in the wider Indo-Pacific (Ministry of Foreign Affairs and Trade, n.d.).

The goals of the 2020 strategy included: building a relationship based on mutual trust that advances the two countries' shared interests; prioritising the need for New Zealanders to have an improved capability for engaging with India; and for New Zealand to make its value proposition to India better known and understood. Stronger and broader cultural connections between New Zealand and India were also to be promoted, and trade progressed as a matter of shared prosperity (Ministry of Foreign Affairs and Trade, n.d.).

The launch of the 2020 strategy was supported by a ministerial visit to India led by Foreign Minister Winston Peters and Trade Minister David Parker in the company of a sizeable delegation. During the visit Peters delivered a speech to the Indian Council of World Affairs titled 'The Indo-Pacific: from principles to partnerships' in which neither the bilateral FTA nor India's eventual decision to withdraw from RCEP were mentioned, but instead he sought to highlight New Zealand and India's 'shared strategic geography' as well as their 'shared commitment to a stable, peaceful, open and secure region'. He noted: 'New Zealand wants to see India take a greater role in international political structures that support global security and regional economic governance' (Peters, 2020).

Unfortunately, the visit and strategy sank from public view almost immediately, with the COVID-19 pandemic hitting just weeks later. With it went all of the bilateral momentum and knowledge-building goals, as the New Zealand Government turned its attention to managing the health crisis, countering the disruptive economic impacts of lockdown measures, restoring disrupted supply chains, securing and distributing vaccines, and managing broader challenges to the rules-based trading system (Parker, 2020).

New Zealand's closed borders also hugely restricted people flows from India. As India grappled with the worst of the COVID-19 pandemic, Indian visa-holders and New Zealand citizens in India were unceremoniously barred from returning to New Zealand. Indians who left New Zealand for deaths, marriages and other significant events were similarly denied re-entry (Bonnett, 2021). The blunt handling of the border closure announcement undid much of the goodwill engendered in the relationship up until that point and naturally caused many to question the sincerity of a New Zealand Government India Strategy that stressed the importance of India as a priority partner, of values, and of warm and close people-to-people linkages.

The signing of an interim FTA between India and Australia, announced on 2 April 2022, further undermined the 2020 strategy by propelling trade back to centre stage. It was lost on few observers that just as New Zealand had finally weaned itself off its fixation on getting an FTA with India, Australia had got a deal across the line — albeit an interim one. The major difference this time, however, was that there was now recognition among senior New Zealand officials that Australia's agreement was not the product of trade negotiators but rather of a whole-of-government shift in the way Australia now viewed India, from a trade opportunity to a critical strategic partner in the Indo-Pacific.

India's New Value Proposition: A Democracy and Indian Ocean Security Partner

Since the emergence of the Indo-Pacific as a geostrategic concept, India's significance as a democracy and security partner in the region has gained increasing prominence and weight. This has been particularly true for the

United States, but also for Japan and Australia, which have come to see India as a critical support partner in the Indian Ocean and as part of an informal arc of democracies that can work together to uphold rules and norms, while promoting regional connectivity and development (Miller, 2021). New Zealand, too, has been part of this shift, but sitting on the periphery.

The increased depth and tempo of defence and security co-operation between India and larger Western partners has opened doors for smaller countries such as New Zealand, which have drawn downstream benefit from the trusted relationships that have been formed by others. While each country continues to maintain its independent foreign and security policy — as India's position on Russia's invasion of Ukraine revealed — these relationships have nonetheless fostered a greater sense of mutual understanding in each other's core strategic interests and outlook. For New Zealand, this has included the opportunity to participate alongside India in defence training exercises and the exchange information in areas of shared interest.

It has also provided openings to partner with India in multilateral security groupings like the Quadrilateral Security Dialogue (or 'Quad') in areas such as COVID-19 pandemic recovery (Sachdeva, 2020). Such initiatives, alongside maritime search and rescue, disaster response and UN peacekeeping, have proven valuable in demonstrating the potential for India and New Zealand to work together in the region, but have not plugged the essential gap that still remains: reframing and elevating the bilateral relationship at home.

Lessons from Australia: Relationship First, Trade Second

Australia's success in its diplomacy with India has its roots in a decision taken in the early 2000s. That decision was to stop using the pursuit of an FTA as the key to unlock a bigger, better relationship with India and to instead focus on direct, targeted trade engagement and broader, shared geostrategic objectives in the Indo-Pacific. In practice, this meant setting aside a number of well-worn bilateral irritants and focusing on areas of capability and commonality.

As the Indian foreign policy scholar Dhruva Jaishankar noted, 'After five decades of testy or distant strategic relations, India and Australia began ... to forge an increasingly co-operative defence and security partnership. The primary drivers were similar concerns about China's rise, behaviour, and assertiveness, as well as converging views about the regional strategic landscape'. He went on to note: 'The decreasing salience of their divergences — Cold War-era geopolitics, India's nuclear status, strained people-to-people ties, and shallow economic and trade links — also helped create more favourable conditions' (Jaishankar, 2020).

After years of visits, speeches and trade expos promoting the potential benefits of a close and comprehensive free trade partnership, Prime Minister Malcolm Turnbull in 2017 commissioned a detailed assessment of Australia's trade and economic relationship with India. Written by the former secretary of the foreign ministry Peter Varghese, and released in 2018, the report put forward a new approach to India — one that focused on services and led with investment across multiple sectors and states. The report found that if Australia considered there to be 'no single major market out to 2035 with more growth opportunities for Australian business than India', then Australia must fundamentally change its game (Varghese, 2018). At the same time, Australia significantly stepped up its resourcing for building and maintaining people-to-people connections through education, film, internships, the arts and sports.

Australia's High Commissioner to India, Harinder Sidhu, observed in 2018 that 'what makes the Strategy interesting and unique ... is how it departs from what I could call the 'standard model' of Australia's economic engagement with Asian partners ... Put simply, India is not China'. The strategy concluded that India's economic development would be driven by consumption and services. Sidhu went on to note: 'There are two key ways in which this conclusion makes a material difference to how Australia has to approach India. One is to recognise the central role of people-to-people links; and the second is to elevate investment links to a higher priority' (Sidhu, 2018).

Australia's experience in and with India offered valuable insights to the Ardern-led Government. Both New Zealand and Australia had traditionally put the pursuit of free trade at the forefront of their bilateral relations, and both had tended to use trade to build the permission space needed to unlock government investment in other areas. Australia's experience with India showed that in fact the reverse was true. Build the relationship first — invest in people-to-people connections and areas of genuine shared strategic interest — and trade will follow (Hall, 2021).

Other countries have also achieved progress in and with India by investing in people-to-people relations, building knowledge and recognising the criticality of face-to-face diplomacy (Ministry of Foreign Affairs, 2023). In 2018 alone, Singapore and India exchanged over 40 ministerial visits, including three at prime ministerial level. Sweden, which has a similar-sized trade relationship with India to New Zealand, has received four prime ministerial level visits from India, including by Prime Minister Modi, since forming diplomatic relations in 1949. By contrast, the last time an Indian Prime Minister visited New Zealand was in 1986 — 37 years ago, despite Prime Minister Modi visiting both Fiji and Australia in 2014.

Even during the COVID-19 pandemic, many countries continued to pursue an active programme of in-person diplomacy with India while maintaining strict social distancing norms. In the two years following Foreign Minister Peters' visit to India in 2020, India hosted approximately 22 leader-level and ministerial visits, including that of Australia's Prime Minister Anthony Albanese, who met Prime Minister Modi in India just one day after he was sworn in as Prime Minister on 23 May 2022. Australian Deputy Prime Minister and Defence Minister Richard Marles also undertook a visit to India, just one month after the election. By comparison, Prime Minister Ardern did not visit India during her entire term in office, from 2017 to 2023. One historic visit was, however, undertaken.

In October 2022, just a few months before Ardern's resignation, India's Minister of External Affairs, Subrahmanyam Jaishankar, visited New Zealand. The visit was notable for three reasons. The first was its focus on New Zealanders of Indian heritage, and in particular Indian students who had borne the brunt of COVID-19 lockdowns and closed borders. During his visit, Jaishankar repeated his call for the New Zealand Government to approach the matter sympathetically. The second was the inauguration of the new Indian High Commission Chancery in Wellington, representing a sizeable investment and positive signal to New Zealand by the Indian Government. And the third and perhaps most striking feature was how low-key the visit was for the first foreign ministerial visit in decades. Although Jaishankar met with Prime Minister Ardern and Foreign Minister Nanaia Mahuta, no significant announcements were made and very little media attention was generated. In short, it largely flew under the radar.

Doing the Same Thing Twice

Jaishankar's visit was emblematic of a wider challenge that has been impacting New Zealand–India bilateral relations over time. It is a relationship full of potential but one that carries the scars of unrequited free trade ambitions on the New Zealand side, recurrent immigration-related irritants on India's, and a lack of in-depth leader-level engagement on both sides. Add the limitations of distance, resourcing and scale, and the relationship continues to appear friendly but rudderless.

The asymmetry in the relationship, coupled with the COVID-19 pandemic, concerns over rising Hindu nationalism under the BJP, India's RCEP withdrawal and, in 2022, India's reluctance to criticise Russia over its invasion of Ukraine, has made the task of assimilating activities, resources and political cultures all the more challenging.

One of the common misconceptions of India in New Zealand is that as it grows, it will naturally align and integrate into the Western liberal world order, further liberalise, and increasingly adopt Western (particularly American) values (Rachman, 2019). This is an outlook shaped by decades of American ascendency and the embedded Western liberal, rules-based system, and never fails to create shock waves when India does not conform (look no further than its stance on Russia). New Zealand, too, has had its own experience of this, stemming from its membership of the Five Eyes intelligence sharing community and the assumption that its foreign policy is largely dictated by the community's larger member states. Both scenarios reveal a lack of understanding of India and New Zealand's foreign policy positions and domestic constituencies.

In New Zealand, media headlines, rather than direct in-person experience through tourism, business or other travel, have disproportionately influenced New Zealanders' perceptions of India. It is often portrayed as a country of extremes, between the exotic or romantic and extreme poverty and calamitous events. In its *Perceptions of Asia and Asian Peoples* survey released in June 2022, the Asia New Zealand Foundation found just 25 per cent of New Zealand adults considered themselves 'somewhat knowledgeable' about South Asia, and only 37 per cent considered the region to be important for New Zealand's future, despite India being on track to have the world's largest population in 2023 and one of the world's largest economies by 2050 (Asia New Zealand Foundation, June 16, 2021).

Getting the Relationship Right

Even if only occasionally publicly acknowledged, India and New Zealand have a genuine stake in each other's futures, as two democracies that achieved independence within months of each other; that supported one another through wartime and peace; and that continue to be quietly glued together by the many thousands of Indians who have decided to call New Zealand home and the many New Zealanders, from cricketers, mountaineers and artists to diplomats and defence personnel, who have played their part in building bilateral relations in India.

As Prime Minister Ardern argued in her 2022 Harvard University Commencement speech, democratic nations cannot take their democracy or their partnership for granted, and occasional differences should not be allowed to manifest into division (Ardern, 2022). Similar words were spoken by Prime Minister Modi in a 2018 speech, when he observed that we live in a world of 'inter-dependent fortunes and failures' and 'no nation can shape and secure it on its own'. He called on countries to build 'bridges of trust' based on respect for sovereignty and territorial integrity, consultation, good governance, transparency, viability and sustainability, and concluded that 'on these principles, we are prepared to work with everyone' (Ministry of External Affairs, 2018).

A New Approach to India in 2023 and Beyond

This chapter began by highlighting New Zealand's predicament in 2003 when it recognised that Asia was going to be critical to its future, but worried that it did not have the right knowledge, skills and policy settings to be able to truly thrive in the region. While relations with North Asia have grown significantly, relations with South Asia, and India in particular, have largely stayed static, swinging between trade and security priorities but lacking a shared strategic outlook. In summing up the outcomes of the 2003 Asia New Zealand Foundation forum, seven points were laid out as a basis for New Zealand progressing its partnerships across Asia. Those points remain as relevant in 2023 — and to the New Zealand–India relationship — as they were twenty years ago:

1. Strong personal and institutional relationships should be at the core of any long-term strategy.

2. Enduring relationships arise from mutual common interests rather than from purely commercial motives.
3. Asia cannot be seen as a single entity. The region's diversity of countries, markets, cultures, languages and history must be individually understood and respected.
4. Knowledge of Asian languages and cultures brings substantial benefits.
5. Positive outcomes come from consistency between policy and practice, co-ordination and collaboration, and by identifying and concentrating on specific opportunities.
6. New Zealand has strengths to play to. An intangible asset is a reservoir of goodwill and trust among Asian countries.
7. Tangible assets include the knowledge and contacts New Zealand's communities of Asian origin, networks such as Chambers of Commerce and sister cities, and members of the New Zealand diaspora and alumni groups throughout the region.

In 2022, as the COVID-19 pandemic eased, the Ardern Government faced a unique opportunity with India. On the one hand, it could have stepped up its investment in India as a strategic partner in the Indo-Pacific, knowing that by doing so, and by developing greater people-to-people connections, trade would be likely to follow. In the end, it decided to stay on the periphery, continuing to observe the rise of India from afar and doing little in practice to substantially develop the partnership or proactively manage irritants.

The sixth Labour Government led by Prime Minister Ardern, however, clearly identified the Indo-Pacific as a region of core strategic interest to New Zealand and tasked New Zealand officials with embedding New Zealand 'as an active and integral partner in shaping an Indo-Pacific order that delivers regional stability and economic integration' (Ministry of Foreign Affairs and Trade, n.d.). The 'NZ Inc' India Strategy explains why India is critical to this endeavour. The task ahead is to put these words into action. As Prime Minister Fraser said in the late 1940s, we have much to gain from fostering a 'free and powerful association' with India, characterised by 'mutual confidence and cooperation in the full respect of the independence, sovereignty, and individuality' (Ministry of Foreign Affairs, 1972, pp. 137–138).

References

Adhia, N. (2015). The history of economic development in India since independence. *Education About Asia, 20*(3). www.asianstudies.org/publications/eaa/archives/the-history-of-economic-development-in-india-since-independence.

Ardern, J. (2022, May 27). Full speech: Jacinda Ardern delivers Harvard University Commencement speech. www.newshub.co.nz/home/politics/2022/05/full-speech-jacinda-ardern-delivers-harvard-university-commencement-speech.html.

Asia New Zealand Foundation (2020). New Zealand and Japan: To our future research report. www.asianz.org.nz/our-resources/reports/new-zealand-and-japan-to-our-future-research-report.

Asia New Zealand Foundation (2021, June). New Zealanders' perceptions of Asia and Asian Peoples. 2020 Annual Survey (p. 34). www.asianz.org.nz/assets/PDFs/Perceptions-of-Asia-2020.pdf.

Asia New Zealand Foundation (2021, June 16). Perceptions of Asia 2020. www.asianz.org.nz/research/perceptions-of-asia-2020.

Bandyopadhyay, S. (2010). *India in New Zealand: Local Identities, Global Relations*. Dunedin: Otago University Press.

Bonnett, G. (2021, December 6). Families left waiting as borders open for tourists: "It's been tough". RNZ. www.rnz.co.nz/news/national/457292/families-left-waiting-as-borders-open-for-tourists-it-s-been-tough.

Didham, R. (2010, April). Future potential and the invisible diaspora: New Zealand and South Asian diasporas (p. 6). www.asianz.org.nz/assets/Uploads/Future-Potential-and-the-Invisible-Diaspora-New-Zealand-and-South-Asia-diaspora.pdf.

Economic Times (2003, June 3). Govt to take only tied aid from allies. economictimes.indiatimes.com/govt-to-take-only-tied-aid-from-allies/articleshow/1854.cms.

Hall, I. (2021). Australia and India in the Modi era: An unequal strategic partnership? *International Politics, 59*, 112–128.

Huang, Y. & Wang, B. (2011). From the Asian miracle to an Asian century? Economic transformation in the 2000s and prospects for the 2010s. Reserve Bank of Australia. www.rba.gov.au/publications/confs/2011/huang-wang.html.

India Today (2016, September 20). Govt reviews impact of trade pacts on economy, employment. www.indiatoday.in/pti-feed/story/govt-reviews-impact-of-trade-pacts-on-economy-employment-690400-2016-09-20.

Indian Express (2016, October 26). Full text: PM Modi on New Zealand Prime Minister John Key's visit to India. indianexpress.com/article/india/india-news-india/full-text-pm-modis-on-new-zealand-prime-minister-john-keys-visit-to-india.

Indian Newslink (2014, November 13). Our communities: Punjabis. indiannewslink.co.nz/our-communities-punjabis.

Jaishankar, D. (2020, September 16). The Australia–India strategic partnership: Accelerating security cooperation in the Indo–Pacific. *Lowy Institute.* www.lowyinstitute.org/publications/australia-india-strategic-partnership-accelerating-security-cooperation-indo-pacific.

Jorgensen, M. (2020, August 12). China is overturning the rules-based order from within. *The Interpreter.* www.lowyinstitute.org/the-interpreter/china-overturning-rules-based-order-within.

Key, J. (2011, October 21). PM launches strategy to open doors to India. www.beehive.govt.nz/release/pm-launches-strategy-open-doors-india.

Key, J. (2016, October 27). NZ and India to strengthen relationship. www.beehive.govt.nz/release/nz-and-india-strengthen-relationship.

Kumarasingham, H. (2010). Independence and identity ignored? New Zealand's reactions to the Statute of Westminster. *National Identities, 12*(2), 147–160.

Laskar, R. K. (2004, June). Respite from disgraceful NDA foreign policy. *Congress Sandesh, 6*(10), 8.

McCully, M. (2009, June 4). *Speech to the Pacific Wave Conference.* www.beehive.govt.nz/speech/speech-pacific-wave-conference.

McDowell, M. & Webb, D. (1998). *The New Zealand Legal System: Structures, Processes and Legal Theory* (2nd ed.). Wellington: Butterworths.

McGibbon, I. (2016, February 1). Asian conflicts — Cold War. Jawaharlal Nehru with Sidney Holland. *Te Ara: The Encyclopedia of New Zealand.* teara.govt.nz/en/photograph/34514/jawaharlal-nehru-with-sidney-holland.

Miller, M. C. (2021, October 13). The Quad, AUKUS, and India's Dilemmas. *Council on Foreign Relations.* www.cfr.org/article/quad-aukus-and-indias-dilemmas.

Ministry of External Affairs, Government of India (2018, June 1). Prime Minister's keynote address at Shangri La Dialogue. www.mea.gov.in/Speeches-Statements.htm?dtl/29943/Prime+Ministers+Keynote+Address+at+Shangri+La+Dialogue+June+01+2018.

Ministry of Foreign Affairs and Trade, New Zealand (n.d.). India–New Zealand 2025: Investing in the relationship. www.mfat.govt.nz/assets/Countries-and-Regions/South-Asia/India/India-Strategy-A5-Final-web-spreads.pdf.

Ministry of Foreign Affairs and Trade, New Zealand (n.d.). Our strategic direction. www.mfat.govt.nz/en/about-us/our-strategic-direction.

Ministry of Foreign Affairs, New Zealand (1972). *New Zealand Foreign Policy: Statements and Documents, 1943–1957.* Wellington: Ministry of Foreign Affairs.

Ministry of Foreign Affairs, Singapore (2023, May 18). India. www.mfa.gov.sg/SINGAPORES-FOREIGN-POLICY/Countries-and-Regions/South-Asia/India.

New Zealand Trade and Enterprise (2011, October). Opening doors to India: New Zealand's 2015 vision. www.mcguinnessinstitute.org/wp-content/uploads/2021/04/GDS077.-Opening-Doors-to-India-New-Zealands-2015-Vision.pdf.

Osisanya, S. (n.d.). National Security versus Global Security. United Nations. www.un.org/en/chronicle/article/national-security-versus-global-security.

Page, J., et al. (1993). *The East Asian Miracle: Economic Growth and Public Policy*. Oxford: Oxford University Press for the World Bank. documents1.worldbank.org/curated/en/975081468244550798/pdf/multi-page.pdf.

Parker, D. (2020, June 8).Trade strategy for the recovery from the impacts of Covid-19. www.beehive.govt.nz/speech/trade-strategy-recovery-impacts-covid-19.

Peters, W. (2020, February 27). The Indo-Pacific: From principles to partnerships. www.beehive.govt.nz/speech/indo-pacific-principles-partnerships.

Rachman, G. (2019, March 4). China, India and the rise of the "civilisation state". *Financial Times*. www.ft.com/content/b6bc9ac2-3e5b-11e9-9bee-efab61506f44.

Rolls, M. G. (2016, September 26). From the margins to the centre: The deepening of New Zealand's relations with India. blogs.lse.ac.uk/southasia/2016/09/26/from-the-margins-to-the-centre-the-deepening-of-new-zealands-relations-with-india.

Round, D. (1980, January–February). Our foreign policy is trade. *New Zealand International Review*, 5(1), 3.

Sachdeva, S. (2020, July 16). NZ joins US-led Covid coalition. *Newsroom*. www.newsroom.co.nz/nz-joins-us-led-covid-coalition.

Seiler, P. E. (1997). *Asian Immigration to New Zealand and the Role of Networks in International Trade*. Master's Dissertation, Massey University, Palmerston North. mro.massey.ac.nz/bitstream/handle/10179/6586/02_whole.pdf.

Sidhu, H. (2018, August 8). High Commissioner's remarks on the "Future of the Australia–India Economic Relationship". Australian High Commission, New Delhi, india.highcommission.gov.au/ndli/HOMspeech080818.html.

Spratt, J. & Wood, T. (2018). Change and resilience in New Zealand Aid under Minister McCully. *Policy Quarterly*, 14(2), 5–31. https://ojs.victoria.ac.nz/pq/article/download/5091/4531/7121.

Sundell, A. (2022, February 11). Visualizing countries grouped by their largest trading partner (1960–2020). *Visual Capitalist*. www.visualcapitalist.com/cp/biggest-trade-partner-of-each-country-1960-2020.

Varghese, P. N. (2018). An India economic strategy to 2035. www.dfat.gov.au/publications/trade-and-investment/india-economic-strategy/ies/index.html.

Waters, G. (2020, February). India and New Zealand: Our story, our future. *Asia New Zealand Foundation* (p. 7). www.asianz.org.nz/assets/Uploads/India-and-New-Zealand-Our-story-our-future.pdf.

Part V

Conclusion: Implications for the Foreign Policy of Ardern's Government

Chapter 12

The Era of COVID-19 and Beyond: Some Reflections on the Implications for the Foreign Policy of Jacinda Ardern's Government

Geoffrey Miller

Few would have suspected that a trip to India by Winston Peters, then New Zealand's Foreign Minister, and David Parker, the Trade Minister, in the final week of February 2020 would be among the final international journeys undertaken by the country's ministers for a very long time.

The coronavirus, as the mysterious new illness that was beginning to sweep the world was usually called at the time — the World Health Organization had only coined the 'COVID-19' name earlier in the month — received little overt attention during the New Zealand ministers' high-profile visit to Delhi and Mumbai. But within a matter of weeks, much of the world would be entering strict lockdowns to try and stave off the worst impacts of the deadly new disease.

The trip by Peters and Parker was promoted as a 'business delegation', but this underplayed its true significance (Parker & Peters, 2020). The potential for a free trade deal with India usually dominated Wellington's view of its relationship with New Delhi, but India's withdrawal from the Regional Comprehensive Economic Partnership a few months earlier, in November 2019, meant that this prospect had all but been extinguished for the time being.

Pre-Pandemic Alignment with the 'Indo-Pacific'

From the Foreign Minister's perspective, there was still a very good reason to proceed with the trip. Arguably, the real aim of the India tour was to cement the reorientation of New Zealand's foreign policy from a trade-driven approach that had dominated since at least the 1990s, to a more ideological one. India was the final member of the Quadrilateral Security Dialogue (or Quad for short) that Peters visited over the 2018–2020 period: he had already made multiple calls on the other members of Australia, Japan and the United States.

Peters' keynote address on the India trip — titled 'The Indo-Pacific: from principles to partnerships' — reflected these aims (Peters, 2020). Since becoming Foreign Minister in 2017, Peters had been seeking to align New Zealand more closely with the United States and other countries that were becoming more sceptical of China's rise. India, which had helped to popularise the 'Indo-Pacific' phrase, was a major geopolitical competitor of China. New Delhi was therefore an obvious next stop on Peters' list of capitals to visit, irrespective of any free trade deal.

To that end, the New Zealand Foreign Minister's speech to the Indian Council of World Affairs endorsed the 'free and open Indo-Pacific' blueprint that the Quad countries were especially keen to advance. Peters situated New Zealand firmly in the Indo-Pacific and linked its interests with India's, pointing to commonalities such as a 'shared strategic geography as well as a shared commitment to a stable, peaceful, open and secure region'.

Telling his audience that 'strategic competition is at levels that we have not seen for decades', Peters said Wellington wanted 'to see an Indo-Pacific that is open and inclusive; that is committed to transparency; that respects sovereignty; that adheres to international law; that upholds freedoms of overflight and navigation; where markets are open; and that is grounded in ASEAN centrality'.

'Pacific Reset'

Even for Peters, getting to this point had taken some time. The Minister had introduced the 'Pacific Reset' as his foreign policy doctrine at a landmark speech to the Lowy Institute in Sydney in March 2018 (Peters, March 1, 2018). The policy was driven in part by concerns over 'Great Power' competition in the region: Peters called the Pacific an 'increasingly contested strategic space, no longer neglected by Great Power ambition, and so Pacific Island leaders have more options'.

Yet for all that, Peters' motivations were complex and probably more pragmatic than ideological in nature in late 2017 and early 2018, when the Pacific Reset was initially developed. Peters was an experienced politician and had already served as Foreign Minister once before, in 2005–2008. He was now also looking for a legacy and a way to make a 'big splash'.

Above all, the Pacific Reset allowed Peters to differentiate himself from his main predecessor, the National Party's Murray McCully, who had become known for his wheeling and dealing far from New Zealand's immediate neighbourhood. Some of the plans led by McCully had paid off — such as New Zealand's election to the UN Security Council for the 2015–2016 period — but they had also resulted in failures and embarrassments such as the ill-fated 'Saudi sheep deal' (Collins, 2020).

For Winston Peters, the Pacific Reset seemed like a way to turn the page on the McCully era. A Pacific focus would give a theme to his term as Foreign Minister that contrasted sharply with his predecessor's ambitions. The refocusing on the neglected Pacific would also provide a convincing argument to request greater resources for the Ministry of Foreign Affairs and Trade (MFAT) from the Labour Finance Minister, Grant Robertson.

Peters' speech to the Otago Foreign Policy School in June 2018 certainly emphasised pragmatism as the main driver behind the shift (Peters, June 29, 2018). In that address, Peters was cautious of ideology and openly expressed reservations about applying the term 'Indo-Pacific' to New Zealand. Peters said 'Asia-Pacific' resonated more with New Zealanders and used the term throughout his speech. He also justified increased spending on the Pacific in investment terms: 'every dollar spent today in the Pacific reduces the risk of expensive interventions in the future, whether military, border security or healthcare'.

Indeed, Peters had secured an enormous boost to MFAT's budget in 2018. Peters won a substantial injection of NZ$900 million in new funding for his ministry, over a four-year period, which included a NZ$700 million boost in foreign aid that would raise New Zealand's rate of Official Development Assistance in its Gross National Income from 0.23 per cent to an eventual high-point of 0.28 per cent, reversing years of declining spending under National-led governments (Nicol-Williams, 2018).

Ideology appeared to become more of a driving factor in New Zealand's international relations as the 2017–2020 Labour–New Zealand First coalition wore on. A key moment was Winston Peters' visit to the United States in December 2018, during which he made a hard-hitting speech at Georgetown University in Washington, DC. that squarely addressed China's ambitions in the Pacific. Peters said: 'larger players are renewing their interest in the Pacific, with an abundant element of strategic competition ... our eyes are wide open to the trajectory and we know that yours are too' (Peters, 2018, December 15).

There were other changes over the 2018–2019 period that aimed to align New Zealand with the more pro-Western camp that was becoming increasingly concerned about China's growing assertiveness in the Pacific. Ron Mark, the Defence Minister and — like Peters — a New Zealand First party MP, announced a decision to purchase the Boeing P-8A Poseidon aircraft that had anti-submarine attack capabilities, for example (Mark, 2018). Mark also revealed a bigger Defence Capability Plan in mid-2019 that involved a collective $NZ20 billion in new spending by 2030 (Mark, 2019). The decisions initiated the first sustained increase in New Zealand's defence spending (as a proportion of GDP) in decades.

Separately, in late 2018, the Government Communications Security Bureau opposed a decision by Spark (New Zealand's biggest telecommunications company) to use Huawei technology in its roll-out of 5G mobile telephone technology, a decision that was part of a co-ordinated approach by the Five Eyes intelligence grouping (Uhlmann & Grigg, 2018).

Peters' foreign travel also became more strategic. Early trips in 2017 and 2018 were to a wide range of destinations, both Western and non-Western — and included a trip to China. But from late 2018 onwards, Peters' travel schedule gradually adopted a narrower focus: there were three trips to the United States, two trips to Japan and no further trips to China. Then, in early 2020, there was the India trip — the final member of the Quad to be visited by Peters, at which he made another, more pro-Western, address.

Ambiguity about New Zealand's Position

There are of course caveats to this interpretation. Peters might have been New Zealand's Foreign Minister, but Prime Minister Jacinda Ardern was a far more prominent international figure from the time of her election in 2017. In response to Peters' shifts, Ardern sought to tread more of a middle ground: in February 2019, she opened a press conference with a six-minute defence of the health of the China–New Zealand relationship, which she called 'robust and mature' (Ainge Roy, 2019). Subsequently, the Prime Minister undertook a short but successful visit to China to meet Xi Jinping in April 2019; Trade Minister David Parker publicly committed New Zealand to China's Belt and Road Initiative in the same month (O'Sullivan, 2019).

The strategic studies specialist Robert Ayson's analysis is that the differing views represented deliberate 'bad cop–good cop' positioning, creating 'wriggle room' for New Zealand (Ayson, 2021, p. 242). Ayson also points to the multilateral and underlying anti-Trump positioning by Ardern at the United Nations in September 2018, for example, along with her public disagreement with Donald Trump over racist statements made by the US president in 2019 (Ayson, 2021, p. 241). Peters seemed to be more enthusiastic about Ardern's meeting with Trump at the United Nations in 2019 than Ardern was herself: Peters issued an unusual press release that headlined Ardern's meeting a 'triumph' and called it a 'diplomatic coup' (Peters, 2019).

COVID-19 as a Turning Point

The tumultuous events of 2020 — especially the COVID-19 pandemic, but also elections in New Zealand and the United States — helped to clarify matters. After the India trip, Peters was effectively grounded as Foreign Minister for the remainder of the parliamentary term by the impact of COVID-19. His duties for several months were focused on organising repatriation flights for New Zealanders stuck overseas and helping foreign nationals in New Zealand to return home. This backroom crisis management role — Peters spent his lockdown weeks in March and April at his rural property in New Zealand's Far North, hundreds of kilometres from Wellington — heavily reduced his visibility (Stuff, 2020).

By contrast, Ardern's stature and media exposure only soared further over the early months of the pandemic. New Zealand's initially successful COVID-19 elimination contrasted with that of the US president. While Trump mused about the efficacy of disinfectant as a COVID-19 treatment method, Ardern's pleas to 'be kind' and work as a 'team of five million' attracted attention and plaudits from around the world.

Ardern's COVID-19 response built on her compassionate but decisive approach that she had already established in her response to the Christchurch mosque attacks of 2019. Ardern's Christchurch Call initiative for curbing terrorist and violent extremist content from the Internet — undertaken in partnership with French President Emmanuel Macron — had helped to further burnish her reputation on the world stage, as had her international travel schedule that included high-profile speeches to the UN General Assembly in New York in 2018 and 2019.

COVID-19 Elimination Advantages and Drawbacks

New Zealand was far from the only country successfully pursuing an elimination strategy during the early phase of the pandemic — Australia, China, Singapore and Vietnam were just some of the other examples from around the Indo-Pacific — but Ardern became a major elimination strategy figurehead. Alongside the Government's science-driven approach and clear communication style, numerous Ardern moments attracted a particularly high level of global media interest. These included her declaration that the Easter bunny was an essential worker (Lee, 2020), to an announcement that she and other ministers would take a 20 per cent pay cut (Ainge Roy, 2020), to her admission that she had performed a 'little dance' when she received news that the virus had been officially eliminated within the community in June 2020 (Menon, June 8, 2020).

By mid-2020, the immediate crisis management phase of the pandemic was transitioning into a 'new normal'. Polls showed that New Zealand voters largely gave Ardern and her Labour Party the credit for the temporary elimination of COVID-19. In most cases, international travel was off the table on account of a strict Managed Isolation and Quarantine (MIQ) system, which heavily limited the numbers of people entering the country.

This would become problematic as time went on, but initially at least, voters were just happy to be safe and for the enormous economic support that the government had provided over the early stage of the pandemic, which included relatively generous wage subsidy payments. Opinion polls showed Labour soaring, while Peters' New Zealand First party sank almost without trace during the election campaign that was held over an extended period from August to October 2020. National, Labour's main centre-right rival, also struggled, despite out-polling Labour as late as February 2020, before COVID-19 took hold (*1News*, 2020).

The 'Covid Elections' of 2020

At the General Election on 17 October 2020, Labour won just over 50 per cent of the vote, giving it an unprecedented absolute majority under New Zealand's Mixed Member Proportional (MMP) voting system that was introduced in 1996. Once the wasted vote was taken into account, Labour commanded 65 seats in the New Zealand Parliament, giving it a healthy majority (at least by MMP standards) to govern alone without any coalition partners.

The implications for New Zealand foreign policy of this landslide win, largely built on Labour's COVID-19 policies, were enormous. Labour's triumph meant the end of the 'outsourcing' of the nuts and bolts of New Zealand's foreign policy to the New Zealand First party; Labour would have the chance to appoint its own Foreign Minister for the first time since Phil Goff held the role from 1999 to 2005 (Peters had claimed the role for New Zealand First when the party supported Labour in 2005–2008).

However, there was still one further vote in 2020 to come that would have a major impact on New Zealand's foreign policy direction — the US presidential election on 3 November. As in New Zealand, the COVID-19 response played a major role in the election campaign, but this time it favoured the challenger rather than the incumbent. Trump's poor management of the United States' COVID-19 response helped to propel Joe Biden into the White House with what was ultimately a decisive victory.

Nanaia Mahuta as New Foreign Minister

A day before the US election, Ardern appointed Nanaia Mahuta as New Zealand's new Foreign Minister. Mahuta was an experienced Labour MP and Minister — she was one of the party's longest-serving MPs and a key figure in the party's Māori caucus — but she had relatively little direct foreign policy experience. However, this freshness and 'blank slate' was part of Mahuta's attraction: she was also the first Māori woman to hold the foreign affairs portfolio and only the second Māori (after Peters) to hold the role. Her appointment in itself, as a Māori woman, attracted significant international interest and was given prominent treatment by news outlets including CNN (Hollingsworth, 2020).

Still, Mahuta's entry into the role was not easy. New Zealand's border restrictions made international travel almost impossible.

The requirement to undertake 14 days of MIQ in a hotel upon return to the country made foreign travel by government MPs politically unpalatable, given the long list of New Zealanders abroad who were still waiting for an MIQ space. The MIQ situation meant that Mahuta was forced to remain in New Zealand and conduct diplomacy via Zoom, rather than undertake the customary inaugural trips as Foreign Minister.

In the early months of her appointment, Mahuta's foreign counterparts were also largely relying on online diplomacy, which provided a level playing field. However, with the arrival of the first vaccines, more regular international travel at Foreign Minister level was beginning to resume by early 2021. In Australia, which adopted a similar MIQ policy to New Zealand, Foreign Minister Marise Payne travelled throughout the pandemic, including to Washington, DC. for the scheduled annual Australia–United States Ministerial Consultations in July 2020 and to Tokyo for a Quad meeting in October 2020 (Dobell, 2020). In May 2021, Payne attended a G7 Foreign Ministers' meeting in Liverpool, while her Prime Minister Scott Morrison attended the G7 in Cornwall in June (Hawke, 2021).

Virtual Diplomacy Impact

Aware of the bad 'optics' that globetrotting ministers would create amidst ongoing controversies over the fairness of the MIQ booking system, Ardern appeared to adopt an all but 'no travel' policy for her government's ministers. The only exception that was made during the first half of 2021 was for Trade Minister Damien O'Connor, who made relatively low-key visits to Brussels and London in June (O'Connor, 2021). The sole purpose of these was to make progress on the free trade deals that New Zealand was negotiating with the European Union and United Kingdom.

The transformation of diplomacy into a virtual affair under COVID-19 was a double-edged sword for both Mahuta and Ardern. While the inability to travel was undoubtedly a barrier, video calls countered the usual difficulties imposed by New Zealand's geographical remoteness and meant both the Prime Minister and Foreign Minister could 'attend' more engagements and hold more meetings with foreign counterparts than would have normally been practical.

COVID-19's Impact on APEC and Expo 2020 Dubai

One example of a virtual meeting that could never have taken place in person was a special APEC leaders' summit on COVID-19 that was called at short notice by Ardern in July 2021. It was the first time in the history of APEC that an additional leaders' meeting had been held, and its existence owed much to Ardern's reputation as a consensus-builder (Miller, July 17, 2021).

But there was no doubt that the impact of virtual diplomacy was beginning to wane, especially as more physical events began to be held globally, such as the G7 in Cornwall in June 2021. One example of the diminishing returns of virtual summits was the fact that while most APEC leaders attended the special online summit on COVID-19 in July 2021 live, President Xi sent only a recorded message (Madhani & McGuirk, 2021).

Even more troubling for New Zealand, the virtual APEC leaders' summit in November attracted nowhere near the amount of attention that the in-person hosting of 21 leaders in New Zealand would have generated. Ardern largely put a brave face on the situation, but even she admitted that 'our ability to put New Zealand on the world stage isn't quite what it would have been, had we had an in-person event' (McKay, 2021).

COVID-19 and the elimination strategy also heavily reduced the impact of New Zealand's $NZ60 million pavilion at what should have been another marquee event, the six-month-long Expo 2020 in Dubai, which began a year late in October 2021. Several hundred MIQ rooms were allocated for attendees, a decision that attracted domestic political criticism, yet still represented a minimal number of New Zealanders for a six-month event (*Radio New Zealand*, 2021). Limited global appetite for travel because of COVID-19 also reduced the number of international visitors generally to Expo 2020, and it was reported that 70 per cent of visitors came from the UAE (Krishna Kumar, 2022).

Increasingly Negative Western Attitudes towards China

Moreover, when it came to China, COVID-19 in many ways marked a turning point in the views of Western publics. Attitudes turned sharply negative, according to Pew Research Center survey data. Pew's findings, released in October 2020 from research conducted in the middle of that year, revealed particularly unfavourable views in New Zealand's closest neighbour, Australia: fully 81 per cent of respondents were unfavourable towards China — a result that was largely mirrored across the 13 other, mainly Western, countries that were covered (Silver *et al.*, 2020).

New Zealand was not included in the Pew survey, but the Asia New Zealand Foundation's 'Perceptions of Asia' survey — released in mid-2021, but based on data collected in October and November 2020 — showed a similar, although not quite as dramatic, trend: 35 per cent of respondents viewed China as a threat or a major threat, up from 22 per cent just a year earlier (Asia New Zealand Foundation, 2021).

It is difficult to look past COVID-19 when it comes to explaining the deterioration in Western attitudes towards China in 2020. However, when the pandemic began, the first lockdown was in Wuhan; subsequent allegations by President Trump that the virus had escaped from a laboratory only added fuel to the fire. In Australia, Prime Minister Morrison called for an investigation into the origins of COVID-19 in April 2020 — which later resulted in China announcing punitive tariffs on Australian wine, barley and other, mainly food-related, exports (*BBC News*, 2020).

Comments by Mahuta and O'Connor on China

It was into this environment that Mahuta stepped as New Zealand's new Foreign Minister in November 2020. After initial coverage, focused mainly on her personal background, an early sign of her intended foreign policy positioning began to emerge. In December 2020, Mahuta gave an interview to *Reuters* in which she said New Zealand could potentially play a mediating role between Australia and China during New Zealand's hosting of APEC events the following year (Menon, 2020, December 15).

Mahuta's suggestion was followed by comments by O'Connor in January 2021, who told CNBC television that Australia 'should follow us and show respect' to China. These comments reportedly provoked a furious reaction from Australian officials (Dziedzic, 2021). In response, the New Zealand Government went into damage control: Ardern quickly distanced herself from the comments (Manch, 2021). O'Connor soon called his Australian counterpart and later issued a statement saying the 'Australia–China relationship will always be a matter for China and Australia' (Patterson, 2021).

Despite this apparent gaffe by O'Connor, Labour's positioning in the first six months of the new majority government did seem to suggest that it was keen to strike a more moderate tone than its predecessor had under the pro-United States Peters. This continued in April, when Mahuta told an audience at the New Zealand China Council that she was 'uncomfortable with expanding the remit of the Five Eyes', after New Zealand had been absent from joint statements on Hong Kong and the origins of COVID-19 (Hollingsworth, 2021). While Mahuta also said in the same speech '[t]here are some things on which New Zealand and China do not, cannot, and will not, agree' — a reference to human rights concerns — it was the Five Eyes remarks that inevitably dominated subsequent media coverage.

Mahuta's admission — made during the question-and-answer session following her speech — sparked a vociferous debate over New Zealand's stance towards China, during which Ardern was called the 'West's woke weak link' by Con Coughlin, the defence editor of Britain's *Daily Telegraph* (Stuff, 2021). And the Australian edition of the '60 Minutes' television current affairs programme asked whether New Zealand was becoming 'New Xi-Land' (Edwards, 2021).

Jacinda Ardern's Gradual Recalibration towards the West

The reaction to Mahuta's rebalancing of the China relationship put Ardern in a difficult position. The ambiguous positioning between herself and Peters towards China — with Ardern largely playing the dove, and Peters the hawk — had worked well partly because of its authenticity. Peters was from the New Zealand First party, while Ardern was from Labour. As coalition partners, the parties could sometimes be expected to have differing positions. Moreover, Ardern and Peters were working together during Trump's time as US president. Trump's crude populism — including his repeated attacks on China — was naturally anathema to Ardern, but more tolerable for Peters, who was himself a natural populist and a holder of nationalist instincts. Writing in 2019, the political scientist David MacDonald found New Zealand First's populism in international relations was applied inconsistently, but noted that Peters vigorously opposed a free trade agreement with China even while New Zealand First was in a governing arrangement with Labour in 2008 (MacDonald, 2019, p. 239).

There might also have been some expectation on the part of Ardern that if she could wait out Trump, the China issue would become more straightforward. After all, a new US Administration might be expected to take a softer tone towards Beijing — akin to the 2009 'reset' policies offered under the Obama Administration towards Russia. However, the opposite happened: upon taking office, Biden immediately appointed Kurt Campbell — the architect of Obama's 'Pivot to Asia' policy — as his Indo-Pacific Coordinator and arranged for the holding of the first Quad leaders' summit. The US pressure on China only increased throughout 2021 — most notably through the launch of the new AUKUS alliance between Australia, the United Kingdom and the United States in September.

Exactly what transpired behind the scenes will be a matter for the history books. One possibility is that Ardern, Mahuta and Labour more generally were still very much in the process of determining what their interpretation of Labour's traditional 'independent foreign policy' should entail. Another is that international pressure that emanated chiefly from the other Five Eyes countries provoked a backtrack. A reversal of sorts from Mahuta's views appeared to take place in May 2021, when Ardern used a keynote speech at the China Business Summit in Auckland to say that New Zealand's differences with China were 'becoming harder to reconcile'. In that address, Ardern cited several sensitive issues, such as human rights in Xinjiang and the backsliding regarding democracy in Hong Kong. Ardern also pointedly noted that New Zealand was a 'strong supporter of the rules, norms and international frameworks that govern global affairs' (Ardern, 2021).

In hindsight, the language used at the China Business Summit was the opening salvo in a series of more pro-Western foreign policy decisions. In July, New Zealand issued a statement alleging that China was sponsoring cyber-hacking (Little, 2021). And in September, Ardern was at best ambiguous about Australia's new AUKUS defence pact: while being clear that New Zealand itself would not be involved, she also appeared to give tacit agreement to the fact that nuclear-powered submarines would now have a presence in New Zealand's immediate region by saying 'we welcome the increased engagement of the UK and US in the region' (McClure, 2021).

The year ended with the release of a particularly hawkish defence assessment, which asserted China was 'seeking to reshape the international system'. In tone and in substance, the document comfortably put New Zealand on the same page as Australia and the United States

(Miller, December 10, 2021). While a similar 2018 document could also be said to have been strongly-worded, Sachdeva notes a key difference: while the earlier document referred to a 'strong and resilient relationship with China' and pointed to collaboration with Beijing on defence-related and security matters, the 2021 edition made no mention of any such arrangements with China (Sachdeva, 2021).

Some Hedging Continues

Of course, this did not mean New Zealand had become a clone of its Five Eyes partners: Mahuta's positioning on the joint statements remained and the Government's ministers dodged calls for a diplomatic boycott of the forthcoming Winter Olympics in Beijing by using New Zealand's COVID-19 border restrictions as an excuse for non-attendance (Sachdeva, 2021). The pandemic had only increased New Zealand's reliance on its primary exports — of which China took 33 per cent — and the New Zealand Government was still keenly aware of the importance of preserving a good relationship with Beijing. More sympathetic positioning towards China emerged over the second half of 2022, when Ardern signalled a visit to China was on the cards and repeatedly emphasised New Zealand's 'independent foreign policy' (Miller, November 14, 2022).

Another sign that New Zealand was still keen to forge its own path came in Mahuta's first foreign trip in November 2021: the trip was book-ended by visits to Five Eyes countries (Australia at the beginning, the US and Canada at the end), but sandwiched in the middle were visits to Indonesia, the UAE and Qatar. Mahuta gave her biggest speech of the trip in Jakarta and used the address to emphasise New Zealand's support of ASEAN centrality. Indonesia had been one of the more vocal critics of the AUKUS deal, and called off a visit by Morrison to Jakarta in response (*Sky News Australia*, 2021).

Negative Impact of COVID-19 Isolation and Virtual Diplomacy

In retrospect, virtual diplomacy and the lack of face-to-face meetings over the 2020–2022 period were perhaps contributing factors to growing global tensions. Fears over contracting COVID-19 led Russian President Vladimir Putin to isolate himself in a protective 'bubble' well beyond the early phase of the pandemic. Meanwhile, in China, President Xi did not travel abroad at all after the pandemic began in March 2020, and one of the few foreign guests he received was Putin himself, at the Winter Olympics in February 2022. The pair issued a 5000-word joint statement at their meeting and declared a 'no-limits' partnership between China and Russia (*BBC*, 2022).

Putin's isolation reportedly enhanced his own sense of paranoia, and may have contributed to his seemingly irrational decision to launch a brutal invasion of Ukraine in February 2022 (Sanger & Troianovski, 2022). In turn, Russia's invasion of Ukraine forced New Zealand to take a much stronger position. Russia itself was a low priority for New Zealand; only around $NZ300 million worth of exports were sold there, making it a relative minnow (Pullar-Strecker, 2022). However, the precedent potential was significant.

Post-Ukraine Rebalancing towards the West

The first sign of a post-Ukraine rebalancing towards the West came in a debate over sanctions: Ardern initially tried to preserve the government's existing stance against autonomous sanctions. However, three days after the invasion, the government gave in and pledged to pass a new Russia Sanctions Act (Miller, March 10, 2022). This was only the start: as the weeks went on, New Zealand found itself sending defensive military equipment to Ukraine. Subsequently, as pressure on the government grew both domestically and from its Western partners, Ardern sent about 70 military personnel and a Lockheed Hercules aircraft to Europe, as well as $NZ7.5 million to the United Kingdom to purchase 'lethal aid' weaponry for Ukraine (Ardern *et al.*, 2022). These were major shifts for New Zealand foreign policy. While New Zealand had long expressed its frustrations over the impotence of the UN Security Council, Ukraine seemed to be the crisis that finally convinced Wellington that it would have to take matters into its own hands.

The first signs of 'spillover' in this new more pro-Western stance came in April and May 2022. In April, Ardern was unusually forthright in her criticism of a security deal announced between China and the Solomon Islands. Equally significantly, she ensured that no differences could be discerned between Wellington and Canberra by repeating Australian phrasing which called the area 'our backyard' (Miller, March 30, 2022). In the same month, Ardern also undertook her first foreign trip since

COVID-19 began, travelling to Singapore and Japan — two of the three Asian countries which had also imposed unilateral sanctions on Russia (Miller, April 19, 2022).

Finally, in May 2022 Ardern gave a keynote foreign policy address on New Zealand's relations with the United States. The speech used New Zealand's support for Ukraine as a springboard to emphasise New Zealand's commitment to what Ardern called the 'rules, norms and international frameworks that govern global affairs'. And several sections of the speech appeared deliberately ambiguous signals about China, while nominally being seen to refer to New Zealand's positioning on Ukraine and Russia. For example, Ardern said that New Zealand had 'held firmly to our independent foreign policy but also to our values. When we see a threat to the rules[-]based order we rely on, we act'.

Beginnings of a New Era?

Looking back, COVID-19 may not have directly changed New Zealand's foreign policy, but it certainly provided the background music for some fundamental shifts. These might have happened gradually over a longer period anyway: Peters' plans immediately before COVID-19 already provided a template. But the polarisation that affected the world in general over the pandemic period — seen in the global debates over lockdowns, masks and vaccines — also affected geopolitics. COVID-19 and the upheaval of 2020 may mark the end point for New Zealand's previous successful strategy of riding the waves of globalisation and viewing foreign policy primarily through a trade lens.

References

Ainge Roy, E. (2019, February 18). Jacinda Ardern disputes reports of diplomatic tensions with China. *The Guardian*. www.theguardian.com/world/2019/feb/18/jacinda-ardern-disputes-reports-of-diplomatic-tensions-with-china.

Ainge Roy, E. (2020, April 15). Jacinda Ardern and ministers take pay cut in solidarity with those hit by Covid-19. *The Guardian*. www.theguardian.com/world/2020/apr/15/jacinda-ardern-and-ministers-take-20-pay-cut-in-solidarity-with-those-hit-by-covid-19.

Ardern, J., Henare, P., & Mahuta, N. (2022, April 11). New Zealand sends C130 Hercules and 50-strong team to Europe to support Ukraine. www.beehive.govt.nz/release/new-zealand-sends-c130-hercules-and-50-strong-team-europe-support-ukraine.

Ardern, J. (2021, May 3). *Speech to China Business Summit.* www.beehive.govt.nz/speech/speech-china-business-summit.

Asia New Zealand Foundation (2021, June 16). Perceptions of Asia 2020. *Asia New Zealand Foundation.* www.asianz.org.nz/research/perceptions-of-asia-2020.

Ayson, R. (2021). New Zealand's foreign and defence policy. In Levine, S. (ed.) *Politics in a Pandemic: Jacinda Ardern and New Zealand's 2020 Election* (pp. 239–250). Wellington: Victoria University Press.

BBC News (2020, November 27). China slaps up to 200% tariffs on Australian wine. *BBC,* www.bbc.com/news/business-55097100.

BBC (2022, February 4). China joins Russia in opposing Nato expansion. *BBC,* www.bbc.com/news/world-asia-60257080.

Collins, B. (2020, February 5). Agencies concede "sobering lessons" from Saudi sheep scandal that damaged NZ's reputation. *1News.* www.1news.co.nz/2020/02/05/agencies-concede-sobering-lessons-from-saudi-sheep-scandal-that-damaged-nzs-reputation.

Dobell, G. (2020, October 19). What's worth 14 days' quarantine for Australia's foreign minister? *ASPI The Strategist.* www.aspistrategist.org.au/whats-worth-14-days-quarantine-for-australias-foreign-minister.

Dziedzic, S. (2021, January 28). New Zealand Trade Minister advises Australia to show China more "respect". *ABC News,* www.abc.net.au/news/2021-01-28/nz-trade-minister-advises-australia-to-show-china-more-respect/13098674.

Edwards, B. (2021, May 31). Australia turns up the heat on NZ's relationship with China. *Democracy Project.* democracyproject.nz/2021/05/31/bryce-edwards-political-roundup-australia-turns-up-the-heat-on-nzs-relationship-with-china.

Hawke, J. (2021, May 6). COVID-19 scare hits G7 foreign ministers' summit in London as delegates test positive. *ABC News.* www.abc.net.au/news/2021-05-06/covid-19-scare-hits-g7-foreign-ministers-meeting-in-london/100119616.

Hollingsworth, J. (2020, November 2). New Zealand's Jacinda Ardern appoints country's first Indigenous female foreign minister. *CNN.* edition.cnn.com/2020/11/02/asia/new-zealand-foreign-minister-intl-hnk/index.html.

Hollingsworth, J. (2021, June 4). New Zealand is a Five Eyes outlier on China. It may have to pick a side. *CNN.* edition.cnn.com/2021/06/03/asia/new-zealand-xinjiang-china-intl-hnk-dst/index.html.

Krishna Kumar, N. P. (2022, March 20). Expo 2020 Dubai achieves massive milestone of 20 million visits. *Al Arabiya English.* english.alarabiya.net/lifestyle/2022/03/20/Expo-2020-Dubai-achieves-massive-milestone-of-20-million-visits.

Lee, A. (2020, April 6). New Zealand PM adds 2 crucial figures to list of essential workers: The Tooth Fairy and Easter Bunny. *CNN.* edition.cnn.com/2020/04/06/world/jacinda-ardern-easter-bunny-essential-workers-trnd/index.html.

Little, A. (2021, July 19). New Zealand condemns malicious cyber activity by Chinese state-sponsored actors. www.beehive.govt.nz/release/new-zealand-condemns-malicious-cyber-activity-chinese-state-sponsored-actors.

MacDonald, D. (2019). Between Populism and Pluralism: Winston Peters and the International Relations of New Zealand First. In Stengel, F. A. *et al.* (Eds.), *Populism and World Politics: Exploring Inter- and Transnational Dimensions* (pp. 227–249). Cham: Palgrave Macmillan.

Madhani, A. & McGuirk, R. (2021, July 17). Pacific Rim leaders agree to step up COVID vaccine sharing. *Associated Press.* abcnews.go.com/Health/wire-Story/pacific-rim-leaders-agree-step-covid-vaccine-sharing-78886921.

Manch, T. (2021, February 3). Jacinda Ardern deflects Australia–China comments with joke about 40-year-old "underarm incident". *Stuff.* www.stuff.co.nz/national/politics/124136962/jacinda-ardern-deflects-australiachina-comments-with-joke-about-40yearold-underarm-incident.

Mark, R. (2018, July 9). New Zealand to buy four P-8A Poseidon Maritime Patrol Aircraft. www.beehive.govt.nz/release/new-zealand-buy-four-p-8a-poseidon-maritime-patrol-aircraft.

Mark, R. (2019, June 11). Defence Capability Plan 2019 released. www.beehive.govt.nz/release/defence-capability-plan-2019-released.

McClure, T. (2021, September 16). Aukus submarines banned from New Zealand as pact exposes divide with western allies. *The Guardian.* www.theguardian.com/world/2021/sep/16/aukus-submarines-banned-as-pact-exposes-divide-between-new-zealand-and-western-allies.

McKay, B. (2021, November 10). Virtual APEC summit frustrates New Zealand. *Australian Associated Press.* www.canberratimes.com.au/story/7505393/virtual-apec-summit-frustrates-new-zealand.

Menon, P. (2020, December 15). New Zealand says willing to be arbitrator in Australia-China spat. *Reuters.* www.reuters.com/article/newwzealand-politics-mahuta-idUSKBN28P0GC.

Menon, P. (2020, June 8). Ardern dances for joy after New Zealand eliminates coronavirus. *Reuters.* www.reuters.com/article/us-health-coronavirus-newzealand-idUSKBN23F0B5.

Miller, G. (2021, December 10). China strategy dominates New Zealand's foreign policy year. *Democracy Project.* democracyproject.nz/2021/12/10/geoffrey-miller-china-strategy-dominates-new-zealands-foreign-policy-year.

Miller, G. (2021, July 17). Jacinda Ardern's APEC diplomacy could be the start of something bigger. *Democracy Project.* democracyproject.nz/2021/07/17/geoffrey-miller-jacinda-arderns-apec-diplomacy-could-be-the-start-of-something-bigger.

Miller, G. (2022, April 19). Jacinda Ardern's trip to Japan and Singapore about more than just trade. *Democracy Project.* democracyproject.nz/2022/04/19/jacinda-arderns-trip-to-japan-and-singapore-about-more-than-just-trade.

Miller, G. (2022, March 10). How significant is New Zealand's new Russia sanctions law? *Democracy Project.* democracyproject.nz/2022/03/10/geoffrey-miller-how-significant-is-new-zealands-new-russia-sanctions-law.

Miller, G. (2022, March 30). New Zealand's Australia-friendly response to China–Solomon Islands security deal. *Democracy Project.* democracyproject.nz/2022/03/30/geoffrey-miller-new-zealands-australia-friendly-response-to-china-solomon-islands-security-deal.

Miller, G. (2022, November 14). Jacinda Ardern's Asia trip rekindles New Zealand's independent foreign policy. *Democracy Project.* democracyproject.nz/2022/11/14/geoffrey-miller-jacinda-arderns-asia-trip-rekindles-new-zealands-independent-foreign-policy.

Nicol-Williams, K. (2018, May 9). "It benefits us" — Almost $1 billion Pacific aid and foreign affairs boost welcomed by aid organisations. *1News*, www.1news.co.nz/2018/05/08/it-benefits-us-almost-1-billion-pacific-aid-and-foreign-affairs-boost-welcomed-by-aid-organisations.

O'Connor, D. (2021, May 13). Trade Minister to travel to UK and EU to progress free trade agreements. www.beehive.govt.nz/release/trade-minister-travel-uk-and-eu-progress-free-trade-agreements.

1News (2020, February 13). February 13 poll: National and ACT hold the numbers to form a government. *1News.* www.1news.co.nz/2020/02/13/february-13-poll-national-and-act-hold-the-numbers-to-form-a-government.

O'Sullivan, F. (2019, April 27). Trade Minister David Parker commits NZ to China's grand plan. *New Zealand Herald.* www.nzherald.co.nz/business/fran-osullivan-trade-minister-david-parker-commits-nz-to-chinas-grand-plan/QOV6SZYQYYGC3JCGRMFHNIWIAY.

Parker, D. & Peters, W. (2020, February 24). Foreign and Trade Ministers to lead business delegation to India. www.beehive.govt.nz/release/foreign-and-trade-ministers-lead-business-delegation-india.

Patterson, J. (2021, January 28). Minister says Australia should follow NZ's lead on China diplomacy. *Stuff.* www.rnz.co.nz/news/political/435364/minister-says-australia-should-follow-nz-s-lead-on-china-diplomacy.

Peters, W. (2018, December 15). Pacific Partnerships — Georgetown address, Washington, DC. www.beehive.govt.nz/speech/pacific-partnerships-georgetown-address-washington-dc.

Peters, W. (2018, June 29). Next steps. www.beehive.govt.nz/speech/next-steps.

Peters, W. (2018, March 1). Shifting the dial. www.beehive.govt.nz/speech/shifting-dial.

Peters, W. (2019, September 24). PM's meeting with Trump a triumph. www.beehive.govt.nz/release/pm%E2%80%99s-meeting-trump-triumph.

Peters, W. (2020, February 27). The Indo-Pacific: from principles to partnerships. www.beehive.govt.nz/speech/indo-pacific-principles-partnerships.

Pullar-Strecker, T. (2022, January 26). Economic impact of Russian invasion of Ukraine on NZ would be "mostly indirect". *Stuff*. www.stuff.co.nz/business/127592162/economic-impact-of-russian-invasion-of-ukraine-on-nz-would-be-mostly-indirect.

Radio New Zealand (2021, August 7). ACT criticises setting aside 400 MIQ rooms for expo attendees. *Radio New Zealand*. www.rnz.co.nz/news/political/448719/act-criticises-setting-aside-400-miq-rooms-for-expo-attendees.

Sachdeva, S. (2021, December 9). Stormy seas ahead in Indo-Pacific — defence assessment. *Newsroom*. www.newsroom.co.nz/stormy-seas-ahead-in-indo-pacific-defence-assessment.

Sanger, D. & Troianovski, A. (2022, March 5). U.S. intelligence weighs Putin's two years of extreme pandemic isolation as a factor in his wartime mind-set. *New York Times*. www.nytimes.com/2022/03/05/world/putin-pandemic-mindset.html.

Silver, L. *et al.* (2020, October 6). Unfavorable Views of China Reach Historic Highs in Many Countries. *Pew Research Center*, www.pewresearch.org/global/2020/10/06/unfavorable-views-of-china-reach-historic-highs-in-many-countries.

Sky News Australia (2021, September 18). PM's trip to Indonesia cancelled amid fallout over aukus alliance. *Sky News Australia*. www.skynews.com.au/australia-news/defence-and-foreign-affairs/pms-trip-to-indonesia-cancelled-amid-fallout-over-aukus-alliance/video/4d36d6d5443d240c5e32f4f8d9e071ef.

Stuff (2020, April 13). Deputy PM Winston Peters fished from his lawn — is that within the rules? *Stuff*. www.stuff.co.nz/national/120986838/coronavirus-deputy-pm-winston-peters-fished-from-his-lawn--is-that-within-the-rules.

Stuff (2021, April 22). Prime Minister Jacinda Ardern labelled the "West's woke weak link" over reluctance to join Five Eyes' China stance. *Stuff*. www.stuff.co.nz/national/politics/124914696/prime-minister-jacinda-ardern-labelled-the-wests-woke-weak-link-over-reluctance-to-join-five-eyes-china-stance.

Uhlmann, C. & Grigg, A. (2018, December 13). How the "Five Eyes" cooked up the campaign to kill Huawei. *Sydney Morning Herald*. www.smh.com.au/business/companies/how-the-five-eyes-cooked-up-the-campaign-to-kill-huawei-20181213-p50m24.html.

Index

A
Abe, Shinzo, 24–25, 31
Accession Working Group, 87
acquire territory, 206
Action Plan, 208
Acton, James, 199, 209
adaptation, 135–136
Adaptation Committee of the UK Climate Change Committee, 135
Advisory Committees, 118
Afghan, 52
Afghanistan, 212
aggression, 212
Agreement on Climate Change, Trade and Sustainability, 81
Agreement on Economic Cooperation with the Separate Customs Territory of Taiwan, Penghu, Kinmen and Matsu, 65
agricultural exports, 68, 77, 209
agricultural trade, 64
agriculture, 152
agriculture sector, 227
aid, xxxv, 166–167, 170, 178, 200, 226, 228

aircraft, 248, 258
airport runway, 167
Albanese, Anthony, 235
Alden, Edward, 77
alert level system, 104, 116, 175
alliances, xx, 206
All India Institute of Medical Sciences, 227
ally, 193
alumni groups, 238
ambiguity, 54
American ascendency, 236
Amul milk pasteurisation plant, 227
Antarctica, 16, 26
Antarctic Treaty System, xxi
anti-submarine, 248
ANZCERTA (Australia–New Zealand Closer Economic Relations Trade Agreement), 65, 76
ANZUS, 26, 52, 139
Aotearoa Action Plan, 84
Appellate Body, 78
application, 113, 114
archaeological sites, 144

266 *Index*

Arctic Circle, 134
Ardern, xxii–xxix, xxxii–xxxv,
    31–32, 34–39, 45–47, 53–54, 79,
    85, 91, 140, 146, 176, 179, 184,
    202, 205, 222–223, 230–231, 235,
    237–238, 249–250, 252–256,
    258–259
Ardern Government, xix, xxiv,
    xxix–xxxi, xxxiv, 52, 56, 63,
    66–67, 69, 73–74, 79–80, 88, 90,
    155, 180, 182, 184, 238
Ardern Labour-led Government,
    177
Ardern-led Government, 234
arms control, 11
arms control efforts, 210
arms race, 197
artificial intelligence (AI), 197,
    209
ASEAN, 26, 45, 66, 74–75, 85, 87,
    209, 229, 246, 257
ASEAN–Australia–New Zealand Free
    Trade Agreement (AANZFTA), 65,
    76, 82
ASEAN Regional Forum, 11
Asia, 57, 83, 119, 220–221
Asia New Zealand, 254
Asia New Zealand Foundation, 165,
    207, 222–223, 236, 237
Asian financial crisis of 1997, 222
Asian Infrastructure Investment
    Bank, 195
Asians, 102
Asia-Pacific, 24, 49, 85–86, 247
Asia-Pacific Economic Cooperation
    (APEC) Summit, xxii, 9, 11–12,
    14, 24, 64, 78, 83–85, 91 107, 179,
    181, 253–254
Asia-Pacific region, xxiii, 64, 69
Asian region, 222
Association of Southeast Asian
    Nations (ASEAN), 9, 24

asymmetric hedging strategy, 202
Atal Bihari Vajpayee, 228
atmospheric carbon dioxide, 137
Auckland, 101, 146, 175, 224
AUKUS, xxxiii, 37–38, 52–53,
    197–200, 208–209, 249, 256–257
AUKUS trilateral security
    arrangement, 193
Australasia, 66, 74
Australia, xxi, xxiv–xxv,
    xxxiii–xxxiv, 16, 18, 26–27,
    30–37, 39–40, 43, 45, 47, 50,
    53–57, 64–66, 74–75, 77–80,
    82, 85, 87–88, 90, 99, 106, 114,
    134, 159, 164, 169, 179, 181–182,
    191, 193–200, 202, 208–209, 211,
    232–233, 235, 246, 250, 252, 254,
    256–258
Australia–China relationship,
    254
Australian, xxvii, 258
Australia/United States–China
    Competition, 203, 208
Australia/United States–China
    relations, 211
Australia/United States–China
    tensions, 207
Australia–United States Ministerial
    Consultations, 252
authoritarian, 177
autonomously sanction, xxxv, 258
Ayson, Robert, 197, 249

B
Baker, Michael, 119
balance of military power, 194
balance of power, 192, 206
balancing, 56
bandwagoning, 56
Bangladesh, 224–225
banks, 135
barriers to trade, 204

Beijing, 183
Belarus, 70
Belt and Road Initiative (BRI), xxv, 31, 45, 50, 196, 249
Bharatiya Janata Party (BJP), 229, 236
Bhutan, 224
Bhutto, Benazir, xxviii
Biden Administration, xxvii, xxxiv, 82, 85–86, 195, 201
Biden, Joe, 37–38, 85, 91, 197, 212, 251
bilateral investment, 229
bilateral partnerships, 222, 224
biodiversity loss, 150
biogeochemical flows, 150
biological threats, 133
Bloomfield, Ashley, 109, 184
body, 77
Boe Declaration, 11
Bogor Goals, 64, 83
Bollard, Alan, xxii
Bombay, 227
Bombay Hills, 224
border, 186
border control, 177
border protection system, 114–115
border security, 247
Bougainville, 167
Brady, Anne-Marie, 30, 177–178, 182
Brazil, 179
Brexit, xxxi, 67–68, 70, 79
Bridges, Simon, 110
Britain, xix, 165, 195, 225, 227–228
British, 23, 32, 224
Brownlee, Gerry, 28
Broz (Tito), Josip, 55
Brunei, 81
bubble, 109
building, 181
building codes, 135

Bullen, Chris, 119
burial grounds, 143
business, 236
Buzan, Barry, 47–49

C

California, 134
Campbell, Kurt, 256
Canada, xxv, 37, 45–46, 69, 74, 76, 78, 81–82, 88, 131, 181, 199, 257
Canberra, 24, 38, 192, 201
cancer, 111
Canterbury Plains, 142, 145–146, 149
carbon dioxide, 132, 134
carbon emissions, 132–133, 152
Cartel, Sinaloa, 134
case contact management, 119–120
Cashmere Estate, 224
Catalinac, Amy L., 139
cemeteries, 144
Central American, 64
Central Epidemic Command Center, 119
Centre for Strategic Studies, 207
Centre of Excellence, 207
Chambers of Commerce, 238
changing climate, 151
chemical weapons, xxiv
Chile, 80–82
China, xxi, xxiv–xxv, xxx–xxxiv, 24–39, 43–57, 64–66, 74–75, 77–78, 81–83, 85–86, 88, 90–93, 104, 136, 164–165, 177–180, 182, 186, 191–197, 199–203, 206, 208–213, 222–223, 228, 231, 234, 246, 248–250, 253–259
China Contemporary Studies Centre, 207
China–New Zealand relationship, 91, 249
China–NZ FTA, 82

China's maritime claims, 195
China's navy, 200
Chinese, 29, 32, 198, 205
Chinese Communist Party, 194, 196
Chinese influence, 33, 195
Chinese military, 231
Chinese New Zealander, 33
Christchurch, xxvi, 175, 224, 231, 250
Christchurch Call to Action, xxvii, 11, 179, 250
Churchill, 226
Civil Defence Emergency Management Act 2002, 174
civil rights, 146
Clark, Helen, xxii, 27, 40, 45, 118
clean energy, 182
climate action, 146, 155
climate action tracker (CAT), 152
climate change, xxiii, xxix, xxxii, 4, 13–15, 81, 131, 133–137, 139, 142, 145–147, 150–152, 154, 163
Climate Change Commission, 152, 154
climate change impacts, 135
Climate Change Response Act 2002, 154
Climate Change Response (Zero Carbon) Amendment Act of 2019, 14, 152
climate crisis, 142
climate implementation plan, 152
climate justice, 146, 147
climate legislation, 154
climate mitigation measures, 147
climate policies, 140–141, 147, 153
climate-related risk disclosure, 135
climate resilience, 15
climate strategy, 140, 151

climate threat, 150
climate transition, 19
climatic patterns, 143
closed borders, 235
coal, 146
coastal erosion, 144
coercive diplomacy, 194
co-governance, 151, 175
collaboration, 238
collectivism, xxiii
Colombia, 82
Colombo Plan for Cooperative Economic Development in Asia and the Pacific, 225
Commonwealth, xxii, 225–227
communication, 109
communication applications, 185
community panel, 118
competition, 212
Comprehensive and Progressive Agreement for Trans-Pacific Partnership (CPTPP), xxi, xxiii, 57, 69, 73–74, 76, 82, 86–88, 230
computer chip shortage, 181
confidence-building, 208
conflict, 201, 206, 212
confrontation, 212
conspiracy theories, 184
constructive ambiguity, 53
Contact Tracing Assurance Committee, 118
contain rising powers, 212
Convoy 2022 NZ, 175, 184–185
conquest, 206
Cook Islands, xxi, 16, 101, 106–167, 178
Cooper, Zack, 54
co-operation, 194, 207–208, 210–212, 238
co-operative approach, 204
co-ordination, 238
COP 26 in Glasgow in 2021, 81

COP 27 at Sharm El Sheikh, 81
Costa Rica, 81, 88
Coughlin, Con, 255
counter-terrorism, 230
COVAX, 18, 106
COVAX scheme, 178
COVID-19, xxix, xxxi–xxxiv, 99–102, 105, 107–108, 110, 153–154, 159, 166, 168, 170, 173–174, 196, 245, 255, 259
COVID-19 All-of-Government Response Group, 174
COVID-19 epidemics, 104
COVID-19 Independent Continuous Review, Improvement and Advice Group, 118
COVID-19 Māori Vaccine and Immunisation Plan, 112
COVID-19 pandemic, xix, 47, 77–78, 84, 163, 231–232, 235–236, 238, 249
COVID-19 pandemic recovery, 233
COVID-19 Protection Framework (CPF), 108, 112, 117
COVID-19 protocols, 159
COVID-19 Public Health Response Act 2020, 174
COVID-19 response, xxviii, 17, 155, 250
COVID-19 restrictions, 160–162, 166
COVID-19 Surveillance Plan and Testing Strategy Ministerial Advisory Committee, 116, 118
COVID-19 Vaccines Global Access Facility (COVAX), 17
CPTPP Commission, 87
cricket diplomacy, 229
crime, 163, 201
criminal activity, 134
crises, xxxiii, 201, 208
crisis management, xxxiii, 250
Crown–Māori relationship, 154

cultural, 145
cultural activities, 162
cultural connections, 231
cultural identity, 148, 150
culturally important sites, 143
cultural sites, 145
cultural values, 111
culture, 148, 238
currency, 93
customs, 230
cyber, 197
cyberattacks, 31
cyber-hacking, 256
cyber, information and space warfare, 195
cyber intrusions, xxv
cyber security, 46, 230
cyber technologies, 209
cyclone, 134

D

2020 Defence Strategic Update, 34
2021 Defence Assessment, 38
dairy co-operative industry, 227
death, 111–112
Death Valley, 134–135
debt, 168
defence, 28, 36–38, 186, 195, 230–231, 233–234, 257
defence assessment, 256
Defence Capability Plan, 248
defence co-operation, 28, 31
defence policy, 29
defence spending, 248
defence training exercises, 233
Defence White Paper (DWP), 25, 28–29
degradation, 150
Delhi, 24
demand for water, 145
democracy, 237, 256
Deng Xiaoping, 45
Department of Defense, 133

270   *Index*

Department of Homeland Security, 132, 133
Department of the Prime Minister and Cabinet (DPMC), 105, 116, 174
deporting, xxvii
deregulating the financial market, 228
deterrence, 186, 212
development, 168, 233
development aid, xxi
development assistance, xxiv, 166
development co-operation, 162
development cooperation funding, 17
development funding, 167
Diaoyu, 25
digital diplomacy, 179
digital economy, 81
Digital Economy Partnership Agreement (DEPA), 81
digital networks, xxvii
digital sector, 209
diplomacy, xxiv, xxix, xxxiii, 186, 200, 204, 208
diplomatic autonomy, xxiv
diplomatic boycott, 257
diplomatic posts, 162
diplomatic relations, 225
diplomatic skills, xxii
Director General of Health, 174
Di Ruggiero, Erica, 146
disaster risk reduction, 136
disasters, 135, 136
discriminatory tariffs, 76
Disinformation Project, 184, 196
diversity, 164
Doha Round' of WTO trade negotiations, 64
domestic extremism, 184
Double Taxation Agreement, 65
dual-use facility, 200
Dubai, 253

Dunedin, 175
Dutch, 37
Duterte, Rodrigo, 54

E
East Asia, 65–66, 74–75, 81–83
East Asia Summit, 11
ecological crisis, 147
ecological degradation, 146
e-commerce, 17, 18, 67, 71, 88, 228
economic, 181
economic coercion, 202, 231
economic competition, 194
economic dependency, 213
economic development, 12
economic diversification, 170
economic governance, 232
economic integration, 238
economic interdependencies, 212
economic leverage, 202
economic management, 168
economic prosperity, 186
economic reform, 168
economic sanctions, 10
economic security, xxxiii, 177, 180–183, 186–187
economic support programmes, 168
economy, 183, 204
Ecuador, 88
education, 169, 222, 229–230, 234
efforts to acquire research, 194
elections, 167, 175
electricity, 146
electronic contact tracing, 114
elimination, 105, 108, 110, 180, 249
elimination strategy, 110, 250, 253
Ellesmere, Lake, 47, 149

emergency response, 136
emissions, 135, 152
emissions reduction, 15
emissions trading scheme, 152
energy, 86
energy cost, 181
engagement, xxxiv
environmental change, 142, 144
environmental health, 150
environmental issues, 14
environmental modification, 150
environmental relationships, 144
Epidemic Response Committee, 105, 109
equity-based decision-making, 120
espionage, 183
ethnically diverse, 222
Europe, 39, 194, 258
European Economic Community, 32, 44, 227
European Union, xxxi, 48, 57, 66, 68–71, 77, 79–82, 177, 185, 199, 201, 252
European Union–New Zealand FTA, 12
excess mortality, 102
exclusive economic zone, 26
exercises, 28
Expo 2020, 253
export restrictions, 78
exports, 65, 68, 75–76, 79–82, 91, 201, 209, 228–229, 257
export subsidies, 64
extreme competition, 212
extremist organisations, xxvii

F

2008 Free Trade Agreement, 31
face-to-face diplomacy, 235
face-to-face meetings, 257
farming, 152

Federal Emergency Management Agency, 132
Fiji, 81–82, 87, 107, 159, 167, 178, 235
Finland, xxi
Fire and Fury: Disinformation in New Zealand, 184
first coalition, 248
fisheries, 89
fishing, 168
fish processing, 167
fish stocks, 168
Five Eyes, xxv, 33–35, 37, 45, 52, 53, 255–257
Five Eyes alliance, xxv–xxvi
Five Eyes intelligence arrangement, 202
Five Eyes intelligence grouping, 248
Five Eyes intelligence sharing community, 236
Five Eyes intelligence-sharing partnership, xxi, xxxiv
Five Power Defence Arrangements, 37, 198
flood, 136, 143, 145
food, 84, 136, 143, 167
food gathering, 143
food safety, 230
Food Standards Treaty, 65
forces exercised, 31
Ford, James D., 143
foreign direct investment, 230
foreign exchange controls, 228
foreign interference, 231
foreign investment, 31
foreign nationals in New Zealand, 249
foreign policy, 186, 187
foreign policy independence, 39
fossil fuel subsidy, 13, 84, 88–89
France, 161, 195, 197

272 *Index*

Free and Open Indo-Pacific (FOIP), 85
freedoms of overflight and navigation, 246
Free Trade Agreements (FTAs), xxi, xxiii, 13, 45–46, 52, 57, 64–65, 70, 75, 79, 81–82, 228–229, 231–233, 255
free trade agreement with Russia, 201
Free Trade Area of the Asia–Pacific (FTAAP), 66, 69
free trade deal, 245, 252
French, xxvi, 79, 250
French Pacific territories, 83
freshwater consumption, 150
FTA with China, 12
FTA with the European Union, xxxi
fuel and food prices, 201

G
G7, 252–253
gambling, 111
Gandhi, Indira, 227
gardens, 143
GATT, xxi, 76
gender issues, 164
geopolitical mindset, xxx
George W. Bush Administration, xxi
geostrategic objectives, 233
Germany, 79, 195
Gisborne, 145
Global Financial Crisis (GFC), 25
Global Health Security Index, 102
globalisation, xx
global public health-care system, 208, 210
global tax system, 208, 210
global warming, 14, 153
Goff, Phil, 251
good governance, 237
governance, 169

Government Communications Security Bureau (GCSB), xxv, 31, 37, 248
great power competition, 194, 204, 208, 247
great power confrontation, 203
great power reassurance, 210
great power rivalry, 205
great power 'spheres of influence', 211
great-power wars, 212
Green Deal, 80
greenhouse gas emissions, 132, 152
greenhouse gases, 151
grey zone conflict, 185
guardians, 149
guardianship, 148
Gulf states, 82

H
hacking, 37
Hansen, James, 132
Harris, Kamala, xix
harvest of fish, 163
Hawaii, 132
health, 164, 169, 186
Health Act 1956, 174
healthcare, 111, 247
healthcare facilities, 110
health checks, 119
health services, 186
health systems, 167–168
hedging, 51–52, 55–56, 193, 257
hedging strategy, xxx–xxxi, 57, 194, 203, 213
Henare, Peeni, 36, 209
Henderson, John, xx–xxi
Higgins, David, 144
high technology, 194
high-tech sector, 192
Hillary, Edmund, 225

Hindu nationalism, 236
HMNZS, 37
Holland, Sidney, 227
Hong Kong, xxv–xxvi, xxxi, 33–36, 38, 46, 64–65, 75, 90, 116, 196, 222, 228, 231, 255–256
Horn of Africa, 134
horticultural work, 169
hospitalisation, 111–112
hospital services, 104, 111, 116
hostility, 210
housing crisis, 183
Huawei, xxv–xxvi, 31, 46, 179, 248
humanitarian, 178–179
human rights, xx, xxix, 33–34, 46, 255–256
human rights abuses, 53
human rights violations, 31, 35

I
Iceland, 81
ideological differences, 195
ideology, 248
immigration, xxiii, 164, 169, 224, 236
immigration policy, 169
import controls, 78
inclusive and stable order in the region, 211
inclusivity, 191, 205
independence, 225, 238
independent foreign and security policy, 233
independent foreign policy, 27, 54, 56, 91, 203, 256, 257, 259
independent New Zealand foreign policy, xx
India, xxxiv, 12, 28, 31, 36, 48, 50, 57, 66, 74–75, 83, 85, 165, 182, 194, 209, 221, 224–228, 230–235, 237–238, 245–246, 248–249
Indian and Pacific Oceans, 197

Indian Council of World Affairs, 231
India–New Zealand 2025: Investing in the Relationship, 231
India–New Zealand Relations, 225
Indian High Commission Chancery, 235
Indian Ocean, 233
Indians, 232
indigenous, xxix, 111
indigenous cultures, 148
indigenous identity, 161
indigenous peoples, 70, 84, 142, 147, 149
Indigenous Peoples Economic and Trade Cooperation Arrangement, 14
indigenous population, 153
indigenous rights, xx, 163
indigenous trade, 13
Indonesia, 56, 161, 165, 178, 222, 257
Indo-Pacific, xxx–xxxi, xxxiii, 24, 35–36, 55–56, 79, 85–86, 178, 192, 195, 200, 202, 206–208, 213, 222, 224, 231–233, 238, 246–247, 250, 256
Indo-Pacific concept, 54
Indo-Pacific Economic Framework (IPEF), 50, 86–87, 182
Indo-Pacific Quad, 208
Indo-Pacific region, xx, xxiv, 39, 50, 186, 194, 203, 205, 209
Indo-Pacific super-region, 48–49, 57
inequality, 146
inflation, 168, 183, 227
influenza, 110
influenza pandemic plan, 102
information, 185
information systems, 120
infrastructure, 164
infrastructure development, 200
Ingham, Tristram, 109

in-person diplomacy, 235
insecurity, 206
institution building, xxxiii
intellectual property, 46, 67, 71, 73
intellectual property rights, 78
intellectual property theft, 183
intelligence, 52, 165, 198
intelligence-sharing, xxvi
intensive care unit (ICU), 102, 117
intercontinental ballistic missiles, 199
interdependence, 204
inter-dependent, 237
interfere, 30
interference, 33
Intergovernmental Panel on Climate Change, 145
Interim National Security Strategic Guidance, 195
International Atomic Energy Agency (IAEA), 199
international crisis-management and quick-response system, 208, 210
international institutions, 26, 208, 210–211
internationalism, xx
international law, 246
international liberal agenda, 210
International Monetary Fund (IMF), 83
International Science Council, 119
international system, 192, 212
international trade agreements, 66, 72
international trade policy, 74
international travel, 252
Internet, 250
interoperability, 33, 198
interstate conflict, 186
invasions, 212
investment, 83, 169, 205, 229, 234, 238, 247
investor[–]state dispute mechanisms' (ISDS), 74, 80

Iran, 93, 104
Iraq, xxi, 52, 212
Ireland, xxi, 146
Islamic State, 52
Islamic State in Syria and Iraq, 49
isolating, 106, 113
Italy, 134

J

Jacinda Ardern's Government, xix, 29, 43, 65, 109, 139, 175, 191, 198, 221, 248
Jaishankar, Dhruva, 233
Jaishankar, Subrahmanyam, 222, 235–236
Jakarta, 37
Japan, 24, 25, 28, 31–32, 37, 45, 53, 69, 74–75, 77, 82, 85, 87–88, 182, 194, 196, 199, 209, 223, 228–229, 233, 246, 248, 259
job losses, 111
John Key/Bill English Government, 90
John Key's Government, 65
Johnson, Boris, 197
journalism, 185

K

Kaiapoi, 144
Kanaks, 161
key, 28–29, 229, 230
Key, John, 28, 140, 228
Khandallah, 224
Kim Jong-un, xxiv
King Tāwhiao, 3
Kiribati, 165
Kirk, Norman, 44
Kiwi–Aussie solidarity, 36
Korea, 45, 64–65, 74–75, 87–88
Korolev, 48
Kupchan, Charles, 211
Kurien, Verghese, 227

L

labour, 27, 29, 33–34, 37, 251, 255–256
labour government, 44, 175, 221, 238
labour-led coalition government, xxii, xxiv–xxv, 230
labour mobility, 163
labour–New Zealand first coalition government, 175, 248
Labour Party, 139, 250
Lancet COVID-19 Commission task force, 119
land ownership, 147
land system change, 150
Lange, David, 27, 44
languages, 238
leadership, xxviii, 119, 180
Lessing, Doris, 221
liberal values, 196
liberal, rules-based order, 204, 231
liberal, rules-based system, 236
Lijian, Zhao, 197
Li Keqiang, xxvi, 46
Lim, Darren, 54
Little, Andrew, 37, 184
loans, 200
lockdown, xxxiv, 105–106, 110–111, 113, 119, 159, 174, 181, 183, 186, 232, 235, 259
locusts, 134
logistic, 181
London, 38
loss of life, 183

M

MacDonald, David, 255
macroeconomic policies, 183
Macron, Emmanuel, xxvi, 79, 250
Mafia, 134
Mahuta, Nanaia, xxix, xxxiv, 34–35, 37, 53–54, 161, 191, 204, 235, 251–252, 254, 257

Mainfreight, 181
mainstream media, 184, 185
MALABAR series of maritime exercises, 208–209
Malaysia, 37, 56, 64, 65, 83, 198, 222, 229
Maldives, 224–225
managed isolation and quarantine (MIQ), 106, 114–115, 117, 252, 253
Manch, Thomas, 53
mandates, 117, 175
manipulation, 185
Māori, xx, xxxi–xxxii, 14, 66–67, 71–72, 80, 101–103, 107, 109, 111–112, 114, 117, 120–121, 135, 141, 147–151, 153–155, 175, 224, 251
Māori economy, 13
Maorification of government, 184
Mapp, Wayne, 28
Marae, Moeraki, 144
marginalisation of communities, 110
maritime claims, 85
maritime patrol aircraft, 30
maritime power, 200
Mark, Ron, 31, 248
market access, 228
market integration, 228
Marles, Richard, 235
masks, xxxiv, 259
Massey University, 227
Matiaha Tiramōrehu, 144
Mauna Loa, 133, 137
Mauna Loa Observatory, 132
McCully, Murray, 28, 247
McKinnon, Don, xxii
Mead, Andrew, 68
media, 185
medical diplomacy, 178
medical supplies, 78
medical support, 167

medicinal plants, 143
medicine, 136, 167
Melanesia, 163, 168
Melanesian people, 161
members of parliament, 33
Menzies, Robert, 226
Merkel, Angela, 79
Mexico, 74, 76, 82, 88
middle, 131
migrant labour, 169
migrants, 229
militarisation, 198
military, xxi, 192–194, 197, 200, 247
military balance of power, 199
military balancing, 204
military base, 200
military build-up, 223
military confrontation, 200
military co-operation, 26, 200, 208
military equipment, 258
military exercises, 198
military forces, 206, 212
military infrastructure, 200
military manoeuvres, 201
military personnel, 258
military power, 202
military spending, 198
military–strategic relationship, xxiv
Minister of Foreign Affairs, 161
Ministry for Primary Industries, 145, 155
Ministry for the Environment, 155
Ministry of Business, Innovation and Employment (MBIE), 174, 176
Ministry of Civil Defence and Emergency Management, 174
Ministry of Foreign Affairs and Trade (MFAT), 72, 86, 91, 247

Ministry of Health, 105, 114–116, 118, 120–121, 174
mis-, dis-, and mal-information, 185
misinformation, 173, 175, 177, 184, 186
missile defence system, 195, 202
missiles, xxiii, 195, 197, 223
mistrust, 206
mitigation, 135–136
mobile telephone technology, 248
mobility restrictions, 183
modelling, 113–114
Modi, Narendra, 230, 235, 237
Moore, Mike, xxii, 64
moral emphasis, xx
moral focus, xxi
Morrison, Scott, xxvii, 32, 36, 179, 197, 252, 254, 257
mosque attacks, xxvii, 250
Mount Everest, 225
movement of commodities, 182
movement of people, 205
Muldoon, Robert, 228
multilateral and institutional architecture, 211
multilateral institutions, xx
multilateralism, xx, xxii, xxxi
multilateral organisations, 204
Multi-Party Interim Appeal Arbitration Arrangement (MPIA), 77
Munich Re, 135
mutual deterrence, 210
mutual distrust, 210

N
2017 National Security Strategy, 202
Napolitano, Janet, 132–133
NASA, 133
national adaption plan, 145

Index 277

National Crisis Management Centre (NCMC), 174
National Democratic Alliance Government, 228
National Emergency Management Agency, 174
National Government, 79
National Health Coordination Centre, 174
National-led governments, 248
Nationally Determined Contribution (NDC), 152–153
National Party, 27–28, 247
National Response Leadership Team, 174
national security, xxv, xxxiii, 27, 29, 173, 176–177, 186–187
National Security Council, 133
National Security Framework, 177
National Security System, 174
NATO, xxii, 28, 48, 202
natural disasters, 135
natural environment, 148–150
naval co-operation, 198
naval forces, 37, 195
naval power, 197
naval ships, 178
navies, 208
Nehru, Jawaharlal, 227
Nelson, 176
Nepal, 224–225
Netherlands, 136
net zero, 14
New Caledonia, 159, 161
New Delhi, 32, 227
New Plymouth, 175
New Progressive and Inclusive Trade Policy Agenda (NPITA), 70–71
New York Times, xxviii
New Zealand, 74
New Zealand–Asia relationships, 165
New Zealand China Council, 255

New Zealand citizens, xxvii
New Zealand citizens in India, 232
New Zealand Climate Change Commission, 142
New Zealand Defence Force (NZDF), 28–29, 176, 178, 208
New Zealand diaspora, 238
New Zealanders of Indian heritage, 235
New Zealand–European Union FTA, 80
New Zealand First, 29–30, 34
New Zealand First party, 248, 250–251, 255
New Zealand Government India Strategy, 232
New Zealand–India bilateral relations, 236
New Zealand–India relationship, 229, 237
New Zealand's 2021 Defence Assessment, 34, 200
New Zealand's Climate Change Commission, 135
New Zealand's communities of Asian origin, 238
New Zealand's Ministry of Foreign Affairs and Trade, 49
New Zealand's naval, 198
Ngāi Tahu, 140–144, 148–153, 155
Ngāi Tahu claim, 151
Ngāi Tahu Settlement of 1998, 151
Ngāti Māmoe, 142
Ngā Toki Whakarururanga, 72–73
Niue, xxi, 16, 106, 178
non-aggression and non-interference pact between Australia/United States and China, 207
non-aligned movement, 56, 226
non-nuclear security policy, xx
non-quota tariffs, 68
non-tariff barriers, 78

Norgay, Tenzing, 225
North America, 184
North American Free Trade Agreement (NAFTA), xxiii
North Asia, 221, 223
North Korea, xxiv, 223
Norway, xxi, 81
nuclear arms, 199
nuclear-free policy, 198–199
Nuclear Free Zone, Disarmament, and Arms Control Act of 1987, xxi
nuclear non-proliferation, 198–199
nuclear-related issues, 230
nuclear status, 234
nuclear strike capability, 199
nuclear weapons, 212, 228
Nye, Joseph, xxviii
NZ–China FTA, 76
'NZ Inc' India strategy, 222, 238
NZ–Korea FTA, 76

O

Obama Administration, 256
Obama, Barack, 49, 132–133
ocean acidification, 143
Oceania, 66
oceans, 163
O'Connor, 254, 255
O'Connor, Damien, 34, 252
OECD, 183
official development assistance, 15, 228, 247
oil, 186
oil and gas exploration, 152
ongoing supply, 180
online diplomacy, 252
online or hybrid diplomacy, 178
Opening Doors to India policy, 229
openness, 191, 205
open polylateralism, 206
Operational Command Centre, 174

operation protect, 176
operations to influence, 30
Ottawa, 184

P

PACER Plus, 82, 83
PACER Plus trade agreement, 64
Pacific, xxiv, xxix, xxxiii, 15–18, 26, 35, 38–40, 48, 50, 53, 83, 101, 106, 114, 117, 120–121, 159–162, 164–170, 179, 247–248
Pacific alliance, 82
Pacific countries, 15
Pacific Deterrence Initiative, 194
Pacific Forum, 159, 163
Pacific Islands Forum, 11, 48, 65
Pacific Islands Forum Fisheries Agency, 163
Pacific Islands Forum Leaders' Declaration on Preserving Maritime Zones in the Face of Climate-Change Related Sea-Level Rise, 15
Pacific Island states, xx–xxi
Pacific Northwest, 131
Pacific people, 102, 107, 112
Pacific region, xxx, xxxii
Pacific Reset, xxiv, 6, 30, 161, 246, 247
Pacific Resilience Approach, 7
Pakistan, xxviii, 224–225, 227
pandemic, xxviii–xxix, xxxiii–xxxiv, 15, 89, 131, 133–134, 136, 167, 180, 183, 258
pandemic control efforts, 183
pandemic diplomacy, 173, 177–180
pandemic preparedness, 102, 119
pandemic response, 116, 173, 177
pandemic response agency, 117
pandemic response capabilities, 120
pandemic strategy, 184

pandemic supplies, 134
Papua New Guinea (PNG), 82, 159, 163, 167, 179
Paraguay, 88
Paris Accord on climate change, 80
Paris Agreement, 15, 19, 153
Parker, David, xxiii, 34, 45, 231, 245, 249
parliament, 110
Parties to the Nauru Agreement Vessel Day Scheme, 168
partnership, 170
Pasifika, 154
Payne, Marise, 252
peacekeeping, xxi, 233
people flows, 232
People's Liberation Army, 28, 197
People's Republic of China (PRC), 23, 30, 40
people-to-people connections, xxxiv, 221, 234, 238
people-to-people relationships, 170, 235
people-to-people ties, 234
perceptions of Asia and Asian peoples survey, 236
personal and institutional relationships, 237
personal contacts, 162, 166
personal protective equipment (PPE), 116, 167, 178, 180–181
personal relationships, 159
Peru, 74, 76, 82
[Peter] Fraser, 226, 238
Peters, Winston, xxiv, 29–30, 32, 45, 47, 70, 161, 231, 235, 245–251, 255, 259
Pfizer–BioNTech mRNA vaccine, 106
pharmaceuticals, 186
Philippines, 25, 54, 134
pivot to Asia policy, 49, 256

planetary boundaries model, 150
planning, 136
plurilateralism, xxxi
polarisation, xxxiv
Police, 167, 174
policy of elimination, 101
political representation, 164
pollution, 149
Polly Atatoa Carr, 154
polymerase chain reaction (PCR) testing, 114–115
Polynesia, 16, 162, 163
Polynesian population, 160
population movement, 186
populism, 255
Portland, Oregon, 131
Port Moeraki, 144
poverty, 146
power co-operation, 193
Powles, Anna, 179
procurement, 116
programmatic cooperation, 211
proliferation, 209
prosperity, 204
protective gear, xxxiii
protest movement, 175
protests, 176, 184, 227
public communication, 175
public diplomacy, 162
public health, xxxii–xxxiii, 100, 102, 104–105, 112, 114, 120, 177
public health specialists, 120
Public Service Act, 154
punitive tariffs, 254
Punjab, 224
Putin, Vladimir, 4, 257–258
Putrajaya Vision 2040, 83–84

Q

Qatar, 37, 82, 257
Quad, xxxiii, 25, 52–53, 246, 248, 252

Quad arrangements, 209
Quadrilateral Security Dialogue, 24, 49, 85, 194, 233, 246
quantum computing, 197, 209
quarantine, 115, 119
quota, 79
quota-free access, 79
quota rents, 80

R
racist statements, 249
Rae, Allan, 68
Raimondo, Gina, 86
Rapid Case Contact Management, 113
rapprochement programmes, 210, 213
reassurance programme, 207
recession, 201
reciprocal restraint, 207
recognised seasonal employer (RSE) schemes, 17, 169
reconciliation, 211
reconnecting New Zealanders to the world plan, 107
refugees, 163
Regional Comprehensive Economic Partnership (RCEP), xxxi, 12, 66, 74–76, 82, 230–231, 236, 245
regional connectivity, 233
regional co-operation, 230
regional economic outlook for Asia and the Pacific, 83
regional peace and security, 208
regional security, 205, 207
regional security complexes, 48
Regional Security Complex Theory (RSCT), xxx, 44, 47
regional stability, 238
regional strategic landscape, 234
regional trade and security agreement, 200

reinsurance, 135
relations between the United States/Australia, 204
relationships between China and Pacific nations, 164
reliance on overseas supplies, 186
renewable energy, 84
renewable sources, 152
Renwick, James, 145
Republic of Korea, 32
requirement to wear masks, 184
Reserve Bank of New Zealand, xxii
resources, 148
resource use, 150
response, 15, 32
response measures, 16
restoration, 149
Ribot, Jesse, 142
Rim of the Pacific (RIMPAC) exercises, 198
rising sea levels, 143
rising seas, 163
risk profiling, 119
Robertson, Grant, 183, 247
Robinson, Mary, 146
Room for the River programme, 136
Rotorua, 175
Royal New Zealand Navy, 36, 208
rules-based international order, xxii, xxx, 24, 35, 77
rules-based international system, 4, 200
rules-based order, xx, xxiv, xxxv, 33, 38, 194, 259
rules-based system, 46
rules, norms and international frameworks, 256
Russia, xxix, xxxii, xxxv, 10, 39, 48, 70, 90, 92, 136, 177, 186, 195–196, 199, 201, 210, 212, 233, 236, 256–259
Russia Sanctions Act, 258

S

2018 Strategic Defence Policy Statement, 46
Sachdeva, 257
Samoa, 106, 159, 167, 178
sanctions, xxxiv, 92–93, 201
Saudi Arabia, 82, 199
Saudi sheep deal, 247
Scarborough Shoal, 25
Schweller, Randall, 56
scientific research, 136
Scott Morrison Government, 90, 196
sea level change, 143
sea level rise, 15, 144
seamen, 224
seasonal workers, 106, 169
sea temperature changes, 143
Secretary to the Treasury, 174
secure, 246
security, xxi, xxx, 36, 38, 40, 47, 49–50, 54–55, 165, 184, 186, 197, 198, 200–202, 209–210, 222–224, 230–234, 257
security and military co-operation, 202
security communities, 212
security concerns, 181
security co-operation, 26, 233
security dilemmas, 206, 210
security information sharing, 31
security partner, 232
self-determination, 204
self-preservation, 203–204
semiconductors, 182–183
Senkaku Islands, 25
sensitive and critical technology, 231
services, 229, 234
services trade, 229
settlers, 224
Severe Acute Respiratory Syndrome (SARS), 222

Shaw, James, 81
Sherman, Wendy, 52, 209
shipborne trade, 201
shipping, 201
shop sector, 164
Sidhu, Harinder, 234
Sikh, 224
Singapore, 37, 64–65, 78, 80–81, 104, 181, 198, 222, 228–229, 235, 250, 259
single economic market, 65
Sino-American relations, 55, 56
Sino-Aotearoa New Zealand relationship, xxxi
Sino-Australia spat, 197
Sino-Australia relations, 196
Sir Peter Gluckman, 119
Sir Sam Neill, xxviii
sister cities, 238
Skegg, David, 105, 119
social cohesion, xxxiii, 173, 175, 177, 187
social injustice, 146
social justice, 146
social licence, 175
socially just, 147
social media platforms, xxvii
social unrest, 183, 185
'soft' and public diplomacy, 179
soft power, xxviii, xxxii–xxxiii, xxxv, 159–160, 162, 165–166, 170, 177, 179, 223
soldiers, 225
Solomonian, Leslie, 146
Solomon Islands, 38, 50, 55, 163, 165, 167, 200, 258
South Asia, xxxiv, 48, 221–222, 224, 236, 237
South China Sea (SCS), 25, 28, 36–37, 50, 53, 85, 195, 197–199, 208, 211

South East Asia, 23, 25, 48, 64–65, 74, 90, 198–199
Southern Ocean, 26
South Korea, 99, 104, 181, 199, 202, 222, 228–229
Southland, 146
South Pacific, xxiv–xxv, 48, 178, 192, 199–200, 231
South Pacific island nations, 198
sovereignty, xxix, 204–205, 231, 237–238, 246
Soviet Union, 24, 27, 55
Spain, 180
special APEC leaders' summit on COVID-19, 253
spiritual, 143, 145
spiritual considerations, 144
sport, 162, 234
Sri Lanka, 224, 225
stability, 213
state of emergency, 105, 174, 227
Statute of Westminster, 225
Steffen, Will, 150
Stockholm Resilience Centre, 150
strategic balance, 200
strategic communication, 186
strategic competition, 195, 248
Strategic COVID-19 Public Health Ministerial Advisory Group, 107, 108
Strategic Defence Policy Statement, xxiv, 30
strategic development, 167
strategic engagement, 178
strategic geography, 246
strategic interests, 231
strategic liberalism, xxxiii, 193–194, 203, 205–206, 208, 211, 213
strategic liberalism, 204
strategic partner, 232, 238
Strategic Public Health Advisory Group, 118
strategic supply chains, 182
strategic vulnerabilities, 208
structural reform programmes, 168
Strutt, Anna, 68
students, 235
submarines, 197, 199, 256
subsidies, 80, 89
superpowers, xxii, 192, 196, 200–201, 212
supply chain disruptions, 201
supply chain issues, 181
supply chain resilience, 182
Supply Chain Resilience Initiative (SCRI), 182
supply chains, xxxi, xxxiii, 16, 18, 86, 91, 136, 173, 186, 197, 205, 232
supply lines, 181
surveillance, 31, 195
sustainability, 237
sustainable development, 81
sustainable development goals (SDGs), 7, 12, 15
Sweden, 99, 235
Switzerland, 81
Syrian war, xxiv

T

Tahu Pōtiki, 141
Taipei, 39
Taiwan, 33–34, 44, 47, 64–65, 75, 88, 99, 104, 119, 164–165, 180, 186, 196, 198, 201, 222, 228
Taiwan Strait, 38, 201
Tang, Shiping, 212
tariff protections, 228
tariff-rate quotas (TRQs), 68
tariffs, xxiii, xxxi, 77, 89
Tauranga, 175
tax, xxxiii
teaching, xxxiii, 207
technologies, 209
Technology Investment Network, 209

telecommunications, xxv, 179, 182
Telegram, 185
Telehealth, 111
telephone consultations, 111
temperatures, 131–132, 134–135
Te Pae Tawhiti initiative, 72, 73
territorial disputes, 194
terrorism, xxvii
terrorist, 250
terrorist attack, xxvi, 231
Te Rūnanga o Moeraki, 144
testing, 113, 115–116
Te Taumata group, 72–73
Thailand, 64–65, 88, 222
the in-quota tariff (TRQ), 68, 79–80
think tanks, 184
Thorhallsson, Baldur, xxi
Three Waters, 175
tight suppression strategy, 108
Tokelau, xxi, 16, 106, 178
Tonga, 106, 178
tourism, 17, 31, 152, 167, 169–170, 181, 183, 202, 236
tourists, xxvii
TPP Agreement, 67, 71
tracking and controlling nano-technology, 184
trade, xx–xxi, xxx–xxxi, xxxiv, 12–13, 18, 32, 43–45, 50, 52, 54, 57, 63, 65–69, 71–72, 75–76, 78, 81, 83–84, 86, 88, 92–93, 164, 169, 182, 186, 193, 196, 200–201, 203–205, 221–224, 226, 228–230, 232–234, 236, 238, 259
trade agreements, 70
trade bans, 196
trade deal with the United Kingdom, 182
trade dependency, 182
trade diversification, 182
Trade Facilitation Agreement, 64
Trade for All, 80

Trade for All Advisory Board, 71
Trade for All Agenda, 71, 84
Trade for All Ministerial Advisory Group, 71
trade liberalisation, 228
trade negotiations, 73
trade policy, 13–14, 70, 72, 86, 90–91
Trade Promotion Authority (TPA), 82
Trade Recovery Programme, 78
Trade Recovery Strategy 2.0, 91
Trade-Related Aspects of Intellectual Property Rights (TRIPs), 89
trade war, 76, 194
trading system, 88, 232
traffic light system, 108, 175
Trans-Pacific Partnership (TPP) Agreement, xxiii, xxxi, 66, 69–70 76, 81, 86
Trans-Pacific Strategic Economic Partnership (TPSEP), 81
transparency, 196, 204–205, 237
transport, 152, 181
transport aircraft, 33
transport costs, 181
trans-Tasman Mutual Recognition Agreement, 65
trans-Tasman relationship, 37
trans-Tasman Travel Arrangement, an Investment Protocol, 65
travel, 168, 179–180, 236
tribunal, 73
Trudeau, Justin, 46
Trump administration, xxiii–xxiv, 26, 33, 194
Trump, Donald, xxiii–xxviii, xxxi, 69, 76–77, 79, 85, 88, 196, 249, 251, 254, 256
trust-building, 207
tuna, 163
Turnbull, Malcolm, 234
Tuvalu, 178

U

Ukraine, xxix, xxxv, 4, 9–11, 39, 48, 186, 201, 210, 212, 233, 236, 258–259
Ukraine War, 91–92
UN Commission on the Limits of the Continental Shelf, 37
UN Convention on the Law of the Sea, 163
UN Department of Economic and Social Affairs, 142
UN Development Programme (UNDP), xxii
UN Framework Convention on Climate Change, 14
UN General Assembly, xxiii, 250
unhealthy dietary, 111
UN Human Rights Council, 31
United Arab Emirates (UAE), 37, 253, 257
United Kingdom, xxxi, xxxv, 36–37, 40, 44–45, 50, 54, 57, 67–71, 79–82, 88, 99, 182, 193, 198, 226, 252, 256, 258
United Kingdom–New Zealand Free Trade Agreement, 12, 14, 79
United Nations (UN), xxxiii, xxxv, 9, 53, 163, 211, 213, 233, 249
United States, xix, xxi, xxiv–xxv, xxvii, xxx, xxxii–xxxiii, 12, 23, 27–28, 30–33, 37, 39–40, 43, 45–57, 66, 69, 73, 76, 79, 81–82, 85–87, 89–92, 99, 132, 136, 165, 177, 192–193, 195–196, 198–199, 201, 203, 205, 208–209, 211–213, 233, 246, 248–249, 256, 259
United States/Australia–China competition, 206
United States–China competition, 212
United States–China economic interchange, 192
United States–China great power competition, 213
United States–China relations, 90, 191, 195–196, 203, 212
United States–China strategic competition, 182
United States–Mexico– Canada (USMCA) Agreement, 88
unlawful maritime claims, 38
unpredictable weather, 163
UN Security Council, xxii, xxxv, 10, 27, 247, 258
uprisings, 227
Uruguay, 88
US, 27, 29, 31, 45, 77, 93, 131, 194, 201–202, 251, 256–257
US forces, 197
US Navy, 195
Uyghurs, xxxi, 33, 35, 90, 231

V

vaccination, 102, 106, 107–108, 112, 116, 119, 163, 168, 175–176, 179
vaccine, xxxiii–xxxiv, 16–19, 89, 99, 106–107, 117, 121, 154, 167, 178–181, 184, 187, 232, 259
Vaccine Alliance Aotearoa New Zealand, 106
vaccine certificates, 108
vaccine diplomacy, 178, 187
vaccine mandate, 107, 184
vaccine or pandemic or medical diplomacy, 179
vaccine pass, 117, 176
vaccine procurement strategy, 180
values, xxii, 161, 170, 206, 259
value system, 148, 155
Varghese, Peter, 234
Victoria, 196
Victoria University of Wellington, 207

Vietnam, 69, 250
violence, 164, 184
violent extremist, 250
virtual diplomacy, 253, 257
virtual summits, 253
virus containment, 183
voices for freedom movement, 184
volcanic eruption, xxvii

W
Wæver, Ole, 47
wage subsidy, 250
Waitangi Tribunal, 66–67, 71–72, 112
Walker, David, 78
Wang, 200
Wanganui River, 149
Wanganui River whānaunga (cousins) in the North, 149
Wang Yi, xxvi, 196
war, 193, 227
warfare exercise, 32
warship, 29
Washington, 24, 200
Washington Declaration in 2012, 28, 52
water rights, 146
water supply, 145
weapons, xxvi, 195
weather events, 15
Wellington, 184–185, 224, 235
Wellington Declaration, 28
West Coast, 146
Western and Central Pacific Fisheries Agreement, 163
West Papua, 161
Westport, 145

Whangārei, 175
White Island, xxvii
whole-genome sequencing, 113
wildfires, 134
Williams, Joe, 101
Winter Olympics, 257–258
wolf warrior diplomacy, 196
woman, xxviii, 111, 251
workers, 17
Working Holiday Scheme, 169
World Bank, 135, 212
World Food Programme, 89
World Health Organization (WHO), 17, 33–34, 47, 106, 118, 185, 211, 245
World Trade Organization (WTO), xxi, xxii, 12, 24, 36, 45, 63, 76–78, 81, 88–89, 181, 212
world view, 149
WTO Appellate, 76
WTO Dispute Settlement Body, xxxi
WTO General Council, 78

X
Xi, 46, 50, 258
Xi Jinping, xxv, 25, 45, 91, 249
Xinjiang, xxxi, 31, 33–34, 36, 38, 46, 53, 90, 196, 231, 256

Y
Yanukovych, Viktor, 48
Yugoslav, 56
Yugoslavia, 55

Z
zero emissions, 152
Zoom diplomacy, 179

Printed in the United States
by Baker & Taylor Publisher Services